COMMUNICATION
THE HANDBOOK

KRISTIN K. FROEMLING Radford University

GEORGE L. GRICE Radford University, *Professor Emeritus*

JOHN F. SKINNER San Antonio College

Allyn & Bacon

Boston   Columbus   Indianapolis   New York   San Francisco   Upper Saddle River   Amsterdam
Cape Town   Dubai   London   Madrid   Milan   Munich   Paris   Montreal   Toronto   Delhi
Mexico City   Sao Paulo   Sydney   Hong Kong   Seoul   Singapore   Taipei   Tokyo

Editor in Chief, Communication: Karon Bowers
Editorial Assistant: Stephanie Chaisson
Senior Development Editor: Carol Alper
Development Manager: David B. Kear
Associate Development Editor: Angela Pickard
Media Producer: Megan Higginbotham
Marketing Manager: Blair Tuckman
Project Manager: Barbara Mack
Managing Editor: Linda Mihatov Behrens
Project Coordination, Text Design, and Electronic Page Makeup: Pre-Press PMG
Senior Operations Specialist: Nick Sklitsis
Operations Specialist: Mary Ann Gloriande
Art Director, Cover: Anne Nieglos
Cover Designer: Anne DeMarinis
Creative Director: Leslie Osher
Manager, Photo Rights and Permissions: Zina Arabia
Manager, Visual Research: Beth Brenzel
Image Permission Coordinator: Joanne Dippel
Photo Researcher: Rachel Lucas

Library of Congress Cataloging-in-Publication Data

Froemling, Kristin K.
    Communication : the handbook / Kristin K. Froemling, George L. Grice, and
John F. Skinner.
        p. cm.
    Includes bibliographical references and index.
    ISBN 978-0-205-46737-2
  1.   Communication—Handbooks, manuals, etc.   I. Grice, George L.   II. Skinner,
John F.   III. Title.
    P90.F75 2010
    302.2—dc22

                                                2009047524

16 15 14 13 12 V056 17 16 15

Allyn & Bacon
is an imprint of

www.pearsonhighered.com   ISBN-13: 978-0-205-46737-2
                             ISBN-10: 0-205-46737-7

For my parents, grandparents, family, and friends who never lose faith in me

For Wrenn, Evelyn, Carol, and Leanne

For Suzanne, Drew, and Devin

BRIEF CONTENTS

CONTENTS

PART **TWO**   Interpersonal Communication

PART **FOUR**   Public Speaking

The word began as the spoken word. Long before anyone devised a way to record messages in writing, people told one another stories and taught each other lessons. Ancient storytellers preserved their cultures' literature and history by translating them orally to eager audiences. Crowds might wander away from unprepared, unskilled speakers, but the most competent, skilled storytellers received widespread attention and praise.

Even today, linked as we are by phone, computer, television, and radio, competent communication continues to be essential. Effectively conveying your message to one or more people can make the difference between success and failure or even life and death. Although most daily communication has less dramatic outcomes, you are still affected by the success or failure of meeting your communicative goals throughout the day.

We created *Communication: The Handbook* with today's communication environment and today's student and instructor in mind. It is a truly unique learning tool that introduces and reinforces the key communication content and is a reference that students will choose to keep and use throughout their college and professional careers. Building on the success of *Mastering Public Speaking*, authors George Grice and John Skinner teamed up with interpersonal communication expert Kristin Froemling, and the result is the introduction to communication textbook you are holding. It exemplifies our belief that communication is not only part of your education but also the way you gain and apply your learning.

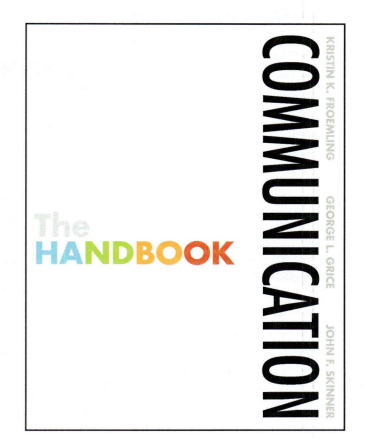

Communication: The Handbook uses a competence approach.

Communication competence and skill development, which instructors tell us are important goals for this course, are emphasized and explained throughout the handbook. By working through the reading and then completing the activities, students will become competent communicators and be well prepared for the wide range of communication situations they will encounter as they continue their college coursework and then launch and succeed in their chosen careers.

For example, in Chapter 3, you will first read about the stages of the listening process; visual learners can see the stages visually laid out in a related flow chart. You can reinforce your competence by applying the concepts you have read about to a listening situation you might encounter as a part of your college studies by completing the associated Applying Concepts/Developing Skills box. Finally, at the end of the chapter, you are prompted to evaluate whether or not you have attained competency in this area.

3d Understanding the Listening Process

The listener is vital to successful communication; without at least one listener, communication cannot occur beyond the intrapersonal level. Remember that any time two people communicate, two messages are involved: the one that the sender intends and the one the li[...]ll receives. These messages will never be identical because p[...] from different experiences that produce different perception[...] stimulus (as noted in Chapter 2). As you examine the steps[...] of listening, you will better understand this concept. Also[...] cause hearing is one of the five senses, the listening process[...] lar to the perception process.

STAGES OF THE LISTENING PROCESS

RECEIVE	SELECT	UNDERSTAND	INTERPRET-EVALUATE	RESOLVE
A stimulus, in the form of sound waves, is received by your body's auditory system.	You determine (consciously or subconsciously) whether to give attention to the received stimulus.	You fit the stimulus into your schemata that best represent that stimulus. The schemata help you to understand the nature of stimulus.	This is the process of judging the reliability of the speaker and quality of the message.	You decide what to do with the information (e.g., accept it or reject it).
Example				
You are in your office and you hear your co-worker calling for you.	*If you are diligently working on a project, you may not hear him. If you do hear him, you may decide to consciously attend to his message.*	*Your co-worker often bothers you about unnecessary things that distract you from your work.*	*You determine that this is another incident in which he is going to waste your time.*	*You tell your co-worker that you will help him in a few minutes.*

Applying Concepts DEVELOPING SKILLS   Analyzing a Recent Interaction

You are having a meeting with your professor in her office. You are discussing the requirements for a research paper that is due in one week. Because your grades are important to you, you are listening intently to what she is saying. Explain how the listening process would apply to this hypothetical interac[...] [...]e [...] listening process different when you are not listening effective[...]

3d Understanding the Listening Process

- There are five stages in the listening process: receiving the message, selecting stimuli to retain, understanding the message, evaluating the message, and formulating a response to the message.

Competence. Can I identify the stages of the listening process? Do I know which stage of the listening process gives me the most problems?

Communication: The Handbook is a practical resource.

This highly readable text incorporates a truly practical approach to communication. Content sections are covered in short, to-the-point chapters that encompass the basics of communication skills and theory. Flow charts provide you with an overview of the information you need to grasp the breadth of issues—the big picture—as well as details to help you understand the depth of the issues. For example in Chapter 10, you will see a flowchart that illustrates the breadth of the speech-making process at a glance; in Chapter 8 you will see the depth of information you need to help you decide how to evaluate varying situations and make the best decision depending on the circumstances.

THE SPEECH-MAKING PROCESS

ANALYZING YOUR AUDIENCE (CHAPTER 10)
Prepare a speech that can be targeted to meet the needs of *your* audience.

GENERATING YOUR TOPIC (CHAPTER 10)
Consider topics that interest you or your listeners, that suit the occasion, and those you encounter in the course of your research.

RESEARCHING YOUR SPEECH TOPIC (CHAPTER 11)
Once you have chosen your topic, research helps you focus it and determine your specific purpose.

SUPPORTING YOUR SPEECH (CHAPTER 11)
Supporting materials give your ideas clarity, vividness, and credibility to make the audience understand, remember, and believe what you say.

ORGANIZING YOUR IDEAS (CHAPTER 12)
Clear organization arranges ideas so that your listeners can rem[...]
It also maximizes your information so that listeners have more [...]
chance to "get" your point.

OUTLINING YOUR SPEECH (CHAPTER 12)
Outlining your speech is the preliminary written work necessar[...]
clear organization of your oral message. When you outline, you [...]
reorganize material, into a pattern that is easy to recognize and [...]

DELIVERING YOUR SPEECH (CHAPTER 13)
Your manner of presenting a speech—through your unique vo[...]
language—forms your style of delivery. *What* you say is your sp[...]
and *how* you say it is your delivery.

CHOOSING THE BEST DECISION MAKING METHOD

Consensus	Majority Rule	Minority Rule	Expert Opinion	Authority Rule
How many people must be involved in making the decision?				
If, in order to remain motivated, all of the group members need to be in favor of a decision to make it successful, then *consensus* is best.	When only a majority of group members need to agree, you can use *majority rule*.	If the situation arises in which a small number of group members can make a decision, such as a committee, then you can use *minority rule*.	If the situation arises in which a trusted expert can make a decision for the group, then you can use *expert opinion*.	In situations in where the group leader can make a decision so that the entire group need not meet, he or she can handle such decisions, thus using *authority rule*.
How quickly does the decision need to be made?				
If a decision needs to be made quickly, consensus may not be appropriate.	If the group members must participate in the decision making, then *majority rule* may be better than consensus.	If the decision needs to be made quickly, but the leader is unavailable or delegates the decision to group members, then *minority rule* can be used.	If the decision needs to be made quickly, but the leader is unavailable or delegates the decision to group members, then *expert opinion* can be used.	If the decision needs to be made quickly and the issue is simple and does not require others to participate, then *authority rule* can be used.

Communication: The Handbook is easy to navigate.

The handbook format, which is unique to the introduction to communication market, makes this text easy to use and navigate. The tabbed dividers provide a color-coded roadmap to the information you need to find. For instance, if you want to read about how relationships form and end, look at the list of topics on the divider for Part Two, Interpersonal Relationships, and find the appropriate section—in this case 6c, "Relationship Development and Dissolution." Now follow the color-coded navigational tabs, printed on the edge of the page, to quickly access information contained in Section 6c.

PART **TWO** Interpersonal Communication

CONTENTS

2 Interpersonal Communication

6c

a trait that ultimately repulsed them. For example, if you are attracted to a person's spontaneity, you might ultimately be irritated by his or her inability to plan.

Rewards. Relational attraction is also determined by the number of rewards you gain from the relationship. You are more likely to form and maintain relationships in which you receive more rewards than you incur costs.

Rewards include both tangible benefits and intangible benefits. A tangible benefit would be sharing rent with someone and an intangible benefit is companionship, for instance.

Costs are anything that you sacrifice for the relationship. If you are not a sports fan, but your friend loves sports, you will sacrifice your time to watch the sports games in exchange for your friend's companionship.

Self-disclosure. **Self-disclosure** occurs when we tell someone something about ourselves. The information we disclose can be unimportant tidbits that we reveal to someone else during small talk (such as television shows and music that we like) or deeply private information (such as our beliefs and values).

We use the amount and type of self-disclosure to measure another person's interest in developing and maintaining a relationship. We will elaborate on the ways self-disclosure affects our relationships in the next chapter.

Applying Concepts DEVELOPING SKILLS Analyzing Your Close Relationships

Consider your closest friend. Which of the six factors listed above attracted you to that friend? What factors can you attribute to the longevity of your friendship? Next, consider your most recent romantic partner. Which factors attracted you to him or her? Now compare the two lists. Are the factors similar or different? Why?

6c Examining Relationship Development and Dissolution

While all relationships have a beginning, they vary with regard to the level of intimacy that is ultimately reached and whether they are maintained. Therefore, this section will discuss methods for examining relationship development and relationship dissolution. These models apply not only to romantic relationships, but also to friendships and workplace relationships.

Communication: The Handbook focuses on managing apprehension.

Students often come to this course with apprehension about communicating in different types of situations: one-on-one, in groups, or in the public context. Rather than limiting the discussion of communication apprehension just to public speaking, our handbook includes a module (a brief, highly readable section containing practical information) in each part to provide specific advice on how to manage communication apprehension in any context and how to feel confident communicating in every communication situation.

MODULE A

Understanding Communication Apprehension

Have you been in a situation requiring you to communicate with one other person, with a group, or in front of an audience and found yourself nervous or anxious? Such a reaction is normal. It's called **communication apprehension**, or "the level of fear or anxiety associated with either real or anticipated communication with another person or persons" (McCroskey, 1977, p. 78).

Communication apprehension is similar in nature to shyness, and it can affect anyone. Even extroverted people can feel apprehensive about communicating in certain situations. Because high communication apprehension can affect a person's communication competence, we will explore the nature of communication apprehension throughout this textbook and offer suggestions about reducing your communication apprehension.

Many people consider communication anxiety only in a public speaking context. But you can also experience a fear of speaking interpersonally, perhaps with a boss or a police officer, or speaking among a group of people (i.e., not speaking up during a meeting).

HIGH COMMUNICATION APPREHENSION

People who have high communication apprehension (CA) are uncomfortable in interactions with another

delivering a speech. As a result of their fear and anxiety, people with high CA will withdraw from or avoid interactions in which they must communicate with others. The person with high CA will not avoid *all* human interaction, but rather will minimize settings in which he or she might experience the type of communication that causes the apprehension.

Example of High CA

Rochelle spends a significant amount of time in her dorm room. While roommates tried at the beginning of the semester to include her in their activities, she declined so often that they stopped asking her to participate. In class she sits in the back of the room and does not ask questions or discuss readings, despite being an

MODULE G

Managing Speaker Apprehension

One form of communication apprehension, public speaking anxiety, affects even people with a great deal of public speaking experience. Perhaps you have experienced public speaking anxiety, too. Many students delay taking a public speaking course because of this anxiety. But with the tips to control your nervousness provided here, you should be able to deliver your speeches confidently and successfully.

James McCroskey has studied the anxieties of public speaking extensively. His data, collected from several thousand students, confirm that public speaking generates greater apprehension than other forms of communication. Nearly three-fourths of college students fall into the "moderately high anxiety" to "high anxiety" range! McCroskey and coauthor Virginia Richmond conclude: "What suggests, then, is that it is 'normal' to experience fairly high degree of anxiety about public speaking. Most people do. If you are highly anxious about public speaking, then you are 'normal.'"

CONTROL YOUR NERVOUSNESS

Your goal should not be to eliminate nervousness. Nervousness is natural, and attempting to eliminate it is unrealistic. Most experienced, successful public speakers still get nervous before they speak.

Some nervousness can actually benefit a speaker. Nervousness is energy, and it shows that you care about performing well. Use that nervous energy to enliven your delivery and to give your

ideas impact. Instead of nervously tapping your fingers on the lectern, for example, you can gesture. Your goal, then, is to control and channel your nervousness.

MODULE F

Managing Group Communication Apprehension

In previous modules, we have talked about communication apprehension (CA) in general (a feeling of anxiety about interacting with others). A general anxiety in all communication settings is called **trait apprehension**.

We have also previously identified two other types of communication apprehension: situation-specific and context-specific apprehension. We discussed situation-specific and context-specific apprehension in terms of interpersonal communication settings.

Another type of communication apprehension is called **audience-specific apprehension**. People who experience this type of CA experience anxiety depending on the audience involved in the setting. You might find that being in class-related groups with peers makes you anxious; someone else may be more anxious in groups of peers in the workplace.

EFFECTS OF GROUP MEMBER COMMUNICATION APPREHENSION ON GROUPS

Several researchers have conducted studies to determine how group members who have high group CA influence groups. McCroskey and Richmond (1988) suggest that members who have high group CA can be more detrimental to a group than high-CA people in other contexts.

Group members with high CA tend to participate less in group interactions (Sorensen & McCroskey, 1977). However, not all high-CA people respond to anxiety through shyness. Some group members will participate in group meetings by making comments that are off-topic (McCroskey & Wright, 1971), with the alleged purpose of creating an impression that they are not able to be productive members of the group.

Jensen and Chilberg (1991) summarized findings regarding high-CA group members. High-CA members are less likely to provide information or to seek information in group meetings. McCroskey and Richmond (1988) noted that high-CA group members make more irrelevant comments during group meetings.

MODULE C

Managing Interpersonal Communication Apprehension

As you read in Module A, *communication apprehension* is a fear or anxiety about speaking to one or more people in any given context. *Interpersonal communication apprehension* exists when a person experiences fear or anxiety about speaking to another person in any setting.

In Module A, we discussed the fact that not everyone is anxious about communicating in every context. McCroskey (1984) suggests that some , which

...h as in ...settings)

...some ...**prehension**, ...th certain ...e asked you ...ect that ...afraid to ...ur ideas ...out how to

...ty reduc- ...information ...to reduce ...es with a ...anaging ...hension.

UNCERTAINTY REDUCTION THEORY

At some point, we all experience a little bit of apprehension in interpersonal communication contexts. Uncertainty reduction theory explains why we are uncomfortable talking to strangers and how we can reduce that apprehension.

Charles Berger (Berger & Calabrese, 1975) is credited with the formation of **uncertainty reduction theory (URT)**, which explains the exchange of information between two people to create understanding and reduce uneasiness or anxiety. Originally, the theory was used to explain how a dyad progressed from stranger to friend. The **uncertainty** in the theory refers to an uneasiness or anxiety about another person or your relationship with that person. In the context that Berger

Communication: The Handbook covers high-interest topics.

The short modules format is also used to cover special information such as how to make small talk, how to conduct an informational interview to collect primary information for a speech, or how to prepare for one of the special occasions you are most likely to encounter during your life: introductions, presentations, acceptances, tributes, and entertainment. The modules are formatted as short sections—about two to four pages—and contain highly practical information to help you get the information you want easily and quickly.

MODULE B

The Art of Small Talk

THE IMPORTANCE OF SMALL TALK

Think back to the first time you met each of your friends. Did you just immediately start self-disclosing important, personal details of your life? How did you know that you wanted to be his or her friend? At some point, you and your friend engaged in small talk. **Small talk** is a conversational tactic whose purpose is to gain basic information that will help you to make a connection with someone.

Mastering the art of small talk can open many doors to your future. Small talk is a powerful instrument for beginning a relationship for two reasons (Gabor, 2001).

1. Engaging in small talk with someone indicates a willingness on your part to talk to the person.
2. Small talk allows people to exchange information in order to discover common interests.

Small talk requires competency in many of the concepts covered in Part One of this handbook: perception, listening, language rules, and nonverbal cues. Therefore, small talk interactions can help you to practice your skills and become a more competent communicator. You will need good conversational skills in every aspect of your life: business, social, and personal.

Why is it so important to remember someone's name?

People feel flattered when you remember their name. Remembering names also shows that you were listening when they are introduced and it builds rapport between you and the other person. When you know someone's name, he or she is no longer a "stranger."

Why do we so often forget a person's name?

most common reason is failing to focus on the
ment of introduction (Gabor, 2001). Meeting
one new can make us so anxious that we are
king more about what we are going to say to the
on than focusing on the introduction.

MODULE H

Interviewing

In chapter 11, you learned how to conduct research to find credible information for your speech. The research sources that you were directed to investigate in that chapter are called *secondary sources* because they report research conducted by other people.

In this module, you will learn how to conduct *primary research*—meaning that you collect information firsthand by asking other people to give you their experiences and expertise regarding your topic. Interviews are one form of primary research that can provide you with valuable information about your topic.

ADVANTAGES OF INTERVIEWS

Depending on your purpose, an interview may be
of firsthand information. Today you
ople by email, instant messaging, or
t rooms, as well as by telephone or
personal interview can aid you in

ed sources are inaccessible, the
nterview may be your only option.
ou have chosen may be so novel that
information is not yet in print or
r topic may also be so localized as to
e or no coverage by area media.

permit you to adapt your topic to
fic audience. Take, for example, the
ycling. If you interview the director
ool's physical plant to find out how
custodians collect and dispose of

each day, you can give your speech a personal touch. You could take your speech one step further by figuring out how much your college could contribute to resource conservation. This shows your audience how this topic affects them directly. You will grab their attention.

- **Personal interviews provide opportunities for you to secure expert evaluation of your research and suggestions for further research.** The experts you interview may challenge some of your assumptions or data. If this happens, encourage their feedback and don't get defensive. Knowing all the angles can only help you give a more thoughtful speech. Near the end of your interview, ask your interviewee to suggest additional sources that will help you better research and understand your topic.

MODULE I

Special Occasion Speeches

We can all count on being called on to deliver a speech on some special occasion. To speak your best at these times, you must consider the customs and audience expectations in each case. You may also not have much time to prepare for special occasion speeches, as sometimes you are called on to give a speech at the last minute.

SPEECH OF INTRODUCTION

One of the most common types of special occasion speeches is the *speech of introduction*—a speech to introduce a featured speaker (not yourself).

The following guidelines will help you prepare such a speech of introduction:

- **Keep focus on person being introduced.** The audience has not gathered to hear you. Keep your remarks short, simple, and sincere.
- **Be brief.** If you can, request and get a copy of the speaker's résumé. This will give you information to select from when preparing your introductory remarks. Highlight key information only.
- **Establish the speaker's credibility on the topic.** Present the speaker's credentials. As you prepare, ask and answer questions such as What makes the speaker qualified to speak on the subject? What education and experiences make the speaker's insights worthy of our belief?
- **Create realistic expectations.** Genuine praise is commendable, just be careful not to oversell the speaker.

- **Establish a tone consistent with the speaker's presentation.** Would you give a humorous introduction for a speaker whose topic is "The Grieving Process"? Of course not. On the other hand, if the evening is designed for merriment, your introduction should help set that mood.

SPEECH OF PRESENTATION

The *speech of presentation* confers an award, a prize, or some other form of special recognition on an individual or a group. Such speeches are typically made after banquets or parties as parts of business meetings or sessions of a convention; or at awards ceremonies. When you give a speech of presentation, let the nature and importance of the award being presented, as well as the occasion on which it is being presented, shape your remarks.

Communication: The Handbook highlights cultural issues.

In each chapter, you are given the opportunity to see the important communication theories and competencies in action in the context of extended examples that illustrate varying "Cultural Connections." For example, in Chapter 1, you will learn about the transactional model of communication and how the various elements of communication interact. Then you will apply these elements to a situation that would be very familiar to you by completing the related "Applying Concepts/Developing Skills" activity. At this point you are ready to apply the theory to a situation that is not likely to be familiar to you by reading the extended example and then answering the questions at the end of the box. In this chapter, the "Cultural Connections" box is called "Analyzing the Transactional Model: Native Americans;" you will practice how to extend your knowledge to a new situation.

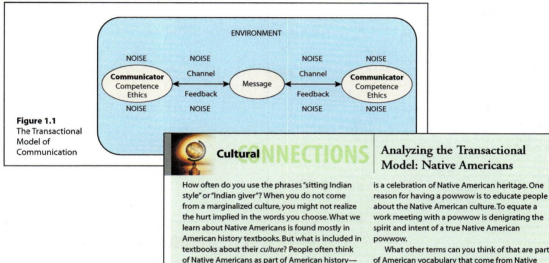

Figure 1.1
The Transactional Model of Communication

Cultural CONNECTIONS

Analyzing the Transactional Model: Native Americans

How often do you use the phrases "sitting Indian style" or "Indian giver"? When you do not come from a marginalized culture, you might not realize the hurt implied in the words you choose. What we learn about Native Americans is found mostly in American history textbooks. But what is included in textbooks about their *culture*? People often think of Native Americans as part of American history—a thing of the past. But Native Americans are still actively celebrating their heritage in many states across the country.

Jo White, a communication major at Radford University, has spent the past ten years researching her Native American heritage. Jo's grandmother was a member of the Seneca tribe in the Iroquois confederacy.

[...] Native Americans [...] to [...] thers [...] part- [...] owwow

is a celebration of Native American heritage. One reason for having a powwow is to educate people about the Native American culture. To equate a work meeting with a powwow is denigrating the spirit and intent of a true Native American powwow.

What other terms can you think of that are part of American vocabulary that come from Native American culture? What terms can you substitute for those to make the statement less offensive?

For a closer examination of Native American culture, Jo recommends that you watch the movie *Smoke Signals*, based on a book by Sherman Alexie.

Application

Referring to Figure 1.1, label all of the elements of the transactional model in terms of Jo's points. At which points in the model are there the greatest opportunities for misunderstandings or friction?

Applying Concepts
DEVELOPING SKILLS

Identifying Elements of the Transactional Model

Using Figure 1.1 as a guide, analyze a lecture given by an instructor in one of your classes. Identify all of the various communication elements that are in effect in this situation.

Communication: The Handbook explores ethical situations.

Ethical issues are presented in much the same way as the "Cultural Connection" boxes. You will first learn about the communication concept and then read an extended example in the form of a box called "Eye on Ethics." Then you are prompted to evaluate how an ethical question comes into play in the situation and answer questions that show how the ethical issues apply to everyday life. For example in Chapter 6, you will learn the theory behind relational development by reading about Knapp's relational model. Then you will read the "Eye on Ethics" box, "The Disappearing Act," to evaluate whether the behavior illustrated by a real-life pop culture personality reflects ethical communication.

Knapp's Model of Relationship Development

In their study of relationships, various communication researchers have formulated models to describe the stages or phases that the relationships go through as they evolve. Relationship development involves the initiation of a relationship between two people, and it continues, developing into a closer, more intimate relationship as the dyad shares personal information and their social networks acknowledge their relationship (whether it is a friendship or a romance).

Mark Knapp (1978) created a relational development model that looks at five stages of relationship development. (See Figure 6.1.)

Stage One: Initiating. In the *initiating* phase, you meet someone who interests you. Perception becomes key as you receive stimuli that catch your attention. The person might be carrying or wearing an object that is similar to yours, or wearing a perfume/cologne that you like. Whatever it is that draws you to that person marks the beginning of the relational development process.

Stage Two: Experimenting. Not all first encounters will lead to experimenting. If you and the other person do not pursue the friendship or romance after that first encounter, then this model no longer applies. If you do hit it off, the *experimenting* stage encompasses getting to know each other. Small talk is a good way to get to know someone. By engaging in small talk (which you read about in Module B), you learn more

6c

Developing   **Dissolving**

5. Bonding
4. Integrating   6. Differentiating
3. Intensifying   7. Circumscribing
2. Experimenting   8. Stagnating
1. Initiating   9. Avoiding
              10. Terminating

Figure 6.1 Knapp's Relational Development Model
Adapted from Mark L. Knapp & Anita L. Vangelisti, Interpersonal communication and human relationships (4th ed.). Allyn and Bacon, Boston, MA. Copyright 2000 by Pearson Education. Reprinted by permission of publisher.

 EYEON**ETHICS**   The Disappearing Act

Pop singer Britney Spears sent K-Fed a text message to tell him that she had filed for divorce. Another musician, Phil Collins, sent his wife a fax to tell her that he had filed for divorce. What about relationships in which a partner just disappears without even a phone call, email, or letter to indicate that the relationship is over?

Most relationships end with a pronouncement by one partner to the other that the relationship is over. Some relationships end with both partners having some idea of the problems that led to the dissolution, but recently another breakup strategy has emerged—the disappearing act. While it could likely be what Cody (1982) calls "behavioral de-escalation," the disappearing act has such important implications for the person who is left behind that it warrants its own category. For those people whose partner "disappears," there is no resolution or understanding.

Application

What are the ethical implications of the disappearing act? Is there a certain amount of time that the couple has been together after which it becomes unethical just to disappear? Are there some situations in which the use of the disappearing act would be ethical? What are those situations?

Communication: The Handbook shows students how to prepare and deliver an effective presentation.

In Part Four, you will systematically work through the steps of the speech making process. Chapter 10 begins with an overview of the entire process; a flowchart, "The Speech making Process," overviews the entire process at a glance. You will then work through the process step by step as you prepare your own presentations. The part culminates with chapters on speaking to inform and persuade and includes annotated speeches that illustrate how students like you applied what they learned through the chapters. You can also log onto MyCommunicationLab.com to view videos of the sample speeches. By the time you have completed the course, you will have had the opportunity to learn a wealth of communication concepts, apply them to real-life situations, develop your communication skills, and attain competence in all the communication contexts. A liberating and lifelong education occurs only through communication with ourselves and those around us. We hope your experiences with this introductory course will prepare you for further studies and whatever career paths you choose.

ANALYZING YOUR AUDIENCE

Prepare a speech that can be targeted to meet the needs of *your* audience.

GENERATING YOUR TOPIC (CHAPTER 10)
Consider topics that interest you or your listeners, that suit the occasion, and those you encounter in the course of your research.

RESEARCHING YOUR SPEECH TOPIC (CHAPTER 11)
Once you have chosen your topic, research helps you focus it and determine your specific purpose.

SUPPORTING YOUR SPEECH (CHAPTER 11)
Supporting materials give your ideas clarity, vividness, and credibility to make the audience understand, remember, and believe what you say.

ORGANIZING YOUR IDEAS (CHAPTER 12)
Clear organization arranges ideas so that your listeners can remember them. It also maximizes your information so that listeners have more than one chance to "get" your point.

OUTLINING YOUR IDEAS (CHAPTER 12)
Outlining your speech is the preliminary written work necessary to foster clear organization of your oral message. When you outline, you organize and reorganize material, into a pattern that is easy to recognize and remember.

DELIVERING YOUR SPEECH (CHAPTER 13)
Your manner of presenting a speech—through your unique voice, body, and language—forms your style of delivery. *What* you say is your speech content and *how* you say it is your delivery.

SAMPLE

Informative Speech
What a Difference a Generation Makes
Elvir Berbic, Radford University, Radford, Virginia

We're living in an age when multiple generations are working side by side in the workplace. According to Zemke, Raines, and Filipczak, authors of the 2000 book *Generations at Work*, generational differences can create problems in the workplace. Everyone in this room may not be from the same generation. I'm a member of the Millennial generation, and I have read extensively about generational differences. Because all of you are part of one of the generations that I'll discuss today, I think you will find the information interesting, too.

> Elvir's topic is apparent by the end of the first paragraph. He also establishes his credibilty and links the topic to his audience.

A generation is defined by historians Neil Howe William Strauss in their book *Millennials Rising* written in 2000 as a "society-wide peer group," born over approximately the same time period, "who collectively possess a common persona" (p. 40). Each generation is characterized by defining historical events, such as 9/11, that happen in their formative years. These events shape the attitudes, beliefs, and values of a generation. The Vietnam War, the Space Shuttle Challenger explosion, and the Columbine shootings are defining moments for each of the three generations I will discuss. Today I'm going to explain several key features that characterize the three most recent generations: Baby Boomers, Generation X, and Millennials.

> This section of the introduction previews the three main points that he will develop in the body of the speech.

The first generation that I'll talk about is the Baby Boomer generation, who were born between the years 1943 and 1960. There are several defining general characteristics of the Baby Boomers. They were the first generation to work 60 hours a week. Baby Boomers are often referred to as the "Me Generation" because they are focused on making themselves better. They go to the gym, get plastic surgery, and purchase self-help material. The Boomers fought for civil rights and diversity. They wanted to create an equal playing field for everyone.

> Here Elvir begins to apply the "4 S's" to his first point. He signposts ("first") and states the idea (Baby Boomer generation). He supports his points with facts and examples.

These general characteristics were born from the core values of Baby Boomers. In the workplace, boomers value hard work and involvement. They are optimistic and team oriented. Both in and out of the workplace, they are concerned with personal gratification and personal growth.

Several other features of Boomers will help us to distinguish them from the other two generations. They buy whatever is trendy, including clothing, plastic surgery, and electronic gadgets. Boomers are the first generation to acquire credit card debt. Boomers typically read *Business Week* and *People* magazine. Their sense of humor is similar to that found in the print cartoon *Doonesbury*.

RESOURCES IN PRINT AND ONLINE

Supplement	Available in Print	Available Online	Instructor or Student Supplement	Description
Instructor's Manual (ISBN: 0205758924)	✓	✓	Instructor Supplement	Prepared by Jimmy Roux, Lynchburg College, each chapter of the Instructor's Manual includes an annotated Instructional Outline that can be used for developing lectures. Discussion Questions, designed to stimulate class discussion, can also be used for assignments, essay questions, or as review questions for an exam. Answers to questions are provided. In addition, you will find In-Class/Out-of-Class Activities and suggestions for Additional Resources. Available for download at www.pearsonhighered.com/irc (access code required).
Test Bank (ISBN: 0205758908)	✓	✓	Instructor Supplement	The Test Bank, prepared by Sandy French, Radford University, consists of approximately 700 thoroughly reviewed multiple choice, completion, matching, and essay questions. Each question has a correct answer/grading criteria (for essay questions only), page reference, and skill designation. Available for download at www.pearsonhighered.com/ irc (access code required).
MyTest (ISBN: 0205758991)		✓	Instructor Supplement	This flexible, online test generating software includes all questions found in the printed Test Bank. This computerized software allows instructors to create their own personalized exams, to edit any or all of the existing test questions, and to add new questions. Other special features of this program include random generation of test questions, creation of alternate versions of the same test, scrambling of question sequence, and test preview before printing. Available at www.pearsonmytest.com (access code required).
PowerPoint™ Presentation Package (ISBN: 0205758932)		✓	Instructor Supplement	Available for download at www.pearsonhighered.com/irc (access code required), this text-specific package, prepared by Ellen Bremen, Highline Community College, provides a basis for your lecture with PowerPoint™ slides for each module and chapter of the book.
Pearson Allyn & Bacon Introduction to Communication Video Library	✓		Instructor Supplement	Pearson Allyn & Bacon's Introduction to Communication Video Library contains a range of videos from which adopters can choose. Videos to choose from cover a variety of topics and scenarios for communication foundations, interpersonal communication, small group communication, and public speaking. Please contact your Pearson representative for details and a complete list of videos and their contents to choose which would be most useful in your class. Some restrictions apply.
Lecture Questions for Clickers for Introduction to Communication (ISBN: 0205547230)		✓	Instructor Supplement	Prepared by Keri Moe, El Paso Community College, this assortment of questions and activities covering culture, listening, interviewing, public speaking, interpersonal conflict, and more are presented in a PowerPoint™ Presentation Package. These slides will help liven up your lectures and can be used along with the Personal Response System to get students more involved in the material. Available at www.pearsonhighered.com/irc (access code required).
Allyn & Bacon Digital Media Archive for Communication, Version 3.0 (ISBN:0205437095)	✓		Instructor Supplement	The Digital Media Archive CD-ROM contains electronic images of charts, graphs, tables, and figures, along with media elements such as video and related web links. These media assets are fully customizable to use with our pre-formatted PowerPoint™ outlines or to import into the instructor's own lectures (available for Windows and Mac).
A Guide for New Teachers of Introduction to Communication: Interactive Strategies for Teaching Communication, Fourth Edition (ISBN: 0205750001)	✓	✓	Instructor Supplement	Prepared by Susanna G. Porter, Kennesaw State University with a new chapter on using MyCommunicationLab by Heather Dillon, Urbana, Illinois, this guide is designed to help new teachers effectively teach the introductory communication course. It is full of first day of class tips, great teaching ideas, outside and Pearson resources, and sample activities and assignments.

Supplement	Available in Print	Available Online	Instructor or Student Supplement	Description
Preparing Visual Aids for Presentations, Fifth Edition (ISBN:020561115X)	✓		Student Supplement	Prepared by Dan Cavanaugh, this 32-page visual booklet provides a host of ideas for using today's multimedia tools to improve presentations, including suggestions for planning a presentation, guidelines for designing visual aids and storyboarding, and a walkthrough that shows how to prepare a visual display using PowerPoint™ (available for purchase).
Pearson Allyn & Bacon Introduction to Communication Study Site (Open access)		✓	Student Supplement	The Pearson Allyn & Bacon Introduction to Communication Study Site features practice tests, learning objectives, and weblinks. The site is organized around the major topics typically covered in the Introduction to Communication course. These topics have also been correlated to the table of contents for your book! Available at www.abintrocommunication.com.
Public Speaking in the Multicultural Environment, Second Edition (ISBN:0205265111)	✓		Student Supplement	Prepared by Devorah A. Lieberman, Portland State University, this supplementary text helps students learn to analyze cultural diversity within their audiences and adapt their presentations accordingly (available for purchase).
The Speech Outline: Outlining to Plan, Organize, and Deliver a Speech (ISBN:032108702X)	✓		Student Supplement	Prepared by Reeze L. Hanson and Sharon Condon of Haskell Indian Nations University, this workbook offers students activities, exercises, and answers to help them develop and master the critical skill of outlining (available for purchase).
Multicultural Activities Workbook (ISBN:0205546528)	✓		Student Supplement	Prepared by Marlene C. Cohen and Susan L. Richardson of Prince George's Community College, Maryland, this workbook is filled with hands-on activities that help broaden the content of speech classes to reflect diverse cultural backgrounds. There are checklists, surveys, and writing assignments to help students succeed in speech communication by offering experiences that address a variety of learning styles (available for purchase).
Speech Preparation Workbook (ISBN: 013559569X)	✓		Student Supplement	Prepared by Jennifer Dreyer and Gregory H. Patton of San Diego State University, this workbook takes students through the stages of speech creation—from audience analysis to writing the speech—and includes guidelines, tips, and easy to fill-in pages (available for purchase).
Study Card for Introduction to Speech Communication (ISBN: 0205474381)	✓		Student Supplement	Colorful, affordable, and packed with useful information, the Pearson Allyn & Bacon Study Cards make studying easier, more efficient, and more enjoyable. Course information is distilled down to the basics, helping students quickly master the fundamentals, review a subject for understanding, or prepare for an exam. Because they're laminated for durability, students can keep these Study Cards for years to come and pull them out whenever they need a quick review (available for purchase).
VideoLab CD-ROM (ISBN:0205561616)	✓		Student Supplement	This interactive study tool for students can be used independently or in class. It provides digital video of student speeches that can be viewed in conjunction with corresponding outlines, manuscripts, notecards, and instructor critiques. A series of drills to help students analyze content and delivery follows each speech (available for purchase).
MyCommunicationLab		✓	Instructor & Student Supplement	MyCommunicationLab is a state-of-the-art, interactive and instructive solution for communication courses. Designed to be used as a supplement to a traditional lecture course, or to completely administer an online course, MyCommunicationLab combines a Pearson eText, multimedia, video clips, activities, research support, tests and quizzes to completely engage students. See next page for more details.

Save time and improve results with mycommunicationlab

Designed to amplify a traditional course in numerous ways or to administer a course online, **MyCommunicationLab** for Introductory Communication courses combines pedagogy and assessment with an array of multimedia activities—videos, speech preparation tools, assessments, research support, multiple newsfeeds—to make learning more effective for all types of students. Now featuring more resources, including MediaShare, Pearson's video upload tool, this new release of **MyCommunicationLab** is visually richer and even more interactive than the previous version—a leap forward in design with more tools and features to enrich learning and aid students in classroom success.

Teaching and Learning Tools

NEW VERSION! Pearson eText   Identical in content and design to the printed text, a Pearson eText provides students with access to their text whenever and wherever they need it. In addition to contextually placed multimedia features in every chapter, our new Pearson eText allows students to take notes and highlight, just like a traditional book.

Videos and Video Quizzes   Interactive videos provide students with the opportunity to watch video clips that portray different communication scenarios, interviews with well-known communication scholars, and sample speeches including both professional and student speeches. Many videos are annotated with critical thinking questions or include short, assignable quizzes that report to the instructor's gradebook.

Self-Assessments   Online self assessments, including SCAM, PRCA-24, and assessments that test introversion, shyness, and communication competence, as well as pre- and post-tests for every chapter, help students to learn about different communication styles and assess their own. The pre- and post-tests generate a customized study plan for further assessment and focus students on areas in which they need to improve. Instructors can use these tools to show learning over the duration of the course.

UPDATED! MyOutline   MyOutline offers step-by-step guidance for writing an effective outline, along with tips and explanations to help students better understand the elements of an outline and how all the pieces fit together. Outlines that students create can be downloaded to their computer, emailed as an attachment, printed, or saved in the tool for future editing. Instructors can either select from several templates based on our texts, or they can create their own outline template for students to use.

UPDATED! Topic Selector   This interactive tool helps students get started generating ideas and then narrowing down topics. Our Topic Selector is question based, rather than drill-down, in order to help students really learn the process of selecting their topic. Once they have determined their topic, students are directed to credible online sources for guidance with the research process.

NEW! ABC News RSS feed   MyCommunicationLab provides an online feed from ABC news, updated hourly, to help students choose and research group assignments and speeches.

NEW! MySearchLab   Pearson's MySearchLab™ is the easiest way for students to start a research assignment, speech, or paper. Complete with extensive help on the research process and four databases of credible and reliable source material, MySearchLab™ helps students quickly and efficiently make the most of their research time.

Cutting-Edge Technology

NEW! MediaShare   With this new video upload tool, students are able to upload group assignments, interpersonal role plays, and speeches for their instructor and classmates to watch (whether face-to-face or online) and provide online feedback and comments at time-stamped intervals. Structured much like a social networking site, MediaShare can help promote a sense of community among students.

NEW! Audio Chapter Summaries   Every chapter includes an audio chapter summary, formatted as an MP3 file, perfect for students reviewing material before a test or instructors reviewing material before class.

NEW! Quick and Dirty Tips Podcast   Through an agreement with Quick and Dirty Tips, MyCommunicationLab now features a RSS Feed of *The Public Speaker's Quick and Dirty Tips for Improving Your Communication Skills*, which covers topics such as conflict, negotiation, networking, pronunciation, eye contact, overcoming nervousness, interviewing skills, accent modification, and more!

Online Administration

No matter what course management system you use—or if you do not use one at all, but still wish to easily capture your students' grade and track their performance—Pearson has a **MyCommunication Lab** option to suit your needs. Contact one of Pearson's Technology Specialists for more information and assistance.

A **MyCommunicationLab** access code is no additional cost when packaged with selected Pearson Communication texts. To get started, contact your local Pearson Publisher's Representative at **www.pearsonhighered.com/replocator**.

ACKNOWLEDGMENTS

Books never reach bookshelves solely based on the work of the authors alone. Although we have tried to speak with one voice for the sake of our readers, the truth is that many voices resonate throughout this text: the voices of our teachers, our colleagues, our editors, and our students. What we know, what we value, and what we write is shaped in part by their influence and insights. Wherever possible, we have tried to acknowledge their contributions. For all their influence on this text we are thankful.

We thank the entire editorial and production staffs at Pearson Allyn & Bacon. Most influential was Carol Alper, our senior development editor, whose wisdom and guidance helped bring *Communication: The Handbook* to its current state. Her thoughtful suggestions and amazing editorial skills were invaluable. We are especially grateful to Karon Bowers whose confidence in our plan, patience with the process, and suggestions for improvements made this book a reality. Thanks to Barbara Mack, our project manager; Lindsay Bethoney, our project editor; Elsa van Bergen, our copy editor; and Rachel Lucas, our photograph researcher.

Many students, authors, and publishers graciously allowed us to quote material in this book. Several graduate students—Cheryl Jordan, Stephanie Murillo, and Hannah Shinault—helped with the beginning research for the book. Thanks to Megan-Dawn Elder-Taylor and Hannah Shinault for recommending their students for sample speeches.

We have benefited immensely from the encouragement and advice of our fellow faculty members at Radford University and San Antonio College.

Communication: The Handbook has been shaped and refined by the close reading and thoughtful suggestions of a number of reviewers. We would like to thank the following reviewers for their comments on this text:

Angie Marie Seifert Anderson, Anoka Ramsey Community College

Karen Anderson, University of North Texas

Peter J. Bicak, Rockhurst University

Dom Bongiorni, Lonestar College, Kingwood

Ellen B. Bremen, Highline Community College

L. Karen Brown, Cape Fear Community College

Carolyn Clark, Salt Lake Community College

Timothy R. Cline, College of Notre Dame of Maryland

Patricia S. Cohill, Burlington County College

Sarah Cole, Framingham State College

Isabel Del Pino-Allen, Miami Dade College

Jean Dewitt, University of Houston-Downtown

Billie Evans, Graceland University

Rolita Flores Ezeonu, Highline Community College

Joyce G. Ferguson, University of North Carolina

Donna L. Friess, Cypress College

Avis P. Gray, Winston-Salem State University

Angela Grupas, St Louis Community College

Kim Gyuran, Modesto Junior College

Deborah Hefferin, Broward Community College

Charlotte Jones, Carroll College

Martin LoMonaco, Neumann College

Marianne Luken, Hawaii Pacific University

Anne McIntosh, Central Piedmont Community College

Shellie Michael, Volunteer State Community College

Melanie Neal, Texas Tech University

Carel Neffenger, Jr., Highline Community College

James L. Parker, Vanderbilt University

Catherine Peck, Chippewa Valley Technical College

Kelly Aikin Petkus, Austin Community College

Evelyn Plummer, Seton Hall University

Debra Rose, Western Piedmont Community College

Natalie V. Safley, Northern Virginia Community College

Pam L. Secklin, St. Cloud State University

Sarah Stout, Kellogg Community College

Eric W. Trumbull, Northern Virginia Community College

Mei-ling T. Wang, University of Sciences in Philadelphia

We also appreciate the many talented individuals who prepared the array of supplemental materials listed in the Resources section in this preface. Their contributions to the effective teaching and learning of communication are immeasurable.

An Invitation

We are interested in your feedback about *Communication: The Handbook*. Please contact us by email at the following addresses:

kfroemlin@radford.edu

ggrice@radford.edu

jskinner@alamo.edu

We look forward to hearing from you.

—Kristin K. Froemling, George L. Grice, and John F. Skinner

Foundations of Communication

Communicating competently is important for many reasons:

- **Communicating effectively can boost your self-esteem and lower your social anxiety.**

- **Feeling more confident in your communicative interactions can benefit your relationships and your career.**

- **Connecting with others is a key to improved communication and stronger relationships.**

Communication competence is a learned skill; you are not born an effective and confident speaker. Therefore, as you read through this book and apply the concepts to your daily interactions, you can become a more competent communicator.

Frequently asked questions

Why do I need to take this introductory communication course? I've been communicating all my life.

My boyfriend and I witnessed the same event, but we sure did not "see" it the same way. Why not?

Why does my girlfriend keep saying that I'm not listening? I've heard everything she said.

Why is it that sometimes when talking to my mother, she doesn't understand some of the words I use?

My instructors say that I need to maintain more eye contact with the audience when I am speaking. What difference does it make if I look at the audience?

PART ONE Foundations of Communication

Elements of Communication

OBJECTIVES

Your communication competence will be enhanced by understanding:

- how the process of communication enables you to focus on simultaneous interactions between yourself and others;
- why the elements of communication help you become a more competent communicator;
- how the universals of communication, when applied to your daily interactions, make you a more effective communicator;
- why communicating ethically will prompt others to consider you to be a competent communicator;
- how your connectedness with others helps you better cultivate and exhibit qualities of competence.

1a Getting Started in Communication Studies

Have you ever thought about the importance of communication in your daily life? Think of your daily interactions. What are the reasons you communicate? With whom do you communicate? In this introductory chapter, we will examine the purposes for communicating and we will define communication. This explanation will serve as the basis for each area of communication that we will cover in this textbook: interpersonal communication, group communication, and public speaking.

Why Do We Need Communication?

In this section, we will explore how communication impacts us in four areas: ourselves, our relationships, our careers, and our society.

WHY DO WE NEED COMMUNICATION?

Communication affects the self.
- Self-esteem and confidence
- Perception skills

Communication improves your relationships.
- Family relationships
- Friendships and romantic relationships
- Marriage

Communication is important to your career.
- Teamwork
- Public speaking
- Interviewing

Communication is important to society.
- International relations
- Politics

Communication affects the self. We must communicate in order to obtain the basic necessities of life: food, shelter, and safety. It also affects us in many more subtle, but important, ways.

■ **Self-esteem and confidence.** In learning about how to communicate effectively, you will gain more confidence in all your communication settings, increase your self-esteem, and create new relationships that can open doors in ways you never dreamed possible.

■ **Perception skills.** Your interpretations and judgments of your own behavior and the behavior of others are called perception. Recognizing your own perceptual inaccuracies is one step toward becoming a more competent communicator.

    For example, one way that you might begin to recognize your own biases and stereotypes is through the *Cultural Connections* boxes in each chapter. By examining a variety of cultures and co-cultures, you understand how communication is influenced by the uniqueness of diverse groups of people. Ultimately, we hope that the knowledge you gain through the *Cultural Connections* segments will help you communicate effectively in your future intercultural interactions.

Applying Concepts **DEVELOPING SKILLS** | **Your Communication Abilities**

What one aspect of your communication would you most like to improve by the end of this course? In what way(s) does this communicative weakness affect your life?

Communication improves your relationships. Talking to others enables you to form many types of relationships that satisfy your need for companionship and helps you to seek employment.

■ **Family relationships.** Researchers have discovered that communication patterns that exist between family members can influence how people communicate with romantic partners and same-sex friends in the future. Adolescents raised in a family that values independent thinking and allows opinions that are not necessarily congruent with the parents are more likely to exhibit more competent interpersonal communication skills with both same-sex friends and romantic partners (Koesten, 2004).

■ **Friendships and romantic relationships.** Studies suggest that communication inaccuracies are common among adult communicators;

communicators achieve no more than 25–50 percent accuracy in interpreting each other's messages (Spitzberg, 1994). What are the costs of ineffective or incompetent communication? According to Spitzberg (1994), there is "convincing evidence that social incompetence and isolation are very damaging, personally, relationally, and socially" (p. 28). People who are unable to communicate effectively and appropriately are more likely to face loneliness and depression along with drug and alcohol abuse and stress. Therefore, being an effective and appropriate communicator is "integral to one's well-being" (p. 28).

■ **Marriage.** According to a study conducted by Roper Starch Worldwide, a "lack of effective communication" was the most frequently cited reason for ending a marriage (NCA, 1998). Of those participating in the study, 44% considered ineffective communication a detriment to their relationship, while the next most frequently reported cause was "money problems" (with 38% citing this as a problem). While we cannot solve your money problems, this book will provide you with the skills to talk with a partner more effectively about a variety of issues in order to enhance your relationship.

Applying Concepts DEVELOPING SKILLS | Communication in Your Relationships

Identify a relationship you enjoy in which you and your partner communicate effectively. What characteristics of the communication in that relationship make your communication effective?

Communication is important to your career. Effective speaking skills enhance your chances of securing employment and then advancing in your career. In a 2005 report, the National Association of Colleges and Employers listed those characteristics that employers consider most important in hiring an employee. Communication skills were at the top of the list (NACE, 2005).

■ **Teamwork.** Many employers require new employees—even those whose job descriptions do not include formal presentations—to have good group communication skills. Studies have revealed that training in teamwork skills can improve team success (Bacon, Stewart, & Silver, 1999; Schilder, 1992; Schullery & Gibson, 2001).

■ **Public speaking.** Although you are likely to spend only a small portion of your communication time at work giving presentations and speeches, your ability to stand in front of a group of people and present your ideas is important to your career success. According to a survey conducted by Speak For Success (2007), female executives were asked to list the most critical skill for career success. Almost every participant in the survey (95%) listed public speaking skills as crucial for success. The survey results revealed the importance of communication skills in the ability to move through the management ranks.

- **Interviewing.** Once you are hired, your communication skills continue to work for you, becoming your ticket to career success and advancement. Using interviews with almost 100 public relations executives, Berger, Reber, and Heyman (2005) reported that having effective communication skills and being proactive were most often cited as the reason for the executive's success in public relations.

Applying Concepts
DEVELOPING SKILLS | **Communication in Your Career**

What role will communication play in your career? Among interpersonal communication, group communication, and public speaking, which do you think will be most important throughout your career?

Find an article in a magazine or journal that discusses speech communication in business or professional environments. Does it cover any issues you had not considered?

Defining Communication

Many people have the misconception that communication is easy because they've been communicating all their lives in a variety of contexts. Also, people erroneously equate communication and talking. However, communication is a complex process that contains many elements. We are not born competent communicators—we must *learn* how to communicate competently. Let's start our journey to becoming competent communicators by defining *communication*.

There are as many definitions of communication as there are communication scholars, but each definition shares common elements. For the purposes of this course, we'll define it as follows: **Communication** is a process of sharing meaning through a continuous flow of symbolic messages. Several terms in this definition may need further explanation.

Process. The focal point of the definition is that communication is a continuing "process."

Shared meaning. When we communicate with others, the purpose is to "share meaning."

Continuous flow. The shared meaning is continuously flowing between the people in the interaction as they "send" information and "receive" feedback. This doesn't mean that they are talking at the same time, but rather that they are continuously communicating, even when they are not talking.

Messages. A "message" is coded in symbols that can be either verbal or nonverbal. *Verbal messages* involve words, while *nonverbal messages* include gestures, tone of voice, and anything else that is communicated without words. Nonverbal feedback could include head nodding (to indicate agreement or to show that we are listening), eye contact (to indicate that we are listening), or gestures (which can be used to substitute for or reinforce words). For instance, if your communication partner appears to be bored with your current topic of conversation, we know that communication has occurred and you may adjust your message in response to the nonverbal feedback.

1b   Examining the Transactional Model of Communication

Over the years, communication researchers have gradually developed a model of communication that helps us visualize the various elements of communication and understand how they work together during an interaction. The Transactional Model has evolved as the most accurate and complete model. (See Figure 1.1.)

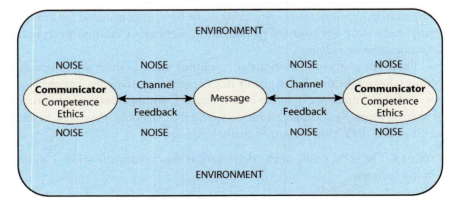

Figure 1.1
The Transactional Model of Communication

Elements of Communication

Let's start by identifying the elements of the transactional model.

Message. A **message** includes any verbal and nonverbal information transmitted from one communicator to another. Verbal messages are transmitted via words. Nonverbal messages are transmitted through gestures, facial expressions, and tone of voice—anything that is not communicated using words.

Communicator. Each person in the interaction is called a **communicator.** Often people misrepresent the communicators in the interaction by labeling them "sender" or "receiver." Those labels do not incorporate the *simultaneous interaction* between the communicators. Each person in the interaction is constantly sending and receiving messages. You do not say something, shut down your brain, and make no facial expressions until your friend responds. As you await your friend's response, you are sending nonverbal feedback that illustrates that you understand what he or she is saying, that you are tired, that you are interested, and so forth.

Channel. We can send messages through a variety of channels. The **channel** is the mechanism used to transmit the message. When we talk about the transactional model of communication, we are typically referring to the face-to-face channel. This means that we are using our voice and our body language as a means of communicating. Other examples of communication channels include telephone, email, IM, blog, and text-messaging. The channel that we use can affect the successful transmission of our message. For example, some channels produce more external noise than others. How many times have you been trying to talk to someone on a cell phone and the message is interrupted by static or a poor connection?

Noise. Messages are often interrupted by noise. **Noise** is anything that interferes with the reception of the message.

- **External noise.** External noise (also called physical noise) is anything outside of the communicators, such as environmental noise. What external noise are you experiencing as you read this chapter?
- **Internal noise.** Internal noise (also called psychological noise) refers to thoughts that you have that keep you from paying attention to the message. Your thoughts could prevent you from focusing on what someone else is saying. Therefore, the person's message was interrupted by your thoughts. For example, during class you might be thinking about what you are going to eat for lunch, or about a romantic relationship problem.

■ **Semantic noise. Semantic noise** occurs when a conversational partner misunderstands or misinterprets something that a partner said, causing them to have a severe reaction. For instance, you might find yourself engaged in the following conversation.

> **YOU:** I was so excited to get my graduate school acceptance letter in the mail yesterday. I have been waiting all week for the mailman to deliver it. My top school accepted me into their graduate program in the fall. Isn't that great?
>
> **YOUR FRIEND:** Mailman?! Mailman?!?! They are called "mail carriers"!

As you can see in this sample conversation, your friend likely didn't hear the remainder of your statement because her attention was diverted by semantic noise upon hearing the politically incorrect term *mailman*.

Applying Concepts
DEVELOPING SKILLS | **Identifying Noise**

Analyze the physical noise present in your classroom. As a listener, how are you affected in receiving the instructor's message? As a speaker, how would you minimize this noise?

Feedback. **Feedback** is response to a message. The feedback arrow in the model (Figure 1.1) points in both directions. Again, this illustrates the simultaneous aspect of feedback. You are both sending feedback to each other, even while you are speaking.

Environment. **Environment** refers to the context in which the communication occurs. There are four dimensions of the environment: physical, temporal, relational, and cultural.

■ **Physical.** The *physical dimension* includes the actual physical setting where the communicators are located. For example, where are you sitting right now? Are you in a noisy, or a quiet location? The physical context can influence conversation. Suppose that you wanted to tell someone something important that you did not want others to know. What location would you choose? Would it be the campus cafeteria or a bench under a tree on campus?

■ **Temporal.** The *temporal dimension* encompasses several aspects of time. First, your interaction could be influenced by calendar time—time of day, day of the week, month of the year. For instance, let's say you want to ask your boss for a raise. Would you approach her first thing in the morning or at the end of the day? Would you choose Monday or Friday to make your request? Why did you choose that time and day? You were using the environment to help influence your interaction.

- **Relational.** The *relational dimension* includes the roles that we play in a given interaction that influence our communication. Let's say that your friend was just hired at your place of employment—as your boss. In what way(s) might that change your communication with her? You might refrain from discussing the amount of time you spend each day IMing with friends while you should be working! The role influences the interaction.

- **Cultural.** As you will see throughout this book, culture is a major influence on communication. If you are talking with someone from another country who has interaction patterns different from yours, you will likely notice the effect of the fourth dimension of environment—the *cultural dimension*. Suppose you are working in a group in another class. If one of the members of the group is consistently late to meetings, you might want to ask yourself if it might be related to cultural differences. Some cultures are less stringent about actual times of day. Instead they arrive *around* the time that is scheduled.

Communication competence. Communication competence is our ability to communicate effectively and appropriately. In each communication interaction, your competence will be on display as will the competence of your communication partner. Differences in competence are evident when one person interrupts the other more frequently. When one person is less communicatively competent, the conversation can become frustrating to the more competent person.

Ethics. Ethics are the standards we use to determine right from wrong, good from bad, in thought and behavior. Part of communication competence is ethical behavior. Each person in the interaction brings with them their ethics, which can influence the interaction. We will elaborate on competence and ethical communication later in this chapter.

Applying Concepts
DEVELOPING SKILLS

Identifying Elements of the Transactional Model

Using Figure 1.1 as a guide, analyze a lecture given by an instructor in one of your classes. Identify all of the various communication elements that are in effect in this situation.

Applying the Transactional Model

Now that we have identified the elements of the transactional model, let's look at how the elements are tied together. The transactional model (Barnlund, 1970) is based on two fundamental concepts regarding the nature of communication.

Simultaneous interaction. **Simultaneous interaction** means that we send and receive messages, both verbal and nonverbal, at the same time. One person is talking—sending both verbal and nonverbal messages— while the other person is sending nonverbal feedback. When you are talking to a friend, the friend is sending nonverbal feedback to you regarding, for example, whether they are interested in the topic of conversation, whether they are paying attention to you, or whether they can hear you.

Mutual influence. **Mutual influence** occurs when nonverbal feedback produces changes in another person's communication. For example, you are talking to a friend and the friend puts his hand to his ear. Your friend is using this nonverbal gesture to indicate that he cannot hear you. Mutual influence is exemplified if you speak louder as a result of your friend's nonverbal message. His feedback changed the way you were communicating with him.

Let's look at a different example. Suppose you are talking about a medical procedure that you saw on the Discovery Health channel last night. Your friend makes a really negative facial expression and covers her ears. The nonverbal feedback should cause you to stop talking about that topic that is too uncomfortable for her to hear.

Applying Concepts
DEVELOPING SKILLS

Identifying Simultaneous Interaction and Mutual Influence

Consider an interaction in your classroom between the instructor and a student. In what way did simultaneous interaction and mutual influence occur? Was the instructor attentive to the verbal and nonverbal behaviors of the students? If your answer is "no," what could the instructor have done to make the communication event more of a two-way experience? If your answer is "yes," give examples to illustrate the instructor's attentiveness to student feedback.

Cultural CONNECTIONS

Analyzing the Transactional Model: Native Americans

How often do you use the phrases "sitting Indian style" or "Indian giver"? When you do not come from a marginalized culture, you might not realize the hurt implied in the words you choose. What we learn about Native Americans is found mostly in American history textbooks. But what is included in textbooks about their *culture*? People often think of Native Americans as part of American history— a thing of the past. But Native Americans are still actively celebrating their heritage in many states across the country.

Jo White, a communication major at Radford University, has spent the past ten years researching her Native American heritage. Jo's grandmother was a member of the Seneca tribe in the Iroquois confederacy.

Just as with any other culture, Native Americans take offense to language that is disparaging to their culture. One usage that particularly bothers Jo (and many other Native Americans) is the misuse of the term "powwow," as in "the department

members are having a powwow." A powwow is a celebration of Native American heritage. One reason for having a powwow is to educate people about the Native American culture. To equate a work meeting with a powwow is denigrating the spirit and intent of a true Native American powwow.

What other terms can you think of that are part of American vocabulary that come from Native American culture? What terms can you substitute for those to make the statement less offensive?

For a closer examination of Native American culture, Jo recommends that you watch the movie *Smoke Signals,* based on a book by Sherman Alexie.

Application

Re-examine Figure 1.1. At which points in the model are there the greatest opportunities for misunderstandings or friction resulting from cultural differences?

1c   Identifying Communication Contexts

A **communication context** is determined by both the environment in which you are communicating and the number of people with whom you are interacting. The environment encompasses a range of variables that can affect interactions—including the physical space or less tangible factors such as culture, relationships that exist between the communicators, or any specific situation that can affect an interaction. For instance, the nature of your communication with friends at a party may be quite different from that between strangers at a party; both are quite different from your communication in class. Throughout this book, we will focus on how the context or environment affects our communication.

The number of people interacting, also considered to be part of the context, can range from one person in intrapersonal communication (communicating with yourself) to many in mass communication (communicating to an audience that could consist of millions of people). Typically communication researchers use the term *level* when they are talking about the number of people taking part in the interaction. We will examine five different contexts or levels of communication starting with the fewest number of communicators and ending with the highest number of communicators.

Intrapersonal communication. **Intrapersonal communication** is communication that takes place within ourselves. Intrapersonal communication is mostly silent in that it is a part of our thought process, but there are times when we might talk to ourselves aloud. We will discuss intrapersonal communication in more detail in Chapter 2, as it is an important part of our development of the self (for example, self-esteem).

Interpersonal communication. As soon as our conversation involves another person, it moves to the second level. **Interpersonal communication** is communication between two people. Interpersonal communication is sometimes called dyadic communication; *dyad* is Latin for "pair." Interpersonal communication is at the heart of relationship building and maintenance. We will examine interpersonal communication in detail in Chapters 6 and 7.

Group communication. Interactions that take place among three to fifteen people are classified as **group communication.** Often these encounters are part of the everyday business environment. We will examine group communication in detail in Chapters 8 and 9.

Public speaking. **Public speaking** occurs when one person speaks face to face with an audience. In public speaking an audience can consist of a small number of people, or hundreds, or even thousands of people and communication is more formal and deliberate. We will examine public communication in detail in Chapters 10 through 15.

Mass communication. The final level of communication is **mass communication,** which involves a sender transmitting a message—often hundreds of thousands to billions—who cannot be gathered in one place. The study of mass communication is beyond the scope of this book, but there are likely courses on the subject available at your college or university.

Applying Concepts
DEVELOPING SKILLS

Applying the Transactional Model in Various Contexts

Draw diagrams that would illustrate an intrapersonal interaction, an interpersonal interaction, a group interaction, a public speaking interaction, and a mass communication interaction. How might the three types of noise influence each of the interactions differently? What environmental factors are likely to be different? Can you think of any element of communication interactions that the transactional model may not account for?

1d Understanding the Universals of Communication

Watzlawick, Beavin, and Jackson (1967) were the first scholars to write down what we refer to as the Universals of Communication (Watzlawick, et al. called them "axioms" of communication). **Universals (or axioms)** are rules or principles of communication interaction that are true of any human communication in any context. Watzlawick, et al. define these as "simple properties of communication" (p. 48).

You cannot not communicate.

Because we are sending messages nonverbally at all times, it is impossible to not communicate. For instance, have you ever asked your boss if it is OK to ask her a question? She says "of course," but then proceeds with what she is doing and does not look up at you. Does her action communicate more information than her response?

We say that you cannot not communicate because messages can be both *intended* (you planned to communicate the message) or *unintended* (you did not plan to communicate the message as it was interpreted by the other communicator).

Applying Concepts
DEVELOPING SKILLS

Identifying Principle One (*You cannot not communicate*) in Your Interactions

Consider one communicative interaction you have had today. Can you identify one aspect of that interaction that would exemplify Principle One?

Principle	Brief Explanation	Example
Principle One: *You cannot not communicate.*	Because we are sending messages nonverbally at all times, it is not possible to not communicate.	You are reading a magazine and your friend asks you a question. You do not hear the question because you are concentrating on your reading. Despite the fact that you have not said a word, your friend will see that you are reading and ask the question later when you are finished reading.
Principle Two: *All communication has a content and a relationship dimension.*	The content dimension represents the words in the message that is communicated. The relational dimension refers to the role(s) that each person plays in the interaction.	Your mother says: "Take out the trash." *Content dimension*: She uses words to communicate that she wants you to take out the trash. *Relational dimension*: She is your mother, so her superior role may compel you to take out the trash more than if a sibling asked the same thing.
Principle Three: *Communication is a series of punctuated events.*	Punctuation is the act of placing emphasis (cause and effect) on a particular communicative act. When two people punctuate a communicative act differently, conflict may result.	Two parents disagree about who was supposed to take their child to soccer practice. The mother thinks she told the father to do it because she had choir practice and the father thinks he told the mother to do it because he took the child the week before.
Principle Four: *Communication is irreversible and unrepeatable.*	Communication is irreversible because once you have sent a message you cannot take it back. Communication is unrepeatable because you can never recreate the same communication situation.	Suppose that you made a negative comment about a co-worker, not realizing that she was right behind you. You cannot take back what you have already said. Celebrating an anniversary at the same location as the previous year will yield very different communication. Your relationship has changed over the year, and your topics of conversation are likely to be different. Therefore, communication is unrepeatable.
Principle Five: *Communication is culture-specific.*	Every culture has unique ways of communicating.	Some cultures believe that the older person in the interaction should initiate a handshake.

All communication has a content and a relationship dimension.

When we communicate with others, we can identify a content dimension and a relationship dimension.

Content dimension. The **content dimension** represents the words in the message that are communicated. For instance, if you ask your roommate to close the door, the content of the message is that you want the door closed and you want your roommate to close the door.

Relationship dimension. The **relationship dimension** refers to the role(s) that each person plays in the interaction. Because you and your roommate are likely to be peers, your roommate might tell you to "Close the darn door yourself." However, if a father asked his son to close the door, the son might be more inclined to obey the father because of the unequal role relationship. The relational dimension is often conveyed through the tone of voice and the power balance in the relationship.

**Applying Concepts
DEVELOPING SKILLS**

Identifying Principle Two (*Communication has content and relational dimensions*) in Your Interactions

Continuing with the same interaction you selected in the previous *Applying Concepts Developing Skills* box, provide a statement that you and the other communicator made. Write it as a brief dialogue. Identify the relationship dimension in the message. Next identify the content dimension. Do you frequently encounter easily identifiable relationship and content distinctions in your interaction with this person?

Communication is a series of punctuated events.

Have you ever been in an argument with a romantic partner about who is correctly interpreting a situation? Typically the argument devolves into a discussion of whose behavior caused the problem in the first place. **Punctuation** is the act of placing emphasis on a particular communicative or behavioral event. Through punctuation, we look at events in terms of cause and effect.

Suppose that Kris and Pat are roommates. When they moved in together, they developed a system for assigning chores that changes each week. One week Kris is in charge of taking out the trash and Pat is in charge of washing the dishes. The next week, they swap chores. Kris washes dishes and Pat takes out the trash. Several months later, the trash is stacked above the top of the trashcan in the kitchen and the dirty dishes have been in the sink for several days. Not surprisingly, an argument ensues. Kris accuses Pat of not taking out the garbage and, naturally, Pat accuses Kris of not washing the dishes.

In situations like the one that Pat and Kris find themselves, it is best to acknowledge that punctuation is occurring. If each individual can see that the other is attributing a different cause for the problem, there might be a chance to move past the blame game and find a solution. Too often, conflict escalates when people get stuck trying to find one person to blame. Ultimately, both people need to acknowledge their roles in the problem and find a way to prevent the same occurrence in the future.

Applying Concepts
DEVELOPING SKILLS

Identifying Principle Three (*Communication is a series of punctuated events*) in Your Interactions

Think of a time when you have been in a disagreement with another person. Are you able to identify whether you and the other communicator were punctuating the event differently? How did the situation conclude? Was there something you could have done to produce a different outcome—whether it was positive or negative?

Communication is irreversible and unrepeatable.

Have you ever said something that you would pay a million dollars to take back? Unfortunately, that is not possible. (And if you have never said anything that you wished you could take back, then you are a lucky person!) Have you ever had such a great interaction with someone that you hoped to have the same interaction the next time you met? Each interaction we have with someone is unique and not repeatable.

Communication is irreversible. Attorneys use this principle to their advantage during trials. How many times have you seen a court drama on television in which the attorney gets a witness to say something that is considered "inappropriate" or "leading"? What does the judge say in response? "Strike that from the record." What is the problem with that? Communication is irreversible. The court reporter can delete the utterance from the official court record of the proceeding, but the jury members heard the statement and it cannot be wiped from their brains like it can be deleted from the court record.

Communication is unrepeatable. Just as communication cannot be taken back, it cannot be repeated. Consider an office manager who needs to meet with several work groups about a new policy for submitting requests for equipment. She prepares a presentation and hopes to use it for every group. She finds that the feedback she gets from each group is different and the same message cannot be used again and again.

We can relate this principle to the temporal dimension of environment. Recall that the temporal dimension includes the location of the interaction in the entire series of interactions you have had with an individual. Every interaction influences subsequent interactions so that no communication can be repeated.

Applying Concepts
DEVELOPING SKILLS

Identifying Principle Four (*Communication is irreversible and unrepeatable*) in Your Interactions

Think of a time when you said something that you wish you could have taken back. How did the other person react to that statement? What was the perception of your statement? What would you have said differently if you were able to erase what you said?

Communication is culture-specific.

The culture in which you were raised plays an important part in your communicative development. You learn about the appropriateness of words, nonverbal cues, and so forth. However, what is acceptable and appropriate in your culture might not be acceptable and appropriate in other cultures. Throughout this book, you will see that cultures have different ways of communicating the same thing.

If you were attending a football game in the United States, not only would you be attending the game Americans traditionally refer to as "football" (as opposed to "soccer," which the rest of the world refers to as "football"), but you would cheer for your team by clapping and whistling. If you were attending a football game in England, you would actually be watching "soccer," and the whistling that you hear is equivalent to "booing" in U.S. culture. Quite a different interpretation of whistling, right? The same nonverbal cue means entirely different things to different cultures.

Applying Concepts
DEVELOPING SKILLS

Identifying Principle Five (*Communication is culture-specific*) in Your Interactions

Explain an encounter with someone when cultural differences influenced the effective transmission and reception of your message. What did you learn from that interaction? Did it influence your subsequent interactions with that person or persons of a similar cultural background?

1e Communicating Ethically

Ethics refers to the standards we use to distinguish right from wrong, or good from bad, in thought and behavior. The ethical framework we choose guides the choices we make in all aspects of our professional and private lives. You should not be surprised that your academic studies include a discussion of ethics. You are, after all, educating yourself to function in a world where you will make ethical decisions daily.

Two principles frame our discussion of ethics.

- **All parties in the communication process have ethical responsibilities.** Assume, for example, that college administrators had denied one of your instructors a requested leave of absence. Assume as well that this instructor, without revealing his or her true motives, used class time to provoke and anger you about inadequate parking or poor food quality in the student center, then led you across campus to take the school president hostage, barricade yourselves in the administration building, and tear up the place.

  Anyone who knew the facts of this case would agree that the instructor acted unethically; it is wrong to manipulate people by keeping your true motives hidden from them. Yet students who let themselves be exploited by participating in such a violent and destructive episode would also share ethical responsibility for what happened. College students, no matter what their age, know that their actions have consequences. As this preposterous example demonstrates, all parties involved in communication share ethical obligations.

In spite of this, communication textbooks often discuss ethics only from a personal perspective, presenting ethical standards as a list of dos and don'ts for the sender of the message. Certainly, you have ethical responsibilities as a communicator, but a speaker-centered approach to ethics is incomplete. Communication, as we suggest throughout this textbook, is an activity shared by all individuals involved in the interaction. As such, all parties have ethical responsibilities. For that reason, we will discuss the ethics of speaking *and* listening.

■ **Ethical speakers and listeners possess attitudes and standards that pervade their character and guide their actions before, during, and after a communication interaction.** In other words, ethical speakers and listeners do more than just abstain from unethical behaviors. Ethics is as much a frame of mind as it is a pattern of behavior. Ethics is not something you apply to one situation; it is a working philosophy you apply to your daily life and bring to all communicative situations.

Consider the actions of the speaker in the following incident that was witnessed in a classroom. Lisa presented a persuasive speech on the need for recycling paper, plastic, and aluminum products. To illustrate the many types of recyclables and how over-packaged many grocery products are, she used as an effective visual aid a paper grocery bag filled with empty cans, paper products, and a variety of plastic bottles and containers. After listening to her well-researched, well-delivered speech, with its impassioned final appeal for us to help save the planet by recycling, the class watched in amazement as she put the empty containers back into the bag, walked to the corner of the room, and dropped the bag in the trash can! After a few seconds, someone finally asked the question that had to be asked: "You mean you're not going to take those home to recycle them?" "Nah," said Lisa. "I'm tired of lugging them around. I've done my job."

You may or may not believe that people have an ethical responsibility to recycle. But regardless of your views on that issue, you likely question the ethics of someone who insists, in effect, "Do as I say, not as I do." Lisa's actions made the entire class question the sincerity with which she spoke. Ethical standards cannot be turned on and off at an individual's convenience.

Throughout this textbook, a feature called "Eye on Ethics" will help you to explore ethical issues in your communicative interactions.

Applying Concepts
DEVELOPING SKILLS

Identifying Ethical and Unethical Communication

Select two individuals prominent on the international, national, state, or local scene whom you consider to be ethical speakers. What characteristics do they possess that make them ethical? Select two people you consider unethical. What ethical standards do they abuse?

1f Communicating Competently

Communication competence is the ability to communicate effectively and appropriately within a given communication context. Communication competence, in essence, involves our ability to communicate effectively and appropriately with others in a variety of contexts. Communication competence is a relatively new concept in the realm of communication research. It first appeared in communication literature in the early 1980s. One prominent communication competence researcher is Brian Spitzberg, whose research

EYEONETHICS | Being Yourself

Sondra is preparing a speech on defensive driving. A drama major, she is comfortable playing all sorts of characters on stage, but the thought of standing in front of an audience and delivering a speech terrifies her. She has visions of herself clutching the lectern, staring blankly at her notes, and mumbling inaudibly. "I'll feel so exposed—I don't think I can get through it just being my ordinary self," Sondra confides to her friends. She asks their help in brainstorming ways to steel herself before she comes to class on speech day.

"An energy drink would perk you up; you'd zip right through your speech before you even had time to get scared," offers Amy.

"Or you could dress like a car crash dummy and deliver your speech in character," jokes her boyfriend, Steve.

What do you think of these suggestions? Could Sondra follow any of her friends' advice and still "be herself" as she speaks?

Application

Given the two principles of ethics discussed in this module, what advice would you offer if you were her friend?

serves as a foundation for the discussion of competence in this module. Throughout the book, at the end of each chapter, we will look at all the communication theory and skills we discuss in terms of how they relate to improving our communication competence.

- **Competence can be *learned.*** By understanding and applying what you read in this book, you can become a more competent communicator! You might hear someone referred to as a "born communicator." There is no scientific evidence to support the existence of a competent communicator gene.

- **Competence is *situational.*** The "born communicator" does not exist, but some people have the natural ability to sense the needs of others and to be savvy about appropriateness in a variety of environments. Our competence changes from situation to situation. We might communicate more effectively and appropriately in interpersonal contexts than group contexts, for example.

- **Competence is *culture-specific.*** One of the main arguments among scholars with regard to communication competence is that behaviors some people consider to be effective and appropriate communicative behaviors might not be considered effective or appropriate to others. Therefore, remember that each culture has its own criteria that identify someone as a competent communicator.

Components of Communication Competence

According to Spitzberg (1994), in any situation we must consider whether a communicative behavior is both effective and appropriate in order for it to be considered a competent communication.

Effectiveness. **Communication effectiveness** is the accomplishment of desired outcomes in a communicative interaction. That is, you need to consider whether or not you accomplish what you set out to accomplish in that interaction.

Appropriateness. **Communication appropriateness** refers to whether or not the communicative behavior was suitable to the given context in which the behavior was enacted. This includes following stated or unstated rules of interaction and norms of behavior for that context. Is it *appropriate* to speak in a normal tone of voice to a fellow classmate during a class lecture? There is a norm in the classroom that speaking to a classmate while the professor is talking (or anyone else who has the professor's permission to speak) is inappropriate because it is rude—especially talking in a "normal" volume rather than a whisper.

Enhancing Your Communication Competence

So where do you start in enhancing your communication competence?

Start with yourself. Analyze your communicative strengths and weaknesses. In what contexts do you feel most comfortable communicating? Perhaps as you work on your competence, you can place yourself into new contexts that will help you to improve your communication.

Watch the communication of others. Among your friends, classmates, and family members, whose communication skills do you most want to emulate? What do they do that makes them effective and appropriate communicators? It is okay to learn from others—even to mimic their behaviors. Of course, you don't want to be annoying or obvious, but it is perfectly acceptable to subtly incorporate those behaviors into your repertoire of skills.

Learn about other cultures. Seek out people who are not like you—those of a different race, ethnicity, age, and so forth. Talk to them and learn about their experiences. They can educate you about things you might not have otherwise learned. How do you know what gestures are appropriate from culture to culture? You could ask individuals from various cultures to answer that question for you. The best way to become more comfortable communicating with people who are not like you is to interact with them. Expand your knowledge about the world and you'll find that you become a more competent communicator because you have some understanding of the world around you. Besides, if nothing else, you'll have plenty of new things to talk about with others!

Learn about your own culture. How do members of your culture use language? What behaviors are considered inappropriate? Does the appropriateness vary depending on the context in which the behavior is enacted? Keep in mind that everyone is unique. Each person in your culture will not act exactly the same.

Applying Concepts
DEVELOPING SKILLS

Assessing Your Communication Competence

Make a list of your communication strengths and weaknesses—be sure to consider both effectiveness and appropriateness. Think of the most competent communicator you know. Identify the strengths of that person's communicative ability that makes him or her effective. How might you integrate those qualities to enhance your communication competence?

ENHANCING COMMUNICATION COMPETENCE

Start with yourself

Watch the communication of others

Learn about others

Learn about your own cultures

Competence SUMMARY

In this chapter, you have learned the following concepts. Check to be sure you have achieved each of the communication competencies.

1a Getting Started in Communication Studies

- Communication is a process of sharing meaning by sending and receiving symbolic cues.
- Messages (both verbal and nonverbal) continuously flow between communicators. You and the other communicator(s) are simultaneously sending and receiving messages.
- Employers seek employees who have good communication skills and can work effectively in groups.

Competence. Can I define communication as a process and focus on the simultaneous interaction between myself and others? Do I pay attention to the other person's nonverbal feedback while I'm speaking? Are the messages I am communicating effective and appropriate, and thus competent?

1b Examining the Transactional Model of Communication

- The Transactional Model is considered the most accurate representation of communication because it illustrates the concepts of simultaneous interaction and mutual influence that are characteristic of interactions.
- Simultaneous interaction means that you and the other person are continually sending and receiving verbal and nonverbal messages.

- Mutual influence refers to the fact that as you receive nonverbal feedback from the other communicator, you adapt your message. If the other person appears to be fidgeting or looking at her watch, do you cut your interaction short or ask if you should continue the discussion later?
- Elements of the transactional model include message, communicator, channel, feedback, noise, environment/context, communication competence, and ethics.

Competence. Can I identify the elements at play when I communicate in various contexts? Can I adapt this process of communication to help me to become a more effective and appropriate communicator?

1c Identifying Communication Contexts

- A communication context is defined by the environment in which you are communicating and the number of people involved in the interaction.
- Intrapersonal communication takes place within ourselves, interpersonal communication occurs between two people, group communication involves three to fifteen people, public speaking can include a small audience or an audience of hundreds of people, and mass communication occurs through a mediated channel to millions of people.

Competence. Can I identify the different communication contexts? Can I distinguish one context from another context?

1d Understanding the Universals of Communication

- You cannot not communicate.
- All communication has a content and a relationship dimension.
- Communication is a series of punctuated events.
- Communication is irreversible and unrepeatable.
- Communication is culture-specific.

Competence. Am I able to explain the five universals of communication and recognize how they can make my everyday communication more effective and appropriate? Can I identify important nonverbal communication cues and cultural differences that may come into play in a communication interaction?

1e Communicating Ethically

- Ethics are the standards by which you determine right from wrong, good from bad. They are a working philosophy that you apply to your daily life and bring to all communicative situations.
- All parties in the communication process have ethical responsibilities.

Competence. Do I understand how ethical behavior and ethical communication will enable me to make more appropriate interactive choices? Will others consider me to be a competent communicator?

1f Communicating Competently

- Communication competence is the ability to effectively and appropriately communicate with others in a variety of contexts.
- Communication competence can be learned and it is situational.
- Effectiveness and appropriateness of communication are the two key factors of communication competence.

Competence. Being an effective and appropriate communicator is integral to your overall well-being. When you recognize your interconnectedness with others, you are better able to cultivate and exhibit qualities of competence, such as effective interaction management and supportiveness.

Review Questions

1. Why is it important to study communication?
2. How does noise influence feedback?
3. What is communication context and why is it important to communicators?
4. Why is communication irreversible and unrepeatable?
5. What are ethics? Why is it important to become an ethical communicator?
6. What is communication competence? How can you become a competent communicator?

Discussion Questions

1. If you were interviewing a candidate to become your employee, what communication skills would you consider to be most important for that employee to possess? How would you rate your own abilities with regard to those skills?
2. Analyze the physical noise present in your classroom. As a listener, how does this affect your reception of your instructor's message? As a speaker, how might you minimize the effect of this noise? If you were redesigning the classroom, what changes would you make to minimize this type of noise?
3. Some instructors do not discuss ethics in the classroom because they believe that "what is ethical to one person is not ethical to another." Do you think that ethics is an important component of communication? How do you think the topic of ethics should be covered in your communication class?

Key Terms

channel *p. 7*

communication *p. 5*

communication appropriateness *p. 21*

communication competence *p. 20*

communication context *p. 11*

communication effectiveness *p. 21*

communicator *p. 7*

content dimension *p. 15*

environment *p. 8*

ethics *p. 18*

feedback *p. 8*

group communication *p. 12*

interpersonal communication *p. 12*

intrapersonal communication *p. 12*

mass communication *p. 12*

message *p. 7*

mutual influence *p. 10*

noise (external, internal, semantic) *p. 7–8*

public speaking *p. 12*

punctuation *p. 15*

relational dimension *p. 15*

simultaneous interaction *p. 10*

universals (axioms) of communication *p. 13*

Understanding Communication Apprehension

Have you been in a situation requiring you to communicate with one other person, with a group, or in front of an audience and found yourself nervous or anxious? Such a reaction is normal. It's called **communication apprehension**, or "the level of fear or anxiety associated with either real or anticipated communication with another person or persons" (McCroskey, 1977, p. 78).

Communication apprehension is similar in nature to shyness, and it can afflict anyone. Even extroverted people can feel apprehensive about communicating in certain situations. Because high communication apprehension can affect a person's communication competence, we will explore the nature of communication apprehension throughout this textbook and offer suggestions about reducing your communication apprehension.

Many people consider communication apprehension only in a public speaking context. But you can also experience a fear of speaking interpersonally, perhaps with a boss or a police officer, or speaking among a group of people (i.e., not speaking up during a meeting).

HIGH COMMUNICATION APPREHENSION

People who have high communication apprehension (CA) are uncomfortable in interactions with another person, in a group, in a meeting, and/or when delivering a speech. As a result of their fear and anxiety, people with high CA will withdraw from or avoid interactions in which they must communicate with others. The person with high CA will not avoid *all* human interaction, but rather will minimize settings in which he or she might experience the type of communication that causes the apprehension.

Example of High CA

Rochelle spends a significant amount of time in her dorm room. While roommates tried at the beginning of the semester to include her in their activities, she declined so often that they stopped asking her to participate. In class she sits in the back of the room and does not ask questions or discuss readings, despite being an above-average student.

According to McCroskey & Richmond (1976), high-CA individuals are perceived as less credible, less socially attractive, and much less influential in their environment than are individuals with less communication apprehension. McCroskey and Richmond suggest that if you are a highly apprehensive communicator and you want to be perceived more positively, you should learn to reduce your communication apprehension.

LOW COMMUNICATION APPREHENSION

People with low communication apprehension (CA) enjoy interacting with others in a variety of contexts. While they may find themselves in a few situations causing them to experience some nervousness (such as delivering a speech to a large audience), they are typically comfortable communicating in most situations.

Example of Low CA

Ileana belongs to many clubs on campus. She is president of her sorority, and she actively participates in community service activities. In the classroom, she sits near the front and center of the room where she can answer her professor's questions and contribute to discussions about readings. People are often heard admiring her ability to deliver speeches to audiences large and small.

Low apprehensives, according to McCroskey and Richmond (1976), are often perceived as more similar, more credible, more socially attractive, and more influential in social situations than high apprehensives.

MODERATE COMMUNICATION APPREHENSION

The majority of people experience moderate communication apprehension. Someone with moderate CA may find that certain situations provoke

anxiety. Perhaps speaking with a superior (e.g., boss or parent) or delivering a speech at a fundraising event causes nervousness for a moderately apprehensive person. Such a person does not withdraw or avoids interaction (like a highly apprehensive individual), but he or she is not as comfortable in all situations as the person with low CA would be.

Example of Moderate CA

Josh enjoys interacting with his wife when he gets home from work. On the weekends, he looks forward to catching up with his friends on the basketball court. However, at work, he is a store manager and is asked periodically to give presentations to other managers in his district. He exhibits some anxiety about peaking in front of a group of people, though he is by no means unable to deliver such presentations.

Because researchers have focused almost solely on high CA and low CA, there is minimal information about how moderately apprehensive communicators are perceived. However, it is widely accepted that it is natural for people to feel some degree of anxiety depending on the situation.

Application: Personal Report of Communication Apprehension (PRCA-24)

Complete the PRCA-24 (Personal Report of Communication Apprehension) below. This popular research instrument measures your communication apprehension in four contexts: speaking in dyads (interpersonal communication), speaking in groups, speaking in meetings, and public speaking.

Personal Report of Communication Apprehension (PRCA-24)

DIRECTIONS: This instrument is composed of 24 statements concerning your feelings about communication with other people. Please indicate in the space provided the degree to which each statement applies to you by marking whether you (1) Strongly Agree, (2) Agree, (3) Are Undecided, (4) Disagree, or (5) Strongly Disagree with each statement. There are no right or wrong answers. Many of the statements are similar to other statements. Do not be concerned about this. Work quickly; just record your first impression.

_____ 1. I dislike participating in group discussions.
_____ 2. Generally, I am comfortable while participating in a group discussion.
_____ 3. I am tense and nervous while participating in group discussions.
_____ 4. I like to get involved in group discussions.
_____ 5. Engaging in a group discussion with new people makes me tense and nervous.
_____ 6. I am calm and relaxed while participating in group discussions.
_____ 7. Generally, I am nervous when I have to participate in a meeting.
_____ 8. Usually I am calm and relaxed while participating in meetings.
_____ 9. I am very calm and relaxed when I am called upon to express an opinion at a meeting.
_____ 10. I am afraid to express myself at meetings.
_____ 11. Communicating at meetings usually makes me uncomfortable.
_____ 12. I am very relaxed when answering questions at a meeting.
_____ 13. While participating in a conversation with a new acquaintance, I feel very nervous.
_____ 14. I have no fear of speaking up in conversations.
_____ 15. Ordinarily I am very tense and nervous in conversations.
_____ 16. Ordinarily I am very calm and relaxed in conversations.
_____ 17. While conversing with a new acquaintance, I feel very relaxed.
_____ 18. I'm afraid to speak up in conversations.
_____ 19. I have no fear of giving a speech.
_____ 20. Certain parts of my body feel very tense and rigid while giving a speech.
_____ 21. I feel relaxed while giving a speech.
_____ 22. My thoughts become confused and jumbled when I am giving a speech.
_____ 23. I face the prospect of giving a speech with confidence.
_____ 24. While giving a speech, I get so nervous I forget facts I really know.

SCORING:

Group = 18 − (1) + (2) − (3) + (4) − (5) + (6)
Meeting =18 − (7) + (8) + (9) − (10) − (11) + (12)
Dyadic = 18 − (13) + (14) − (15) + (16) + (17) − (18)
Public = 18 + (19) − (20) + (21) − (22) + (23) − (24)
Overall CA = Group + Meeting + Dyadic + Public

An overall score between 80 and 120 indicates you are **high** in communication apprehension.
An overall score between 51 and 79 indicates you are **moderate** in communication apprehension.
An overall score between 24 and 50 indicates you are **low** in communication apprehension.

FROM: "Personal Report of Communication Apprehension (PRCA-24)," pp. 40-41, from *An Introduction to Rhetorical Communication* by James C. McCroskey. © 2006. Reproduced by permission of Pearson Education, Inc.

Perception of the Self and Others

Your communication competence will be enhanced by understanding:

- how you form perceptions so that you can work toward reducing your tendency to stereotype and instead treat each person as an individual;

- the types of personal biases that inhibit perceptual accuracy so you can become more objective in attributing motives for behaviors;

- the influences on your perceptions—in order to help you to better understand yourself;

- the importance of engaging in perception checking to help you keep the lines of communication open between you and the person with whom you are communicating.

2a   Understanding Perception

Perception is the process of assessing information in your surroundings. It is important in your daily interactions. The information you use to form perceptions comes from stimuli that arouse your senses. You might see a hairstyle, smell freshly baked cookies, or hear a familiar voice. You notice how others react to your behavior. These stimuli are interpreted in your brain and become a part of your perception.

In the previous chapter, you learned about the concept of punctuation. As you may recall, punctuation occurs when you attribute a different cause for behavior than another person does. For instance, you might misinterpret a friend's help as a hindrance, while the friend intends merely to help. You might also have a different view of what caused a particular problem. You and a sister could be arguing. From your perspective, there was no nastiness until your sister raised her voice. But from her perspective, it was *you* who started the nastiness by raising your voice. Both of these scenarios represent a difference in punctuation, and thus, a difference in *perception*.

Consider the scene of a car accident. It is highly likely that each eyewitness has a different perception of the events leading to the accident. This will be especially true for the two people involved in the accident—each will probably blame the other for causing the crash.

Why are there so many different sides to each of these scenarios? Because we never perceive stimuli directly. Our senses pick up the stimuli, which are *filtered* through our brain, and subsequently are altered by our previous experiences and knowledge. The altered interpretation becomes a perception. Later in this chapter, we will see how perceptions are altered by various influences on perception. But first, let's look at the three stages of the perception process.

2b Identifying the Stages of the Perception Process

The stages of perception occur almost simultaneously. Stage models often imply a linear, progressive process that could be stretched over an extended period of time. But, as you read about these stages, you will see how all three can occur within a mere second or two of time (perhaps even less than one second!).

Stage One: Stimulation

Stage One is stimulation in which your senses are activated by a sound, smell, noise, or touch that triggers the perception process. Given all that you encounter in your environment, you cannot possibly pay attention to every stimulus. Try this: Feel the clothes on your skin, the shoes on your feet, the book in your hands; hear the noises in your room; smell the scent of the room; and taste the food or drink in your mouth. Can you perceive all of this at once? Doubtful. Because you cannot attend to every stimulus in your environment, you engage in *selective perception*.

Selective perception. **Selective perception** occurs when you attend to some stimuli and not others. Some stimuli characteristics may capture our attention more than others; here are those we perceive most readily.

- **Intensity.** Typically, we are prone to noticing things that are of greater *intensity* than normal, such as things that are brighter or louder. Advertisers use this behavior to their advantage. Did you ever notice that commercials are often louder than regular programming? Advertisers hope that if you walk out of the room you will still hear the commercial. Commercials often contain loud noises and flash bright objects. The commercial might start with the crashing sound of breaking glass or the loud sneeze from someone with a cold. These louder items draw our attention.

- **Novelty.** We also notice things that are *unusual*. Despite the newer trend toward punk-inspired appearances, most people still react to a person with a bright blue Mohawk hairstyle or whose body is covered in tattoos or piercings. The first author of this textbook has several rabbits as pets. One of the rabbits enjoys playing in the grass outside. To keep him from getting away, she puts a leash on him. Needless to say, this draws many a double-take from passers-by! How often do you see a rabbit on a leash?

- **Repetition.** *Repetition* is another factor involved in selective perception. Things that we see or hear over and over tend to resonate in our minds. That's why seeing someone who looks familiar may catch your attention. Advertisers know that repetition is a key to persuasion. The more you hear something, the more you tend to remember it. The same is true for perception: the more you see or hear something, the more likely you are to notice it.

- **Motivation.** Another factor that determines what stimuli we attend to is our *motives*. Suppose that you are romantically attracted to someone. You likely hang on every word that the person says or every gesture that the person makes trying to determine if that person would reciprocate your romantic desires. Therefore, you are more likely to notice if the person sits closer to you or talks about "future" events together because of your motive; you are interpreting cues to determine, in this case, attraction. Therefore, the motive that you bring to a communicative interaction can skew your attention to all behavioral cues, and/or you could misinterpret cues to fit your motives.

Selective exposure. The second part of Stage One is selective exposure. **Selective exposure** is when we consciously expose ourselves to certain viewpoints that are consistent with our own. This could include maintaining friendships with people who share similar beliefs, or exposing ourselves only to messages that are consistent with our own beliefs. If you are a Democrat, you might visit only Web sites that espouse those ideals. The same is true if you are a Republican. In this instance, you are limiting your exposure to other points of view.

Applying Concepts DEVELOPING SKILLS | Analyzing Your Selective Exposure

Selective exposure is when you consciously expose yourself only to viewpoints that are consistent with your own. List three ways to expand your exposure to viewpoints that are less consistent with your own. Pick one and take steps to do it to widen your exposure.

Stage Two: Organization

During Stage Two, organization, your brain organizes the stimuli into pockets of knowledge called **schemata**. You develop schemata over time based on your experiences, and schemata change as your experiences change. For example, you may refine your "definitions" of expectations for friendships, who you think you are, and characteristics of a loving romantic relationship.

Peter Andersen conducted many research studies examining cognitive schemata. Based on his research, he developed six categories of schemata that guide our interactions: cultural, situation, self-schemata, state, interpersonal, and relational schemata.

Cultural schemata. **Cultural schemata** are based on your ethnic heritage and your familial experiences. According to Andersen (1993), cultural schemata guide what you consider to be appropriate behavior. This knowledge base includes cultural differences that influence how you interact with others. For instance, in the United States, it is considered appropriate to shake hands when you meet someone new or greet someone you know. In some other cultures, it is more appropriate to kiss each other on the cheek. Your cultural upbringing dictates what you consider to be appropriate behavior. Therefore, when you experience behavior that you would consider inappropriate in your culture, you tend to view negatively the person who is violating your cultural norm.

Situation schemata. **Situation schemata** refer to the appropriateness of a behavior in a given context. In other words, are public displays of affection appropriate in church, synagogue, or mosque? In the classroom, is it appropriate to speak without asking permission?

Self-schemata. A third category is **self-schemata**, which enable you to organize stimuli based on your own personality traits. If you consider yourself to be extroverted, then in social situations you will be excited to meet new people. But if you consider yourself to be introverted, then you might avoid social situations. Therefore, you understand your own behavior based on your understanding of who you are and how others relate to you.

State schemata. The fourth category involves **states schemata**, or an individual's physical or emotional conditions. States include things like anger, happiness, or hunger. State schemata are internal, while situation schemata are external. When you perceive someone's state behavior, you might adjust your communication accordingly. If the other person is grumpy, you might wait to ask him or her for a favor.

Interpersonal schemata. **Interpersonal schemata** include other people's characteristics and how you react to them. An important aspect of this category is the *valence*, or positive or negative quality, of the behavior. If you meet someone whose behavior you deem negative, then you are likely to attribute additional negative qualities to the person. For instance, if someone violates your personal space, you will likely react negatively to him or her. You might step backward to regain a comfortable physical distance, or avoid that person in the future because you believe he or she possesses other negative qualities, such as being unintelligent or unfriendly.

Relational schemata. The final category of schemata is relational schemata. When you judge the appropriateness of a behavior, you are more likely to view it from the appropriateness of the behavior in that particular type of *relationship* between the communicators than from any other aforementioned quality. Andersen suggests that relational schemata are the most influential of the six schemata. **Relational schemata** differ from interpersonal schemata in that relational schemata deal with how you view relationships, while interpersonal schemata concern another person's personality characteristics. Relational schemata allow you to use your understanding of relationship structures to understand behavior. What is the appropriate behavior in a friendship? Is it appropriate to display affectionate behavior toward a new romantic partner in public? The answers to these questions are based on your relational schemata.

To recap, when your senses are stimulated through sight, sound, touch, or smell, your brain must categorize that stimulus in order to make sense of it. Schemata offer the brain a means for quickly organizing the stimuli you encounter. If it were not for schemata, you would spend a large part of your day attempting to understand each stimulus as a brand new piece of information rather than being able to understand the stimulus quickly by comparing it to previously categorized stimuli.

Applying Concepts
DEVELOPING SKILLS | Analyzing Your Schemata

How are your schemata influential in how you organize stimuli? What factors of your culture influence your interpretation of stimuli? As you read, Andersen considers relational schemata to be the most influential of the six schemata on your formation of perceptions. Which of the six do you consider most influential? Why?

SIX CATEGORIES OF SCHEMATA

Schemata category	Explanation	Example
Cultural Schemata	Guide what you consider to be appropriate behavior based on your heritage and your familial experiences.	Using appropriate nonverbal communication for greetings
Situation Schemata	Guide your behavior based on the appropriateness in a given context.	Exhibiting appropriate behavior in the classroom or at a funeral
Self-Schemata	Guide how you understand your own behavior based on your own personality traits.	Avoiding social situations, if you are introverted, or seeking them if you are extroverted.
State Schemata	Guide your interpretation of behavior based on an individual's physical or emotional conditions.	Understanding what it means to be sad, angry, or anxious
Interpersonal Schemata	Determine your reaction based other people's characteristics and valence of the behavior.	Adjusting your personal space based on whether you view a person positively or negatively
Relational Schemata	Concern your view of relationships and allow you to use your understanding of relationship structures to understand behavior.	Behaving appropriately in a friendship or a new romantic relationship

2b

Cultural CONNECTIONS | Perception of Time

A cultural difference with regard to perception is the perception of time. In the United States (and most Western cultures), time plays an important role in our daily lives. We live by schedules. If you have an appointment at 1 p.m., you are expected to arrive at the designated meeting place by 1 p.m. However, not all cultures are "clock watchers."

Asian Indian cultures have a different perspective on time. An Indian student who takes classes at a U.S. university may show up late for class. Naturally, this might cause a problem with the professor who expects students to show up to class on time. The Indian student knows that he must be at class, but time is relative for him and his culture. He will show up somewhere near the appointed time.

Some Hispanic cultures are also less restricted by the clock when it comes to social gatherings. If a Hispanic family holds a celebration for Cinco de Mayo, for instance, they will tell the guests to be there one hour earlier than they want guests to arrive. They know that if they tell the guests that the party starts at 2 p.m., guests will not arrive until 3 p.m. So if they want guests to arrive at 2 p.m., then the invitation will say that the party starts at 1 p.m.

Application

Other cultures that are less bound by time include Turkish and Italian cultures. Do you know of any other cultures that have a different perception of time?

Stage Three: Interpretation-Evaluation

The third stage is interpretation-evaluation. Once you categorize the stimulus, you interpret and evaluate the information by comparing the new stimulus to previously experienced stimuli, which are stored in schemata. This stage is referred to as interpretation-evaluation (with a hyphen in between) because it is impossible to interpret stimuli without simultaneously evaluating them. It is in this stage that you engage in generalization and stereotyping—two ways that you interpret and evaluate stimuli.

Generalization. When you generalize stimuli, you are comparing the stimuli to previously experienced stimuli. The **generalization** is a statement in which you categorize something as representative of an entire group. For instance, Canadians like hockey. Generalizations are not problematic until you take them to an extreme and treat every similar stimulus as if the generalization were a fact.

Stereotyping. A generalization taken too far is a stereotype. **Stereotyping** is when you react to a person by assuming he or she is a representation of a generalization. Let's use the Canadian example again. Instead of making a statement that Canadians like hockey (generalization), a stereotype would be treating every Canadian you meet as a hockey fan. You might meet a person who says he is from Canada and say, "Then you must love hockey!" That response represents a stereotype. You have evaluated the Canadian based on a generalization. Not every Canadian likes hockey. Every person possesses unique qualities. By stereotyping someone, you treat the person as a member of a group rather than as an individual person with independent thoughts and behaviors.

Influences on interpretation. There are several possible influences on your *interpretation* of events.

- **The degree to which you are involved with a person or the event.** If you like someone and you are interpreting his or her behavior toward you, you might assume that the mere fact that he or she is talking to you must mean that the attraction is mutual. However, if you were not attracted to the person, perhaps you wouldn't concern yourself with whether the person is attracted to you.

- **Relational satisfaction.** When you are happy with a relational partner (whether it is a friend or romantic partner), his or her annoying habits are endearing. But, if you are unhappy with the relationship, the annoying habits are unbearably irritating, and might contribute to you ending the relationship.

- **Past relational experiences.** If you have had trust issues in previous friendships or romantic relationships, then you might misinterpret a new friend or romantic partner's behavior as untrustworthy.
- **Your expectations about the other person's behavior.** If you expect that your roommate is going to be mad at you, then you might interpret her coming home and slamming doors to be directed toward you. In actuality, she might have just received a bad test grade or had a bad day.

Applying Concepts DEVELOPING SKILLS | **Analyzing Your Interpretations**

For any given day, make a list of the instances where you have engaged in a generalization. Did any of the generalizations cross the line to stereotyping? If so, what could you have done to avoid the stereotype?

THE STAGES OF PERCEPTION			
	STAGE ONE: STIMULATION	**STAGE TWO: ORGANIZATION**	**STAGE THREE: INTERPRETATION-EVALUATION**
Explanation of the stage	Senses are activated by sound, smell, noise, or touch	Brain organizes stimulus into schemata	Interpret and evaluate information by comparing new stimulus to previously experienced stimuli
Attributes of the stage	Selective perception Selective exposure	Schemata: Cultural Situation Self-schemata State Interpersonal Relational	Generalizations Stereotypes

2c   Understanding Perceptual Biases

In the previous section, we examined the issues and events that might influence your formation of perceptions. But what might influence the perceptual process as a whole? In this section we will examine how perceptions can become biased.

Halo Effect and Reverse Halo Effect

The process of inferring additional positive qualities to someone based on a known positive quality is called the **halo effect**. For example, if you know that someone is a volunteer for a nonprofit organization, you might conclude that she must also be friendly, intelligent, and caring. The positive quality of volunteerism could cause you to infer those additional positive characteristics of the person herself.

The reverse is true as well. When you infer additional negative qualities about someone based on a known negative quality, you are engaging in the **reverse halo effect**.

What is the problem with relying on the halo effect or the reverse halo effect? While the observations might help you to make a quick evaluation of another, it causes you to focus on only a few qualities of that person. Our initial impressions are typically the result of someone's appearance. Based on this initial observation of a person's appearance, you assign positive or negative adjectives to the person, and this dictates your assumptions about other characteristics before you have a chance to learn more.

Applying Concepts **DEVELOPING SKILLS**	Analyzing Perceptual Biases

Too often we rely on our assumptions about people based on one or a few known characteristics. What if the volunteer mentioned above donated money to charities for the sole purpose of getting a big tax break? Would that change your perception of her?

Similarly, if you assume that someone has negative qualities because of an initial negative impression, you usually try to avoid interactions with him or her. Therefore, you could miss out on cultivating a relationship with the person.

Can you think of a situation in which you used the halo effect or the reverse halo effect? Did you ever change your perception of the person with continued communication? Explain.

Perceptual Accentuation

Perceptual accentuation occurs when you see only what you expect and want to see. The phrase "rose-colored glasses" illustrates this perceptual bias. Research has shown that we consider people that we like to be more physically attractive than those people we do not like. In this case, we want to believe that our friends are attractive because they are our friends! Therefore, we may see more (or less) than what actually exists.

EYEONETHICS | Attractiveness Bias

A number of specials on television news magazine show over the past decade have examined employer bias toward hiring the more physically attractive candidate for a job. In fact, scholarly research findings are consistent with the hidden camera "eyewitness" footage of the more attractive candidate being hired. Unfortunately, the attractiveness bias, in which one person is overlooked in favor of a more attractive person, still exists.

Luxen and Van de Vijver (2005) report that both men and women favor attractive opposite-sex candidates. Interestingly, women prefer less attractive female candidates over more attractive ("highly attractive" according to the authors) candidates. Chiu and Babcock (2002) found similar results for employers in Hong Kong. They discovered an "attractiveness bias" for entry-level positions. In other words, the more attractive candidate was hired in the entry-level positions. Additionally, Chiu and Babcock report that female candidates are preferred over male candidates.

Application

Given what you have learned about perceptual bias in this chapter, are these ethically acceptable situations? Would you consider hiring someone based solely on her or his looks? What are some of the consequences of attractiveness hiring?

Primacy Effect and Recency Effect

The order in which we receive information also can bias our perceptions. Primacy and recency effects are opposites. **Primacy effect** explains the impact of first impressions—what we see first exerts the most influence on our perception. Therefore, if your professor was in a bad mood on the first day of class, you might have the perception that he or she is mean and unapproachable. The power of the primacy effect is important to keep in mind when you meet someone for the first time.

The **recency effect,** on the other hand, says that what occurs most recently exerts more influence on our perceptions. One venue in which this effect is evident is a political debate. Each candidate has time to make a closing statement. The candidates want to give their statement last because it will likely be the information voters will remember because of its recency in their minds. The same is true for court cases. Defense attorneys get the advantage of making closing statements last, which allows their arguments to be most recent in the mind of the jury.

2d   Examining Influences on Perception

We have already noted that you never directly perceive anything. Many elements in your environment influence your perceptions. Those elements are categorized below.

Self-Perception

There are several components that comprise your self-perception. Let's look at these components and see how they influence how you perceive yourself. Figure 2.1 should help you to visualize how the components work together to form your self-perception.

Self-concept. Self-concept is how you describe yourself subjectively. Your self-concept is created by others' perceptions of you. You reflect on the statements and behaviors others make about you when you examine who you think you are.

Social comparisons. Your self-concept is also shaped by **social comparisons**, which is when you judge yourself against your peers, siblings, friends, and others. When you get a graded test returned, what is the first thing you want to know? Probably the class average on the test! Why? You want to compare *your* grade to the *average* grade of the class. You are comparing yourself to the average person in the classroom. In another context, you might judge your sense of fashion by comparing your clothing to the clothing worn by your friends or the clothing worn by supermodels.

Self-esteem. Another aspect of self-perception is **self-esteem**, or the value that you place on yourself. People with high self-esteem have a high degree of self-confidence and self-worth. People with low self-esteem have a low degree of self-confidence and self-worth. In the book (and movie based on the book) titled *A Hitchhiker's Guide to the Galaxy*, a robot named Marvin the Paranoid Android has low self-esteem. He believes that no one likes him and that he has bad luck. His self-esteem drives his behavior. He places little value on himself and, therefore, he often puts himself in harm's way because he doesn't care if anything happens to him.

Self-awareness. Self-awareness, the third aspect of self-perception, represents the extent to which you know yourself. You might think that you would never run into a burning building. But have you ever been faced with that situation? What if there were children screaming in the building? However, you might also know your limits. You might know for certain that

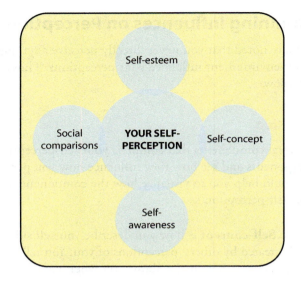

Figure 2.1
Components of
Self-Perception

you would never bungee jump off of a 500-foot cliff. Or you might know that you would do anything necessary to save the life of an animal. All of this self-knowledge culminates in your self-awareness, which can influence your perception of yourself. If you know that you would never intentionally do anything unethical, but you find yourself having behaved unethically, how will you modify your self-perception?

Personal Experiences

If you were once homeless or know someone who was homeless, then you might perceive a homeless person on the street differently (perhaps feeling more sympathy) than someone who has no personal experience with homelessness (who might look at the person as a menace). As you go through life and experience a variety of occurrences and behaviors, you'll notice that your personal experiences shape your perceptions.

Third-party Influences

Parents. The likes and dislikes of your parents shaped your perceptions when you were a child—perhaps they still do.

Friends. Friends influence our perceptions in that their opinions are important to us. Suppose that Jane finds someone she is romantically interested in. Jane thinks that the guy is extremely attractive. She asks her friend Martha what she thinks of him. Martha points out that he has really hairy arms and big ears, and she professes to find him unattractive. Martha's opinion influences Jane's perception of the previously attractive guy. Before she only noticed his blue eyes, nice build, and cool clothing. With Martha's observations, Jane now perceives other aspects of the guy's appearance as less attractive.

Professors. Feedback from teachers can help shape how we perceive ourselves. A professor might approach you and suggest that you think about pursuing a graduate degree. You never thought much about your ability to succeed in grad school. But now that an esteemed, credible person has told you that you would be the perfect graduate student, your perception of your abilities changes for the better!

Media. The media influence our perceptions. *Agenda setting theory* states that the media don't tell us what to think, but rather what to think about. They serve as the gatekeepers of newsworthy information. They tell us what they believe we need to know. How a news story is framed can greatly influence our perceptions of the event or situation. For instance, many soldiers and civilians come back from Iraq talking about how much has been accomplished since the fall of Saddam Hussein's dictatorship. They become dismayed at the media coverage of the Iraq war because the media focuses almost solely on the violence and deaths of U.S. soldiers. With the focus solely on violence and death, the audience's perceptions of the war can be easily influenced.

Media influence doesn't stop at news coverage. Think of how much television programming has changed just in the past decade. With shows like *Ellen* and *The L Word*, the gay lifestyle is becoming more acceptable. The media (in the form of television executives and television studios) have changed many people's perception of gays.

Physical Conditions

Personal comfort. Your comfort level in terms of room temperature, seating, and hunger, for example, can determine what aspects of your environment you attend to. If you are sitting in a classroom that is too warm and has uncomfortable desks, you are less likely to attend to the professor's lecture and more likely to attend to your uncomfortable physical state. Thus you miss out on important information.

Physical limitations. People who use a wheelchair are likely to have different perceptions of various campus locations. Ease of access to buildings can influence how they perceive the administration of the school. Of course, there are building codes that dictate wheelchair access to buildings, but that doesn't always mean that those entries are easily maneuvered or in the most convenient locations.

Psychological Conditions

One of the more profound influences on perception in romantic relationships is psychological condition. If you are smitten with someone, you are more likely to notice the person's positive nonverbals and positive statements about you than his or her negative ones. Likewise, if you dislike someone, you are likely to perceive what he or she says as negative. Or, more likely, you will avoid that person altogether.

As we noted earlier, Marvin the Paranoid Android in *The Hitchhiker's Guide to the Galaxy* is always depressed. His depression taints his perception of everything that goes on around him. The same is true for humans who are depressed or unhappy. Think of the times when you are with people who are in a bad mood. They often allow their bad mood to taint their perceptions of everything all day long.

Self-fulfilling Prophecy

A **self-fulfilling prophecy** occurs when you make a prediction about the outcome of a situation and you act on that prediction as if it were true, thus making the predicted outcome more likely to occur. If you have heard the phrase "self-fulfilling prophecy," it likely existed in a negative context. Self-fulfilling prophecies actually can have positive or negative consequences. For example, when you predict that you are not going to pass a test, you are likely to act on that prediction causing you to fail the exam. By internalizing the prediction, you could freeze when you get the test, causing the failing grade.

It is also possible to make a positive prediction, act on it as if it were true, and create the positive outcome. Suppose that Gene is attending a party that he knows Barb, the woman he is attracted to, will be attending. During the day of the party, Gene might predict that if he gets the opportunity to talk to Barb, she will be attracted to him, too. At the party, Gene's confidence works to his advantage because he is able to create and sustain a meaningful and interesting conversation with Barb. The result is that she accepts his request to go on a date. This self-fulfilling prophecy comes true!

You can also influence the behavior of others through **other-imposed prophecies**, in which your predictions about their behavior cause you to act toward them as if the prediction were true. Gene could have started with a negative prediction—that Barb would not be interested in talking to him—and ended up not meeting her because he was emitting negative nonverbal cues that caused Barb to stay away from him. The other person reacts to your behavior, causing the prediction actually to come true.

Applying Concepts
DEVELOPING SKILLS | Examining Your Perceptual Influences

Which of the perceptual influences—self-perception, third-party influences, physical conditions, psychological conditions, or self-fulfilling prophecies—do you more easily notice throughout your day? Are there one or more influences that are almost unnoticeable to you? What makes some of these influences more apparent than others?

2e Engaging in Perception Checking

Given the number of influences on your perceptions, it is best to engage in perception checking. **Perception checking** involves asking others for clarification or validation of your perceptions. Typically, the need for perception checking involves the observation of a person's repeated behavior. Let's look at an example:

> Vicki is normally smiling, laughing, and happy. Lately, her IM away message contains lyrics to songs about how hard life is and other depressing topics. After noticing this behavior for several days, Joan calls Vicki to remind her that if she ever needs to talk, she is always available. Vicki thanks her, but reveals nothing. Vicki continues to sound depressed on the phone and in person. If you were Joan, what would you do?

Unfortunately, many people would respond by asking Vicki, "Are you mad at me?" or "What did I do wrong?" Such responses are self-centered and not focused on the other person. They create a defensive situation in which the other person might feel accused of doing something wrong or might be angry with you for being so self-centered. When asking these types of questions you are engaging in mind reading. You are essentially telling Vicki that you *know* that her problem involves you. So what should Joan say to Vicki?

- **Describe the behaviors you are encountering.** The key to beginning a conversation in which you check your perceptions is to use descriptive language. Therefore, Joan might say, "I have noticed that your away messages have been regularly depressing. And I have noticed that your nonverbal cues mirror that depression."

- **Suggest possible reasons for the behavior.** After you have made descriptive statements (and not accusations or statements that create defensiveness), you should suggest possible reasons for the behavior. Joan could suggest, "I know you have been under a lot of stress with your coursework lately. I also know that your grandmother has been in the hospital." By providing some suggestions, you are showing that you have noticed other aspects of Vicki's life experiences, but also that you do not necessarily consider her behavior to have anything to do with you.

- **Ask for clarification.** When you have suggested reasons for the behavior, you need to ask for clarification. So Joan might follow her suggestions about the origin of Vicki's behavior with, "Is anything bothering you that you would like to talk about? I am worried about you."

When you are uncertain of the purpose of someone's behavior, it is important to seek understanding. Perception checking allows you to verify your observations and interpretations of the behavior. Perception checking involves describing the behavior, suggesting reasons for the behavior, and asking for clarification. When you ask for clarification, you are giving the other person an opportunity to elaborate on his or her thoughts and feelings.

Applying Concepts DEVELOPING SKILLS | Practice in Perception Checking

Write a role-playing script that would effectively check the characters' perception(s) in these situations.

- Your partner walks into the room and turns on the TV without even saying "hello." You assume she must be annoyed with something you said.
- Your co-worker walks by your desk and puts down a stack of papers. He only utters a sigh as he walks away. You wonder if you forgot a deadline.
- You approach your instructor after class to ask a quick question about an upcoming assignment. The instructor snaps an answer at you before walking out the door. You wonder if you said something insulting to him or if he doesn't like you.

Competence SUMMARY

In this chapter, you have learned the following concepts. Check to be sure you have achieved each of the communication competencies.

2a Understanding Perception

- Perception is the process of assessing information in your surroundings.
- We do not directly perceive stimuli, but rather we examine it through our previous experiences and knowledge.

Competence. Can I define perception?

2b Identifying the Stages of the Perception Process

- The three stages in the perception process are stimulation, organization, and interpretation-evaluation.

- The perception process begins when you receive a stimulus—you hear, see, or smell something, for example. Two components of the stimulation stage are selective attention and selective exposure.

- Once you have received the stimulus and paid attention to it, you must understand what you are hearing, seeing, or smelling. In the organization stage, your brain compares the stimulus to your schemata to determine how to react.

- When you understand what you are sensing, you can interpret and evaluate it. The brain naturally generalizes stimuli in order to shortcut the understanding process. However, assuming generalizations to be true for each person you meet is called stereotyping.

Competence. Am I able to interpret stimuli accurately (from sensing a stimulus to evaluating the stimulus), and in the process reduce my stereotyping and treat each person I interact with as an individual?

2c Understanding Perceptual Biases

- Other perceptual biases include halo effect and reverse halo effect, perceptual accentuation, primacy and recency effects.

Competence. Am I able to understand how I attribute meaning to my own behavior and the behavior of others? Recognizing my perceptual biases can help me attempt to be more objective in attributing motives for behaviors.

2d Examining Influences on Perception

- You never directly perceive anything, but several elements influence your perceptions.

- Your perception of yourself is shaped by others' perceptions of you and your own perception of yourself. Self-perception is one influence on your general perceptions.

- Personal experiences, third-party influences, physical and psychological conditions, and self-fulfilling prophecies can influence your perceptions.

- Self-fulfilling prophecy occurs when you make a prediction about the outcome of a situation and then act on that prediction as if it were true. As a result, your prediction is more likely to occur.

Competence. Do I understand what influences my perceptions and therefore better understand myself? Do I have the self-knowledge that enables me to gain more confidence in myself? Has this confidence transferred to my communication with others, which can also be enhanced?

2e Engaging in Perception Checking

- The best way to know if you have accurately attributed motives for someone's behavior is to engage in perception checking.
- Perception checking involves more than simply asking "Am I right?" It involves describing the other person's behavior(s), suggesting potential reasons for that person's behavior(s), and asking for clarification of the behavior(s).

Competence. Do I second-guess the motives for someone's behavior, or do I communicate with that person based on accurate attributions that I verify by engaging in perception checking?

Review Questions

1. Explain the stages of perception.
2. What is the difference between selective attention and selective exposure?
3. What is the difference between a generalization and a stereotype? How are schemata related to generalizations and stereotypes?
4. Name three influences on perception.
5. What are the differences between "self-concept," "self-esteem," and "self-awareness"?

Discussion Questions

1. You develop schemata over time based on your experiences. Therefore, schemata change as you expand your experiences. What are some factors that influence how, when, and why your own personal schemata change?
2. A self-fulfilling prophecy occurs when you make a prediction about the outcome of a situation and act on that prediction as if it was true, thus making the predicted outcome more likely to occur. How does self-esteem affect the self-fulfilling prophecies that we make?

Key Terms

Listening

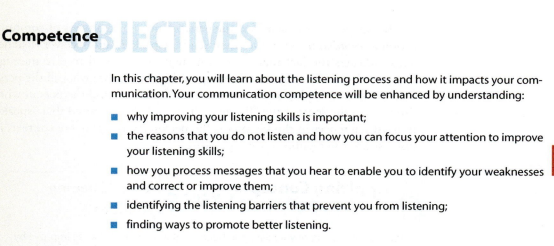

In this chapter, you will learn about the listening process and how it impacts your communication. Your communication competence will be enhanced by understanding:

- why improving your listening skills is important;
- the reasons that you do not listen and how you can focus your attention to improve your listening skills;
- how you process messages that you hear to enable you to identify your weaknesses and correct or improve them;
- identifying the listening barriers that prevent you from listening;
- finding ways to promote better listening.

3a

3a   The Importance of Listening

Listening is an important skill for effective communication. Yet, most of us are poor listeners. You probably remember playing the game of "Telephone" when you were a child. Someone whispered a phrase or sentence to another person, who whispered it to the next one, and so on. The last person to receive the message then said it aloud. Usually, the final message bore little resemblance to what the first person whispered, and the group laughed at the outcome.

Unfortunately, examples of poor listening exist in areas of life where the results are often far from humorous. You can probably think of several examples of problems, or at least embarrassing situations, caused by your own ineffective listening. You asked a question the teacher had just answered. Or, you didn't realize that a complete sentence outline of your informative speech was due a week before you were scheduled to speak.

Each day, we send and receive both oral and written messages. Of the four roles we perform—speaker, listener, writer, and reader—we spend more time listening than doing any of the other actions. College students, for example, spend approximately 53% of their communication time listening (Barker, Edwards, Gaines, Gladney, & Holley, 1980). For example, we listen to others talk, we watch TV, and we hear other noises around us. While you have taken several courses teaching you to read and write, you have probably never taken a course in listening. In short, you have received the least training in what you do the most!

It will probably not surprise you, then, to learn that most of us are inefficient listeners. In fact, immediately after listening to your professor's lecture, chances are high that you will remember, at most, only 50% of what you heard, and two days later you will remember only 25%.

In Chapter 1, we identified the participants in the process of communication as *communicators* rather than sender (speaker) and receiver (listener). This indicates the fact that we simultaneously send and receive messages. However, in our discussion of listening in this chapter, we will call the person who is communicating at any moment the "speaker," and the person who is listening to the speaker the "listener." It should also be noted that "speaker" in most references in this chapter is the person speaking in any context, not just a speaker in a public speaking setting.

Applying Concepts **DEVELOPING SKILLS**	**Your Listening** Abilities

What is one aspect of your listening behavior that you would like to improve by the end of this course? In what way(s) does this listening weakness affect your life?

3b Why Don't We Listen?

Think of all of the reasons that prevent you from listening effectively. What are they?

- **Message overload.** Message overload occurs when you have received so much new information that you are tired from the listening process. The exhaustion caused by message overload can turn you into a lazy listener.

- **Preoccupation by thoughts.** You might have relational problems that are consuming your thoughts. Perhaps you are worried about something—an upcoming test, a friend, your health. When you are preoccupied, your brain is unable to attend to the auditory stimuli that you encounter.

- **Inadequate effort.** You might be tired or sick and do not have the energy necessary to listen. One instance in which this is unacceptable is when you refuse to expend the energy necessary to listen to someone with a heavy speaking accent. Students often criticize instructors who speak English as a second language because they "can't understand" the person. Too many times it is the student who does not want to pay attention closely in order to understand the speaker. This is unfortunate because the student misses out on important knowledge that the instructor has to offer.

- **Semantic distractions.** Listeners may be confused with the meaning of a word they haven't seen or heard, one they have seen in print but have never heard spoken, or a word the speaker is mispronouncing. If a student gave a speech about her native country, Eritrea, without showing that word on a visual aid, most listeners would probably begin wondering, "How do I spell that?" "Have I ever seen that word on a map before?"

"Is the speaker pronouncing correctly a word I've always heard mispronounced?" These thoughts divert you from the serious business of listening to a speech filled with new and interesting information.

- **External noises.** When someone coughs during a lecture, you might be unable to hear what the speaker is saying. There might be an emergency vehicle passing by the building with sirens blaring, thus causing you to not hear what your friend is saying.

- **Hearing problems.** A hearing disability can prevent you from receiving aural stimuli.

- **Rapid thought.** This is one human condition that affects us all. Humans are capable of processing 400 to 500 spoken words per minute. The average person only speaks between 125 and 190 words per minute (Mayer, 1994). That is a major difference! This means that, depending on the situation, you may be able to listen at a rate of four times faster than a person speaks! As a result, you can get bored and move your attention back and forth between what the speaker is saying and some extraneous message, perhaps a personal problem that concerns you. Of course, that can create major misunderstandings.

Applying Concepts
DEVELOPING SKILLS

Your Listening Skills and Technological Advances

Think about the various technological advances in the past two decades, such as widespread mobile phone availability and the Internet. How have these technologies influenced your listening skills—both positively *and* negatively? What technologies typically have a negative influence on listening in general?

3c Examining Listening versus Hearing

Does the following situation sound familiar? You are watching *The Daily Show with Jon Stewart*, listening to a CD, or doing Economics homework when one of your parents walks by and tells you to put out the trash. Fifteen minutes later that person walks back to find you still preoccupied with television, music, or homework, and the trash is still in the kitchen. Your parent asks, "Didn't you hear me?" Well, of course you did. You heard the request to put out the trash just as you heard Stewart joking about politics, Stevie Ray Vaughn playing a riff, the dog barking at a passing car, and the air conditioner clicking on in the hall. You heard all of these things, but you might not have been *listening* to any of them.

What is the difference between listening and hearing? **Hearing** is the continuous, natural, and passive process of receiving aural stimuli. It is the act of the sound waves hitting your eardrums. **Listening** is the intermittent, learned, and active process of giving attention to aural stimuli. Listening is the process of assigning meaning to what you hear.

These two activities differ in at least four important ways.

Listening Is Intermittent

Listening is not a continuous activity, but occurs only from time to time when you choose to focus and respond to stimuli around you. Hearing, on the other hand, is a continuous function for a person with normal hearing ability.

Listening Is a Learned Skill

Listening must be taught and learned. Unless you were born with a hearing impairment or lost your hearing at some point in your life, hearing is a natural capacity for which you need no training. You hear sounds before you are born; fetuses grow accustomed to certain voices, noises, and music. For this reason, pediatricians advise new parents not to tiptoe or whisper around the infant they have just brought home from the hospital. The child is already used to a lot of noise and must grow accustomed to the rest of it. Throughout your life, you will hear sounds even as you sleep.

Listening Is Active

Hearing means simply receiving an aural stimulus. The act of hearing is passive, continuous and natural; it requires no work. Listening, in contrast, is active. It requires you to concentrate, interpret, and respond—in short, to be involved. You can hear the sound of a fire engine as you sit at your desk working on your psychology paper. You listen to the sound of the fire engine if you concentrate on its sound, identify it as a fire engine rather than an ambulance, wonder if it is coming in your direction, and then turn back to your work as you hear the sound fade away.

Listening Implies Using the Message Received

Audiences assemble for many reasons. You choose to listen to gain information, to learn new uses for existing information, to laugh and be entertained, and to be inspired. There are literally thousands of topics you could listen to. The perceived usefulness of the topic helps determine how actively you will listen to a speaker. Listening implies a choice; you must choose to participate in the process of listening. However, keep in mind the context in which you are listening. Have you pondered the effects of inactive listening in a close friendship? Deciding that a topic is unimportant or uninteresting to you can have lasting effects on a relationship.

Applying Concepts **DEVELOPING SKILLS**	**Teaching Effective Listening Skills**

Do you think listening is a skill that should be taught more frequently in schools? Explain your response. How would you incorporate listening instruction into a class? Would you have activities to help students learn to listen more effectively? Would you have a separate course that just discusses effective listening skills?

3d Understanding the Listening Process

The listener is vital to successful communication; without at least one listener, communication cannot occur beyond the intrapersonal level. Remember that any time two people communicate, two messages are involved: the one that the sender intends and the one the listener actually receives. These messages will never be identical because people operate from different experiences that produce different perceptions for the same stimulus (as noted in Chapter 2). As you examine the steps in the process of listening, you will better understand this concept. Also note that because hearing is one of the five senses, the listening process is quite similar to the perception process.

Receive Stimuli

The first step in listening is to *receive* sounds. In face-to-face communication, we receive sound waves set in motion through the air by the speaker; on the telephone, those same sound waves are transmitted electronically. In both cases, the first step in listening to the speaker is receiving the sounds, the auditory stimuli. In other words, accurate *hearing* is the first step in effective listening.

Select Stimuli

Individuals *select* different stimuli from those competing for their attention, a phenomenon called **selective attention**. When the police gather reports from various witnesses to a traffic accident, they often find conflicting information.

Each bystander's report will be shaped by where the person was standing or sitting, what the person was focusing on at the moment of impact, how the person was feeling, and a host of other factors. Each witness has a selective perception of the event.

In public speaking situations, the audience reacts in a similar way. One person in the audience may focus primarily on what speakers are saying, another on their tones of voice or their gestures, still another on what they are wearing or even on the distracting hum of the heating system. You may even be distracted by internal noise, such as worrying about an upcoming chemistry exam or trying to resolve a conflict with your roommate. As William James said more than 100 years ago, our view of the world is truly shaped by what we decide to hear.

Understand the Message

Once you have received the aural stimulus, you must decode it. To do this, you, first, attach meanings to stimuli and, second, begin fitting the message into your framework of existing knowledge and beliefs (what we referred to in Chapter 2 as "schemata"). To *understand* a speaker, you must consider both the message's content and its context. Is the speaker attempting to inform or persuade you? Is the speaker serious or joking? In short, what are the speaker's intentions?

It is easier to judge the context of communication when you listen to friends rather than to strangers. When you communicate with your friends, you can tell whether they are joking, upset, or teasing by their facial expressions or tones of voice, but you cannot always tell with strangers. You know your friends well and are more familiar with their cues.

At this stage, the listener is paying careful attention to those verbal and nonverbal symbols and their meanings. You also *filter* what you hear through your own experiences. Think of your schemata as a sieve. Your brain runs the stimulus through the schemata sieve (the filter) and picks out information that is similar to a given schemata. What is left in the sieve is what your brain examines to add meaning to the stimulus.

Evaluate the Message

Before acting on the message you have decoded and understood, you *evaluate* it. *Evaluating* is the process of judging both the reliability of the speaker and the quality and consistency of the speaker's information. If the speaker is someone you know, you reflect on the history of that person's interactions with you. Has the person ever tried to deceive you? If the speaker is a stranger, you often gauge the person's credibility based on the nonverbal cues of communication.

Is the speaker making eye contact with you? Does he or she speak fluently, without unnecessary pauses or filler words?

However, it is important to remember to withhold evaluation until you have heard the speaker's entire message. In other words, if you begin to evaluate the message before you have heard the speaker amend what he or she is saying, you risk misinterpreting the speaker's thoughts. It is always best to respond to a message after you have given the speaker a fair amount of time to speak.

Determine Your Interpretation

The final step in listening, *resolving*, involves deciding what to do with the information you have received. As a listener, you can resolve to accept the information, reject it, take action on it, decide to investigate it further, or just try to remember the information so that you can resolve it later.

You should refrain from forming your response mentally while the speaker is still talking. Otherwise you could miss valuable information that the speaker is imparting. Therefore, after the speaker has stopped

STAGES OF THE LISTENING PROCESS				
RECEIVE	**SELECT**	**UNDERSTAND**	**EVALUATE**	**RESOLVE**
You receive a stimulus, in the form of sound waves, that is received by your body's auditory system.	You determine (consciously or subconsciously) whether to give attention to the received stimulus.	You fit the stimulus into your schemata that best represent that stimulus. The schemata help you to understand the nature of stimulus.	You judge the reliability of the speaker and quality of the message.	You decide what to do with the information (e.g., accept it or reject it).
Example				
You are in your office and you hear your co-worker calling for you.	*If you are diligently working on a project, you may not hear him. If you do hear him, you may decide to consciously attend to his message.*	*Your co-worker often bothers you about unnecessary things that distract you from your work.*	*You determine that this is another incident in which he is going to waste your time.*	*You tell your co-worker that you will help him in a few minutes.*

talking, you can respond to the message. It is important to not interrupt the speaker (one of the barriers to effective listening that we will discuss momentarily).

Obviously, you do not consciously go through and dwell on each of these five steps each time you listen to someone. As the significance of the message increases for you, however, you become more involved in the process of listening—a point each speaker should remember.

<table>
<tr><td>

Applying Concepts
DEVELOPING SKILLS

</td><td>

Analyzing a Recent
Interaction

</td></tr>
</table>

You are having a meeting with your professor in her office. You are discussing the requirements for a research paper that is due in one week. Because your grades are important to you, you are listening intently to what she is saying. Explain how the listening process would apply to this hypothetical interaction. How is the listening process different when you are not listening effectively?

3e   Identifying Barriers to Effective Listening

You have learned about the listening process and why we don't always listen. In this section we'll identify some of the bad habits of listening. Do you recognize any of these as your own bad habits?

Pseudo-listening

Saying "uh huh" periodically to the speaker when you are really not paying attention is a form of **pseudo-listening**, or pretending to listen. In what circumstances do you engage in pseudo-listening? It often occurs when a speaker is preoccupied or uninterested. However, the act can cause hard feelings between you and the speaker, who may end the conversation upon catching you pseudo-listening.

Selective Listening

How often do you find yourself in a conversation in which someone is telling the same story you have heard more often than you care to remember? Perhaps the topic has shifted to something that you have no interest in. You may resort to engaging in **selective listening**, which occurs when you pay attention to the speaker only when the topic of conversation changes to something that interests you.

Stage-hogging and Interruptions

When you interrupt someone, you are essentially conveying that what you have to say is more important than what he or she is saying. Interruptions are a form of **stage-hogging**, which occurs when you turn the topic of conversation away from what the speaker is discussing and toward yourself.

Sidetracking

How many times have you caught yourself drifting off into your own little world during a lecture or while someone is talking to you? That is known as **sidetracking**—allowing something that someone says to distract you. For example, your nutrition professor might start talking about the detriments of eating bacon because of the high fat content. This statement makes you think about what you will have for lunch and whether it might contain bacon. All the while you are missing the next part of the lecture!

Physical Distractions

Have you ever told someone that he or she was being so loud that you couldn't hear yourself think? If so, you were commenting on one obstacle to effective listening: physical distraction. *Physical distractions* are interferences coming to you through any of your senses, and they may take many forms: glare from a sunny window, chill from an air conditioner vent, or the smell of formaldehyde in your anatomy and physiology lab.

Physiological Distractions

Physiological distractions have to do with the body. Any illness or unusual physiological condition is a potential distraction to effective listening. A bout of flu, a painful earache, or fatigue after a sleepless night all place obvious and familiar limitations on our willingness and ability to listen.

Factual Distractions

College students, who should be among the most adept listeners in our society, are often hampered by *factual distractions*, listening disturbances caused by the flood of facts presented to them in lectures. You may be tempted to treat each fact as a potential test question. But this way of listening can pose problems. For example, have you ever taken copious notes in your World Civilization class only to realize later that, although you have lots of facts, you missed the key ideas? Students and other victims of factual distractions sometimes listen for details, but miss the general point that the speaker is making.

3f   Promoting Better Listening

Once you understand the barriers to effective listening, you can develop a plan of action to improve your listening behavior and that of your fellow communicators. A major theme of this book is that each party in the communication process has a responsibility to promote effective communication. Promoting better listening should be a goal of both the sender and the receiver of the message.

The following suggestions will help you become a more effective listener. As you master these suggestions, you will find yourself understanding and remembering more of what you hear.

Desire to Listen

Your attitude will determine, in part, your listening effectiveness. Some topics will interest you; others, no doubt, will not. Good listeners, however, begin with the assumption that each interaction can potentially benefit them.

Focus on the Message

Your first responsibility as a listener is to listen attentively to the speaker's message. Yet a speaker's message competes with other, often quite powerful, stimuli for your attention. Sometimes speakers themselves create distractions. Effective speakers can help listeners focus on the message by eliminating distracting mannerisms and by incorporating nonverbal behaviors that display immediacy (or draw in listeners and make them feel that the speaker is concerned about them).

Understand the Speaker's Point of View

When speakers and listeners come from different cultures, the chances for misunderstanding increase. Differences in language, education, and customs challenge listeners to work especially hard at understanding the speaker's message and intent. These differences are often evident in today's multicultural classroom. Some foreign students, for example, come from educational environments that are more structured and formal than the typical American college classroom.

Learning about cultures that are different from your own can help you to better understand the speaker's point of view. Pay particular attention to the feature *Cultural Connections* in each chapter to learn more about cultures with which you may be unfamiliar.

3f

Reinforce the Message

In this chapter, you learned that humans can process up to 500 words per minute, but that most people speak between 125 to 190 words per minute. Therefore, as a listener, you must find a way to maintain attention to the speaker.

You can fill some of this time and better focus on the message by mentally repeating and paraphrasing what the speaker is saying. You use repetition when you state exactly what the speaker has said. Paraphrasing the speaker's message involves putting the speaker's ideas into your own words. By doing this you become actively involved in message transmission.

Provide Feedback

A listener can enhance the communication process by providing feedback to the speaker. Although there is a greater opportunity for verbal feedback in interpersonal and group contexts, it is nevertheless also possible in public speaking settings. The effective speaker will especially read the nonverbal cues of the listener(s) to assist in the continuation of the message. If you understand the message and nod to acknowledge that, the speaker can continue. If you appear perplexed, that signal could prompt the speaker to explain the idea more fully before moving to the next point.

Withhold Judgment

Many of us have a problem withholding judgment. We hear something and immediately label it as right or wrong, good or bad. The problem is that once we do that we cease to listen objectively to the rest of the message.

It is difficult for you to withhold judgment, of course, when you listen to a speech advocating a position you strongly oppose. Topics student speakers sometimes discuss include legalization of drugs, capital punishment, abortion, flag burning, euthanasia, gun control, and embryonic stem cell research. You may even find it difficult to listen to a speech opposing your view without silently debating the speaker. Yet, as you mentally challenge these arguments, you miss much of what the speaker is saying. If you can suspend evaluation until after speakers have presented and supported their arguments, you will be a better listener.

Actively Listening

Active listening is the process of paraphrasing a speaker's message and conveying understanding of that message back to the speaker. Active listening is an important aspect of interpersonal communication and relationship building. There are three steps in the active listening process.

- **Paraphrase the speaker's message in your own words.** Paraphrasing, putting the speaker's message in your own words, serves several purposes. You show speakers that you are actually listening to them. It enables you to check to make sure that you have accurately understood what they are saying. And similarly, you provide the speaker with an opportunity to clarify or amend your interpretation of what they are saying.

- **Express understanding of the speaker's feelings.** In addition to paraphrasing the content of the message, you should also clarify your interpretation of the speaker's feelings. Expressing understanding prevents you from challenging those feelings. No one likes to hear that he or she shouldn't feel a certain way about something. Validate the other person's feelings.

- **Ask questions.** Ask follow-up questions to clarify the speaker's message. This prompts the speaker to elaborate on thoughts and feelings without feeling defensive.

Let's look at a hypothetical scenario to test your active listening skills. Of course, you are reading and not listening. But, suppose that you are attending the birthday party of your close friend. You find her in another room looking like she is going to cry. You ask her what is wrong, and she says, "It's my birthday, and I'm so upset I could cry." What would be your reaction?

a. "Don't be sad about getting older. You should have fun on your birthday!"

b. "Let's go have a lot of cake and ice cream. That will make you feel better!"

c. "But everyone is out there looking for you."

d. "You seem pretty sad about something. You know, it's okay to feel bad on your birthday. What has made you so upset?"

If you would respond with a, b, or c, then you would not be engaging in active listening. Response "a" presumes that you know why she is upset—because she is getting older. But, it also chastises her for being upset by telling her that she *should* be having fun. Response "b" sounds like a great plan, but

EYEONETHICS | Right of Refusal

As she listened to Jeff's speech on the importance of rap music, Crystal found some of the lyrics he recited to be obscene and sexist. As she continued listening, she thought to herself, "These lyrics are offensive. I refuse to listen to them at home, so why should I be forced to listen to them now?" So, Crystal stood up and walked out of the classroom during Jeff's speech.

Application

Was it appropriate for Crystal to leave the classroom? Should audience members in your class have the freedom to listen or not to listen to certain speeches? Are there some topics for which walking out is an unacceptable form of feedback to the speaker? If so, what are some of these topics? What should guide a listener's decision to take such actions?

Some people attend political speeches and turn their chairs so that their backs face the speaker. Is this an ethical form of protesting the speech? If one of your classmates planned to protest your speech topic, would you rather that he not show up to your speech, walk out in the middle of the speech, or turn his chair so his back faced you throughout your speech?

What about heckling a speaker? Of course, in the classroom setting the instructor usually controls the heckling (or actually, you each police each other—who wants to get heckled when they are giving a speech for a grade?!). However, in a public setting, you are not always protected from hecklers. Is heckling acceptable feedback? Are there any ethical responsibilities that the heckler should consider?

In this chapter, you learned about the importance of listening and withholding judgment until the speaker has finished his or her thoughts. How do these three forms of protest (walking out, showing your back, and heckling) influence listening? Don't forget that there are other people in the audience along with the protesters.

you are pretending that whatever is bothering her will go away by merely eating cake and ice cream (if only that would solve all of our problems!). In response "c" not only do you ignore her pain, but also you make her feel guilty about it!

Response "d" best exemplifies active listening. She hasn't said much yet, so there isn't a lot to paraphrase. But, your first sentence acknowledges that there is something wrong (in essence, you are paraphrasing her emotions). The second sentence expresses understanding of her feelings by letting her know that it is okay to feel bad on her birthday. And, the final statement of the response is a follow-up question. Through the question, you are allowing your friend to elaborate on what is making her so upset.

Active listening is also an important component to diffuse conflict. One of the main complaints from people during an argument is that the other person doesn't understand their point of view. When you show your opponent that you are trying to understand the problem by paraphrasing his or

Cultural CONNECTIONS

High- and Low-Context Cultures

Cultures can be described as high or low context. In a **high-context culture** much of the communication information is implicitly conveyed by the context of the situation. In a **low-context culture**, the information is stated explicitly. Members of a high-context culture spend a great deal of time getting to know one another. Such a close relationship allows them to speak to each other using fewer words. Think of it like a romantic relationship or a best friendship in which the two people know each other so well that they can finish each other's sentences.

In a low-context culture, its members do not get to know each other as intimately, thus creating the need for more explicit explanations in communication. Japan is considered a high-context culture, while the United States is considered a low-context culture.

Misunderstandings between management and employees can result when you mix high- and low-context cultures in the workplace. Kim and Paulk (1994) studied the communication between Japanese and American co-workers at a company that manufactures computer peripheral devices.

Japanese workers were frustrated with their American managers because American managers would give explicit instructions to the Japanese workers about the completion of a task. The Japanese workers considered this insulting to their intelligence. They interpreted the American manager's explicit instruction as a sign that they are not smart enough to know how to complete the task on their own.

Similarly, Japanese managers were frustrated with their American workers because the Americans asked too many questions and expected too much direction to complete tasks. Likewise, the American workers felt slighted by their Japanese managers who were not willing to talk to them.

Application

Which of the suggestions for promoting better listening would you recommend for the workers at this corporation?

her message and asking follow-up questions, you are more likely to come to a quicker resolution to the problem. If both parties in the conflict engage in active listening, misunderstandings can be kept to a minimum and each party can be sure that messages are accurately interpreted.

Applying Concepts
DEVELOPING SKILLS

Actively Listening in Your Interactions with Others

Think of a recent conversation in which you could or should have used active listening. Summarize the interaction. How would you change what you said to make it active listening? In what way(s) would the interaction have been impacted by the use of active listening?

Competence SUMMARY

In this chapter, you have learned the following concepts. Check to be sure you have achieved each of the communication competencies.

3a The Importance of Listening

- You spend more time each day listening than you do speaking, writing, or reading.
- Immediately after listening to someone, you will remember only 50% of the message. Two days later, your memory of the message is reduced to 25%.

Competence. Do I know why listening is a fundamental part of my daily communication?

3b Why Don't We Listen?

- There are several reasons that you may not be listening effectively: message overload, preoccupation, inability or lack of desire to exert effort to listen, semantic distractions, external noises, and hearing problems.

Competence. Can I identify the reasons why I do not listen? Can I use these reasons to improve my listening skills?

3c Examining Listening versus Hearing

- Hearing is the continuous, natural, and passive process of receiving aural stimuli.
- Listening is the intermittent, learned, and active process of giving attention to aural stimuli.

Competence. Do I understand the difference between listening and hearing?

3d Understanding the Listening Process

- There are five stages in the listening process: receiving the message, selecting stimuli to retain, understanding the message, evaluating the message, and formulating a response to the message.

Competence. Can I identify the stages of the listening process? Do I know which stage of the listening process gives me the most problems?

3e Identifying Barriers to Effective Listening

- We identified seven barriers to effective listening: pseudo-listening, selective listening, stage-hogging/interruptions, sidetracking, and physical, psychological, and factual distractions.

Competence. Do I know which barriers to effective listening I most often exhibit? Have I learned how to alleviate my reliance on those barriers?

3f Promoting Better Listening

- Several suggestions for becoming a better listener are provided in this chapter, including cultivating a desire to listen, focusing on and reinforcing the message, providing feedback, withholding judgment, and actively listening.
- Active listening enables you to make sure that you have accurately understood the message while also communicating to the other person or persons that what they say is important to you.

Competence. Have I implemented these suggestions to improve my daily listening behavior?

Review Questions

1. What are some reasons we do not listen?
2. Explain the difference between listening and hearing.
3. What is a semantic distraction?
4. Describe the process of listening.
5. What are four ways in which you can promote better listening?

Discussion Questions

1. What are some ways to overcome barriers to effective listening?
2. Having read the chapter and analyzed your listening skills, in what ways does listening impact your personal relationships? In what context(s) do you find your listening skills are strongest? Weakest?

Key Terms

active listening *p. 63*

hearing *p. 54*

high-context culture *p. 64*

listening *p. 54*

low-context culture *p. 64*

pseudo-listening *p. 58*

selective attention *p. 55*

selective listening *p. 58*

sidetracking *p. 59*

stage-hogging *p. 59*

The Power of Language

OBJECTIVES

In this chapter, you will examine the nature of language by exploring the functions and power of language. Your communication competence will be enhanced by understanding:

- how the functions of language help you to appreciate the importance of language;
- ways that a competent communicator considers his or her words carefully to avoid misunderstandings or hurting someone's feelings;
- how to speak clearly using specific and familiar language, while being sensitive to the needs of others by putting people first and avoiding sexist language;
- ways of avoiding powerless speech to enable you to sound more credible;
- how to create supportive communication climates in which all communicators feel comfortable interacting.

4a

4a Identifying the Functions of Language

Speakers of English have access to the richest vocabulary on Earth, largely because we have adopted words so freely from other languages. In fact, three out of five words in English come from a foreign tongue (Parshall, 1995). As a result, the revised *Oxford English Dictionary* is huge, containing 615,000 words. That is more than three times as many words as the German language contains and more than six times the number of words available to the French (Bryson, 1990). People who speak English can achieve degrees of subtlety and nuance that are impossible in most languages. How we use words makes us stand out from others. Language empowers us, and we can employ it to serve both ethical and unethical purposes.

Studying language is important because the more you know about it, the greater influence you will have as you communicate. The language we use fulfills at least five functions (Jakobson, 1964).

Communicate Ideas

"Humans are alone on the planet in their use of language to communicate" (Balter, 2001). Our language can communicate an infinite number of ideas because it has a structure of separate words. Unlike the sounds most animals make to signal danger, for example, our language allows us to specify the type of threat, the immediacy of the danger, and any number of other characteristics of the situation (Barber, 1965). As long as the speaker and the listener attach similar referents to the words they use, the two can communicate indefinitely.

Send Messages About Users

Our vocabulary reveals aspects of our educational background, our age, and even what area of the country we call home. In addition, language expresses the feelings or emotions of the speaker. The words you select communicate how you feel about both your listeners and the subject under discussion. Which of these terms suggests the strongest emotion, for example?

crisis   dilemma   problem

Crisis suggests a more powerful feeling than do the other terms. Language can carry considerable emotional impact, and the words you select carry messages—sometimes obvious, sometimes subtle—about your background and the nature and strength of your emotions.

Strengthen Social Bonds

Precisely because it communicates ideas and emotions between people, language serves a social function. For example, we often use language to identify ourselves as part of a particular group. Think of the slang expressions you use around friends to signal that you are a member of a certain group and in the know. Many of these utterances are fun and harmless.

Other language serves a social function when spoken in unison. A group of kindergarten students reciting the alphabet or counting from 1 to 20 strengthen their group identity and celebrate the group's accomplishment. Adults repeating a pledge or prayer experience similar group feelings. Or consider the words we use to greet one another. The exchange "Hi, how are you?" and "Fine, how are you doing?" may be a hollow, automatic social ritual. Nevertheless, such rituals acknowledge the social bond that exists even between strangers.

Serve as an Instrument of Play

You have to love the name The Wailin' Jennys, three talented Canadian singer-songwriters (none named Jenny). Our language not only works, it also entertains. Many linguists believe we all vocalize as children partly because it just feels and sounds good. Luckily, we do not entirely lose that capacity for play as we mature. The jump-rope chant, the forced rhyme of much rap music, and the rapid-fire lyrics of a hit single used in a car commercial are all examples of language used mainly for the sheer fun of its sounds.

Check Understanding

When in doubt, we as speakers will sometimes check with our listeners to see whether they are decoding a message similar to the one we intended. For example you might ask someone, "Do you understand?"

When you want to send a very clear message, you would use language with clear denotations. **Denotation** is the dictionary definition of a word. On other occasions, you speak to get a message across, but also to convey it in an especially vivid way. When your purpose is to signal your feelings about a subject, you use language with strong connotations. **Connotation** is the emotional association that a particular word has for an individual listener. Your choice will depend on the purpose of your speech.

Language has many registers, from chatty and confidential to simple and direct, complex and technical, lofty and formal. You speak differently to different people, depending on the environment, the subject under discussion, and your relationship with your listeners.

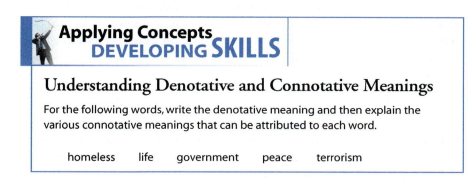

Applying Concepts
DEVELOPING SKILLS

Understanding Denotative and Connotative Meanings

For the following words, write the denotative meaning and then explain the various connotative meanings that can be attributed to each word.

homeless   life   government   peace   terrorism

4b   Exploring the Nature of Language

In the previous section, we introduced the concepts of denotative and connotative meaning, which are crucial to the decoding of words. As part of the decoding process, we must understand the nature of language.

Language Is Symbolic

A **symbol** stands for something else. Symbols can be pictures, drawings, or objects. The police officer's uniform and squad car are symbols of the authority of the police. Symbols also include the names of things, people, and events. Your name is a symbol that represents you.

Words are symbols that are conventionally agreed upon to represent certain things, people, and events. Some words refer to concepts, such as freedom, existentialism, and justice. It is important to recognize that words are "conventionally agreed upon," meaning that the majority of people use the same word to stand for the same thing. If words were not conventionally agreed upon, we would have no way to communicate with one another because we would be using different words to communicate about the same thing.

Words simplify the amount of information needed to communicate. For example, if Jane bought a new chair today, the word *chair* simplifies her message. She doesn't have to tell you that she bought a new *object with four legs upon which people sit*. The word chair has been conventionally agreed upon by English-speaking people to represent an object upon which people sit.

Words enable us to communicate about things that are not physically present. Jane can tell us about her new chair without our having to go to *see* the chair. We know the general concept of a chair and need not be bothered to witness it for ourselves. Similarly, *words enable us to communicate about the past and the future*. "Chair" is a vague concept, but words allow us to talk about Jane's *previous* chair without having to see it. We can reminisce about the past and dream about the future. If we are using common words (in the same language, of course), we are able to communicate about things that are not directly in front of our eyes.

Language Is Subjective

Beyond symbols and words is meaning. **Meaning** is the relationship between the symbol (typically a word) and the thing that it represents. There are several key characteristics of meaning:

Meanings are in people, not in words. People conventionally agree which symbols can be put together to make words. The word *chair* means nothing—the letters *c, h, a, i,* and *r* do not inherently mean "an object upon which you sit." People ascribe meaning to words and symbols.

Words have more than one meaning. Words have both denotative and connotative meaning based on the experiences and knowledge of the person encountering the word. *Freedom* has a finite number of definitions in the dictionary, but typically means existing without constraints. The word *freedom* means different things to different people. If you have been imprisoned, you likely have a different connotative meaning for *freedom* than someone who has never been imprisoned. If you have lived in a country that does not have the same liberties as found in the United States, *freedom* might mean something different to you.

Meanings are more than words and gestures. We can have a basic understanding of what people are saying to us by looking at the context in which the words are used and by looking at the way they are saying those words. But, just as we discussed with perception, everyone engages in communication from the basis of their own experiences. Therefore, much of what we say remains unspoken.

As society and culture changes, so do common meanings for words and their acceptable usages. The "political correctness" movement is a prime example of this characteristic of meaning. As our societal and cultural values evolve, we conventionally agree which words are no longer appropriate. A *secretary* is now an *administrative assistant*. A *mailman* is a *mail carrier*. The word *bad* can now mean "not good" or "good"!!

4b

No word is inherently "good" or "bad." As stated above, the shift in language from gender-specific words, such as *fireman*, to gender-neutral words, such as *firefighter*, illustrates this characteristic of meaning as well. It is no longer politically correct to refer to a firefighter as a fireman—because women are firefighters, too.

Of course, this quality also pertains to swear words. Society has deemed several "four-letter words" to be "bad" words. An episode of *South Park* entitled "It Hits the Fan" provides an excellent illustration of how society changes the meaning of words. During the episode, a popular network program decides to break the swear word moratorium by saying the word "shit" on television. Because the popular program used the swear word, everyone agrees that it is now okay to say "shit." By the end of the episode, the South Park kids note that it is no longer fun to say that word because it's no longer a bad word. It became part of acceptable everyday language.

Words do not have authority, people do. This characteristic is similar to the first characteristic we mentioned—that meanings are in people, not in words. If your roommate asks you to take out the trash, the words themselves are not compelling you to take out the trash. Rather, your relationship with your roommate and the potential repercussions of *not* taking out the trash are what compels you to consider the request.

Words have no meaning or reality apart from the person using them and responding to them. Again, we give symbols conventionally agreed-upon meanings. The letters themselves do not inherently mean anything. They are just letters that sit next to each other. People give the meaning to the words.

Communication is clearest only when the interpreters involved attach similar referents to the message being communicated. You can, no doubt, think of experiences you have had when people misinterpreted what you said because they attached different referents to your words. The most important thing to remember about the process of communication is this: Words and other symbols have no inherent meaning. People have meaning; words do not. The word takes on the meaning that each interpreter attaches to it.

Language Is Rule-governed

4b

Rules abound in the English language. **Syntactic rules** dictate what letters can go together to form a word. Words contain consonants and vowels. Some languages may look odd to you because they have different rules for how letters can form a word. For instance, Slavic languages use many more consonants than vowels.

The meaning of words is guided by **semantic rules**. We agree that a *chair* is an object on which you sit. We know that a *desk* is an object that usually has four legs, a solid top, and an open frame at which we can sit on a chair. Semantic rules dictate the meaning of the words.

Cultural CONNECTIONS | Connotative Meanings

Countless jokes and situation comedy plots revolve around interpreters who attach different referents to the same symbol. Yet the consequences can also be serious and divisive. Consider the experience of Muslim-American Zayed M. Yasin, the Harvard student whose graduation speech was one of the three choices of the selection committee in the spring of 2002. The furor began when the campus newspaper, the *Harvard Crimson*, published the titles of the three student commencement speeches. Yasin's speech, to be delivered less than nine months after September 11, 2001, was titled "Of Faith and Citizenship: My American Jihad." His aim, he said, was to rescue the word *jihad* from extremists who had co-opted it to justify terrorism. He defined the term as a spiritual quest, "the determination to do right and justice even against your personal interests" (HNN Staff, 2002). Among the definitions of the Arabic word are "striving," "effort," and "struggle," but many of those who protested the selection of Yasin's speech equated the term *jihad* with a "holy war." After the protests began on this campus, Yasin met with members of the selection committee, retitled his speech, "Of Faith and Citizenship" for the printed program, and delivered the text of the speech without changing a word (CNN.com, 2002).

Application

How does this incident illustrate denotative and connotative meanings? Discuss the ways in which this incident exemplifies the fact that language is subjective.

Pragmatic rules guide the context of words. Typically, to decode the meaning of words you look at the context in which the word is used. Think of all of the words that sound the same, but are spelled differently, like *pear* and *pair*. The context guides the meaning of the word, especially if you are hearing spoken words.

Applying Concepts DEVELOPING SKILLS | Regional Variation in Meanings

The words *soft drink, pop, soda,* and *coke* all refer to the same thing. Your use of one of those words over another depends on the region of the country in which you were raised.

Consider colloquialisms, or regional meanings for words. What words are used where you live that might be different from words used in other regions of the country? How did you discover that the different words actually had the same meaning?

4c Communicating Effectively

Words are sometimes compared to tools and weapons, and, in a sense, you draw from that arsenal every time you speak. The words you choose help determine your success in communicating with others. Three principles should guide your use of language and make you a more effective communicator.

Use Language Correctly

When you use language incorrectly, you run the risk of sending unintended messages, as well as undermining your credibility. Poorly worded ideas are sometimes evaluated as poor ideas, although this may not be the case. For example, one public speaking student, concerned about the increase in sexually transmitted diseases, encouraged her listeners to commit to "long-term monotonous relationships." We hope she meant to use the word *monogamous*.

The list entitled Using Language Correctly provides guidelines to avoid miscommunication. These strategies will help you detect and correct errors. Not only will your speaking improve, but you may also save yourself some embarrassment. As Mark Twain noted, "The difference between the right word and the almost right word is the difference between lightning and the lightning bug."

USING LANGUAGE CORRECTLY

Use these few simple guidelines to avoid miscommunication.

- Make a note of grammatical mistakes you hear yourself and other people make in casual conversation. Attentive listening is a first step to improving your use of language.
- When you are unsure of a word's meaning, consult a dictionary.
- If you have a question about proper grammar, refer to a handbook for writers.
- In a public speaking setting, when practicing your speech, record it and play it back. Listen for mistakes you may not have noticed as you were practicing.

4c

- Prior to a speech, practice in front of friends and ask them to point out mistakes.

Use Language Clearly

Language use must not only be correct, it must also be clear. To achieve clarity, you should use language that is specific and familiar. If you sacrifice either criterion, your language may confuse others.

Use specific language. Many of our communication problems spring from the fact that there are always two messages involved whenever two people are communicating: the message that the speaker intends and the message that the listener infers or interprets. If you tell your instructor that you missed an assignment deadline because you were "having some problems," you leave yourself open to a wide range of possible interpretations. Do you have health problems, family troubles, or stress from a personal relationship? These and other interpretations are possible because *problem* is an abstract term.

To clarify your ideas, use the lowest level of abstraction possible. Words are not either abstract or concrete, but take on these qualities in relation to other words. Look at the following list of terms, for example.

class

college class

college communication class

COMM 110: Introduction to Communication

COMM 110 at Radford University

COMM 110 with Betty Kennan at Radford University

The term at the top of this list is more abstract than the one at the bottom. As we add those limiting, descriptive words, or qualifiers, the referent becomes increasingly specific. The lower the level of abstraction used, the more clearly the listener will understand the speaker.

Suppose you were giving a speech on how citizens can protect their homes from burglaries, and you made the following statement:

> Crime is rampant in our city. Burglary alone has gone way up in the past year or so. So you can see that having the right kind of lock on your door is essential to your safety.

4c

What is wrong with this statement? The language is vague. What does *rampant* mean? How much of an increase is "way up"—15%, 50%, 400%? Is "the past year or so" one year, two years, or more? What is "the right kind of lock"? As a speaker you should help your audience by making these ideas more concrete. After some research, you might rephrase your argument like this:

> Last week I spoke with Captain James Winton, head of our City Police Department's Records Division. He told me that crime in our city has increased by 54% in the last year, and the number of burglaries has doubled. We can help deter crime by making our homes burglar-proof, and one way of doing this is to make sure that all doors have solid locks. I brought one such lock with me: It's a double-keyed deadbolt lock.

Notice the improvement in the second paragraph. Your message is clearer, and with that clarity you would gain added credibility as a speaker.

Use familiar language. Your language may be specific but still not be clear. If the people with whom you are interacting are not familiar with your words, communication is impaired.

The use of jargon can undermine clarity. **Jargon** is the special language of a particular activity, business, or group of people. What, for example, are the meanings of the following acronyms: BRB, ROFL, and FWIW? If you participate in Internet chatrooms, message boards, or instant messaging (IM), you probably quickly interpreted these letters as the phrases: "be right back," "rolling on the floor laughing," and "for what it's worth." If you lack much online experience, however, this unfamiliar jargon thwarts effective communication. If you inform your classmates on the development of maglev trains, you will probably also need to tell them that *maglev* is short for "magnetic levitation" and then explain what that means.

If you are certain that the people with whom you are communicating know such terms, jargon presents no problem. In fact, it is usually quite specific and can save a lot of time. Jargon can even increase your credibility by indicating that you are familiar with the subject matter. If you have any doubts about whether someone knows the jargon, however, either avoid such terms or define each word the first time you use it.

Use Language Ethically

Ethical communicators neither exclude nor demean others on the basis of their race, ethnicity, gender, sexual orientation, disability, age, or other characteristics. Their language is inclusive, unbiased, and respectful. At least three principles should guide you as you become a more inclusive communicator (*Publication Manual of the American Psychological Association*, 2001; Maggio, 1997).

Consider people's preferences. *When referring to individuals and groups of people, use the names by which they wish to be called.* Acceptable terms when referring to race or ethnicity include African American or black; Asian or Asian American; Native American or American Indian; white or Caucasian; and Hispanic, Latino, or Chicano. Refer to individuals' sexual orientations, not their sexual preferences. *Lesbians, gay men*, and *bisexual women and men* are acceptable terms. Address females and males who are 18 years or older as women and men, not girls and boys. Not everyone with these characteristics favors the terms listed, and you should consider those preferences when you address a specific audience. Your goal, though, should be to respect individuals' rights to choose what they wish to be called.

Put people first. *Use the "people first" rule when referring to individuals who have disabilities.* As the name implies, we should place people before their disabilities. Avoid calling someone a disabled person, an epileptic, or an AIDS victim. Instead, refer to a person with disabilities, a person with epilepsy, or a person who has AIDS.

Avoid gender bias. *Avoid using language that is gender biased.* The issue of gender bias is particularly pervasive and problematic. Gender bias occurs when language creates special categories for one gender, with no corresponding parallel category for the other gender. *Man* and *wife*, for example, are not parallel terms. *Man* and *woman* or *husband* and *wife* are parallel. Other examples of nonparallel language are *nurse* and *male nurse*, *chairman* and *chairperson*, and athletic team names such as *The Tigers* (the men's team) and *The Lady Tigers* (the women's team).

Perhaps the most common display of gender-biased language comes from the inappropriate use of a simple two-letter word: *he.* Sometimes called the "generic he," this word is used to refer to men and women alike, usually

4c

with the fallacious justification that there aren't acceptable alternatives without cluttering speech with intrusive phrases such as "he and she" and "him and her." Fortunately, this assumption is false.

Communicators exhibit fairness when they express their ideas and examples in language that treats others equally and fairly. The strategies discussed in this section should help you communicate in a way that uses inclusive language and respects others. If you'd like to learn more about how to use bias-free language, consult a dictionary such as *The Bias-Free Word Finder: A Dictionary of Nondiscriminatory Language*, by Rosalie Maggio. Speaking inclusively is an ethical obligation for those who value civil discourse.

4c

Applying Concepts DEVELOPING SKILLS | Encountering Gender-biased Language

List some examples of gender-biased language (other than those listed above) that you hear occasionally or frequently. How could you rephrase each word to make it gender-neutral? Why are the gender-biased words that you listed considered unethical? For instance, what about those words is problematic?

EYEONETHICS | Doublespeak

In his book *The New Doublespeak, William Lutz* writes about the unclear and misleading language used in our society. In recent speeches and public statements, politicians have used phrases such as "revenue enhancement," "receipt proposals," and "wage-based premiums" when they mean taxes. Business leaders have referred to "laying off workers" as "work reengineering." Military spokespersons sometimes speak of "neutralizing the opposition" to avoid using the word *killing*, and "improvised explosive device" instead of *bomb*.

Lutz argues that the use of such phrases is unethical because "The clearest possible language is essential for democracy to function, for it is only through clear language that we have any hope of defining, debating, and deciding the issues of public policy that confront us."

Application

Do you agree with Lutz's position, or do you think it is legitimate for speakers to use this kind of language if it helps them achieve their purposes? Can you think of a time when the use of such "doublespeak" would be appropriate? In general, what ethical guidelines should speakers use to govern their choice of language?

4d   Understanding the Power of Language

From the previous section on using language ethically, you can see the power of language. The words we use, while they do not have power apart from the person using them, can create severe negative reactions in others.

Names that we use to refer to a person or a group of people can shape the way that others think of us. Names can also shape the way we view ourselves and the way we act. In Chapter 2, we examined self-concept and self-esteem. The names people call you or the labels they use to describe you have considerable influence on how you view yourself. If you continually hear teachers tell you that you are smart and could do well in a graduate program, you will likely allow that to influence how you feel about yourself and, perhaps, your interest in graduate school. Therefore, the positive labels influence the way you view yourself and the way you act.

Powerless Language

The use of **powerless speech mannerisms**, words and phrases that deflate the strength and confidence of your message, can greatly diminish your credibility and your perceived competence. There are several types of powerless speech mannerisms that invade people's speech.

Hedges include phrases like "I think," "kinda," and "I guess." These are phrases that make you seem unable to make a decision or to take a stand. A sample statement would be, "We *kinda* need that report by tomorrow." Well, do you need the report tomorrow, or don't you? In this example you can see that hedges can render your statements confusing and nonspecific.

Tag questions work similarly in degrading your ability to speak with confidence. Tag questions are tacked onto the end of statements that sound confident. However, the questions take the power out of the statement by making you appear wishy-washy. Examples of some tag questions include: "right?" "isn't it?" and "shouldn't we?" Here's an example of a tag question in use: "We should write a letter of complaint to the vice president to express our displeasure with this new policy, *don't you think*?" Can you see how the question tacked at the end of that powerful statement reduces all the power of the statement?

Hesitations **are signs of weak communicators.** Hesitations, like "uh" and "well," can drain the power of your message. Consider the following sample interaction:

BOSS: What do you think we should do?

YOU: Well, *uh*, we should write a letter, *uh*, to the vice president to express our displeasure, *uh*, with the new policy.

What do you think the boss's impression is of you after this statement? You are not speaking with confidence. Your hesitations not only deflate your confidence, but they also make you appear intimidated by your boss.

Disclaimers **are denials.** When people start sentences with disclaimers, it is as though they are setting you up for something. Doesn't it make you nervous when someone starts a sentence with "I probably shouldn't say this, but . . .?" Disclaimers immediately deflate your message, and they often put the listener into a defensive state. Worse yet is the disclaimer, "You aren't going to like this, but . . ." Talk about making someone defensive! How would you expect someone to react to such a disclaimer?

Applying Concepts
DEVELOPING SKILLS

Eliminating Powerless Language in Your Communication

Which of the types of powerless language do you use most frequently? What are some ways you can attempt to eliminate that powerless language from your communication?

Confirmation and Disconfirmation

Powerful and powerless language is also evident in the concepts of *confirmation* and *disconfirmation*. As we discussed earlier, names and labels that are derogatory are demeaning to the person or group of people to whom they refer. **Disconfirmation** occurs when you ignore the presence of others and ignore who they are as persons. Three common "isms" are examples of disconfirmation: *racism, sexism,* and *heterosexism*. Language that incorporates the "isms" implies that a person does not exist outside of his or her race, sex, and sexual orientation. Disconfirmation is different from rejection. With rejection, you are still acknowledging the other person's existence. Rejection is synonymous with disagreement. However, disconfirmation denies the person's existence. Examples that we have used earlier in this chapter apply here as well: *mailman,* *policeman*, and *lady doctor*. The first two terms deny the presence of women who are mail carriers and police officers. The use of *lady doctor* implies that the norm is a male doctor. More women than men are becoming doctors these days. So the use of *lady doctor* is antiquated as well.

Instead of using disconfirming statements, competent and ethical communicators strive for **confirmation**, statements acknowledging the presence and acceptance of those with whom they are communicating. Understanding the origin of many disconfirming statements enables communicators to avoid using them. Many gays and lesbians react negatively to the label *homosexual* because of the origin of the word. For a long period of time, homosexuality was listed as a mental disorder in the DSM-IV-TR (Diagnostic and Statistical Manual of Mental Disorders). As you might recall from *Cultural Connections* in Chapter 1, the phrase "sitting Indian style" is disconfirming to Native Americans. Instead, a confirming statement would be "sitting cross-legged." Merely changing a few words can make all the difference in how our message is interpreted by others.

In her book *The Future of White Men and Other Diversity Dilemmas*, Joan Lester explores the power of language. She makes a profound statement that summarizes well our discussion of the power of language and ethical uses of language.

> Noticing what language is used all around us, and what language we use ourselves, is a major step toward becoming more inclusive. As we become more inclusive in our words, we usually find our thinking and then our actions reflect the shift. Because we have to think about what we are saying. (1994, p. 83)

A common reaction to the discussion of confirming statements is, "I have to worry about *everything* I say now." Lester reminds us that as we use inclusive (confirming) language, it becomes more routine for us. And, more importantly, our actions reflect that shift in language usage. Understanding the effects of words and phrases is an important step toward becoming a competent communicator.

Applying Concepts
DEVELOPING SKILLS | Developing Confirming Feedback

What disconfirming word do you find yourself using most often? Develop a plan to attempt to erase that disconfirming word from your vocabulary. What word could you substitute? What is the typical reaction from others when you use the disconfirming word?

4e Creating a Supportive Communication Climate

Another important aspect of communication is **climate**, or the tone of the interaction. Climate can influence how each person communicates. Two components of climate are the *valence* of the interaction and the *disclosure* in the interaction. Valence is the positivity or negativity of the communication. Disclosure is the act of communicating information to someone else.

Gibb (1961) categorized climate as defensive or supportive. In a **defensive climate**, communication is likely to be negative and communicators do not feel comfortable communicating freely. Communicators in a defensive climate may also feel as though their reactions are limited.

In a **supportive climate**, communication is likely to be positive and the communicators feel comfortable communicating freely. Communicators feel free to state their positions without potential for negative reactions.

CREATING A SUPPORTIVE COMMUNICATION CLIMATE

Defensive Behavior	Supportive Behavior
Evaluation A message judging the other person or placing blame on the other person	*Description* Objective statements that do not assign blame
Superiority Communicating as though you are better than the other person	*Equality* Communicating with respect for the other person
Control Statements indicating that you know how the other person should act, think, or feel	*Problem Orientation* Indicating that you will work on a solution to a problem with the other person
Strategy Deceptive or manipulative statements	*Spontaneity* Messages that are instantaneous and free from deception/manipulation
Neutrality Statements of indifference	*Empathy* Feeling as the other person feels (putting yourself in the other person's shoes)
Certainty Close-minded statements indicating an unwillingness to consider other perspectives	*Provisionalism* Indicating a willingness to hear all sides of the story before making a judgment

Several types of defensive and supportive communication serve to set the climate, or tone, of the interaction. Gibb outlines six defensive behaviors and six supportive behaviors, and encourages you to avoid defensive behaviors in favor of supportive behaviors.

In order to illustrate defensive and supportive communication, let's use the following examples.

Defensive Communication Example

You never do the dishes! Every day you just put your dishes in the sink and expect them to wash themselves. If you weren't so lazy, you could spend one minute rinsing the dishes and putting them in the dishwasher. Instead, they pile up and, if I don't wash them, they get moldy and attract bugs. The other day a cockroach ran across the counter and my friend was so disgusted that he left. I don't care how busy you are with your work. You have made this place a disaster!! Now fix it!!

Supportive Communication Example

I have noticed that you have not been rinsing your dishes and putting them in the dishwasher. The problem is that when friends come over to visit, the dishes are piled up and moldy. Often that causes bugs to gather and it is embarrassing. I know that you have been busy lately, but I am not sure if that is the reason you haven't had time to clean your dishes. Is there some way that we can resolve this problem and make our place bug-free?

Evaluation versus description. **Evaluation** is a defensive behavior in which the communicator judges (positively or negatively) the other person and/or places blame on that person. Evaluation statements are characterized by the use of the word *you*, as in "You never do the dishes!" When someone confronts you with such statements, how do you react? Most likely you will react defensively by either shouting back your own evaluation statement or attempting to justify your actions. In either case, a defensive reaction merely escalates the defensive communication and, thus, the negative climate of the interaction.

Description is a supportive behavior using objective statements that do not assign blame in the situation. To avoid a defensive climate use description instead of evaluation. Description is typically characterized by the use of "I" statements rather than "you" statements. Therefore, in the Supportive Communication Example, the person is describing the situation without assigning blame (you are, essentially, stating that the roommate has created the situation, but in a way that would be less likely to elicit a defensive reaction).

Superiority versus equality. **Superiority** is a defensive behavior of communicating as though you are better than the other person. A lot of evaluation statements also illustrate superiority. In the Defensive Communication Example, the speaker is telling the other person what to do and acting as though he or she has the authority to talk down to the offender.

Rather than assuming you are better than the other person (and thus communicating that superiority), you should use statements of equality. **Equality** is a supportive behavior that lets the other person know that you respect him or her and that you do not consider yourself superior. Supportive communication is often characterized by equality in a nonspecific way. By using description and not assigning blame, you are showing the offender that you respect her and will not talk down to her—that you consider the other person an equal.

Control versus problem orientation. **Control** is a defensive behavior communicating that you know how the other person should act, think, or feel. In the Defensive Communication Example, the speaker is assuming that the offender does not wash the dishes on purpose (expecting the dishes to wash themselves) and the speaker tells the offender how to act to fix the situation.

Instead of using control statements, you should use problem orientation. **Problem orientation** suggests to the other person that you work on a solution to the problem together. Problem orientation typically uses "we" statements because that shows a desire to work together. The example ends with the speaker suggesting that "we can resolve this problem" and not telling the offender what to do.

Strategy versus spontaneity. The use of strategy, or strategic messages, is a defensive behavior. **Strategy** includes any message that is deliberately deceptive or manipulative. A communicator who withholds information, makes up stories, or distorts messages, he or she is using strategic communication. Suppose the speaker in the Defensive Communication Example had simply said, "It sure is hard to get a glass of water when the sink is full of dishes." That is a strategic message because he is attempting to manipulate the person into cleaning the dishes in order for the sink to be useable. Rather than outright asking the person to clean the dishes, a strategic message would *imply* that the dishes needed to be cleaned.

The opposite of strategy is **spontaneity**, or messages that are instantaneous and free from deception or manipulation. In the example above, the speaker exhibits spontaneity when he admits embarrassment as a result of the dish situation. He is not blaming the other person for that feeling, but rather he is *owning* that feeling of embarrassment.

Neutrality versus empathy. **Neutrality** is a defensive behavior which includes statements of indifference. A communicator who conveys a lack of interest in what the other person says is displaying neutrality. In the Defensive Communication Example, the speaker indicates indifference, or neutrality, regarding the offender's personal situation.

Empathy is the opposite of neutrality. **Empathy** is feeling as the other person feels, or putting yourself in another person's shoes. It involves imagining what the other person is going through and how that might feel. When you express empathy with the other person, you are creating common ground from which you can build a solution to the problem. The speaker in the Supportive Communication Example says, "I know that you have been busy lately," which illustrates an understanding of the offender's personal situation. The speaker acknowledges that there may be extenuating circumstances that are causing the dirty dishes problem.

Certainty versus provisionalism. A person who uses **certainty** leaves no room for interpretation. Think of certainty as a close-minded behavior and unwillingness to consider any other perspective. Every statement in the Defensive Communication Example illustrates certainty to some degree. The speaker is clearly unwilling to consider any reason other than the sheer laziness of the offender as the cause of the situation.

Instead, the speaker should use provisionalism, which is an open-minded perspective. A person who uses **provisionalism** is indicating a willingness to hear all sides of the story before making a judgment. In the Supportive Communication Example, the speaker suggests a possible motive for the offending behavior ("I know you have been busy lately . . ."), but reserves judgment until the offender has time to explain ("but I am not sure if that is the reason . . .").

Keep in mind that defensive and supportive behaviors are not all verbal messages. Nonverbal communication can be supportive and defensive, too. Rolling your eyes at someone (when not used in a humorous way) can create a defensive climate. Some scholars would argue that crossing your arms in front of your body is a defensive behavior that indicates certainty and superiority. What other nonverbals would you characterize as defensive or supportive?

Have you ever been in an interaction with someone who continually uses defensive communication despite your efforts to change the climate from defensive to supportive? What did you do, or, if faced with such a situation, what would you do? It is often easier to fall into the defensive communication trap than to continue to use supportive behaviors in the face of opposition. However, it is also difficult for most people to continue to be defensive and nasty towards a person who is trying to be nice. So if you find yourself in this situation, stand your ground and continue to use supportive messages. If nothing else, you will leave the interaction knowing that you did the right thing.

4e

One note of caution: do not confuse defensive climate, communication, and behaviors with conflict. Conflict is inevitable in any relationship, and is typically not a negative relational event. However, defensive communication is a negative relational event because the negative and sometimes nasty language can erode trust and respect between two people. Because trust and respect are important foundations for healthy relationships, any behavior that can erode trust or respect is detrimental to the continued existence of the relationship.

Applying Concepts
DEVELOPING SKILLS

Changing a Communication Climate from Defensive to Supportive

The setting is a restaurant, and a customer's order contains meat when she specifically asked for no meat. Create a dialogue between the customer and the server. Have the customer use defensive communication and the server attempt to change the climate by using supportive communication. Is it possible for the server to change the behavior of the customer? Why or why not?

Competence SUMMARY

In this chapter, you have learned the following concepts. Check to be sure you have achieved each of these communication competencies.

4a Identifying the Functions of Language

■ The more you know about your language, the more effective you will be as a communicator.

■ Language serves many functions, including communicating ideas, sending messages about communicators, and strengthening social bonds.

■ Words have denotative meanings, or dictionary definitions, and connotative meanings, including the emotional association a person attributes to a word.

Competence. Can I identify the functions of language? In what ways will knowing the functions of language make me a more competent communicator?

4b Exploring the Nature of Language

■ Language is symbolic, subjective, and rule governed.

■ Words enable you to simplify the amount of information needed to communicate; they allow you to communicate about things that are not present and about the past and the future.

- Meaning is the relationship between the symbol and the thing it represents. There are several characteristics of meaning.

Competence. Can I explain the characteristics of meaning so that I can better communicate my messages to others? Will I be able to carefully choose my words to avoid misunderstandings or hurting someone's feelings?

4c Communicating Effectively

- As part of using language correctly, learn the appropriate usage of new words and continually refresh your memory of grammar rules.
- Specific language conveys meaning more effectively than vague language does. Using language that is familiar to the person or persons with whom you are speaking can strengthen the connection between or among you.

Competence. Do I speak clearly using specific and familiar language? Am I sensitive to the needs of others and do I avoid sexist language?

4d Understanding the Power of Language

- While words do not have meaning or power apart from the people using them, words can create severe negative reactions in others.
- The use of powerless speech mannerisms (hedges, tag questions, hesitations, and disclaimers) can make you look less competent and less confident.
- Disconfirmation occurs when you deny the existence of another person or ignore who he or she is as a person. Instead you should use confirmation, which occurs when you acknowledge the individuality of the person and accepting him or her.

Competence. Do I incorporate confirming messages into my communication with others? Have I eliminated disconfirming messages?

4e Creating a Supportive Communication Climate

- The climate, or tone, of an interaction can influence how each person communicates. Climate consists of the valence (positivity or negativity of the communication) and the amount of disclosure (not necessarily disclosure about yourself) in the interaction.
- A defensive climate is one in which communicators do not feel comfortable communicating freely. In a supportive climate, communicators feel free to communicate and the messages are more positive.

Competence. Do I effectively use communication to create a supportive communication climate in which all communicators feel comfortable interacting? Do I know how to change a defensive situation into a supportive one?

Review Questions

1. What are the three characteristics of language? Explain each.
2. Explain the difference between connotative and denotative meanings.
3. Why do we say that language is subjective?
4. When trying to create a supportive climate, why is it important to use "I" statements as opposed to "you" statements?

Discussion Questions

1. How can the use of powerless speech mannerisms diminish credibility and competence?
2. Why is it important to be able to use language correctly? What determines the language you use?
3. Think of a time when you felt you were engaged in a defensive climate. What characteristics of the communication led you to label it defensive? Did you try to change the climate of the interaction or did you choose to react defensively? How could you have made that interaction more supportive?

Key Terms

certainty *p. 86*

climate *p. 83*

confirmation *p. 82*

connotation *p. 71*

control *p. 85*

defensive climate *p. 83*

denotation *p. 71*

description *p. 84*

disconfirmation *p. 81*

empathy *p. 86*

equality *p. 85*

evaluation *p. 84*

jargon *p. 77*

meaning *p. 72*

neutrality *p. 86*

powerless speech mannerisms *p. 80*

pragmatic rules *p. 75*

problem orientation *p. 85*

provisionalism *p. 86*

semantic rules *p. 74*

spontaneity *p. 85*

strategy *p. 85*

superiority *p. 85*

supportive climate *p. 83*

symbol *p. 71*

syntactic rules *p. 74*

words *p. 71*

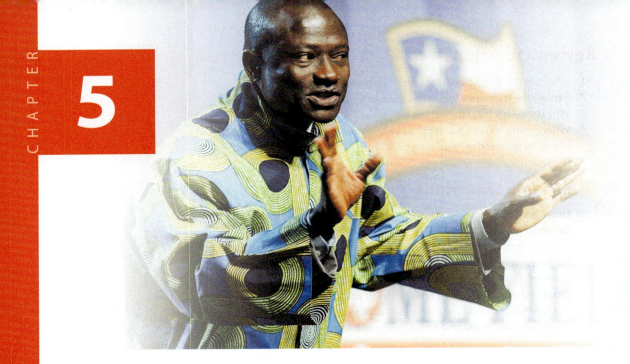

5

Nonverbal Communication

In this chapter, you will learn about the nature of nonverbal communication by identifying the types and functions of nonverbal messages. Your communication competence will be enhanced by understanding:

- how nonverbal cues can be misinterpreted and that they may even be unintentional;
- the importance of considering the context in which nonverbal cues occur to avoid making hasty conclusions about their meaning;
- why you should create a positive first impression with someone you have just met.

5a Understanding the Principles of Nonverbal Communication

We learn how to communicate from the time that we are born. While children do not have the physical ability to speak until around 16 to 18 months, a new trend in child-rearing is to teach children sign language so that they can communicate *before* they can speak. That's right—the sign language that Robert De Niro's character was teaching the baby in the movie *Meet the Fockers* was not just a joke. Many parents are using sign language as a means of communicating with a baby. So it appears as though our first communicative messages are largely nonverbal.

You should recall from Chapter 1 that nonverbal communication is an essential element in the communication process. **Nonverbal messages** are messages that are sent without using words. Gestures, tone of voice, facial expressions, and vocal fillers ("um" and "uh") are examples of nonverbal communication.

Can you think of a time when you called a friend and asked how they were doing? The friend replied (with a sad voice), "Oh, I'm fine." Did you believe that reply? The nonverbal tone of voice (sad voice) conveyed the true meaning of the message, despite the fact that your friend was trying hard to mask the sad feelings. Our nonverbal messages are often beyond our conscious control.

In this chapter, we will explore the principles, types, and functions of nonverbal communication. By identifying all of the nonverbal messages that you are capable of sending, you can become a more competent communicator.

Your nonverbal behavior communicates a great deal of information concerning your feelings about what you say and your reactions to the messages of others. In particular, four principles of nonverbal communication help account for the importance of speech delivery.

Nonverbal communication can be deliberate or unintentional.

You do certain things deliberately to make other people feel comfortable around you or attracted to you. You dress in colors and fabrics that flatter you or make you feel comfortable. When speaking or listening to others, you look them directly in the eyes. You smile when they tell you good news and show concern when they share a problem.

On the other hand, you may have habits of which you are unaware. You fold your arms, assuming a closed and defensive body position, or jingle your keys when nervous. You can control only those things you know about. Therefore, the first step in becoming a more competent communicator is to identify and isolate any distracting nonverbal behaviors you exhibit. You might recall from Chapter 4 that people are generally not good listeners. If you display distracting nonverbals, your listener(s) might pay more attention to those annoying movements than to your message.

Nonverbal cues are cultural.

Cultural differences abound when it comes to nonverbal communication. Standing at a bakery in Paris, France, you can't resist the aroma of long, golden loaves of bread hot from the oven. Unable to speak French, you get the clerk's attention, point to the loaves, and hold up two fingers, as in V for victory. The clerk nods, hands you three loaves, and charges you for all three. Why? The French count from the thumb, whether it is extended or not.

Nonverbal messages are trusted more than verbal messages when the two conflict.

A supervisor at work tells you privately that she is impressed with your work, but then doesn't allow you to speak at staff meetings. A person keeps saying, "I love you," but never does anything to show consideration for you. Would you doubt the sincerity of these people? Most people certainly would.

We have each been interpreting and responding to other people's nonverbal communication for so long that we lose sight of its significance. But we are reminded of the importance of nonverbal communication when someone breaks a nonverbal rule. One of these rules demands that a person's words and actions match. Suppose Doris walks reluctantly to the front of the classroom, clutches the lectern, stands motionless, frowns, and says, "I'm absolutely delighted to be speaking to you today." Do you believe her? No. Why? Doris's speech began not with her first words, but with the multiple nonverbal messages that signaled her reluctance to speak. Nonverbal messages should complement and reinforce verbal ones. When they do not, as in Doris's case, actions speak louder than words. We tend to trust the nonverbal message to help us answer the question, "What's really going on here?" As a result of this, one final principle of nonverbal communication becomes extremely important.

Nonverbal messages can be ambiguous.

You stare out the window while delivering your speech because you feel too nervous to make eye contact with your listeners. The audience, however, assumes that you are bored and not really interested in speaking to them. Even though it may be far from the truth, your audience's perception that you are disinterested is the more important factor in this situation.

Applying Concepts DEVELOPING SKILLS | Cultural Nonverbal Differences

Consider an incident in which you were communicating with someone from another culture. In what ways did your nonverbal communication differ from the other person? How did those differences affect your interaction?

Aware of these principles of communication, we can see that our nonverbal messages can be as ambiguous as our verbal messages. Let's take a look at the different types of nonverbal communication in order to see how that ambiguity is created.

5b Identifying Types of Nonverbal Communication

There are many types of nonverbal communication. We can send messages through channels such as facial expressions, gestures, eye contact, artifacts, and not saying anything at all!

Applying Concepts DEVELOPING SKILLS

Identifying the Nonverbal Cues That You Use

Before reading this section, think of all of the times during the day that you deliberately use nonverbal messages to convey meaning. Make a list of the nonverbal cues that you use and then list the reasons why you used them. As you read through this section, see how many of the nonverbal cues on your list are represented in the text below.

Paralanguage

Paralanguage includes *tone of voice* and utterances, which are vocal but not verbal. As we mentioned at the beginning of the chapter, if a friend sounds sad when telling you that she is "fine," her paralanguage tells you that her verbal message is not exactly truthful. For an excellent example of how tone of voice can determine the meaning of a word, watch the movie *BASEketball* with Trey Parker and Matt Stone. At a key point in the movie, their two characters get in a fight. The entire fight is comprised of the word *dude*. They have an entire "conversation" by changing their tone of voice when they respond to each other with *dude*.

Vocal segregates and *disfluencies* are two vocal but not verbal examples of paralanguage. Vocal segregates are parts of words, such as "uh-huh" and "shhhh." They are not "real" words, but we know what someone means when they use these parts of words, or segregates. Disfluencies are also called "fillers." Disfluencies are utterances that fill up a pause in speaking—such as "uh," "um,"—or words, such as "like." People often use disfluencies to indicate that they are not yet finished speaking.

Proxemics

The use of space to communicate is known as **proxemics**. Each person has a "personal bubble" as some call it, or the distance in which you allow others to be near you. **Protection theory** says that your personal space is defined by you and how safe you feel having people of varying relationship levels close to your body. Your definition of personal space is based on your cultural norms, personal experiences and preferences.

Levels of distance. There are four levels of proxemics (Hall, 1990).

- **Intimate distance—touching to 1 foot.** People with whom you are very close—close friends, family, romantic partners—are allowed to be close enough to feel your breath on their face. For example, these people would be allowed to hug you. It is unlikely that you would be comfortable allowing someone you just met to be that close to you. However, personal distance is cultural, as we'll see.

- **Personal distance—1 to 2 feet away.** You are close enough to shake hands. Friends are typically allowed into this level of distance where you can still remain protected and untouched.

- **Social distance—3 to 5 feet away.** This distance, reserved for acquaintances and co-workers, allows you to be close enough to carry on a conversation, but far enough away to maintain a safe distance from someone with whom you do not have a close relationship. You might note that when you meet someone, you both lean forward to shake hands, but then you step back to maintain the social distance.

- **Public distance—5 feet or more from the other communicators.** Public distance is typical in public speaking settings or formal speaking settings. There is a "barrier" of space that separates the speaker from the audience.

Think of where your instructor stands in the classroom. Does he or she stand at the front of the classroom? Is there about 5 feet between the instructor and the first row of desks? Classrooms are usually set up with public distance in mind. How about when you talk to your instructor after class? How much space would you estimate exists between the two of you? Would you say it is about 3 to 5 feet? In the U.S. culture, that would be considered acceptable. If your instructor were to stand less than 3 feet from you, would it make you nervous? Why? You would likely feel nervous because you don't know the instructor as well as your friends, who would be allowed to stand within 3 feet. As you communicate with different people today, note where each person is standing or sitting in relation to you. Do you think the distance is appropriate for the type of relationship you have with that person?

One theory that helps us to understand how these levels of personal distance work is equilibrium theory. **Equilibrium theory** states that the more intimate the relationship, the closer you allow the person into your personal space. Hence, the intimate distance is reserved for those people we like *a lot* or even *love*. Likewise, social distance is reserved for people you do not know well.

Territoriality. Proxemics is not confined to personal space. Humans are also **territorial**, meaning that they protect their "space" or their "things." Two types of territorial behavior are "home field advantage" and "markers."

- **Home field advantage.** *Home field advantage* is the comfortableness that you feel in your own surroundings. Because you feel most comfortable in your own living or working space, you might prefer to hear or deliver bad news in those surroundings.

- **Markers.** *Markers* are objects that we use to mark our territory. When you go to class, does everyone sit in the same seat each class period, despite the fact that you do not have assigned seating? If so, do people get agitated if someone sits in "their" seat? Perhaps it is *you* who gets agitated! What do people do when they get to class early? They leave markers to show that they are occupying a particular seat. A student might come into the classroom, leave a book bag and coat on a chair, and leave the room to get a drink or use the restroom. Everyone knows that the seat is "occupied," so they sit elsewhere. Would you dare move the things and take the seat?

Applying Concepts DEVELOPING SKILLS	Your Personal Space
Write down some observations about your use of personal space. Consider the levels of distance and how they relate to the people in your environment. Then examine your territoriality. Do you sit in the same seat in the classroom each day? If you briefly leave the room, do you leave markers?	

Artifacts

How have you decorated your apartment, house, or bedroom? If you have an office, what personal items do you have displayed? **Artifacts** are objects that convey information about us. We litter our environment with artifacts that communicate about our personality and likes.

A documentary entitled, *Home Movie* by Chris Smith (2001), examines the homes of five people. Each home is unique and offers insights into the type of person who owns and lives in it. One house is owned by a couple obsessed with cats. They have platforms near the ceiling that run all along the walls of the house for the cats to walk on. All of the artifacts in the house are cat-related. Another gentleman has a house that is completely electronic. Doors open like they do in *Star Trek*. Even the soap dispenser in his bathroom is electronic—he pushes a button and a mannequin arm comes out of the wall and drops soap on the counter! The man is an electrician who has made his living building all-electrical houses. Chris Smith truly captures the essence of how artifacts communicate about a person!

What kind of car (if any) do you drive? What does your car communicate about you? Many college students own used vehicles that are cost-effective (i.e., low or no car payments). Others drive expensive cars such as BMWs and Mercedes. What do those types of cars communicate? How about the interior of a person's car? That often tells more about the person than the type of car! Does the person keep an immaculate car, or do you have to peel a week-old McDonald's wrapper off the passenger seat?

As you can see, we possess many artifacts that communicate about us. In fact, we consciously and subconsciously display these items. The first author of this textbook has a veritable pop culture museum in her office—containing things such as Pez, talking Homer Simpson and Crocodile Hunter dolls, and an authentic Michael Jackson doll (which would be worth a lot of money had her younger brother not ripped his clothes off to see if he was anatomically correct!). She has cartoons and posters all over her walls, and a live rabbit running around. One of her colleagues has nothing on his walls and stacks of papers all over his desk and the floor (and for stack, think disorderly pile). What would be your interpretation of these two professors based on their space decoration?

Personal Appearance

Similar to artifacts is personal appearance. **Personal appearance** includes how you look in terms of physical appearance and clothing.

Clothing. Often the *clothing* we wear sends nonverbal messages to others. Do you dress neatly or do you look like you just rolled out of bed? In what situations do you take more pride in your personal appearance? Why do you choose those times and not others? Do you wear the latest fashions or whatever is most affordable? Based on what you wear, what do you think you are communicating about yourself?

Body type. We often judge people based on their body type. What adjectives do you associate with overweight, athletic, medium-build, or anorexic body types? Those are the meanings you associate with this category of nonverbals.

Body adornments. In the past decade, *tattoos and body piercings* have become more popular. There are even some folks who have the "plugs" in their ears—the disks that slowly enlarge the hole in their ear. Do you have a tattoo or a piercing? Why or why not? When you make perceptions about someone who has a tattoo, are your perceptions based on the tattoo in general, or the specific picture that is inked on their skin? What about piercings? Do your perceptions of the person depend upon *where* the piercing is located? How about the number of tattoos or piercings?

5b

5b

Kinesics

The use of body movements, or gestures, to communicate is known as **kinesics**. There are several categories of kinesics.

Emblems. Emblems are nonverbal substitutes for words. If you want to say "okay" nonverbally, what hand gesture do you use? There are a couple of ways to communicate okay in the United States—either a "thumbs up" or the index finger and thumb in a circle with the other three fingers held up. What if you want to say "peace"? Usually that is two fingers held up in a "V" with the palm forward. Keep in mind that emblems *replace* words.

Illustrators. Illustrators are body movements that accompany nonverbals. When we want to add emphasis to a message, we use illustrators. If you ask someone to "come here," you might say "come here" along with a hand motion toward your body. The nonverbal gesture and verbal message occur simultaneously.

Affect displays. A third category of kinesics is affect displays, which are facial expressions used to show emotion. We smile or frown to indicate happiness or sadness. According to Ekman and Friesen (1975), we use facial expressions to exhibit six primary emotions: happiness, sadness, surprise, fear, anger, and disgust or contempt.

Regulators. Regulators maintain, monitor, and control the speaking of another person. Regulators include a head nod to indicate understanding or to show agreement with the speaker and eye contact to show interest in the speaker. If you want to speak during class, how do you show that nonverbally? Classroom etiquette normally dictates that you raise your hand if you want to speak in class. We use eye contact to indicate when we are finished talking. For example, when your instructor asks a question of the class, what is the first thing most students do in response? They look down at their desks. Why? If the instructor makes eye contact with you, you feel compelled to answer the question. It is a natural reaction for regulating interaction.

Adaptors. The last category of kinesics is adaptors, which are designed to satisfy some need. For instance, you might need to scratch an itch, or push hair out of your eyes. Often in public speaking settings, nervous mannerisms fall under this category. A speaker might twist a ring, twirl hair, or jingle change in a pocket. These body movements become an outlet for their nervousness, or a way of satisfying the need to combat the nervousness.

Eye Communication

We can communicate a lot just with our eyes. We have already mentioned eye communication within the context of eye contact as a regulator of communication. First, as we have said, we use eye contact *to monitor the feedback* of others and *to signal a conversational turn.* Both of these functions help us regulate interactions. Similarly, we use eye contact *to show interest in and attention to a speaker.*

Aside from regulating interactions, our eyes serve other functions in communication. Eye contact can *signal the nature of a relationship.* Research has shown that we look more at people that we like than at people that we do not like. Eye contact also allows us *to compensate for physical distance.* When you are attempting to communicate with people from across the room, eye contact becomes an important element in the communication process. You need to observe their facial expressions and gestures, and to watch their lips if they are trying to say something.

Cultural CONNECTIONS | Presidential Nonverbal Faux Pas

5b

On her first trip to Europe as a member of the First Family in April 2009, Michelle Obama stirred controversy when she put her hand on Queen Elizabeth's back. Royal etiquette forbids the touching of the Queen or her family. However, in this case, the Queen was the first to put her hand on Michelle Obama's back. Therefore, some would argue that Mrs. Obama's reciprocal hand on the back was acceptable.

In 2005 President George W. Bush met with Russian President Vladimir Putin in Bratislava, Slovakia. When the President arrived, he was greeted by Slovakian officials. Because it was cold, President Bush had gloves on his hands. He shook the hands of the officials and went about his business. However, what he didn't realize is that he had violated Slovakian etiquette, which dictates that when leaders meet they shake with bare hands. The flesh of each person touches. Later that night, President Bush greeted officials properly—with nothing on his hands.

There seems to be at least one nonverbal faux pas in each President's history. When leaving the funeral of Secretary Ron Brown, President Bill Clinton was videotaped joking and laughing with another gentleman who had also attended the funeral. As soon as the President saw that he was being videotaped, he immediately changed his demeanor—from laughing to crying. Of course, most people would consider it inappropriate to laugh and joke at a funeral.

President Richard Nixon made a famous presidential faux pas that is often cited as a reason to know the culture of the people with whom you are interacting. When Nixon got off Air Force One in Latin America, he waved to the crowd by raising both arms high in the air and making an "okay " sign. Instead, in Latin America, the "okay " sign is considered a vulgar gesture.

When you visit foreign countries, even those for whom English is the predominant language, it is important to remember that there can be different interpretations for nonverbal cues as well as for words and phrases.

Application

How could the individuals in these examples have prevented those intercultural blunders? What are some other nonverbal gestures that are different in the United States than they are in other countries?

Silence

It is not just what we say, but what we do not say that can communicate volumes. Silence is a type of nonverbal message that can be used for a variety of functions. Sometimes it is best to not say anything. Silence *allows time to think* before speaking. Similarly, you have probably heard the saying, "If you don't have anything nice to say, don't say anything at all." Silence can *prevent the communication of certain messages*—something that you might later regret saying.

Silence can be used *to hurt others*. Giving the silent treatment—or not speaking to the other person—is often used as a conflict management strategy. Any conflict management strategy that hurts the other person is certainly not going to help solve the problem. Similarly, silence can *communicate emotional responses*. For instance, a mother might ask her son to clean his room. Since he is annoyed by the request (because in his mind it is really a "command"), he might use silence to indicate his disapproval of that request.

There are other, less negative uses for silence. Shy people might use silence as a *response to personal anxiety* experienced in social interactions. And, believe it or not, some people simply *have nothing to say*! So their silence merely reflects that fact.

Applying Concepts
DEVELOPING SKILLS | Your Use of Silence

How do you deliberately use silence on a regular basis? How do others react to your use of silence? Do they accurately attribute meaning to the silence?

Chronemics

The use of time to communicate is known as **chronemics**. We each use time in different ways. Some people are habitually *early*. What does that communicate to you? Perhaps the person is nervous about making sure they are there at the appointed time, so they arrive early. Or maybe the person is being considerate by not making the other person wait. Some people are always *on time*. What does that communicate? They are punctual and considerate? Others are chronically *late*. Some are five or ten minutes late, while others typically can be more than thirty minutes late! What message are the late arrivers sending? Are they showing that they are more important than you? Are they displaying their lack of organization?

Chronemics are cultural. Some cultures, such as Indian cultures, are not bound by the time on the clock. People of these cultures know where they need to be and around what time they should be there.

Applying Concepts
DEVELOPING SKILLS | Understanding the Use of Time

Are there instances when it is acceptable in the United States to be late? When is it okay to be late? What does it mean to be "fashionably late"? Of course, fashionably late is best used for attending parties or gatherings—not for a job interview! Why do we consider lateness at parties to be acceptable, but not at a job interview?

Haptics

Haptics involves the use of touch to communicate. Touch can communicate several messages. Again, it is always important to consider the context in which touch is used to determine which message is being communicated.

Communicating emotion. We use touch *to communicate positive emotions*, such as love, happiness, and caring. We might hold hands or hug to display those emotions.

Communicating demeanor. We use touch *to indicate playfulness*. When you are joking with others, you might lightly tap them on the arm as you say, "I'm just kidding." In what other contexts might you use touch to indicate playfulness?

Communicating control. We often use touch *to control* children. We hold their hands when crossing the street to prevent them from getting hurt. We also put our arms across their chests to communicate "stay here," to prevent them from running in front of a car, for instance. In more negative contexts, you can shove someone whom you want to move out of your way. Or you might push someone from behind if you want that person to move more quickly. These are also instances in which we might use touch to control adults.

There are also more neutral forms of touch.

Cultural rituals. For instance, we use touch in *ritualistic* ways. We shake hands when we meet someone (as a greeting) and when we are leaving. Some people will hug and/or kiss a friend, family member, or romantic partner as a greeting. Some cultures kiss cheeks as a ritual greeting for strangers or close friends.

Performing a task. Another neutral form of touch is *task-related* touch. Doctors use task-related touch all day long. We might help someone into or out of a car. When people fall, we help them up; that touch, too, is task-related. Have you had a friend ask you to feel her forehead because she thinks she has a fever? That touch is task-related, too.

Olfactics

The use of smell to communicate is called **olfactics**. The use of cologne or perfume communicates something about you. You choose a particular scent for a reason. Perhaps you choose the scent that is most popular at the time. When trying to sell your house, it is recommended that you bake a batch of cookies prior to a showing. The smell of the cookies makes people feel more "at home." As you can see, smell can communicate a lot.

TYPES OF NONVERBAL COMMUNICATION

Paralanguage	Tone of voice and utterances, which are vocal but not verbal	• Vocal segregates, or parts of words that communicate meaning, such as "uh-huh" and "shhhh" • Disfluencies, or sounds that fill a pause in speaking, such as "uh," "um," and words such as "like"
Proxemics	The use of space to communicate	• Each person's "personal bubble"
Artifacts	Objects that convey information about us	• The kind of car you drive • How you decorate your living space • Personal items you display
Personal appearance	How you look in terms of physical appearance	• Clothing • Body type • Body adornments
Kinesics	The use of body movements, or gestures, to communicate	• Emblems—nonverbal substitutes for words • Illustrators—body movements that accompany nonverbals • Affect displays—facial expressions used to show emotion • Regulators—gestures to maintain, monitor, and control the speaking of another • Adaptors—gestures that satisfy some need
Eye communication	The use of the eyes to communicate	• To monitor feedback • To signal a conversational turn • To show interest in and attention to a speaker • To signal the nature of a relationship • To compensate for physical distance
Silence	The lack of making a sound	• Allows a person time to think before speaking • Prevents the communication of certain messages • As a way to hurt others • As a response to personal anxiety • Simply having nothing to say

(continued)

5b

Chronemics	The use of time to communicate	• Some people are chronically *early* • Some people are always *on time* • Others are habitually *late*
Haptics	The use of touch to communicate	• Communicating emotion • Communicating demeanor • Communicating control • Cultural rituals • Performing a task
Olfactics	The use of smell to communicate	• The use of cologne or perfume • The smell of the food to make people feel more "at home"

5c

**Applying Concepts
DEVELOPING SKILLS** | Reviewing Your
Nonverbal Cue List

How many of the nonverbals on your list from the *"Identifying the Nonverbal Cues That You Use"* Applying Concepts Developing Skills exercise (p. 93) are identified in the text? Which, if any, of the nonverbals that are mentioned in the chapter did you not have on your list? Did any of the nonverbal cues mentioned in this chapter surprise you? For example, were you surprised to learn that smell is a nonverbal cue?

The nonverbal messages that you witness each day will fall under one of the categories that are mentioned above. But, as you have seen from the explanation of the different types, nonverbals serve many functions.

5c Examining the Functions of Nonverbal Cues

Nonverbal cues serve several functions. As you read about each function, try to think of other examples of each function.

Substitute

Nonverbal cues *substitute* for verbal messages. Instead of saying something, we can often use a gesture to replace the words. What occasions would require a nonverbal substitute? If you are in a crowded place and cannot hear verbal messages, you would use a nonverbal substitute. The same is true for a context in which you are not supposed to talk, such as the library.

Reinforce

Nonverbals can *reinforce* verbal messages. We can use nonverbals to emphasize our verbal message. If you are angry, you might use tone of voice (or even volume) in addition to pounding your fist on a table to reinforce your angry verbal words.

Regulate

As has been noted many times in this chapter, nonverbals *regulate* conversations. You use eye contact to signal turn-taking cues or raise your hand in class to indicate that you would like to speak.

Contradict

Sometimes we use nonverbals to *contradict* our verbals. In this instance, we are trying to tone down our verbal message or to show that we are joking. For example, say you hated the movie *Pearl Harbor*. You might say, "Oh *Pearl Harbor*. That was a *great* movie." Your intonation on the word *great* and your lip curling contradict your words. Thus the listener realizes that your verbal message was not accurate and you really did not like the movie.

Indicate a Relationship

We use nonverbals to signify a *relationship*. You wear a wedding ring to symbolize your marriage. Police officers wear uniforms to indicate their relationship with citizens. Holding hands indicates the nature of your relationship with someone, as does kissing or hugging.

Deceive

Nonverbal cues can be used to *deceive* others. You might mask your sadness so as to not ruin a party, for example. Suppose Sally is trying to deceive her boyfriend, Joe. She might use a smile and a pleasant tone of voice to persuade him that she is telling the truth (when in fact she is trying to convince him of a lie).

Manage Identity

Finally, we use nonverbal cues for identity management, also known as impression management. **Identity management** is the deliberate use of nonverbal cues to help form and manage others' perceptions of you. You might wear a particular brand of clothing, color your hair purple, or speak in a particular tone of voice.

Identity management is based on the concepts of perceived self and presenting self. Your **perceived self** is the person you believe you are. **Presenting self** is your public image, or the perception you want others to have of you. It is possible for your presenting self and your perceived self to differ. Are you self-confident, or do you just want others to believe that you are self-confident? Maybe you are painfully shy (perceived self), but you give others the impression that you are confident and social (presenting self) in order to get a job.

There are several characteristics of identity management.

- **We create multiple identities.** We are not talking multiple personalities, but rather multiple identities. You might behave one way in front of your parents and an entirely different way with your friends. These are two "identities" that you have created and are managing.

- **Identity management is collaborative.** Our identities are shaped and adjusted depending on our interactions with others. Our behavior is often shaped by the behavior and messages of the people with whom we interact.

- **Identity management is sometimes outside of our control.** Have you ever interacted with someone you didn't like but you were unable to mask your dislike? Sometimes we think we can control our nonverbal communication, but some nonverbal communication is subconscious. Through identity management, we might attempt to create the impression that we like someone, but our subconscious brain does not always cooperate.

Why do you engage in identity management? There are social norms that dictate appropriate behavior and appearance in certain environments. For example, in a business setting, it is important to be courteous to a customer. You are also supposed to dress neatly.

We also attempt to attain personal and relational goals. You may put on your best clothing and use your best manners on a first date in order to impress the person. You might look to gain respect from others or to control someone.

How do you manage others' impressions of you? The use of cell phones has provided additional behavior to use when interpreting the behavior of others. If you are eating lunch with a friend, and your friend leaves the table to use the restroom, what do you do? Most people grab their cell phone and either call someone, text someone, or start playing a game. We want the people around us to get the impression that we are important—so important that the second we have a moment alone, we have important calls to make or messages to send.

In face-to-face communication, we usually manage impressions through mannerisms, appearance, and setting. Mannerisms can include proper etiquette. We can clean ourselves up and use our appearance to create impressions. And, as we mentioned earlier in this chapter, we can manipulate our surroundings, such as our office, to communicate a particular identity.

5c

5d Putting Nonverbal Communication into Action

One of the more well-known theories of nonverbal communication is expectancy violations theory. Having read this chapter, you are able to identify the different types of nonverbal cues. **Expectancy violations theory** explains why you react to people in different ways based on their nonverbal communication. At the core of expectancy violations theory (EVT) is proxemics, or personal space. Remember that earlier in this chapter we discussed personal space using protection theory, which states that your personal space is defined by you and how safe you feel having people of varying relationship levels close to your body. Your definition of personal space is shaped by your cultural norms and personal experiences.

Expectancy

An **expectancy** is what you predict or expect to occur. EVT explains how you react when someone enters your personal space, or violates your expectations—in this case, your expected personal space. According to Judee Burgoon who, along with colleagues, formulated EVT, there are three conditions of expectancy: context, relational factors, and communication characteristics (Burgoon & Hale, 1988). Context is the setting, nature, and norms of the interaction. Relational factors include similarity, status, and familiarity. Finally, communication characteristics include physical appearance, competency, and personality. These three factors influence what you expect to occur. For example, if you are at your home and your friend comes to visit you, receiving a hug from the friend would not be unexpected (unless you or your friend do not hug and/or you do not have a close friendship).

Valence

Another factor of EVT is the **valence** of the violation, or the positive or negative value assigned to the unexpected behavior regardless of who engages in the behavior. When someone acts in an unexpected manner, you are prone to interpreting the behavior. You will ultimately change your perception of the person based on the valence of the violation and your attitude toward the person before the violation.

Suppose that your boss comes to your desk to talk to you. In the process of discussing a client, she stands only about 2 inches away from you—a clear violation of personal space as it was defined earlier in this chapter. Therefore, you perceive this behavior as a violation of your expectation of personal distance in the workplace. Once you have interpreted the violation, you will determine how you feel about the violation.

EVT states that if you view the person positively, then the violation will be viewed positively, and you may even like the person more. If you view the person negatively, then the violation will be viewed negatively, and you will likely increase your negativity toward the other person as a result.

Prior to the violation in the example above, if you liked your boss and felt as though she were looking out for your best interests, you might interpret the close proximity as a reassurance of her commitment to helping you succeed in your job. However, if you and your boss have communicatively sparred on occasion and there is open animosity between you, then you will likely view the close proximity as condescending, and thus dislike her more than you did before.

Ambiguous Behaviors

But what if the meaning of the behavior is unclear? What if you do not know how to interpret her unexpectedly close proximity? According to Burgoon and EVT, you will interpret the behavior based on the social consequences of the behavior. Burgoon calls this *communicator reward valence*, or the outcome of your mental list of potential gains and losses from the relationship. It is the sum of the positive and negative attributes of the person and his or her ability or potential to reward or punish you in future situations.

When assessing *reward potential*, you are influenced by the person's personal appearance, abilities, and status. Assessment of *punishment potential* includes the overall perception of the person's nonverbal messages that indicate disapproval and disconfirmation, for instance.

In situations of ambiguous violations (violations in which you are unsure of their valence), you look at the social context for clues to the meaning of the violation. For example, when assessing your boss's proximity violation, you would look at the social context for clues. If your boss violates your personal space while smiling and giving you encouragement on your current project, then you will likely view the violation positively. But if your boss violates your personal space while sternly reminding you of your mistakes on previous projects, you will likely view the violation negatively. The reward potential of the first example is encouragement from your boss. The punishment potential of the second example is being fired for continued mistakes. Your judgment of the ambiguous behavior is based then on reward and punishment potential.

There are advantages and disadvantages of EVT. EVT is a widely cited theory of nonverbal communication, and it provides us with some understanding of the interpretation of nonverbal violations. However, it is not yet fully developed. For instance, EVT does not account for touch violations. Burgoon has found that touch violations are ambiguous, and EVT does not provide a reliable prediction for the outcome of touch violations.

Applying Concepts
DEVELOPING SKILLS | Violating Expectancies

How do the various types of nonverbal communication provide clues to the meaning of an expectancy violation?

Competence SUMMARY

In this chapter, you have learned the following concepts. Check to be sure you have achieved each of these communication competencies.

5a Understanding the Principles of Nonverbal Communication

- Nonverbal communication can be deliberate or unintentional, but few nonverbal signals have universal meaning.
- When a person's verbal and nonverbal messages conflict, you tend to trust the nonverbal message. It is also difficult to avoid your message being misunderstood if people pay more attention to your nonverbal message.

Competence. Do I know how my nonverbal cues may be misinterpreted based on the cultural experiences of the other person?

5b Identifying Types of Nonverbal Communication

- There are many types of nonverbal communication: paralanguage, proxemics, artifacts, personal appearance, kinesics, eye communication, silence, chronemics, haptics, and olfactics.

- Proxemics, or the use of space to communicate, is defined by the amount of space that exists between you and another communicator. The four levels of proxemics are intimate, personal, social, and public. The less distance between the two people, the more intimate (or close) the relationship.

- Kinesics are body movements or gestures. They are categorized as emblems, illustrators, affect displays, regulators, and adaptors.

- Silence has many meanings. You can use silence to indicate that you need time to think about your response, to hurt others, to prevent the communication of certain messages, to communicate emotional responses, to indicate personal anxiety, or because you simply do not have anything to say.

- Haptics, or the use of touch to communicate, can have many positive connotations. Touch can indicate positive emotions, playfulness, and control. Touch can also be ritualistic and task-related.

Competence. Can I distinguish among the different types of nonverbal cues that I use? Am I considering the context of the nonverbal message when interpreting the message?

5c Examining the Functions of Nonverbal Cues

- There are several functions of nonverbal cues. A nonverbal cue can be a substitute for a word, reinforce a verbal message, contradict a verbal message, regulate communication, and manage identity.

- Nonverbal cues can indicate a relationship, deceive others, and help to manage how others perceive you.

Competence. Do I know the functions of nonverbal cues? How will I use that knowledge to aid me in being a more competent communicator?

5d Putting Nonverbal Communication into Action

- Expectancy violations theory provides an explanation for why we react positively or negatively when someone violates our personal space. An expectancy is what you expect to happen or how you expect someone to behave.

- If you have positive impressions of people prior to their violating your personal space, your impressions of them will become more positive after the violation. If you have negative impressions of people prior to their violating your personal space, your impressions will become more negative after the violation.

- If you have no prior impression of the person, you will consider social consequences of the violation by accumulating a mental tally of gains and losses from the potential relationship with that person.

Competence. Why should I refrain from passing judgment until I've gained necessary information? What is the importance of nonverbal cues in assessing expectancy violations?

Review Questions

1. What are the principles of nonverbal communication?
2. Explain paralanguage.
3. How does equilibrium theory explain proxemics?
4. Explain how haptics, artifacts, and proxemics serve to signify a relationship.
5. Distinguish between the perceived self and the presenting self.
6. For what reasons do we engage in impression management?

Discussion Questions

1. Proxemics is the use of space to communicate. Why is this important to communication?
2. Impression management is the deliberate use of nonverbal cues to help form and manage others' perceptions of you. Based on the concepts of perceived self and presenting self, what are some ways you use impression management to influence perceptions of yourself by others? For what purposes do you use impression management? How does impression management relate to self-esteem and self-concept?

Key Terms

artifacts *p. 96*

chronemics *p. 101*

equilibrium theory *p. 95*

expectancy *p. 107*

expectancy violations theory *p. 107*

haptics *p. 102*

identity management *p. 105*

kinesics *p. 98*

nonverbal messages *p. 91*

olfactics *p. 102*

paralanguage *p. 94*

perceived self *p. 106*

personal appearance *p. 97*

presenting self *p. 106*

protection theory *p. 94*

proxemics *p. 94*

territorial *p. 95*

valence *p. 108*

The Art of Small Talk

THE IMPORTANCE OF SMALL TALK

Think back to the first time you met each of your friends. Did you just immediately start self-disclosing important, personal details of your life? How did you know that you wanted to be his or her friend? At some point, you and your friend engaged in small talk. **Small talk** is a conversational tactic whose purpose is to gain basic information that will help you to make a connection with someone.

Mastering the art of small talk can open many doors to your future. Small talk is a powerful instrument for beginning a relationship for two reasons (Gabor, 2001).

1. Engaging in small talk with someone indicates a willingness on your part to talk to the person.
2. Small talk allows people to exchange information in order to discover common interests.

Small talk requires competency in many of the concepts covered in Part One of this handbook: perception, listening, language rules, and nonverbal cues. Therefore, small talk interactions can help you to practice your skills and become a more competent communicator. You will need good conversational skills in every aspect of your life: business, social, and personal.

INTRODUCTIONS

Remembering someone's name when you first meet is an important skill that very few individuals have mastered.

Why is it so important to remember someone's name?

People feel flattered when you remember their name. Remembering names also shows that you were listening when they are introduced and it builds rapport between you and the other person. When you know someone's name, he or she is no longer a "stranger."

Why do we so often forget a person's name?

The most common reason is failing to focus on the moment of introduction (Gabor, 2001). Meeting someone new can make us so anxious that we are thinking more about what we are going to say to the person than focusing on the introduction.

Focus on the moment of introduction.

Give your full attention to the introduction. Don't think about what you are going to say next—*just listen.* When you hear the name, repeat it aloud. If they say their name and it is an unusual name, ask them to spell it and explain that you want to be sure to remember it. Be sure to use the person's name throughout the conversation and at the conclusion of the conversation. Not only does it personalize your conversation, but also it reinforces your memory.

BEGINNING THE CONVERSATION

You want your conversation partners' first impression of you to be positive. Before you utter a single word, potential partners will interpret your nonverbal cues.

After you have been introduced to someone, you may want to begin a conversation him or her. You should pay attention to your nonverbal cues and construct ritual questions to start the conversation.

Nonverbal Cues

Boothman (2000) asserts that you need less than 90 seconds to make someone feel comfortable and willing to engage in conversation with you. In order to capture someone's attention, you have to appear likable, sincere, and trustworthy. These qualities can be evoked through: your presence (your appearance and body language), your attitude (what you say and how you say it), and how you make people feel.

Before you utter a single word, potential conversational partners will interpret your nonverbal cues. Each of the following nonverbal cues can help you to project a friendly, approachable image that will encourage people to begin and sustain a conversation with you.

- **Facial expressions.** Focus on making sure that you are not frowning or sulking. When you smile, you are demonstrating an open attitude

to conversation because a smile is equated to friendliness (Gabor, 2001).

- **Eye contact.** Direct eye contact with others indicates that you are listening (but this does not mean staring). Eye contact also serves as a turn-taking cue in conversations. When finished speaking, you typically look at your conversational partner so that they know it is their turn to speak.

- **Open body posture.** You should avoid crossing your arms in front of your body. Keep your arms at your sides. Remember that as you make your way around a room full of new people, you want your hands to be ready for handshakes at all times.

- **Handshakes.** To make a good first impression, be the first to extend your hand in greeting a new person. When you finish your conversation, you should also offer a handshake (and a smile). This leaves both of you feeling good about your interaction. Remember that not all cultures treat handshakes as we do in the United States.

Ritual Questions

Someone has approached you to meet you. You extend your hand and introduce yourself. Now what? You need an icebreaker.

Ritual questions are a series of easy-to-answer questions that allow you to gather basic information about the other person. It is best to create a "stockpile" of ritual questions that you commit to memory so that small talk is less intimidating. If you have a series of questions that you ask people in order to get to know them, then you are never left thinking, "What do I have to say to this person?"

You can also create your ritual questions on the spot if you have a list of possible topic ideas.

- **Comment on something interesting about the person.** What is she wearing, doing, or carrying? Perhaps she is wearing a T-shirt or sweatshirt with your alma mater's name across it. What a great way to start a conversation with her!

- **Be sure to listen to "free information," the information that the other person provides in answers to your questions.** Instead of worrying about what to ask next, *listen* to the free information you are receiving and let that guide your conversation. Learning to do this will greatly alleviate the anxiety of talking with someone you have never met.

- **Remember that the other person is also looking for free information.** So don't make the conversation sound like an inquisition. Be sure that you are also self-disclosing basic information about yourself.

Sample Ritual Questions

1. That is a great sweater. Did you make it?
2. I see that you are using a PowerBook. Are you a veteran Mac computer user?
3. How do you know the host/hostess?

SUSTAINING THE CONVERSATION

Hot button issues are areas of interest that create enthusiasm in the person with whom you are talking. Gabor (2001) suggests that you find out the other person's hot button issues including work, hobbies, a new job, upcoming trips, or career goals. As with free information, you should share your hot button issues as well. Be sure to include facts, examples, and locations so that your conversational partner has a lot of free information to question you about.

Sample Hot Button Topics

Travel	School	Sports	Television
Hobbies	Interest	Movies	Technology
	Science	Cooking	

Changing Topics

Changing topics of conversation is easier than you think. Because you have gathered a lot of free information from the other person, you can refer to previously revealed free information by commenting on it or asking a closed ritual question.

One fruitful area for conversation topics is current events. Current events provide you with a new pool of topic ideas by allowing you to ask the other person what he or she thinks about a particular event or relating what the other person is saying to something you read recently. As always, be sure that you are staying away from controversial or taboo topics. Stick to something less controversial, like reality television, as opposed to launching into an argument over politics. Current events do not always have to be about politics.

RoAne (1997) says that if we are "well-read," then we are more likely to recognize names of important people, companies, products, and so forth. It is not so important that you remember where or why you heard those names, but rather that you just know that you have heard them. Just the recognition provides the opportunity to ask a question about it.

Conversation Killers

RoAne (1997) discusses several topics and behaviors that can bring the conversation to an abrupt end. Avoid the following:

- **One-upmanship.** Trying to appear better than the other person is not going to help you to cultivate a positive environment.

- **Stretching the truth.** Give accurate information about yourself. Lying or exaggerating about your abilities or experiences will come back to haunt you if you should want to have an honest relationship with the person in the future.

- **Complaining.** No one wants to hear you whine.

Tried Everything?

What if you are trying to have a conversation and the other person is just not cooperating? Boothman (2000) suggests that after about three questions, if the other person is just not responding positively, then move along. Be cordial, wish the person a good evening, and find someone more willing to engage in small talk. Not everyone that you meet and greet will be open to conversation.

CONCLUDING THE CONVERSATION

Concluding the conversation can be difficult, especially if you are enjoying the conversation, or worse, if some of your conversational partners talk incessantly. Here are a few pointers for ending the interaction on a positive note.

- **When the time is right to end the conversation, begin to send signals that you are ready to leave.** You could stand up if you are sitting down, or begin to indicate verbally that you are moving along. Just be sure to be somewhat subtle and avoid being rude.

- **If you want to see them again, be specific about seeing them again.** For instance, "How about lunch next week?"

- **Remember to use people's names when you say goodbye.** Not only will they be flattered that you cared enough to remember, it will help you to remember their name in the future.

- **Don't forget your positive body language.** Incorporate eye contact, a smile, and a handshake in your departure.

Interpersonal Communication

There are several reasons we form interpersonal relationships. Relationships fulfill our personal needs (Schutz, 1958).

- **Need for inclusion. We want to feel a sense of belonging.**

- **Need for control. We need to possess some degree of influence in our environment.**

- **Need for affection. We want others to like us.**

Through interpersonal relationships, we can simultaneously satisfy our own needs and those of someone else.

Frequently asked questions

Why do I form relationships with some people I meet and not others? (See Chapter 6, page 117.)

Am I the only person who gets nervous talking to another person I do not know well? (See Module C, page 142.)

Can conflict ever be positive in a relationship? (See Chapter 7, page 146.)

Does communication in online relationships differ from communication in face-to-face relationships? (See Module D, page 171.)

Do men and women really communicate differently? (See Module E, page 175.)

CONTENTS

PART **TWO** Interpersonal Communication

Introduction to Interpersonal Communication

OBJECTIVES

In this chapter, we will explore interpersonal communication by examining the dynamics of interpersonal relationships. Your communication competence will be enhanced by understanding:

- with whom and why you form interpersonal relationships, which will help you to understand better how your communication influences the development of a relationship;
- how relationships develop and dissolve to help you to determine communication behaviors that are appropriate to particular stages or phases in your relationship;
- the influence of dialectics on relationships so you can better communicate with your relational partner in order to successfully negotiate the tension;
- why you disclose and when you disclose, in order to know when it is appropriate to make self-disclosures in your relationships.

6a

6a Defining Interpersonal Communication

In Chapter 1, we defined *communication* as a process of sharing meaning by sending and receiving symbolic messages. While this definition is broad enough to encompass all types of communication, from interpersonal to group to public speaking to mass communication, in this chapter we examine interpersonal communication in particular. Therefore we need a more specific definition.

Interpersonal communication is a process by which two people exchange meaning by simultaneously sending and receiving symbolic messages. The elements of interpersonal communication are similar to all types of communication—people exchange meaning by sending and receiving verbal and nonverbal messages. What makes interpersonal communication different is that it involves just two people.

- **Impersonal communication.** Some researchers (e.g., Stewart, 2006) distinguish between impersonal communication (communication between strangers such as customers and grocery store clerks) and interpersonal communication because the number of prior interactions with the other person shapes the current interaction and the level of intimacy.
- **Interpersonal communication.** Other researchers believe that your communication with a grocery store clerk is not fundamentally different from the communication between you and a friend, family member, or romantic partner.

- **Communication with strangers—impersonal vs. interpersonal.** In this text, we'll assume that these differences do not diminish the fact that when you are talking to a stranger, you are still exchanging meaning with one other person by sending and receiving symbolic messages. Therefore, while this section on interpersonal communication will focus primarily on family members, friends, romantic partners, and colleagues, the same principles also apply to communication with a stranger. Let's face it, your friends, romantic partners, and colleagues were once strangers to you, right?

Applying Concepts
DEVELOPING SKILLS

Identifying Interpersonal Communication

Create a fictional dialogue between two people or recreate an actual dialogue you recall. Now rewrite the dialogue to include a third person. How does the conversation change when the third person is included?

6b Forming Interpersonal Relationships

Humans have an innate need for companionship. If we did not have this need, we would not experience loneliness. It is natural for people to form "pair bonds," which is an anthropological way to say "romantic couples." The need to procreate and care for children fuels the need for companionship. This is not to suggest that people are unable to be independent or that everyone will feel the need to have children. We are merely stating that people are unable to be alone all of the time forever.

Why Do We Need Relationships?

William Schutz (1958) identified reasons why we form interpersonal relationships; these relationships help us fulfill our personal needs. A **need** is a strong desire that must be met for a person to feel a sense of satisfaction. Schutz defines three needs that we fulfill through relationships.

Need for inclusion. The need for **inclusion** is the desire to be wanted. When we form and maintain a relationship with someone, we experience an implied connection between us and the other person. In other words, the person *wants* to be with us. Thus, inclusion also refers to feeling like a valuable person.

RELATIONSHIP FORMATION

Why Do We Need Relationships?

We all have a need for

- inclusion by others.
- control in our environment.
- affection from others.

With Whom Do We Form Relationships?

We form relationships with people

- who are in close proximity to us.
- who are similar—they share our interests, beliefs, and values.
- whom we find attractive.
- whose appearance attracts us.
- who have opposite or complementary features to our own.
- whom we think will give us relational rewards.
- who are somewhat flawed—without perfect competency.
- with whom we can self-disclose—share information about ourselves.

6b

People with whom you are in a relationship will ask your opinion and keep you informed about what is going on around you. Therefore, you meet your need for inclusion from this person.

Need for control. The need for **control** is the need to have some influence in what occurs in your environment. When relational partners ask for your opinion or seek your guidance, you have a sense of empowerment that is manifested in the need for control.

Need for affection. **Affection** is a basic human need to be liked and esteemed. When others want to spend time and to maintain a relationship with us, we feel liked by them. Thus, interpersonal relationships satisfy our need to be liked, but they also satisfy your relational partner's need to be close to someone.

Applying Concepts
DEVELOPING SKILLS | Relationships and Needs

Identify the needs that one of your close friendships fills for you. Does your list match up with Schutz's list?

With Whom Do We Form Relationships?

Of all of the people you meet, how do you determine with whom you will form friendships? Romantic relationships? Co-worker relationships? Let's look at six factors that influence with whom we form relationships.

Proximity. Proximity refers to the geographic distance between us and another person. We form relationships with people who live near us, enroll in the same classes, or work for the same organizations. While we might be separated by geographic distance, the Internet puts us in virtual proximity to each other. We might subscribe to the same dating site (such as match.com or true.com), blog, or chat room. Our interests, or our similarities, have put us into contact despite the geographic distance.

Similarity. Similarity is the degree to which we and our dyadic (or interpersonal) partner share interests, beliefs, and values. When we know that someone is similar to us, we can more confidently infer that he or she might like us because of the similarity factor. If you meet someone at a Star Trek convention, then you can more confidently infer that he or she will like you, too, because you have similar interests. We like those who like us. Thus we are attracted to people who are like us.

Attractiveness. Upon first meeting someone, our initial impression is often based on physical attractiveness. Therefore, it would stand to reason that physical attractiveness would play a part in relational development. Interestingly, Bosson and Swann (2001) discovered that physical attractiveness is important only in potential dating relationships and not important in the initiation of friendships. They found that "people who had rated themselves at average levels of physical attractiveness . . . wanted their dating partners to rate them as more attractive" (p. 73). However, people wanted their platonic friends to view them as they saw themselves.

Complementarity. So what about the idea that opposites attract? Another factor of relational attraction is complementarity, or the attraction between two people who have opposite features. The complements could be in beliefs and values (e.g., opposing political beliefs) or they could be behavioral (e.g., one person is punctual and the other person is perpetually late).

However, the complements can lead ultimately to the end of the relationship. While it is possible to be attracted to someone who is not like us, the likelihood that it will last is small. Felmlee (1998) researched "fatal attraction" in romantic relationships. She discovered that many people break off relationships because a trait that initially attracted them to the person is a trait that ultimately repulsed them. For example, if you are attracted to a person's spontaneity, you might ultimately be irritated by his or her inability to plan.

Rewards. Relational attraction is also determined by the number of rewards you gain from the relationship. You are more likely to form and maintain relationships in which you receive more rewards than you incur costs.

Rewards include both tangible benefits and intangible benefits. A tangible benefit would be sharing rent with someone and an intangible benefit is companionship, for instance.

Costs are anything that you sacrifice for the relationship. If you are not a sports fan, but your friend loves sports, you will sacrifice your time to watch the sports games in exchange for your friend's companionship.

Self-disclosure. **Self-disclosure** occurs when we tell someone something about ourselves. The information we disclose can be unimportant tidbits that we reveal to someone else during small talk (such as television shows and music that we like) or deeply private information (such as our beliefs and values).

We use the amount and type of self-disclosure to measure another person's interest in developing and maintaining a relationship. We will elaborate on the ways self-disclosure affects our relationships in the next chapter.

Applying Concepts DEVELOPING SKILLS | Analyzing Your Close Relationships

Consider your closest friend. Which of the six factors listed above attracted you to that friend? What factors can you attribute to the longevity of your friendship? Next, consider your most recent romantic partner. Which factors attracted you to him or her? Now compare the two lists. Are the factors similar or different? Why?

6c Examining Relationship Development and Dissolution

While all relationships have a beginning, they vary with regard to the level of intimacy that is ultimately reached and whether they are maintained. Therefore, this section will discuss methods for examining relationship development and relationship dissolution. These models apply not only to romantic relationships, but also to friendships and workplace relationships.

Knapp's Model of Relationship Development

In their study of relationships, various communication researchers have formulated models to describe the stages or phases that the relationships go through as they evolve. Relationship development involves the initiation of a relationship between two people, and it continues, developing into a closer, more intimate relationship as the dyad shares personal information and their social networks acknowledge their relationship (whether it is a friendship or a romance).

Mark Knapp (1978) created a relational development model that looks at five stages of relationship development. (See Figure 6.1.)

Stage One: Initiating. In the *initiating* stage, you meet someone who interests you. Perception becomes key as you receive stimuli that catch your attention. The person might be carrying or wearing an object that is similar to yours, or wearing a perfume/cologne that you like. Whatever it is that draws you to that person marks the beginning of the relational development process.

Stage Two: Experimenting. Not all first encounters will lead to experimenting. If you and the other person do not pursue the friendship or romance after that first encounter, then this model no longer applies. If you do hit it off, the *experimenting* stage encompasses getting to know each other. Small talk is a good way to get to know someone. By engaging in small talk (which you read about in Module B), you learn more

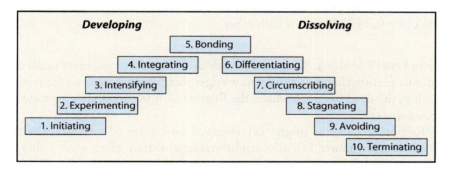

Figure 6.1 Knapp's Relational Development Model

Table 2.1 "A Model of Interaction Stages," p. 34, from *Interpersonal Communication and Human Relationships* by Mark L. Knapp & Anita Vangelisti. © 2009. Reproduced by permission of Pearson Education, Inc.

about your similarities and differences and whether or not you want to pursue a relationship.

Stage Three: Intensifying. Having determined that you and your new acquaintance have a lot in common or have a number of reasons to continue the relationship, you enter the *intensifying* stage. During this stage you are beginning to express your desire to continue the friendship or build a deeper romantic relationship.

You might engage in **secret tests**, presenting the other with inconspicuous challenges that will provide proof of commitment to your friendship or romance (Baxter & Wilmot, 1985). For example, you could ask a third party whether the partner says positive things about your relationship. You could do something to make the partner jealous to gauge his or her reaction. Or you could joke with the other person about progressing to a more serious relationship.

The intensifying stage is about telling someone how you feel, whether overtly or covertly, and finding out how he or she feels about you.

Stage Four: Integrating. If the person indicates a desire to continue to spend time together (thus intensifying the friendship) or wants to become monogamous romantic partners (perhaps moving from a friend to a romantic partner), the dyad then moves to the *integrating* stage.

During this stage, others view the two people as a dyad or a couple. If one appears at a social function without the partner, people ask the whereabouts of the partner. Perhaps you and a co-worker who have become friends start to go to non-work-related functions together.

The social circles of each partner begin to merge. Routines and rituals of the friendship or romance develop. The dyad or couple might create nicknames or personal idioms for each other.

Stage Five: Bonding. When the friends or the romantic partners make a symbolic gesture that publicly acknowledges their commitment to the relationship, the dyad or couple enters the final stage of relational development, the *bonding* stage.

Romantic couples might get engaged and married to show their public commitment. Friends might name children after each other. Colleagues might sign a contract to start a new business together. Each of these is a public acknowledgment of the commitment to the other person.

Applying Concepts
DEVELOPING SKILLS

Identifying Development Stages in Relationships

Choose one of your closest friends. Can you identify the stages of relational development in your friendship? Did you skip any stages? Why or why not?

Now examine a previous or current romantic relationship. Identify the stages of your relational development. Did you skip any stages that you may not have skipped in your friendship formation?

What are some factors that contribute to the skipping of stages by relational partners (friends, romantic partners, co-workers, etc.)?

Knapp also outlined the five stages of relationship dissolution. All relationships do not experience dissolution, and not all relationships that engage in the beginning stages of dissolution will dissolve. However, as you may have experienced previously, some relationships do not last a lifetime.

Stage Six: Differentiating. At some point in a relationship, the individuals in the dyad may feel the need to distinguish themselves from their relationship, and *differentiating* occurs. In other words, one person may want to have his own identity outside of the relationship. Spending all your time with a relational partner can create boredom because neither of the individuals brings any new or unique experiences to the dyad. Therefore, one person may decide to join a bowling league without the partner. In this example, the person is attempting to do something to maintain his or her own identity, and not always be identified as part of the dyad. However, such an action does not signify the end of the relationship. Instead, the desire to do something different without the partner could actually strengthen the relationship.

Stage Seven: Circumscribing. If the dyad experiences a decrease in the quantity and quality of communication, they move into the *circumscribing* stage. Dissatisfaction with the relationship becomes more evident to the relational partners. The partners do not yet openly express their dissatisfaction, nor do they engage in complete avoidance.

Stage Eight: Stagnating. When communication between partners subsides, very little growth can occur in the relationship and we say that the relationship is *stagnating*. With stagnation the relationship exists merely in name only.

Stage Nine: Avoiding. When the partners discover that the stagnation is too painful to continue to experience, they may begin *avoiding* communication with each other. With less communication and less contact, the relationship will be hard to resurrect at this point.

Stage Ten: Terminating. Ending, or *terminating*, a relationship can be quick or it can be a long process, depending on the closeness and length of the relationship. Cody (1982) reported that the longer the partners were in a relationship, the more likely one person is to justify the end of the relationship. Thus if the relationship did not last for long, the partners may not feel the need to justify its end.

Stage models assume that most relationships are linear and therefore progress through a series of similar stages or phases. The dyads can skip over stages or go back and forth between stages, returning to a previous situation. For example, if a romantic couple decides to "cool things off," the stage model would exemplify this as a movement from the integrating stage back to the experimenting or intensifying stages.

A flaw of the stage models is that, although the couple is no longer trying to get to know each other, the model asserts that both partners again experience the same patterns of communication that are typical of that stage. We will contrast Knapp's stage model with the structural-helical model in the next section.

Applying Concepts
DEVELOPING SKILLS | **Identifying Stages of Relational Dissolution**

Think of friendships that you have had over the years that have ended. Can you identify Knapp's stages of relational dissolution? Were there stages that did not occur?

Now consider previous romantic relationships (if applicable). Are romantic relationships more likely to go through all of the stages of relational dissolution? Or are friendships more likely to go through all of the stages? Or are they equal in the number of stages? Explain your response.

Structural-Helical Model: Conville's Model of Relational Development and Dissolution

An alternative approach to examining relational development and dissolution is through the structural-helical model (Conville, 1991), which addresses the weaknesses of stage models. The *structural-helical model* suggests that relationship development is irreversible—a dyad can never return to the same point (that is, stage) because the context will be different (a different point in the relationship and a different point in history).

Think of the helix as a metal spring, as illustrated in Figure 6.2. The dyad might experience similar recurring situations, such as anniversaries, but the situations will never be exactly the same. Time has progressed, which corresponds to following the spiral path of a spring, and during that time the dyad has had additional experiences that influence the communication in their relationship.

The structural-helical model incorporates the dynamic nature of communication and the influence of time and communicative experiences within the dyad. In contrast, stage and phase models focus more on events that mark the progression through developmental or dissolution stages.

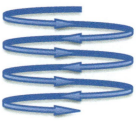

Figure 6.2
Structural-Helical Model

The continuation of time in a relationship is represented by the spiral path of the spring. Instead of progressing through linear stages or phases think of the progression as a continuous flow.

6c

Applying Concepts
DEVELOPING SKILLS

Examining a Friendship

Use the structural-helical model to explain a relationship with one of your friends. Are there issues, events, etc., that recur in your relationship? Does the structural-helical model help you to explain your friendship better than the stage models would? Why or why not?

EYEONETHICS | The Disappearing Act

Pop singer Britney Spears sent K-Fed a text message to tell him that she had filed for divorce. Another musician, Phil Collins, sent his wife a fax to tell her that he had filed for divorce. What about relationships in which a partner just disappears without even a phone call, email, or letter to indicate that the relationship is over?

Most relationships end with a pronouncement by one partner to the other that the relationship is over. Some relationships end with both partners having some idea of the problems that led to the dissolution, but recently another breakup strategy has emerged—the disappearing act. While it could likely be what Cody (1982) calls "behavioral de-escalation," the disappearing act has such important implications for the person who is left behind that it warrants its own category. For those people whose partner "disappears," there is no resolution or understanding.

Application

What are the ethical implications of the disappearing act? Is there a certain amount of time that the couple has been together after which it becomes unethical just to disappear? Are there some situations in which the use of the disappearing act would be ethical? What are those situations?

6d Relational Dialectics

Are there recurring issues in your friendships, romantic relationships, and family relationships that you can identify? Perhaps you and your friend have to negotiate time that you spend together versus time that you spend with other friends or a romantic partner. Do you struggle with deciding what information about your life you should keep private or share with a parent? These "issues" are at the heart of relational dialectics (Baxter, 1993).

Relational dialectics suggest that relationships are influenced by opposing forces (or tensions) that change throughout the lifespan of the relationship and are managed through communication between relational partners. According to relational dialectics, many tensions exert influence on the communicative nature of these relationships. Relational partners need to manage these tensions and negotiate and renegotiate them over time. Let's look at three dialectical tensions.

Autonomy–Connectedness

The **autonomy-connection dialectic** looks at the amount of time the dyad spends together or apart.

For example, at the beginning of their romantic relationship, Sally and Juan liked to spend a lot of time together. In fact, they often did so to the exclusion of their other friends. But, this is normal. As they got to know each other, Sally's friends were concerned about her lack of interest in them. Juan felt the same way. So Sally and Juan decided that they would not spend all of their time together, but that they would have certain days/times designated for their friends. Of course, this dialectic will need to be renegotiated from time to time as other situations arise.

Predictability–Change

The **predictability-novelty dialectic** reflects the amount of change versus routine in the dyad's relationship.

Using the same dyad as above, do Sally and Juan go to dinner with friends every Friday night and stay in on Saturday night? If so, they are rather predictable. If you were looking for either Sally or Juan, you would know that they would not be home on Friday night.

Some couples like more novelty, or uniqueness, in their relationship. They don't have scheduled, routine outings. They might take a road trip one weekend and stay home the next weekend.

Neither predictability nor novelty is better than the other; each dyad determines how they handle change in their relationship.

Openness–Closedness

The **openness-closedness dialectic** involves the amount of self-disclosure expressed between the two people in the relationship. Openness implies full disclosure of everything to your relational partner. Closedness implies the opposite—not disclosing anything to your relational partner.

In a relationship, do you avoid "taboo topics" (Baxter & Wilmot, 1985) or do you maintain complete openness? **Taboo topics** are those that you and your relational partner avoid because of the negativity that they create. Identifying them is a way of managing the tension of openness-closedness.

TYPES OF DIALECTICAL TENSIONS

Autonomy—Connectedness: Tensions between time spent together and time spent apart
Predictability—Novelty: Tensions between stability or change in the relationship
Openness—Closedness: Tensions between self-disclosing or not

Applying Concepts
DEVELOPING SKILLS | Analyzing a Dialectical Tension

The autonomy-connection dialectic can be problematic for romantic long-distance relationships. Given the hyper-conscious attention given to long-distance relationships by romantic partners, negotiating this dialectic could be problematic. What if one partner likes to go out and be social—even when his partner is in town visiting? What if his partner prefers to spend time together alone? Perhaps she thinks he can spend time with his friends when she is not around. How would you manage this dialectical tension?

6e   Understanding the Dynamics of Self-Disclosure

Self-disclosure, voluntarily revealing information about ourselves to another, aids in the development and management of interpersonal relationships.

Self-Disclosure in Interpersonal Relationships

Many communication scholars consider willingness to self-disclose a sign of attraction. As a person increases the personal nature of self-disclosures, he or she is indicating trust in you and an interest in continuing the relationship.

Factors that influence self-disclosure. Several factors may influence a decision about whether or not to self-disclose information to another person.

- **Dyadic effect.** Typically, if one person in the dyad self-discloses, the other person is socially persuaded to reciprocate. This is called the *dyadic effect*. People are often motivated to reciprocate the self-disclosure to "level the playing field" so to speak.

  If an acquaintance tells you something personal about herself, that puts you in a one-up position; you have control of the relationship because you know more about her than she knows about you. However, if you reciprocate the self-disclosure, then you bring equality to the relationship by balancing the self-disclosures. Subsequently, neither party knows more about the other.

- **Topic.** The *topic* of the self-disclosure also influences the likelihood of disclosure. Something that is extremely personal—that few people, if any, know about—might be omitted from your everyday conversation.

  As your relationship develops, you and your dyadic partner will disclose more personal information. One reason is that you are developing trust as your relationship grows; thus you may feel as though you can trust the person with more private information.

- **Valence.** Closely related to the topic of your self-disclosure is *valence*, or the positive or negative quality of the self-disclosure. Positive disclosures, which make us look good or favorable, are more common than negative disclosures, which make us look unfavorable.

  If you made a good grade on an exam, you are likely to disclose your grade to others. If you did not make a good grade, you are not as likely to disclose your grade. Of course, there are people who consider bad grades to be "cool," and in that sense, they think that they are making "positive" self-disclosures.

- **Receiver relationship.** Our *relationship* to the receiver may determine the topic and valence of the disclosure. We are more likely to make disclosures about our most basic likes and dislikes (all positive, of course) to acquaintances than we are with close relational partners (to whom we would disclose more personal information). You are more likely to reveal your views about a controversial topic like abortion to people you know well rather than to complete strangers.

- **Communicator's sex.** A person's *sex* can influence the type and amount of self-disclosure. According to Reis (1998), women are more likely to self-disclose than men, and men are more likely to self-disclose to female friends than to male friends. However, men and women make negative self-disclosures almost equally—and those negative disclosures are few.

6e

Reasons for self-disclosure. Why do we choose to self-disclose to some people and not to others? There are several reasons we disclose information.

- **Catharsis.** We might disclose for catharsis, or getting something off our chest. If we have done something that a friend, romantic partner, or colleague would not like, we could begin to feel guilty about it. Therefore, to relieve the guilt and subsequent stress, we tell the other person what happened.

- **Self-clarification.** Self-clarification is talking to another person to clarify your feelings or thoughts about an issue. Have you ever wanted to talk something out with another person? Perhaps you know of someone in your workplace who is stealing office supplies. You disclose this to your friend (who does not work with you) and ask about whether or not to notify a supervisor.

- **Self-validation.** There may come a time when you have done something wrong and you want some verification that what you did was not abnormal or strange. Self-validation is seeing whether you have done the right thing. You could turn to your closest friend to seek self-validation, or seeing if you had done the right thing. Your friend could tell you if he or she would have done the same thing in the same situation.

- **Reciprocity.** One of the factors that determines self-disclosure is also a reason for self-disclosure—reciprocity. Reciprocity is the need to counter disclose to someone based on the dyadic effect.

- **Impression formation.** Impression formation is a process by which you attempt to manipulate the perception that others have of you through your self-disclosures. When you go to an employment interview, you will likely wear a suit or professional outfit and groom yourself in order to promote the most favorable, professional impression for the potential employers.

- **Relationship maintenance.** Relationship maintenance and enhancement is another reason for self-disclosure. We might reveal positive information about ourselves in order to make another person more attracted to us, thus enhancing the relationship. But we also continue to self-disclose to our friends, family members, co-workers, and romantic partners to maintain the relationship. Continuing to self-disclose shows others that you continue to trust them and want to share information with them.

- **Manipulation.** As many of these reasons point out, we might use self-disclosure as a means of manipulation. Suppose you are the boss at a local bottling plant. Two-weeks before his annual review, your assistant informs you that his mother has just been diagnosed with leukemia and his world is in a tailspin. There are a few negative behaviors that need to be pointed out in his annual review. However, now that there is a reason to feel bad for the assistant, you might decide to put off including negative information in his review. It is possible that the assistant told you this in order to manipulate you as you put together his review.

Applying Concepts DEVELOPING SKILLS | **Reasons That You Self-disclose**

What are the primary reasons that you self-disclose with an acquaintance? Close friend? Family member? Romantic partner? Do you self-disclose for different reasons depending on the type or intimacy of the relationship? Why or why not?

Rewards of self-disclosure. You may find that when you tell someone something you are rewarded in some way. Some of the rewards include:

- **Knowledge of yourself.** We might find that we gain a better knowledge of ourselves. Perhaps hearing yourself talk about something you did will help you to understand your own behavior.

- **Physiological health.** Earlier we mentioned catharsis as a reason for self-disclosure. With catharsis comes better physiological health. Stress can cause a disruption in our sleeping patterns and can make us more susceptible to illnesses. You might find that after you get something off your chest you will be less stressed and can reap the reward of better health.

- **Coping with a problem.** Along those same lines, self-disclosure might help you to better cope with a problem. Talking about a situation might allow you to better think it through and bring some perspective to the situation. Other people may have advice or a different perspective that can help you to cope.

- **More meaningful relationships.** Many researchers argue that self-disclosure adds meaningfulness to our relationships and aids in relationship maintenance. By disclosing to others, as stated previously, we are essentially telling them that we trust them with personal information and that we want to continue the relationship. Therefore, the more we disclose, the deeper the intimacy of the relationship.

Dangers of self-disclosure. Although there are a lot of rewards to self-disclosure, that doesn't mean that there aren't accompanying risks.

- **Personal risks.** We could face personal risks. What we reveal may cause someone to get angry or even to become violent and harm us physically or psychologically. The other person could use the information to manipulate our behavior in the relationship.
- **Relational risks.** We may also encounter relational risks. Our self-disclosure could be received negatively and could cause the other person to reject us and the relationship. You could disclose something to a romantic partner about a close friend. The romantic partner could tell the close friend about the disclosure and you could lose the friendship and/or the romantic relationship.
- **Professional risks.** We may lose a job as a result of self-disclosure. The military's "don't ask, don't tell" policy is the perfect example of professional risks linked to self-disclosure. Enlistees who disclose to a fellow enlistee that they are gay can be discharged and not allowed to re-enlist if the fellow enlistee reports the self-disclosure to a superior officer.

6e

SELF DISCLOSURE

Factors that Influence Self-Disclosure	Reasons for Self-Disclosure	Rewards of Self-Disclosure	Dangers of Self-Disclosure
Dyadic effect	Catharsis	Knowledge of yourself	Personal risks
Topic	Self-clarification	Physiological health	Relational risks
Valence	Self-validation	Coping with a problem	Professional risks
Receiver relationship	Reciprocity	More meaningful relationships	
Communicator's sex	Impression formation		
	Relationship maintenance		
	Manipulation		

Cultural CONNECTIONS | Cultural Influences on Self-Disclosure

Cultural differences regarding self-disclosure can be examined from collectivist and individualist perspectives. Recall that a collectivist culture is one that emphasizes group needs and group success. Members of the collectivist culture are likely to sacrifice their own accomplishments for the sake of the group. An individualist culture is ego-driven, emphasizes the individual, and is characterized by competition between members of a group. Because disclosures are often about personal information and personal achievement, there is more open disclosure in individualist cultures because of the emphasis on the accomplishments of the individual. Collectivist cultures disclose less than individualist cultures because they tend not to emphasize personal experiences.

Yum and Hara (2006) explored self-disclosure as a component of relational development in Internet relationships. The focus of the study was to determine if there were differences among Koreans, Japanese, and U.S. Americans. Yum and Hara used social penetration theory to study the breadth and depth of self-disclosure as the online relationships developed.

Results of their study indicated that culture does play a role in the perception of self-disclosure. Among all three cultures, self-disclosure was associated with relational quality. However, Americans were more likely than Korean and Japanese participants to associate self-disclosure with trust. In other words, Americans perceived increased self-disclosure with increased trust, whereas for Koreans, as self-disclosure increases, trust decreases. For Japanese participants, there was no relationship between self-disclosure and trust.

Yum and Hara attribute these findings to the individualist and collectivist cultures of the Americans, Koreans, and Japanese. They suggest that the collectivist culture of Korea may consider self-disclosure a negative behavior and, perhaps, an indication of inappropriate behavior.

The components of social penetration theory— breadth and depth—seem to affect relationship development among the American participants more than Koreans or Japanese.

Application

How do you think self-disclosure differs in face-to-face interactions and online interactions among these three cultures? Would you argue that culture has more influence on self-disclosure than the channel of communication?

Applying Concepts DEVELOPING SKILLS

Identifying Rewards and Risks of Your Self-disclosures

Without revealing details, describe a situation in which one of your self-disclosures was rewarding. In what ways was it rewarding? Next, describe a situation in which you encountered risks for a self-disclosure. In what ways was it dangerous? If you cannot (or are unwilling to) identify your own self-disclosures in this application, use someone else's situation. However, do not identify that person by name.

Social Penetration Theory

Altman and Taylor's (1973) **social penetration theory** describes relational development based on self-disclosure. As a relationship develops, self-disclosure increases in both breadth and depth.

- **Breadth. Breadth** refers to the number and variety of topics covered in the self-disclosures.
- **Depth. Depth** is the amount of information you disclose about each of those topics, including the significance and private nature of the disclosure.

In a relationship with a co-worker, you might have little breadth and low depth, meaning that you discuss only a few topics in superficial discussions. With a close friend, your disclosures may have tremendous breadth and depth; you would discuss any topic with him or her and discuss those topics in depth. You may discuss some topics in more depth than others.

Figure 6.3 provides a model to represent social penetration. Altman and Taylor suggest that you think of social penetration as an onion. Each layer of the onion represents more depth of the self-disclosure. The more divisions you make in the sides of the onion, the more breadth or range of topics that are covered. According to the theory, the development of the relationship is represented by the progression from the outer portion of the model to the center.

Social penetration theory (SPT) is based on several observations.

1. People share less personal information at the beginning of a relationship, and share increasingly more personal information as the relationship progresses.

2. Reciprocity is important at the outset of the relationship. Both people in the dyad need to share increasingly personal information for closeness to develop.

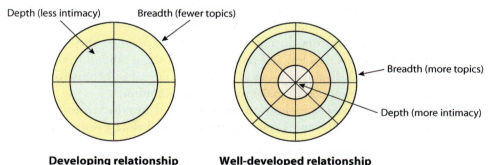

Developing relationship   **Well-developed relationship**

Figure 6.3 Model of Social Penetration Theory

Consider the layers of an onion as representing the breadth and depth of information you share with someone. You can see that the developing relationship is characterized by sharing commonly known information about yourself to someone else. In a well-developed relationship, the partners share more intimate information about themselves on a variety of topics.

3. As the dyad progresses into the deeper layers of the "onion," self-disclosure slows down. As you get to know someone, you are sharing a lot of information on a variety of topics. When closeness increases, the disclosures are fewer, but more personal.

Applying Concepts
DEVELOPING SKILLS

Applying Social Penetration Theory to Your Friendship

Consider your closest friend. Using Altman and Taylor's model, draw an illustration of the breadth and depth of the self-disclosure in your friendship including both the topics of breadth and depth of your discussions. Now illustrate your relationship with a new friend. In what ways are your models different? How would your model differ if you were illustrating your relationship with a family member?

6e

Competent Self-Disclosure Through Self-Monitoring

Self-monitoring is reading our environment and adjusting our communication accordingly. Our ability to self monitor appropriately is an important component of communication competence. When you go to the library, do you behave differently than when you go to the food court on campus?

The Self-Monitoring Inventory (see page 138) provides us with a way of measuring our level of self-monitoring, which ranges from high to low.

High self-monitors are able to go into a particular context and change their behavior to match the appropriateness of the context. High self-monitors might curb their cursing in their workplace, where such language is often not acceptable. However, when going to a party with friends, high self-monitors might express themselves freely.

Low self-monitors do not change their behavior as they encounter different contexts. If a low self-monitor swears when around friends, then that person is likely also to swear at work. Of course, just because you swear anywhere you want doesn't make you a low self-monitor.

Knowing when and how to self-disclose is key to self-monitoring. Competent communicators consider the following before self-disclosing.

- **Nature of the disclosure.** The *nature of the disclosure* considers both the topic and the valence of the disclosure. Are you communicating negative or positive information?

- **Location.** Are you in an appropriate *location* to make your disclosure? If you are disclosing to a romantic partner that you are in love with someone else and plan to break up with him or her, is it appropriate to do that in a public place?

- **Timing of the disclosure.** If your romantic partner is rushing to the hospital because her father just had a heart attack, is that an appropriate *time* to disclose your love for someone else?

- **Relationship with the other person.** Your disclosure should also be dependent upon your *relationship with the other person*. The information you share about yourself to another person should become more personal as you get to know that person.

- **Motivations.** Your *motivations* should also guide your disclosures. Is your intention to harm the other person? Manipulate the other person? Are you genuinely concerned about the other person, and so would your disclosure improve your relationship? A competent communicator uses self-disclosure positively rather than as a means to manipulate or hurt another person.

- **Possible burdens of self-disclosure.** Thinking about your motivations, your relationship with the other person, and the nature of your disclosure will give you a chance to consider the *possible burdens* of the self-disclosure. Will your disclosure put the other person (or you) at risk personally or professionally?

6e

KNOWING WHEN AND HOW TO SELF-DISCLOSE

	Explanation	Example
Nature of Disclosure	What is the topic and valence of the disclosure?	Are you disclosing negative information?
Location	Where do you plan to disclose the information?	Will you be in a crowded place?
Timing	Are there any extenuating circumstances that might complicate the disclosure?	Is the person to whom you plan to self-disclose having a bad day?
Nature of Relationship	What is your relationship with the other person? How well do you know the person?	Is the person your best friend?
Motivations	Why are you self-disclosing the information to someone?	Do you intend to harm the other person by self-disclosing to them?
Possible Burdens	Is your self-disclosure likely to burden the other person?	Are you disclosing information about an illegal activity that might put the other person in a position of having to withhold information from the police?

Applying Concepts
DEVELOPING SKILLS

Determining Your Level of Self-monitoring

Use the Self-Monitoring Inventory to determine whether you are a high, moderate, or low self-monitor. Does the level of your self-monitoring influence your interpersonal relationships? How could low self-monitors learn to adjust their communication to fit each environment they encounter?

SELF-MONITORING INVENTORY

INSTRUCTIONS: The following statements concern personal reactions to a number of different situations. No two statements are exactly alike, so consider each statement carefully before answering. If a statement is true, or mostly true, as applied to you, circle the T. If a statement is false, or not usually true, as applied to you, circle the F.

1.	I find it hard to imitate the behavior of other people.	T	F
2.	I guess I put on a show to impress or entertain people.	T	F
3.	I would probably make a good actor.	T	F
4.	I sometimes appear to others to be experiencing deeper emotions than I actually am.	T	F
5.	In a group of people, I am rarely the center of attention.	T	F
6.	In different situations and with different people, I often act like very different persons.	T	F
7.	I can only argue for ideas I already believe.	T	F
8.	In order to get along and be liked, I tend to be what people expect me to be rather than anything else.	T	F
9.	I may deceive people by being friendly when I really dislike them.	T	F
10.	I'm not always the person I appear to be.	T	F

SCORING: Give yourself one point for each of questions 1, 5, 7 that you answered F. Give yourself one point for each of the remaining questions that you answered T. Add up your points. If you are a good judge of yourself and scored 7 or above, you are probably a high self-monitoring individual; 3 or below, you are probably a low self-monitoring individual.

From "The Many Me's of the Self-Monitor," by Mark Snyder, *Psychology Today*, March 1983, p. 34. Reproduced by permission of Mark Snyder.

In this chapter, you have learned the following concepts. Check to be sure you have achieved each of the communication competencies.

6a Defining Interpersonal Communication

- Interpersonal communication is a process by which two people exchange meaning by simultaneously sending and receiving symbolic messages.

Competence. Can I identify ways in which I maintain interpersonal relationships to satisfy my needs for inclusion, control, and affection?

6b Forming Interpersonal Relationships

- Interpersonal relationships satisfy our need for inclusion, control, and affection.
- We are attracted to people based on a number of factors, including proximity and similarity.

Competence. Do I notice the reasons for forming relationships with the people with whom I interact?

6c Examining Relationship Development and Dissolution

- Stage models examine the evolution of relationships through the movement between stages of development and dissolution.
- The structural-helical model suggests that relationships do not progress through stages, but rather that they are better envisioned by the structure of a metal spring.

Competence. Am I able to identify the stages or phases in my relationships? Can I explain the difference between the stage/phase models of relational development and dissolution and the structural-helical model of relationship maintenance as it pertains to my relationships?

6d Relational Dialectics

- Dialectical theory suggests that each relationship experiences dialectical tensions that must be continually negotiated through communication in order to maintain the relationship.
- Dialectical tensions involve integration (time spent together), change (amount of change in the relationship), and expression (amount of self-disclosure).

Competence. Can I distinguish between the three types of dialectical tensions? Am I able to identify how each tension has influenced one friendship and one familial relationship?

6e Understanding the Dynamics of Self-Disclosure

- Several factors influence self-disclosure: dyadic effect, topic, valence, receiver relationship, communicator's sex.

- There are many reasons for self-disclosing in addition to rewards and dangers of self-disclosure.

- We can examine relational development that results from self-disclosure using the theory of social penetration. As the relationship progresses, the partners will notice an increase in the breadth and depth of the topics they disclose.

- Self-monitoring is the ability to read the environment appropriately and to adjust our communication accordingly. Self-monitoring ranges from high to low.

- There are several factors to consider before making self-disclosures.

Competence. Do I know why I self-disclose? Can I identify how self-disclosure differs depending on the type of relationship I have with the other person? Am I a high self-monitor or a low self-monitor?

Review Questions

1. Can interpersonal communication occur between strangers? Why or why not?
2. How does the Structural-Helical Model differ from the stage models?
3. What are three key dialectical tensions in relationships?
4. Explain the dyadic effect. What role can it play in interpersonal communication?
5. What rewards can come from self-disclosure?
6. What is self-monitoring?

Discussion Questions

1. According to the relational development model, during the intensifying stage, one or both parties may engage in secret tests to gauge the other's commitment to the relationship. Can you think of a time when you have done this or when this was done to you? What type of test did you use? Did that change the overall nature of the relationship?
2. In what ways can guilt lead to self-disclosure?
3. Consider your own interpersonal communication style. Are you a high, medium, or low self-monitor? What role does your environment play in your level of self-monitoring?

Key Terms

Managing Interpersonal Communication Apprehension

As you read in Module A, *communication apprehension* is a fear or anxiety about speaking to one or more people in any given context. *Interpersonal communication apprehension* exists when a person experiences fear or anxiety about speaking to another person in any setting.

In Module A, we discussed the fact that not everyone is anxious about communicating in every context. McCroskey (1984) suggests that some people have **context-specific apprehension**, which means that only in certain contexts (such as in interpersonal settings or public speaking settings) do they feel anxiety about communicating.

McCroskey (1984) also suggests that some people experience **situation-specific apprehension**, which occurs in particular settings or with certain people. For example, your boss may have asked you to come to her office to talk about a project that she'd like you to help with. You might be afraid to come off as too assertive when giving your ideas about the project, so you are nervous about how to communicate with your boss.

Through an examination of uncertainty reduction theory, you will learn ways to gather information about another person or situation in order to reduce your apprehension. The module concludes with a discussion of additional approaches for managing your interpersonal communication apprehension.

UNCERTAINTY REDUCTION THEORY

At some point, we all experience a little bit of apprehension in interpersonal communication contexts. Uncertainty reduction theory explains why we are uncomfortable talking to strangers and how we can reduce that apprehension.

Charles Berger (Berger & Calabrese, 1975) is credited with the formation of **uncertainty reduction theory (URT)**, which explains the exchange of information between two people to create understanding and reduce uneasiness or anxiety. Originally, the theory was used to explain how a dyad progressed from stranger to friend. The **uncertainty** in the theory refers to an uneasiness or anxiety about another person or your relationship with that person. In the context that Berger intended, the uncertainty exists because the dyad did not know each other.

You may have experienced uncertainty reduction at some point in your life. Suppose a stranger sitting next to you on a train started a conversation with you. You might feel uncertainty about communicating with the stranger because you don't know her motives for talking to you or you are worried about saying or doing something that might offend her (such as shaking her hand, which could be offensive if she is from another culture where hand-shaking is not a greeting ritual).

Uncertainty reduction theory describes how you gain knowledge about each other, thereby *reducing* uncertainty and enhancing your ability to predict the behavior of the other person. You might find that you are more comfortable with people you know because you can predict how they will react to you and to various situations. But with strangers you have to be careful about the words you use and the behaviors you enact to prevent insulting them or making them uncomfortable. That is the primary source of uncertainty.

In what instances might you feel the need to reduce uncertainty? You could be new to a company and feel anxious about breaking communication norms of that workplace. Likewise, any time you enter into a new relationship or a new group, you could feel some measure of apprehension. Of course, as you get to know the person or people, that uncertainty dissipates.

According to Berger, the key to reducing uncertainty is communication. When we disclose information about ourselves to another person, we feel more comfortable in the interaction. The more information we have about the other person, the less uncertainty we feel.

URT provides three strategies to uncertainty reduction. In a situation in which you experience uncertainty, you might use a passive, active, or interactive strategy. Suppose that you just started a new job and you have just met Bob, who works in the cubicle next to you. How might you use each of the three strategies to reduce your uncertainty about your new workplace?

A **passive strategy** is when you *observe* another person's behavior. You see how someone acts with other people (to see if a person acts differently around other people) or what someone talks about with other people.

SCENARIO: At your new workplace, you could observe how Bob interacts with co-workers. You could pay particular attention to how he greets them. Does he address each by a first name (Sam) or a formal name (Mr. Jones)? That could help you feel more comfortable when you meet people because you will know the proper protocol for greetings. What topics does Bob talk about with co-workers? This could help you determine what is appropriate workplace talk so that you do not worry about saying the wrong thing. You could also observe how Bob interacts with the boss. Do they engage in polite conversation, or is it always work-related conversation?

Keep in mind that gathering information through a passive strategy does not provide you with concrete evidence for effective and appropriate behavior. In Chapter 2 you learned that we each perceive the same situation in different ways, based on our previous experiences. You could misinterpret how two people are communicating, especially if you are not close enough to hear everything they are saying. Also, you may be observing only part of the interaction, and the portion you observe could be interpreted out of context.

When is it appropriate to use a passive strategy if we cannot be confident about the knowledge we gain from its use? You could be in a situation where you have not yet met anyone, so directly questioning strangers would seem inappropriate. For example, when you arrive for an interview, you probably do not know anyone there. As you wait to meet the interviewer, you might "scope out the scene" to see if the people who work there are people you would want to interact with on a daily basis.

There are situations in which it is not possible to observe another person. When that is the case, you can use an active strategy to gain some initial information. An **active strategy** involves asking a third party for information. The third party would be someone directly connected to a person or a situation.

> SCENARIO: You ask Bob to have lunch with you. During lunch, you ask Bob about appropriate forms of communication with the boss. You inquire about how people ask the boss for time off from work. You might want to know whether the boss is approachable during the day or prefers to have a scheduled meeting.

By asking Bob questions about other people in the workplace, the information you gather will be less ambiguous than what you might get through a passive strategy. However, there is still the risk that Bob's perceptions and observations have been tainted by previous experiences. For example, if Bob went to school with your boss, then their relationship might be very different from the relationship you would be expected to have with the boss. If Bob was denied a raise recently, his perceptions of the boss could be skewed.

When is the active strategy appropriate to use? You might find the active strategy useful if you are seeking information about someone who is a higher status than you. You might not feel comfortable asking the boss some of the questions that you can ask Bob, especially if you are trying to create a good first impression. When it comes to wanting to know how to approach someone, as in the scenario, asking a third party might be less threatening than confronting the person and asking them directly.

An **interactive strategy** occurs when you communicate face-to-face with the person for whom you wish to reduce uncertainty. You ask questions directly rather than going to another person for information.

> SCENARIO: You could ask your boss questions about appropriate workplace behavior and communication. You could ask her directly if it's appropriate to call co-workers by their first names. You could ask her if workers are free to spend a few minutes socializing with co-workers during the workday.

In some situations, an interactive strategy is more beneficial because the person will appreciate that you haven't gone behind her back to find the information. It can also cultivate a stronger relational bond between you because you have set precedence for open and direct communication.

Applying Concept
DEVELOPING SKILLS

Uncertainty Reduction

SCENARIO: You see someone from across the room and the person looks like someone you would like to get to know better.

Explain how you would use each of the three uncertainty reduction scenarios to gain information that will reduce your apprehension in the situation.

ADDITIONAL STRATEGIES FOR MANAGING INTERPERSONAL COMMUNICATION APPREHENSION

Learning how to engage in small talk appropriately and effectively is one method for decreasing your interpersonal communication apprehension. Some people find apprehension in small talk situations.

Some people do not like to be in a setting where they have to interact with people they do not know. You might think to yourself, "What am I going to say?" In Module B, you learned the importance of creating a list of potential small talk questions or topics *before* an interaction. If you are prepared to interact with a stranger (or anyone), then you do not have to focus on what you are going to say because you will already have a plan.

You also learned in the small talk module about how to soften your nonverbal cues to make yourself more approachable. Many times we are nervous about communicating with another person because we are self-conscious about how we look. We think another person might not approach us because of the way we look. If you keep in mind that your nonverbal messages could be communicating a desire to be left alone, then some conscious attention paid to your nonverbal cues could reduce your apprehension and improve your interactions. Keep in mind the concept of self-fulfilling prophecy from Chapter 2. If you think no one will talk to you, and your nonverbal cues reflect that attitude, then it is likely that no one will talk to you because your nonverbals indicate that you are unapproachable. Therefore, you have created the very situation that you feared.

Starting a conversation with a stranger or acquaintance can be intimidating. *Cognitive restructuring* can help you to reduce interpersonal apprehension just as it can with other forms of communication apprehension. For example, if you look at an interaction as an opportunity to talk to someone who could be influential in your life, you might be more inclined to talk. You could also envision a positive interpersonal encounter that allows you to feel more confident in approaching someone else.

Cognitive restructuring is all about training your mind to think in a different, more productive way. Imagine yourself being more confident when speaking to others. Replace a negative thought ("She is not going to want to talk to me.") with a positive thought ("I have several interesting topics to talk to her about."). Think about the strategy or strategies you will use when communicating with another person. The more you can believe in your abilities, the more comfortable you will become when communicating in interpersonal contexts.

Applying Concept DEVELOPING SKILL

Managing Your Apprehension

In what ways could you use these suggestions on your first day at a new job? Which of the suggestions discussed seems to be the easiest to practice and implement? Which seems most difficult?

CHAPTER

7

Relational Conflict

7a **Defining Conflict**
Components of Conflict
Phases of Conflict

7b **Exploring Positive and Negative Consequences of Conflict**
Positive Consequences of Conflict
Negative Consequences of Conflict

7c **Identifying Types of Conflict and Conflict Issues**
Conflict Types
Conflict Issues

7d **Examining Approaches to Conflict Management**
Potential Conflict Outcomes
Five Traditional Approaches to Conflict
Management

7e **Managing Conflict**
Conflict Management Styles
Aggressiveness Versus Argumentativeness
Unproductive Strategies for Managing Conflict

Cultural CONNECTIONS Fistfighting as a Conflict
Management Strategy

7f **Examining Interpersonal Conflict: John Gottman versus John Gray**
Gottman's Four Horsemen of the Apocalypse

EYE ON ETHICS Moral Conflicts
John Gray's Interpersonal Conflict Perspective

In this chapter, you will explore the dynamics of conflict in relationships and strategies of conflict management. Your communication competence will be enhanced by understanding:

- why it is important to communicate conflict to another person;
- how identifying the type of conflict you are experiencing can enable you to devise a better approach to managing or resolving the conflict;
- how the five approaches to conflict management can provide you with a number of ways to manage or resolve conflict;
- why knowledge of the positive aspects of conflict can help you to feel more comfortable engaging in conflict with another person;
- how you can avoid aggressiveness in favor of assertiveness and argumentativeness;
- how your ability to identify negative communication patterns during interpersonal conflict events can enable you to find ways to shift the conversation to more positive patterns of interaction.

7a

7a Defining Conflict

It would be impossible to go through life without conflict unless you were to live alone in isolation. Therefore, it is important to understand the nature of conflict and how to manage it.

How would you define conflict? Think of all of the situations that could be labeled "conflict." Does your list include only interpersonal conflict? Remember that countries can be in conflict, too. How else might you expand your list?

Components of Conflict

Conflict can occur between two people or among a group of people, even between groups of people. Regardless of the context, how we define conflict does not change. **Conflict** occurs when the goals of interdependent people are incompatible and at least one person communicates to the other(s) about the incompatibility.

As we examine several key words in the definition of conflict, let's consider a scenario. Jane and Jack are co-workers who are assigned to plan the company's annual family day.

Goals. Goals are whatever it is that each party is attempting to attain. In our example, Jane and Jack share the same overarching goal of wanting to have a successful event. However, their individual goals—different ideas about the theme of the event—could be at odds. Jane wants to have a retro theme (e.g., 1980s) and Jack wants to have a circus theme.

Interdependence. Parties in a conflict must be interdependent, meaning that the actions of one party influence the actions of the other party. The actions of one party must have consequences for the other party; otherwise there is no conflict. Because the parties are interdependent, they can benefit or harm each other, and they may vary in their desire to cooperate or compete to attain their goal(s). Therefore, interdependence is an important component of conflict because it affects the conflict management process.

Communication. Until one person communicates about the conflict, neither knows that they are involved in conflict. If Jane and Jack do not express their ideas and recognize how different they are or if one merely accepts the other one's idea, then there is no conflict. But if there is communication about the difference in their ideas, then conflict occurs.

Phases of Conflict

To see the importance of communicating conflict, let's examine phases of conflict. Pondy (1967) suggested that conflict occurs in five phases. Keep the Jane and Jack scenario in mind as we follow their conflict through these phases.

Latent conflict. **Latent conflict** occurs when underlying conditions are present that could cause conflict. At the beginning of the project, Jane and Jack spend time individually thinking about a theme for the event. During this phase, they are experiencing latent conflict because they are not yet aware that their goals are incompatible.

Perceived conflict. **Perceived conflict** occurs when one or both parties become aware of the incompatible goals. At this point, overt conflict has not yet occurred. There is just the perception of differences. When Jane and Jack meet the next day to begin planning the event, Jack tells Jane about his great idea for a circus theme. He's quite certain that this is the perfect theme. At this point, Jane realizes that there is going to be conflict. She is just as certain that the circus theme is the worst theme. Thus, they are in the perceived conflict phase.

Felt conflict. **Felt conflict** involves the emotional impact of the perceived conflict. This phase is the combination of perception and awareness, or latent and perceived conflict. The parties involved consider strategies for managing the conflict. Again, at this point overt conflict has not yet occurred. Jane begins to get knots in her stomach with the realization that this project is going to be more difficult than she imagined. She begins determining how best to communicate her concerns to Jack.

Manifest conflict. When conflict is communicated, the dyad or group moves into the phase of **manifest conflict**. The conflict can be communicated in a number of ways, but ultimately the communicators create either a supportive or a defensive climate (review the discussion in Chapter 4). How the parties communicate about the conflict will have an enormous impact on their ability to manage or resolve the conflict and on the fate of their communication and their relationship after the conflict. In this phase, Jane tells Jack about her idea to have a retro theme for the event. In addition, she tells Jack that the circus theme is too kid-focused and inappropriate for single employees and employees who are married without kids. Jack says he's so certain that the circus theme is better that he won't acknowledge Jane's idea. Now the conflict has been communicated.

Conflict aftermath. The residual effects of the communication and behaviors that occurred during the conflict episode are called **conflict aftermath**. The parties will, either individually or together, determine whether the conflict was productive or unproductive. If Jack and Jane devolve into petty personal attacks rather than looking at the facts of the issue, then there will likely be residual hard feelings. It's even possible that Jack would quit his job in order to distance himself from Jane. On the positive side, Jack and Jane could find that their ability to work through conflict to complete their assigned task enhanced their working relationship.

Applying Concepts
DEVELOPING SKILLS | Applying the Phases of Conflict

Situation: Your boss asked you to complete a report by tomorrow. You have been working on it all day and are quite proud of what you have written. At the end of the day, you find out that a co-worker completed the report without your knowledge and turned it in to the boss. The boss may pass you up for a promotion since she thinks that you didn't do your job. What would you do?

Using the scenario, identify the parties in conflict and list their incompatible goal(s). Then create a storyline in which you explain how you would respond in this situation. Within your storyline, label the points at which you reach perceived, felt, and manifest conflict.

PHASES OF CONFLICT

LATENT CONFLICT

Underlying conditions are present that could create conflict.

PERCEIVED CONFLICT

One or both parties in the conflict realize that their goals are incompatible.

FELT CONFLICT

The emotional impact of the conflict that results from the perception and awareness of the existence of incompatible goals.

MANIFEST CONFLICT

Incompatible goals are communicated between interdependent parties.

CONFLICT AFTERMATH

Residual effects remain after the conflict has been managed or resolved.

7b Exploring Positive and Negative Consequences of Conflict

Many people consider conflict to be a negative relational event. However, we can see that there are both positive and negative consequences of conflict.

Positive Consequences of Conflict

Here are three positive aspects of conflict.

Encouraging solutions. Conflict forces people to examine a problem and come up with a solution. In group communication, this is important because the conflict can enable the group to create a better solution than the one resulting from everyone just going along with the group leader's ideas.

Reducing stress. When you confront and discuss problems, you are preventing the hostility and negativity from building up inside of you. Conflict can be cathartic because it allows you to get things off your mind instead of causing you endless stress.

Maintaining relationships. When you attempt to manage or resolve conflict with someone, you are indicating that the relationship you have with that person is worth keeping. If you didn't care about the other person, then you wouldn't stick around and argue with them, right? Therefore, engaging in conflict can be a means of relational maintenance.

Can you think of additional positive consequences?

Negative Consequences of Conflict

What would you consider to be the negative consequences of conflict? Here are two of them.

Negative regard. Conflict can produce *negative regard* for your opponent. Negative regard comes especially if you and your opponent are resorting to personal attacks. You may also come to resent the opponent for continuing the conflict.

Creating distance. If the negativity continues, then you will likely feel the need to distance yourself from your opponent. You might avoid the opponent or refuse to speak to him or her. Either way the distance might cause more resentment and further damage the relationship.

Applying Concepts
DEVELOPING SKILLS

Analyzing Positive and Negative Aspects of Conflict

Why do people consider conflict to be negative? Now that you know the positive consequences of conflict, how would you persuade others to view conflict in a more positive way?

7c Identifying Types of Conflict and Conflict Issues

While it might seem logical for conflict to exist or not exist, there are actually a number of different types of conflict. If you consider previous conflicts in which you have been involved, you might be able to see how they differ.

Conflict Types

Let's examine different types of conflict. Keep in mind that any particular conflict can be categorized under one or more of these types.

Real and unreal conflict. Conflict can be labeled as real conflict or unreal conflict (Lulofs and Cahn, 2000). **Real conflict** is an actual conflict situation in which both parties acknowledge that they have incompatible goals. Conflict that is communicated is classified as real conflict.

Unreal conflict occurs when one person misperceives a conflict situation or that the conflict doesn't really exist. There are three types of unreal conflict.

■ **False conflict. False conflict** occurs when you think that there is a conflict, but upon discussing it with the other person, you find out that conflict never existed. Suppose that your co-worker is in a bad mood. Your initial reaction is to think that he is angry with you because you criticized his business plan in yesterday's meeting. Later in the day you ask if he is okay. He tells you that his wife lost her job yesterday and that he is concerned about how they are going to survive financially.

> *Conflict outcome.* At this point, you realize that you have experienced false conflict because you believed that conflict existed when it really did not. Communicating your concerns to the other person rather than making assumptions about the potential existence of a conflict can prevent the development of hard feelings between you and the other person.

■ **Displaced conflict.** When you direct the conflict toward the wrong person, you have **displaced conflict**. People often take their anger out on someone who has nothing to do with the source of the problem. Spouses take their anger out on each other despite the fact that their problem is work-related. Displaced conflict most frequently occurs with a person with whom you have a close relationship, such as a friend or a romantic partner. Why? Well, your close relational partners are "safe targets" who will not run at the sign of displaced conflict. One responsibility of close relational partners is to give aid and comfort in times of need. Therefore, the partner will likely allow the displaced conflict as part of his or her role in the relationship. But, do not forget that *always* taking your anger out on an innocent relational partner is not acceptable and will likely not be tolerated for a lengthy period of time.

> *Conflict outcome.* Displaced conflicts are typically acknowledged when the person who is angry apologizes for taking anger out on the other person. If the unintended target grows tired of endless displaced conflict, the conflict could become a real conflict.

■ **Misplaced conflict.** When people are arguing about the wrong issues, it is called **misplaced conflict**. Arguing about the real issue might be too painful. Therefore, people choose to argue about "safe" issues that are less painful. For example, a married couple might argue about what movie to see rather than emotional issues (such as lack of affection) because a movie is a "safer" issue.

> *Conflict outcome.* Resolving misplaced conflicts can be difficult because the relational partners are not dealing with the underlying issues in their relationship (e.g., emotional issues). Until the underlying issues are managed or resolved, the "safe" issues will continue to exist.

While displaced and misplaced conflict might sound similar, there is a distinct difference between the two conflict types. Displaced conflict involves directing anger toward a "safe" *person*, whereas misplaced conflict involves directing anger toward a "safe" *topic*.

**Applying Concepts
DEVELOPING SKILLS** | Confronting Displaced Conflict

7c

In many close relationships, displaced conflict can become problematic. When one person in the relationship continually directs anger at the other person, the target's patience wears thin. Construct a dialogue to address someone who is continually displacing his or her anger or discontent (with someone else or about something else) on you. It can be a hypothetical or a real situation.

Content and relational conflict. You may recall that in Chapter 1 you learned that all communication has both content and relational dimensions. It would stand to reason then that two types of conflict are content conflict and relational conflict. Although content and relational conflict are both potentially "real" conflicts, we examine them here to provide another context for understanding misplaced conflict.

Content conflict emphasizes tangible issues, such as money, events, or people. These tangible issues are typically external to the parties involved in the conflict. Spouses can argue about which movie to see. This is a content conflict if they are truly fighting about the movie rather than a relational issue, such as dominance or control.

Relational conflict involves relational issues such as control and power. Suppose that Emma and Eve are sisters. Emma is 3 years older than Eve. Their mother tells Emma to be sure that Eve cleans her room. Emma reminds Eve of this chore. Eve responds with a typical sibling response, "You're not my mother." Eve is not necessarily angry about the act of cleaning her room (which would be content conflict), but rather she is angry that her sister is telling her to clean her room. Therefore, they are experiencing relational conflict because there is disagreement about who is in control.

Most conflicts involve a combination of content and relational conflict. The married couple who experiences content conflict by arguing about what movie to see could also be experiencing relational conflict. Perhaps one spouse always picks the movie (and chooses everything they do) and there is perceived inequity in the relationship. That is a relational conflict.

> *Conflict outcome.* So what do you do in this situation? How do you manage or resolve this conflict? It is imperative that both parties separate the content and relational conflict and deal with each separately. If there is an underlying relational issue, that should be addressed first, as the resolution of that conflict could also resolve the content conflict. This is true for any relationship type. Dealing with each type of conflict on its own can help create a quicker solution.

Take the case of Jack and Jane (the co-workers in the previous section). Would you characterize their conflict as content or relational? Given that there are not many details provided about each party in the conflict, the most appropriate answer is that they are experiencing content conflict. Jack and Jane have different ideas about the theme of their company event. But what if Jane has always been pompous and portrayed a sense of superiority around Jack? If Jane's behavior prompts Jack to "fight" to get her to agree to use his theme, would they be experiencing relational conflict as well as content conflict? The struggle over dominance and control would become the relational issue.

Jack and Jane would need to separate the content and relational conflict (and address each separately) in order to come to a resolution that could prevent future conflicts of a similar nature. That is the best-case scenario. However, it's not likely that Jack will confront Jane about her pompous behavior. If he does not address the relational issue, but they manage to come to a solution about the content issue (the theme of the event), then there is a greater potential for future conflict that centers on the relational issue of Jane's pompous behavior.

Substantive and nonsubstantive conflict. Substantive conflict deals with issues that are potentially harmful to the relationship. However, not all conflict involves a potential threat to the relationship. With **nonsubstantive conflict** there is no real issue involved. We have seen substantive conflict examples illustrated in each of the sections in this chapter. Now, let's take a closer look at two types of nonsubstantive conflict.

Relating Misplaced Conflict and Relational Conflict

Rick and Steve have been friends for 10 years. A year ago Rick hired Steve to work for his company. This created a new dimension in their friendship. Not only were they friends, but they now have a working relationship characterized by unequal roles (i.e., superior-subordinate). Steve has always been competitive with Rick. They became friends when they were playing on the same softball team. Their competitive nature was the foundation of their friendship. Recently, Rick has become concerned because Steve is continually undermining him at work. Rick gives Steve assignments with particular outcomes clearly stated, but Steve changes the assignments to reflect how he thinks they should be accomplished. Rick must confront Steve about the conflict.

Create a dialogue in which Rick and Steve work to manage or resolve their conflict.

■ **Bickering.** *Bickering* occurs when two relational partners snap at each other and is exemplified by the continual exchange of "yes it is" and "no it isn't." It's really about picking at the other person instead of arguing about something substantive and evident. Something as simple as the temperature outside or leaving dirty socks on the floor can lead to bickering. Here's an example of bickering:

HUSBAND: "Why do you always leave your dirty socks on the kitchen floor?"

WIFE: "I don't leave my socks on the kitchen floor."

HUSBAND: "Yes you do. You always leave your dirty socks on the kitchen floor."

WIFE: "I don't always leave my socks in the kitchen. Tell me one time other than today that you have found my socks in the kitchen."

HUSBAND: "Yesterday."

WIFE: "That's not true."

And, of course, the dialogue continues in this manner until one person changes the subject or leaves the interaction.

Conflict outcome. Continued bickering could transform the non-substantive conflict into a substantive conflict if one person communicates negative feelings about the bickering.

■ **Competition.** Relational partners might challenge each other in some playful way, thus creating *competition*.

> *Conflict outcome.* Competition can, however, lead to substantive conflict if the competition becomes personal.

**Applying Concepts
DEVELOPING SKILLS**

Identifying Instances of Nonsubstantive Conflict

In what way(s) can false conflict be nonsubstantive conflict? How can you link displaced conflict to nonsubstantive conflict? Explain your responses to these two questions.

Conflict Issues

Until now we have mostly been concerned with the nature of the conflict, but not the issues that are under debate. Let's now have a look at what types of issues can cause conflicts. An *issue* is the object of the conflict. Issues can be categorized as behavioral, normative, personality, and moral conflicts.

Behavioral conflicts. **Behavioral conflicts** involve control over tangible issues, such as resources or interests. These types of conflicts are often categorized as real and substantive because they are overt issues that have the potential to harm the relationship. Behavioral conflicts can include control over how money is spent, where to vacation, or whose family will visit during the holidays.

Normative conflicts. **Normative conflicts** exist when there is some question regarding the rules and norms of the relationship. Relational issues are known as normative conflicts. Typically these revolve around things that you believe you should receive from the relationship but do not. Normative conflicts can also include unreasonable expectations. Overall, normative conflicts deal with the rules of the relationship and how and why those rules are broken.

Personality conflicts. **Personality conflicts** typically involve behaviors or beliefs and values. You may have felt personality conflicts on occasion. You can probably identify conflicts that were minor and temporary, such as a group member who has an annoying habit of cracking her knuckles continually. But you may also have experienced personality conflicts that are much

7c

more serious. You may have had a group member who believed that he was smarter and better than the rest of the group. He may have taken over a project and completed it "his" way without regard for the views and work of the other group members. As you can imagine, personality conflicts that involve beliefs and values are much more difficult to resolve.

Moral conflicts. Finally, some conflict issues involve morality. **Moral conflict** exists when there are moral implications involved in the conflict. The example above of the group member who takes over the group project and does it his way is also creating a moral conflict. Is it acceptable for him to take over the project? Suppose that he plagiarized a large portion of the project, putting the rest of the group members in a moral dilemma. Until the parties can get past the issue of who is right and who is wrong, the conflict cannot be resolved.

We can examine conflict by categorizing the type of conflict into real versus unreal, content versus relational, or substantive versus nonsubstantive, and we can examine the issues involved in the conflict. The next section outlines traditional approaches to conflict management.

7d

| Applying Concepts DEVELOPING SKILLS | Identifying Conflict Issues |

Create a scenario for each of the conflict issues discussed in this section. They can be actual or hypothetical situations. Of your scenarios, which one would be the easiest to resolve? Which would be the most difficult to resolve? Explain your response.

7d Examining Approaches to Conflict Management

Conflict is often talked about as "resolved." However, conflict is complex. Unless the conflict can be solved to the satisfaction of both parties, the conflict is really just "managed" (Thomas, 1976). Thus it is more useful to discuss approaches to managing conflict rather than resolving it.

Potential Conflict Outcomes

The five conflict management approaches we will examine can be classified based on the projected outcome of the conflict. Conflict outcomes can be lose-lose, win-lose, lose-win, or win-win. Lose-lose means that both parties lose and neither gains from the solution. Win-lose and lose-win occur when one party benefits from the solution at the expense of the other party. Win-win strategies are characterized by benefits for both parties in the solution.

Distributive agreements. **Distributive agreements** are solutions that "distribute" the benefits unevenly. Lose-win or win-lose are distributive agreements because one person gains and the other loses in the solution. With distributive approaches, only one person can "win." Avoidance, accommodation, and competition are approaches to conflict management that can be classified as distributive in nature. In each of those approaches, either both parties lose or only one party wins (Pruitt & Rubin, 1986).

Integrative agreements. **Integrative agreements** are based on the assumption that there is a way to approach the conflict so that both parties benefit from the solution. The main concerns of both parties are integrated into the solution so that they obtain a win/win outcome. Collaboration is the ultimate integrative strategy because each party gets his or her most important issues included in the solution. Compromise is considered a partial integrative agreement because with compromise each party must give something up in order to create a solution. However, each party gets some of what he or she wants, which makes it a type of integrative agreement (Pruitt & Rubin, 1986).

Five Traditional Approaches to Conflict Management

There are five traditional approaches to conflict management: avoidance, accommodation, competition, collaboration, and compromise (Thomas & Kilmann, 1974). The approaches differ with regard to the level of concern for the self and concern for other (as in the other person involved in the conflict with you). See Figure 7.1 for a grid that visually describes the five approaches.

Avoidance. **Avoidance** occurs when you refuse to confront the conflict or manage it. Avoidance is high concern for self and low concern for other. This would include refusing to talk about the issue or avoiding the person all together. Avoidance is high concern for self because avoiding behavior usually makes the actor feel better. However, it shows low concern for the other because you are negating the other person's ability to manage or resolve the conflict; doing so would make you uncomfortable.

Accommodation. **Accommodation** exists when you give in to someone else's wishes (or demands) in order to resolve the conflict. Accommodation is low concern for self and high concern for other. In this case, you have low

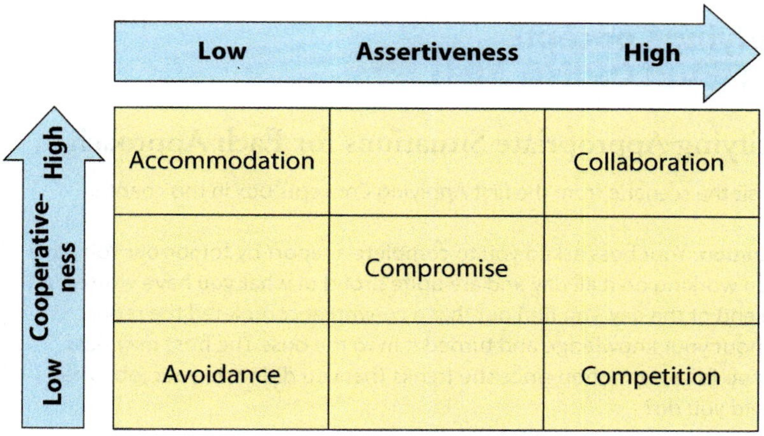

Figure 7.1 Traditional Approaches to Conflict Management

Adapted from K. W. Thomas (1976). "Conflict and Conflict Management" in M. Dunnette (Ed.), *Handbook of Industrial and Organizational Psychology*, Chicago: Rand-McNally. Reproduced by permission of Leaetta Hough.

concern for yourself because you are not standing up for your own rights. Instead you are giving in to the other person. Because the other person gets exactly what he or she wants, you have high concern for other(s).

Competition. When you assert your own rights with little (or no) concern for the other person, you are engaging in **competition**. Therefore, it is classified as high concern for self and low concern for other. Your goal is to have the conflict resolved in the way that you want it resolved.

Collaboration. Collaboration is reached when both parties in the conflict get what they want. Therefore, it is high concern for self (because you get what you want) and high concern for other (because the other person gets what he or she wants).

Compromise. In a **compromise**, each party must give up a little of what they want. Note that *each* party sacrifices. That is what creates the equality of concern for self and concern for other. Because each party gives up something, there is *moderate* concern for self and other—no one person is winning or losing. A compromise is considered a partial collaborative agreement.

Keep in mind that there is no one best way to approach conflict management. In other words, collaboration is not better than competition. Some situations do not allow for collaboration. Therefore, approaches to conflict are situational.

Identifying Appropriate Situations for Each Approach

Let's revisit the scenario from the first Applying Concepts box in this chapter:

Situation: Your boss asked you to complete a report by tomorrow. You have been working on it all day and are quite proud of what you have written. At the end of the day, you find out that a co-worker completed the report without your knowledge and turned it in to the boss. The boss may pass you up for a promotion since she thinks that you didn't do your job. What would you do?

Which of the five approaches to conflict management would be most effective in this situation? Which approach would be least effective? Which approach would you be most comfortable using if this scenario were real?

7e   Managing Conflict

Most people rely on just one or two conflict styles in every conflict situation. However, some people make use of all the styles depending on the conflict. As with the approaches to conflict, there is no one best conflict management style; competent communicators choose the style that best fits the situation. There are five conflict management styles.

Conflict Management Styles

Nonassertiveness. **Nonassertiveness** is an unwillingness to manage the conflict. Avoidance and accommodation are approaches to conflict that exemplify the nonassertiveness style. When you do not stand up for your rights or show concern for your own needs, you are displaying nonassertiveness. You might avoid the conflict or give in to the other person's solution.

Indirect communication.   When you hint or imply something that you want someone to do rather than asking directly, you are engaging in **indirect communication**. Suppose that Lucy and Taniesha are sitting in Taniesha's living room. Lucy is cold, but she doesn't want to ask directly to have the ceiling fan turned down. So Lucy says, "Gosh, it's so cold in here." The implication is that Lucy wants Taniesha to turn off the ceiling fan. The use of indirect communication can cause conflict because the other person might get angry that you do not directly ask for what you want. However, you might use indirect communication when you want to save face for the other person or if you want to offer self-protection.

Passive aggression. Communicating your dissatisfaction with something in a disguised manner is called **passive aggression**. Sometimes during a conflict, one person sighs loudly to indicate frustration and disgust with the conversation. The sigh is a form of passive aggression. The reason you might use passive aggressive behavior is because you could claim that the other person is misinterpreting your behavior, thus saving face for yourself. In the case of the loud sigh, you could claim that you were merely taking a deep breath. However, passive aggressive behavior has drawbacks. First, the passive aggressive behavior might not work. Perhaps your conflict partner didn't hear your sigh. Second, you can create resentment. If your partner knows you well enough to know that you don't normally take loud, deep breaths, then he or she may resent your sighing in the middle of a conflict situation.

Direct aggression. **Direct aggression** ranges from personal attacks to teasing and swearing to physical violence. Direct aggression includes yelling or actually hitting or hurting the other person. Of course, the use of personal attacks and physical violence could definitely result in resentment by the object of the aggression.

7e

Asssertiveness. **Assertiveness** is the willingness to stand up for your rights without infringing on the rights of others. It is the opposite of nonassertion. When using assertiveness, you are stating clearly and honestly what you want. At the same time, you are making sure that you are not harming the other person by using personal attacks or physical violence. And, there is a balanced conversation between you and the opponent because you have a concern for the rights and needs of the opponent.

Aggressiveness Versus Argumentativeness

There is an important difference between being argumentative and being aggressive, despite the fact that many people use those terms interchangeably. **Aggressiveness** exists when one person intentionally inflicts psychological or physical harm on the opponent with the goal of winning the argument. There is little or no concern for the rights and needs of the other person. Aggressiveness is a type of disconfirmation because you are not acknowledging the opponent's feelings or needs.

Argumentativeness is quite different. If you are argumentative, you are more interested in crafting your argument than you are with insulting or harming your opponent. **Argumentative** people are willing to verbalize and defend their viewpoint. People who are highly argumentative state their positions on controversial issues and they are more resistant to persuasion. Why might they be more resistant to persuasion? Highly argumentative people are used to arguing and analyzing viewpoints. Therefore, they are better able to identify persuasive messages.

People who are low in argumentativeness are more likely to avoid arguments and are more susceptible to persuasive messages. They do not have the practice in analyzing arguments that we see with the highly argumentative person.

Unproductive Strategies for Managing Conflict

There are two unproductive conflict management strategies (DeVito, 2009) that people often employ in a conflict situation. Why do they? Because they usually work.

Silencers. **Silencers** are used to prevent the continuation of the argument. Silencers include crying or yelling really loudly. The intention with crying is to turn the attention away from the argument and onto the person who is crying. Yelling loudly or out-shouting someone is another silencer. For example, if you and your opponent are stating your positions at the same time, one of you will speak louder than the other in an attempt to get the softer-speaking person to stop talking.

If silencers can end an argument, why are they considered unproductive? The main purpose of silencers is to end the conversation about the conflict. Therefore, the partners are no longer focused on managing or resolving the conflict. As stated previously, silencers draw attention away from the argument and onto the person invoking the silencer.

Gunnysacking. When you keep minor conflicts with another person to yourself, but then unload them all at one time during a major conflict, you are **gunnysacking**. Imagine Matt walking through life with a sack over his shoulder. Every time his partner Pat does something to irritate Matt, he puts that irritation in his sack. The sack, of course, is a metaphor for Matt's body, which is storing the suppressed displeasure with these irritations. At some point, Matt will reach the point at which he cannot fit any more irritations in his "sack." Therefore, he unloads the sack onto Pat—meaning that Matt will remind Pat of all the irritating behaviors he has put up with over a certain period of time.

The problem with gunnysacking is that it is not present-focused. The focus is on the past rather than on the current conflict. If Matt and Pat are arguing about who should take out the trash, it is inappropriate for Matt to remind Pat of all of the negative behaviors he has endured recently. By bringing up past behaviors, Matt draws attention away from the current conflict and disperses it into the past.

Applying Concepts
DEVELOPING SKILLS

Applying Styles to Conflict Scenarios

Situation: Suppose that your family has a gathering every Memorial Day. It's the one time of the year that everyone can get together at the same time. You just found out that your favorite band is having a concert that weekend about five hours away. When you tell your family that you are going to the concert instead of the family gathering, they are upset. What would you do?

In this situation, which of the conflict management styles would be most appropriate to use? Which would be the most inappropriate? Explain your answers.

Cultural CONNECTIONS

Fistfighting as a Conflict Management Strategy

You might think that our senators and congressional representatives are too focused on partisan issues and not focused enough on bipartisan agreements. But, at least our legislators are not prone to resolving conflict with a fistfight!

From time to time there are news reports about ideological feuds in parliaments (legislative body similar to our House or Senate) around the world that erupt into physical violence. The legislators sometimes resort to punching, and have been known to shove, spit, and pull the hair of their opponents.

Some of the countries where physical fighting has erupted among politicians are Thailand, Russia, Ukraine, Taiwan, Mexico, Indonesia, Republic of Guinea-Bissau, and Kyrgyzstan.

Interestingly, in 2005 the prime minister of Canada, Paul Martin, challenged the (then) new Conservative Leader Stephen Harper (who would later become Canada's prime minister) to reform the etiquette in Canada's House of Commons. At the time, legislators were trading verbal insults shouted in angry tones. Physical violence had not yet erupted. Martin was attempting to diffuse the verbal attacks before they became violent.

Application

If you watch the British parliamentary procedures on BBC, you will notice that the politicians shout quite frequently. What is it about the U.S. legislative branch that prevents physical violence as a means of resolving ideological battles? Certainly there have been times when politicians have shouted in the House or Senate, but in recent decades, fistfights have not been common. Are there cultural norms that prevent the use of physical violence in the legislative bodies in the United States? How would you explain the relative calm that exists in U.S. congressional debates?

7f Examining Interpersonal Conflict: John Gottman versus John Gray

Until this point, we have examined conflict approaches and conflict management styles that can be applied in interpersonal *and* group contexts. In this section, we'll focus solely on interpersonal relationships.

John Gottman and his wife, Julie Schwartz Gottman, created a laboratory in Seattle, Washington, where they study the interaction of romantic couples. They call it the "Love Lab." Gottman has accumulated more than 20 years of scientific research that he has used to understand how couples communicate in conflict situations. As a result, he can predict with 90 percent accuracy whether the relationship will dissolve or end in divorce. While there is an emphasis on *marriage* in Gottman's writings, all of these concepts can be applied to nonmarital romantic relationships as well. In Figure 7.2, you can see a side-by-side comparison of John Gray and John Gottman.

Gottman's Four Horsemen of the Apocalypse

Based on Gottman's extensive research data, he has identified four negative behaviors that, when displayed frequently, can predict the demise of an interpersonal relationship. He calls these behaviors the Four Horsemen of the Apocalypse (a metaphor based on the four horsemen whose arrival precedes the end of the world).

Criticism. **Criticism** involves attacking someone personally by attacking the person's personality or character. Typically criticism involves blaming the person for a negative event or behavior. Criticism is different from complaining. **Complaining** is merely stating something that you do not like. Here is the difference between a complaint and a criticism:

> *Criticism:* "You never take me out to dinner anymore because you're too cheap."
> *Complaint:* "We never go out to dinner anymore."

Gottman considers complaining to be one of the most important (and healthiest) communicative behaviors in a relationship. He claims that it makes the relationship stronger in the long-run because the complaints are not suppressed.

Contempt. **Contempt** takes criticism one step further and adds *intention* to hurt or insult a person with a personal attack, or criticism. In the example of criticism above, the person may just be using the insult ("too cheap") as a way of persuading the other person to go out to dinner.

Moral conflicts are conflicts that involve moral implications. You may find your-self in a situation in the future (or perhaps you have been faced with such a situation already) in which you are faced with a moral dilemma. Suppose that your boss has asked you to include an article in your monthly newsletter that you know he took from an online article. But he wants you to put his name on a byline so that it looks like he wrote it.

You look at your boss with concern, and he replies, "If you don't like your job you can always find another one." The implication, of course, is that you write the newsletter article with his name on the byline or you will be fired.

This is a moral conflict because you have to decide if you are going to commit plagiarism willingly. Your boss has put you in an unenviable position.

Application

What would you do? What if there were many alternative jobs available? Would that make it easier to quit and not commit plagiarism? What if there were very few alternative jobs available? How would that affect your decision?

However, if the speaker purposefully called the other person "cheap" in order to hurt that person's feelings of that person, then the remark is an example of contempt.

Defensiveness. **Defensiveness** occurs when a person is compelled to explain the motives for his or her behavior. Gottman provides several types of defensive behaviors: *denying responsibility, making excuses,* and *whining.* When faced with a partner's complaint, a defensive response would be to *counter the complaint* with a complaint of your own. Another defensive strategy is *repeating yourself,* in which you continuously repeat your position rather than listening to and understanding the other person.

Stonewalling. **Stonewalling** is an avoidant behavior that occurs when you cease to communicate with the other person. This could include ignoring or avoiding that person.

Identifying a couple of these behaviors in your relationship does not mean that the relationship is doomed. And, even if you identify all four in a relationship, the relationship is not necessarily going to dissolve. How the couple communicates in order to rectify the negative behavior is what is most important. Turning the defensive climate into a supportive climate can bring about change in the relationship resulting in more positive communication.

According to Gottman (1994), "a lasting marriage results from a couple's ability to resolve the conflicts that are inevitable in any relationship" (p. 28).

John Gray's Interpersonal Conflict Perspective

If you haven't read John Gray's (1992) book, *Men Are from Mars, Women Are from Venus*, then you may have heard of the book. His initial book spawned a "Mars and Venus" empire—from additional books to board games (e.g., *Mars and Venus on a date*, 1997). Gray's empire is built on his understanding of men and women and how they communicate. For example, he suggests that after a long day at work, men want to come home and go to their "cave." The cave is the room that is designated as "his" room or domain. The man needs to unwind before engaging in talk with his spouse. Women, on the other hand, want to come home and talk with their husband about the day's events. The vastly different behaviors create conflict. Gray's solution is to recognize that men and women are different and that each must respect those differences and learn to live with them.

A tremendous number of people have heeded the advice of John Gray. However, the problem is that Gray never researched human behavior or human communication. His books are so popular because they are based on sex stereotypes—women like to talk *a lot* more than men, for instance. Stereotypes can be easy to see, which is why he has been able to establish a successful Mars and Venus empire. However, stereotypes are dangerous if used in this way because you can end up treating the person as a stereotype rather than as an individual.

There are likely many women who come home from work and would prefer to go to a "cave" to unwind before engaging in conversation. Similarly, there are likely many men who look forward to coming home and sharing their day's experiences with their wives. Assuming that all men have to go to a "cave" and all women have to talk can create additional conflicts unintentionally.

7f

Applying Concepts DEVELOPING SKILLS | **Examining Interpersonal Conflict**

Situation: Your romantic partner is having lunch with an ex-romantic partner. You have told your partner previously that you are uncomfortable with their friendship. Your partner goes to the lunch despite your request to cancel the lunch. What would you do?

Using the situation above, create a dialogue in which the couple discusses the incident. Include in your dialogue an example of each of the four horsemen from Gottman's conflict approach. Be sure to label each behavior as such in the dialogue.

ISSUE	GOTTMAN	GRAY
Academic versus best-selling book	*Why Marriages Succeed* (55,000 copies)	*Men Are from Mars, Women Are from Venus* (6 million + copies)
Cardinal rule of relationships	What people think they do in relationships and what they actually do are two different things.	Men and women are fundamentally different.
Criteria for successful marriages	Making mental maps of each other's world	Heeding gender stereotypes
Criteria for failing marriages	Heeding gender stereotypes; reactions to stress	Gender differences in communication style
Number of couples formally studied	760+	None

Figure 7.2 John Gottman vs. John Gray

Adapted from *Psychology Today*, November/December 1997.

Competence SUMMARY

In this chapter, you have learned the following concepts. Check to be sure you have achieved each of the communication competencies.

7a   Defining Conflict

■ In order for conflict to exist, the parties in the conflict must be interdependent and have incompatible goals. This means that the parties must rely on each other in some way and that a goal cannot be reached because of the actions of the other party.

■ If one party does not communicate to the other about the incompatibility, then there is no conflict. Only after the incompatibility is communicated does conflict exist.

■ There are several phases of conflict: latent, perceived, felt, manifest, and conflict aftermath.

Competence. Can I explain the important components that make a situation a conflict? Can I identify the phases of conflict?

7b Exploring Positive and Negative Consequences of Conflict

- There are many positive and negative consequences of conflict. Conflict can be positive if it helps people to examine a problem and come up with a solution or if it keeps negativity from building.
- Conflict can be negative either because you feel increased negative regard for the other person or the relationship could end.

Competence. Can I explain the negative *and* positive consequences of conflict?

7c Identifying Types of Conflict and Conflict Issues

- Conflict can be real or unreal; content or relational; and substantive or nonsubstantive.
- Each conflict situation involves an issue, or the object of the conflict. Issues can be categorized as behavioral, normative, personality, and moral conflicts.

Competence. If presented with a conflict scenario, can I correctly identify the type of conflict that exists? Can I distinguish the different issues that are involved in a conflict?

7d Examining Approaches to Conflict Management

- Approaches to conflict management include avoidance, accommodation, competition, collaboration, and compromise. There is no one best way to manage conflict; therefore none of these five approaches is any better than the other.
- Each approach differs with regard to the level of concern for self and the level of concern for the other party.

Competence. Which approach to conflict management do I most often exhibit? Can I distinguish the differences between the approach I use and the other approaches?

7e Managing Conflict

- Conflict management styles include nonassertion, indirect communication, passive aggression, direct aggression, and assertiveness. People often use a variety of styles depending on the situation.
- An important distinction is the difference between aggressiveness and argumentativeness. People who are aggressive are typically inflicting psychological or physical harm on their opponent, and thus have no regard for the

opponent. Argumentativeness refers to the desire to argue one's position while you maintain concern for the other person.

■ Unproductive conflict management styles (silencers and gunnysacking) can create more harm than good in attempting to manage conflict.

Competence. Which conflict management style do I tend to use? Can I explain the difference between aggressiveness and argumentativeness. How can I prevent using unproductive conflict management styles?

7f Examining Interpersonal Conflict: John Gottman versus John Gray

■ Gottman's Four Horsemen of the Apocalypse are four conflict behaviors that can signal the demise of the relationship: criticism, contempt, defensiveness, and stonewalling.

■ Gray bases his understanding of men and women on stereotypes. His philosophy on conflict is that men and women need to embrace their differences in order to avoid conflict.

Competence. Can I identify Gottman's four horsemen in a conflict setting? Can I apply Gray's interpersonal conflict perspective to relational conflict?

Review Questions

1. What are the key parts of the definition of conflict?
2. During which phase of conflict is the conflict communicated?
3. Explain the three types of unreal conflict.
4. Relate content and relational dimensions of communication and content and relational conflict.
5. Provide an example of substantive conflict and an example of nonsubstantive conflict.
6. Explain the five approaches to conflict and label each one as distributive or integrative.
7. List one positive aspect of conflict and one negative aspect of conflict.
8. Explain the difference between aggressiveness and argumentativeness.
9. Why are silencers and gunnysacking unproductive conflict management strategies?
10. Which is better for a relationship: complaining or criticizing?

Discussion Questions

1. This chapter listed two types of unproductive conflict management strategies—silencers and gunnysacking. Can you identify other unproductive conflict management strategies?
2. In the workplace, would you identify any of the five approaches to conflict as more effective than others? If so, why?
3. Create a scenario in which two people go through the five phases of conflict.
4. What role do defensive and supportive climates play in conflict management?
5. Discuss the differences between John Gottman's and John Gray's work on conflict. Whose findings do you believe are more credible?

Key Terms

accommodation *p. 158*

aggressiveness *p. 161*

argumentative *p. 161*

assertiveness *p. 161*

avoidance *p. 158*

behavioral conflict *p. 156*

collaboration *p. 159*

competition *p. 159*

complaining *p. 164*

compromise *p. 159*

conflict *p. 147*

conflict aftermath *p. 149*

contempt *p. 164*

content conflict *p. 153*

criticism *p. 164*

defensiveness *p. 165*

direct aggression *p. 161*

displaced conflict *p. 152*

distributive agreements *p. 158*

false conflict *p. 152*

felt conflict *p. 148*

gunnysacking *p. 162*

indirect communication *p. 160*

integrative agreements *p. 158*

latent conflict *p. 148*

manifest conflict *p. 149*

misplaced conflict *p. 152*

moral conflict *p. 157*

nonassertion *p. 160*

nonsubstantive conflict *p. 154*

normative conflict *p. 156*

passive aggression *p. 161*

perceived conflict *p. 148*

personality conflict *p. 156*

real conflict *p. 152*

relational conflict *p. 153*

silencers *p. 162*

stonewalling *p. 165*

substantive conflict *p. 154*

unreal conflict *p. 152*

Computer-Mediated Communication

Computer-mediated communication, or CMC, covers a wide variety of interpersonal contexts using digital technology. CMC can include messages sent to others via email, instant messaging, blogs, chat rooms, and newsgroups. More recently, social networking sites such as Facebook and MySpace as well as Twitter have become popular ways to connect and reconnect with others.

In Chapter 6, we examined the reasons that people form relationships. Since the first online dating site was launched, more and more people each year are joining dating sites to meet significant others. You may recall the discussion of what attracts us to some people and not others. Some of the criteria for choosing people with whom you will form relationships can be created online. You and other members are joining the site (thus in the same proximity) for the same reasons (similarity). You can also further explore your similarities with other dating site members indirectly through viewing a member's profile or directly through email or instant messaging (IM) with the member.

Various forms of CMC are also used to maintain relationships. Partners (friends or significant others) can keep in touch via social networking sites, instant messaging, and emails. Companies can create virtual workplaces where employees can conduct business via IM and email.

In Chapter 6, you read about the "disappearing act" and saw how CMC can also be used to nd a rela-

tionship. People send text messages or email to break up with a significant other or to end a friendship.

CMC AND THE TRANSACTIONAL MODEL OF COMMUNICATION

You may recall from Chapter 1 that communication is transactional because there is simultaneous interaction and mutual influence between two or more people. CMC differs from face-to-face communication in the channel used to transmit messages, the lack of nonverbal feedback, and the timing of feedback. We listed above the different CMC channels available for us to use to communicate with others. Written communication, which comprises CMC, lacks nonverbal cues from which to derive further meaning from the message. And, depending on the form of CMC that you are using, feedback can be delayed, perhaps indefinitely (if you are using email, for example), or it can be slightly delayed (if you are using instant messaging). Therefore, we categorize types of CMC as asynchronous or synchronous.

Asynchronous Forms of CMC

Asynchronous forms allow you to send and receive messages when the other person is not logged in or able to receive the information. Email is one example because you send a message to a receiver, who reads it at his convenience and sends a response at his convenience. Newsgroups and blogs are also asynchronous because members can post information for other members to read when they have time.

Social networking sites and online dating sites tend to be more asynchronous (if you are not using the instant messaging feature). You can post messages and information on Facebook and MySpace for your friends and family to see when they log into the site. On a dating site you can "wink" at someone who catches your attention or you can send him or her an email. Twitter sends messages to your followers, but the reaction is not necessarily instantaneous.

An advantage to asynchronous forms of CMC is that the communicator has time to carefully craft a message before sending it. Thus email messages tend to be more thoughtful and well written than synchronous forms of CMC. An obvious disadvantage is the time span between the exchange of emails.

Synchronous Forms of CMC

Synchronous forms of CMC allow you to communicate directly and immediately with another person or groups of people. Responses are designed to be instantaneous. Instant messaging is a common form of synchronous CMC. Two people can communicate with each other as fast as it takes for them to type a

message and hit "send." Chat rooms are a group-oriented form of synchronous CMC. Members of a chat room log in to communicate with other chat room members. The purpose of the chat room varies from social support (e.g., cancer patients) to viewer interaction (e.g., chat rooms associated with television channels).

These two types of synchronous CMC are the closest mediated channels to telephone and face-to-face. They offer the ability to have a direct connection with the other person that can allow for immediate feedback from the other person.

An advantage of synchronous forms of CMC, as we have stated, is that it allows for more instantaneous communication than asynchronous forms do. A disadvantage of synchronous CMC is that users tend to type quickly, making errors and use abbreviations such as "brb" (be right back) or "ttyl" (talk to you later) that can be confusing for new users of synchronous channels. As a result, there is an increased chance for miscommunication.

Applying Concepts
DEVELOPING SKILLS

Forms of CMC

Consider the different types of relationships you have (family, friends, coworkers). In which relationships are you more comfortable with asynchronous forms of CMC and in which relationships are you more comfortable with synchronous forms?

INTERPERSONAL COMMUNICATION AND CMC

One of the premier researchers of CMC is Joseph Walther. Through his study of online communication, Walther reported that CMC often becomes hyperpersonal communication. **Hyperpersonal**

communication refers to "communication that is more intimate and social than that found in equivalent, offline interactions" (Rabby & Walther, 2003, p. 142). According to Walther (1996), people using CMC will create images of the other persons despite never having met them in reality. They overattribute characteristics to others, thus idealizing them.

Consider the fact that users of CMC are able to carefully construct the messages that they send to another person. Thus, they are able to create a persona that may or may not be similar to how the person behaves or interacts in person. Thus it is possible that people are more confident and competent online because they have greater control over how they can present themselves and take the needed time to construct effective messages.

Today more than ever we are initiating relationships with people we meet online. Relationships range from acquaintance to friendship and romantic partners. Family members and friends often reconnect through virtual means, such as email and social networking sites.

For many people, online relationships are formed and maintained through CMC. In fact, some people never meet in person or even talk via telephone. How are online relationships maintained with no face-to-face contact? Walther (1992) proposed the social information processing theory. **Social information processing theory** assumes that people adapt to the medium that they have available for communication. Thus, if they are able to communicate only via email, then they adapt their communication and expectations accordingly. However, according to Walther, when there is a lack of nonverbal communication, especially in asynchronous CMC, the two people will take longer to get to know each other.

When people get to know each other, they start with a high level of uncertainty, or feelings of discomfort resulting from not knowing the other person. To reduce our uncertainty in face-to-face relationships, we can watch how the person acts in different contexts or ask questions of the friends who know the person. Because CMC channels lack nonverbal cues in addition to a lack of shared social circles, people are forced to use more direct means of obtaining information to reduce uncertainty. Thus, we ask more direct questions of the person to reduce our uncertainty about them. Interestingly, according to Tidwell and Walther (2000), CMC partners who used direct questioning and self-disclosure to reduce uncertainty rated each other more favorably than face-to-face partners who used direct questioning and self-disclosure (as cited in Rabby & Walther, 2003).

The **social information and deindividuation (SIDE) theory** (Lea & Spears, 1992) states that because of the lack of nonverbal cues and visual anonymity, CMC users become deindividuated in relational formation. In other words, rather than being a real person, each person is merely text on a screen. According to this theory, as you interact online with those whom you have never met and have no picture of, you imagine them to look however you want them to look. Lea and Spears argue that people's identities are comprised of their personal and social identities.

According to SIDE, users make overgeneralizations about the people with whom they are interacting (like *perceptual accentuation* from Chapter 2). As such, users interpret messages favorably by "filling in the blanks" about the other person in positive ways (Rabby & Walther, 2003). In addition, users have the ability to present themselves as they wish to be seen (remember *impression management* in Chapter 5). Therefore, the resulting image tends to be nothing like how the person looks and behaves in person.

Interestingly, if you and the person with whom you are engaging in CMC are members of the same online group, you are likely to be equally attracted to any other member of the group.

Applying Concepts
DEVELOPING **SKILLS**

Using CMC

Go to an online dating site (Yahoo! Personals is free of charge). Choose one personal ad and explain the ways in which the person has used pictures and language to create a particular identity of himself or herself.

In other words, the members of the group are considered equivalent and interchangeable. Therefore, the attraction that you feel toward the person is likely to be misperceived as "personal attraction" because of perceptual accentuation. It is an attraction that you would likely feel toward any member of that group.

KEY TERMS

asynchronous *p. 172*

computer-mediated communication *p. 171*

hyperpersonal communication *p. 172*

social information and deindividuation
  (SIDE) theory *p. 173*

social information processing theory *p. 173*

synchronous *p. 172*

Gender and Communication

If you think about your interactions with members of the opposite sex, would you characterize your communication behaviors as being different? There are endless jokes about how women and men communicate, and each joke plays to the stereotyped differences in their communication. Are we different? If so, in what ways are we different?

In this module, we will explore sex and gender differences in communication. However, it is important to keep in mind that when you talk to someone you should always treat him or her as an individual rather than a stereotype. Wood refers to the tendency to view people through stereotypes as "essentializing." When you engage in essentializing, you are ignoring the individual communicative behaviors that make each person unique.

DISTINCTION BETWEEN SEX AND GENDER

At the outset, it is important to distinguish between *sex* and *gender*. *Sex* is determined by the physiological and biological characteristics that make us "male" or "female." *Gender* is determined by the psychological components of masculinity, femininity, androgyny (high in masculinity and femininity), or undifferentiated (low in masculinity and low in femininity). Gender is more complex than sex in that gender can be learned and is socially constructed. While a person can surgically change from male to female or vice versa, sex is still a physiological trait.

GENDERLECT STYLES

According to Deborah Tannen (1990) in her book entitled *You Just Don't Understand*, men and women communicate differently. In fact, Tannen suggests that male and female communication styles should be considered culturally distinct with neither style identified as superior to the other. *Genderlect* (created from the word *dialect*) is a term she uses to remind us that communication between men and women is a form of cross-cultural communication.

Connection versus Status

Tannen's (1990) distinctions between men and women are based on what she calls the "connection" versus "status" difference. Women are raised to nurture others by considering their feelings and concerns. Their emphasis is on connection through cultivating and maintaining relationships. On the other hand, men are raised to be independent and drawn to achievement. They are driven by a need for status, to be respected by others.

Rapport Talk versus Report Talk

Tannen (1990) states that women are more predisposed to "rapport talk," in which they focus their communication on nurturing relationships, while men are more predisposed to engage in "report talk," where their concern is detailing events of the day (again, part of the need for status and respect).

When telling something to another person, women are more interested in (and thus, they often expect) relating an understanding of their situation. Men are more interested in giving advice. So if a wife tells a husband about an argument that she had at work earlier in the day, the husband is likely to respond with advice on how he would have handled the argument. Most of the time, the wife is merely venting her frustration about the situation and not seeking advice. Thus, you can see how such a misunderstanding could create negative feelings between the wife and husband.

Cooperative Overlap versus Power Play

When women interrupt, according to Tannen (1990), they are engaging in cooperative overlap, where they shape and continue the discussion. The interruption is a sign of rapport rather than a power play. The female, through the interruption, may be showing agreement or support. For males, interruptions are perceived as power plays; they take control of the conversation. Given the competitive nature of men, according to Tannen, when interrupted, men are likely to respond negatively and take back control of the conversation. Again, you can see how the differences in the usage and interpretation of interruptions can create arguments between men and women.

Thus, there are two forms of genderlect: feminine and masculine. Women can adopt a masculine genderlect and men can adopt a feminine genderlect. Because the concept of genderlect is more about masculine and feminine communication styles, sex is not as important as gender.

	Feminine Genderlect	Masculine Genderlect
Connection vs. Status	Emphasizes connection between two individuals. The focus is on developing and maintaining relationships. Relationships are developed and maintained through talk.	Emphasizes status in a relationship. The focus is on independence and competitiveness. Relationships are developed and maintained through shared activities (e.g., bowling league).
Rapport Talk vs. Report Talk	Focus of communication is on nurturing relationships (rapport talk). Emphasis in rapport talk is communicating understanding and seeking understanding from others.	Focus of communication is on transfer of information (report talk). Emphasis in report talk is giving advice.
Cooperative Overlap vs. Power Play	Feminine interruptions are considered "cooperative overlap" because the interruptions are meant to shape and maintain the conversation.	Masculine interruptions are considered "power plays" because the purpose of the interruption is to take control of the conversation.

DO MEN AND WOMEN REALLY COMMUNICATE DIFFERENTLY?

Whether or not men and women truly communicate differently is a hotly debated topic in the field of communication. In fact, Dindia (2006) argues that the differences are so slight that, instead of being from different planets (as John Gray, 1992, suggests in his *Men Are From Mars, Women Are From Venus* series), men and women are not only on the same planet, but also in neighboring states (Men are from North Dakota and women are from South Dakota).

Gray's empire is built on sex stereotypes. Stereotypes, which you learned about in Chapter 2, are generalizations about people that are taken as fact. The sex differences that Gray discusses are based on the stereotype of women being submissive and nurturing and men being dominant and competitive. If sex stereotypes are accepted as fact, then stereotypes become standards for behavior (Canary & Emmers-Sommer, 1997). For Gray, the differences are biological, and thus we would call them sex differences. However, genderlect styles are psychological and socially constructed so we call them gender differences.

The concept of genderlect styles (Tannen, 1990) represents the idea that boys and girls are raised in gendered speech communities that cultivate the gendered communication differences that we see in men and women in adulthood. Dindia (2006) argues instead that boys and girls are not segregated in childhood, but rather they interact together in school, at home with siblings, and in other social arenas. Additionally, she claims that the biosocial perspective on gender differences best describes any true gender differences.

The *biosocial perspective* states that sex differences are the combination of biological differences and culture (Wood & Eagly, 2002). Biological differences come from the fact that men are physically stronger and larger than women, and that women's activities are often tied to their childbearing physiology. As Dindia (2006) argues, "Cultural conventions, including gender roles, the division of labor, patriarchy, and so on, arise as a result of biological differences between women and men and the perceived limits these biological differences place on women and men" (p. 16). Thus, if the biological differences were nonexistent, then the cultural differences would be as well.

Applying Concepts
DEVELOPING SKILLS

Identifying Sex and Gender Differences

Consider your communication with your friends. Characterize a male friend and a female friend in terms of their genderlect style. If you have a sibling, characterize the communication between you and a sibling. In your sibling communication, are there sex or gendered communication differences?

Group Communication

Why do we need to learn about group communication? There are several aspects of group communication that can aid you in future group work.

- **Employers expect employees to have learned effective group skills in their college education.**

- **Groups can satisfy personal needs, such as the need for inclusion, as well as professional needs.**

- **Groups are better at solving problems than individuals are.**

- **Learning about group communication can help you to have more positive and productive group experiences in the future.**

Frequently asked questions

Does my group need to set goals? (See Chapter 8, page 186.)

We've been given a problem and asked to create a solution to the problem. Where do we start? (See Chapter 8, page 194.)

Is it normal to feel anxious about talking with my group members? (See Module F, page 207.)

How can I be an effective group member? (See Chapter 9, page 212.)

Is there any way to make meetings more productive? (See Chapter 9, page 223.)

CONTENTS

PART **THREE** Group Communication

Introduction to Groups
and Decision Making

OBJECTIVES

In this chapter, you will learn the fundamentals of group communication—including an examination of the components of group culture and the processes of problem solving and decision making in groups. Your communication competence will be enhanced by understanding:

- how to pinpoint where problems in group development began in order to resolve them;
- how setting goals from the beginning will help your group on the path to success;
- how to enhance the effectiveness of the group by identifying cohesiveness issues in your group and improving cohesiveness;
- effectively managing conflict by creating thoughtful solutions to problems and making the most effective decisions;
- how to create more effective group decisions by following the process of group decision making and using meeting time productively;
- how to produce effective solutions by using the problem solving process and the reflective thinking model.

8a   Introduction to Group Communication

Groups are so prevalent in our society that it is estimated that there are more groups in America than there are people (Patton & Downs, 2003). Not only are groups plentiful, they are also influential. Groups shape our society and our behavior. Government, businesses, educational institutions, and other organizations depend on groups to gather information, assess data, and propose courses of action. Our families and our close friends function as groups that give us counsel and support in times of need.

Because groups significantly influence our lives, it is essential that groups communicate effectively. Unfortunately however, many of us have difficulty mastering small-group communication skills. Estimates are that professionals lose 31 hours a month—nearly four workdays—in unproductive meetings (SMART Technologies ULC, 2004). Clearly, poor group communication can be costly.

Defining Group Communication

As you may recall from Chapter 1, we defined group communication as interactions among 3 to 15 people. As we delve more deeply into our study of group communication, we need to refine and expand the definition.

Group communication occurs when between 3 and 15 individuals with interdependent goals and an assigned or assumed leader meet and interact over time. Let's examine the components of this expanded definition.

Group size. The focus of the chapters in this section will be on *small* group. Three is the minimum number of individuals that can be classified as group communication. When two people interact, it is *interpersonal* communication, and dyadic conversation differs greatly from group communication. Turn-taking and feedback are two communication dynamics that exemplify the differences between interpersonal and group communication.

The upper limit for group communication is 15 (Socha, 1997). More than 15 people creates a group that is so large that it breaks into smaller groups, such as cliques, because communication as one group is too difficult. The smaller groups help to facilitate conversation and task completion more efficiently.

Interdependent goals. Individuals must be working toward similar goals in order for there to be a reason for the group to exist. In the workplace, for example, the goal could be the creation of a marketing plan. There must also exist interdependence, which creates the need to work together to accomplish mutual goals, such as the creation of a marketing plan. The cohesiveness of the group is partly determined by its progress toward fulfilling the group goal(s).

Time frame. The groups that we will examine in this section are groups that meet over a period of time. These groups develop roles and norms that are unique to the group. Groups that meet only one time do not have the same interaction characteristics mainly because they have little need to maintain good relations with each other.

Leadership. Groups typically have a leader. The leader can be assigned or assumed. An assigned leader is appointed to that role by a person in authority. Workplace groups may have a leader who is appointed by the boss of the group members. An assumed leader is a person who, through communication within the group, emerges as the leader of the group. Consider your membership in a group that had no appointed leader. You and the other group members likely looked to one member of the group for guidance and support. Perhaps that person was you. Whether appointed or assumed, a leader emerges when a majority of people in the group rely on one member for guidance. We will discuss leadership and group roles more thoroughly in the next chapter.

8a

Why Do We Need to Learn about Groups?

Groups exist in all contexts of life. You may belong to groups that meet your individual needs, such as a book club. In the workplace, it is almost inevitable that you will be asked to work in a group, for example, to create a solution to a company problem. In college, your professor might require you to work on a group presentation. By better understanding how groups function, you can become a better group member.

To become an effective employee. If you have not yet worked in a group or on a group project, then you almost certainly will at some point in your life. Professors use group work as a means of teaching you how to deal with others in attaining group goals and completing tasks. Why? In the workplace, you will be working in groups and you should know how to make your group as efficient and effective as possible. Second, employers seek employees with good group communication skills—because they will be working in groups.

There are several studies that indicate that group communication skills are essential in the workplace.

In 2006, the American Association of Colleges and Universities (AACU) surveyed business leaders on important skills that a college graduate should possess in the workplace. The business leaders ranked group communication skills in diverse groups as one of the most important skills (www.aacu.org).

The Gallup Organization conducted a survey asking people to rate 13 work-related skills. Over 80% of the respondents listed "dealing with people" and "critical thinking" as essential for success in the workplace (Lyons, 2003).

Many studies have revealed that training in group communication skills can improve a group's success (e.g., Schilder, 1992; Schullery & Gibson, 2001).

Possessing good group communication skills and the ability to work well in groups are essential skills for getting and keeping a job. Aside from employment benefits, group communication serves several other purposes listed next.

To provide a venue for meeting personal needs. As we have said in previous chapters, humans have needs that must be met, including inclusion, affection, and control.

- **Inclusion.** Inclusion is the need to belong or to be identified with others. Clearly groups are well-suited to fulfill inclusion needs.
- **Affection.** Affection is the need for love and esteem from others. Group members might not "love" you, but you could feel affinity for other group members and that affinity could be reciprocated.
- **Control.** Control is the need to exert power over other people and/or your environment. Fulfilling control needs in a group likely depends on your role within the group. However, there are several forms of power that can create control. For example, expert power is derived from your knowledge of a particular topic. If that expertise is helpful to the group, you might become an influential group member, and thus fulfill some of your control needs.

You may have noticed that needs that can be fulfilled by group membership are similar to the needs we fulfill by engaging in interpersonal relationships. Groups allow you to fulfill inclusion needs better than interpersonal relationships; because group membership provides identification with others, you meet inclusion needs faster in a group than with individual relationships.

To effectively solve problems. Suppose you were assigned the task of finding a solution to the lack of parking on your campus. (Our favorite response to parking problems is offered by college presidents who say, "We don't have a parking problem, we have a walking problem.") What solutions would be on your list? If you worked within a group, you would likely come up with a much more extensive list of solutions. Groups are better at problem solving than individuals because group members have a combined bank of knowledge and experiences, and these can be used to come up with solutions that one person might never have considered. A group can see the flaws and biases in ideas that you might be unwilling or unable to see when you work independently.

To combat negative attitudes toward group work. Because we are members of many groups and groups are such an integral part of our daily lives, we can take the group process for granted. As a result the group becomes less effective over time. Many people complain about disliking group work, especially in the classroom. Susan Sorensen (1981) created the term "group-hate" to label the "sincere dislike for any group activity in the academic settings." However, if people understood the characteristics of effective groups, they might find group work less stressful.

Also illustrative of many people's genuine dislike for groups is the results of a survey conducted by *USA Today* (November 15, 2004). Respondents were asked what task they would prefer over attending a meeting. Fifty-four percent of workers said they would rather mow the lawn, 25% would rather visit a dentist (yikes!), and 23% would prefer reading the phone book.

Applying Concepts DEVELOPING SKILLS | What's In It for You?

Revisit the list you created for the previous application. For each group you have listed, write a statement about why you are a member of that group. In other words, what does membership in that group provide for you?

8b Identifying Types of Groups

We can label small groups as primary or secondary groups. Before we define these two types of groups, it is important to note that these labels are not mutually exclusive. A group can be categorized as both primary *and* secondary.

Primary Groups

A **primary group (or socially-oriented group)** exists to fulfill our basic needs for inclusion and affection. Group members typically have long-term affiliations within these groups. Can you think of an example of a primary group? Some examples include your family, a sorority or fraternity, friends (cliques). Any tasks these groups perform are less important than the affiliations created within the group.

Secondary Groups

A **secondary group (or task-oriented group)** is focused on doing work, such as accomplishing a task or solving a problem. There are several types of secondary groups.

- **Activity groups.** Activity groups enable members to participate in a particular activity, such as in book clubs or gaming clubs.

- **Personal growth groups.** Personal growth groups include self-help and therapy groups, such as AA or cancer survivor groups.

- **Problem-solving groups.** Problem-solving groups are designed to address a concern or condition. For example, a problem-solving group might form among members of a community who are interested in finding ways to implement a recycling program in their town.

- **Self-directed groups.** Business and professional organizations are increasingly using work groups to accomplish their objectives. A type of task-oriented group becoming increasingly common in the business world is the self-directed work group. Such work groups manage themselves, in addition to getting work done.

Having read about the different types of secondary groups, it is easy to see how some groups could be categorized as both primary and secondary. Your book club may start as a secondary group where the focus is on discussing a book read by all of the members. However, over time, the group members might also become a primary group as members develop close relationships and do things together outside of book discussions.

Applying Concepts
DEVELOPING SKILLS

What Are Your Primary and Secondary Groups?

Review your list of groups again, and label each group as primary or secondary. If you label a group as secondary, indicate the type of secondary group that applies. Have the groups changed from primary to secondary (or vice versa) in the time you have been a member? With which type of group do you prefer to associate?

8c Understanding Group Culture

When a group of people with an interdependent goal meets over time, they form unique characteristics through their communication. Their communication creates a **group culture**, which is the personality and beliefs of the group. In this section we'll examine the components of group culture: goals, norms, cohesiveness, and conflict.

You may notice that each group that you belong to is different. If you have completed several classes for which you have had to perform group work, you probably noticed those differences. Even if you had the same group members from class to class, there will likely be a different group culture depending on the task. For example, the leader of the group might change when the nature of the task and goals change. Each group member might have different areas of expertise, and when the tasks change, the leader changes in order to have the most knowledgeable person leading the group.

Establishing a Group

Group development is centered around two concerns: task concerns and socioemotional concerns. Task concerns include any talk about what the group will *accomplish* and how they will accomplish it. Socioemotional concerns deal with the *personal aspects* of the group, such as stability and harmony among group members. The group will cycle between task and socioemotional concerns throughout its existence.

There are two phases of group development.

Formation phase. In the first phase, called the **formation phase**, group members are getting to know each other, thus the primary emphasis is on socioemotional concerns. During this phase, the group members vie for different roles in the group. If the group can move quickly through this phase, they will have more time to focus on their task(s). A group can move quickly if the members focus first on getting to know each other, and then on the task concerns. Perhaps including an icebreaker exercise to get to know group members would facilitate the development of personal relationships and take care of socioemotional concerns. If there is a lot of infighting among members, too much time will be consumed with socioemotional concerns and the group output could be compromised as a result.

Production phase. In the **production phase**, the group has reached socioemotional maturity and is able to focus on task concerns. When groups do not have to spend excessive amounts of time on socioemotional concerns, then they can be more efficient in their work production.

Setting Group Goals

Remember that group members share common, interdependent goals. A **goal** is an objective that a group or individual strives to achieve. The goal refers to the outcome that the group or individual seeks. Goals can vary, depending on a variety of factors, including group culture and the personal needs of members.

At this point, it is important to distinguish between a goal and a task. A **task** is an action or activity that the group performs to help them reach a goal. Tasks can be initiated by a group member or assigned by a group leader. The goal of a class group might be to earn a B on their group presentation. To reach that goal, the group members perform tasks. For example, one task could be for two of the group members to conduct research on their presentation topic. That task helps to get them closer to the goal of earning a B.

There are several types of goals that a group can set.

Personal goals. Problems in the group can arise when personal goals conflict with group goals. A **personal goal** is an outcome that an individual group member strives to achieve. One group member may have a personal goal of earning an A in the course. Some other group members may be striving only for a C. Therefore, the group goal to achieve a B on the group presentation is in conflict with the personal goals of earning an A. Perhaps you or someone you know has been in a similar situation. What was the end result? Did you or the person you know compromise the personal goal or work to achieve something more than the group goal?

Group goals. There are two types of group goals—achievement goals and maintenance goals.

- **Achievement goal.** An **achievement goal** describes the outcome that the group intends to produce. The goal of earning a B on the group's final presentation is an achievement goal.

- **Maintenance goal.** A **maintenance goal** identifies an objective of the group to strengthen or maintain the group. For example, the group might have the maintenance goal of completing their assigned task with a satisfactory level of cooperation.

  There are three common examples of maintenance goals. First, the group may have the goal of keeping the group together through to the end of accomplishing its achievement goal. This is the most common maintenance goal. A second example is to ensure the continued existence of the group after the achievement goal is accomplished. Finally, the group may decide to strive to strengthen the group by seeking higher cohesiveness.

Like personal and group goals, achievement goals and maintenance goals can often come into conflict. In order to ensure the survival of the group, it might be necessary to balance both achievement and maintenance goals.

Clear and attainable goals. It is important that the group sets clear and attainable goals. If your group will continue to work together for a lengthy time period, your group might want to take long-term goals and break them into several short-term goals. The attainment of goals increases satisfaction in the group and thus group cohesiveness. Therefore, several short-term goals will give the group several chances to succeed.

Goals should be written and clearly worded so that all group members understand them. But most importantly, the goals should be achievable. Attempting to achieve a goal that is unattainable is setting up the group for failure.

Applying Concepts
DEVELOPING SKILLS

Identifying Group Goals

Choose a group from your list in which you are currently a member. List the goals of the group (if the group has no stated goals, list what you think the group would consider to be their goals). Now label each goal as task, personal, achievement, or maintenance.

Establishing Group Norms

Over time, groups develop **norms**, or informal rules, for general behavior and role expectations. Norms are not typically stated directly by members (as rules would be), but they are worded as rules (hence they are *informal*). Members become aware of group norms when someone violates that norm or makes an observation about it. You can witness the group's reaction to the norm violation for clues about the norm. If someone in the group wants to address the norm, then it is vocalized. But most norms are unstated. For example, if the norm is that group members can show up late to a meeting without punishment, then the norm is likely unstated. In other words, the group would not state a rule that members can show up to meetings whenever they feel like it. That would be unproductive. In this case, the unstated rule is the norm.

Categories of norms. There are two categories of norms that guide and regulate the behavior of group members.

- **General norms. General norms** direct the behavior of the group as a whole. Therefore, general norms apply to everyone in the group. For example, group members should arrive on time for meetings. (Remember that norms are stated as rules.) Here's another example: group members should be dressed professionally at meetings.

- **Role norms. Role norms** direct behavior for specific roles within the group. Therefore, the role norms pertain only to the individual(s) who performs that role in the group. For example, the group leader should create and distribute an agenda prior to the meeting.

8c

Confirming existence of norms. Norms are often created without the awareness of any of the group members. If norms exist at the subconscious level, then how do you know that they exist? As stated above, the violation of a norm and the members' reactions to that violation are the reason you know that the norm exists.

There are two factors you should note when looking for the existence of a norm: frequency and whether or not violating the norm is punished. Suppose that you notice that Shavon, your co-worker, routinely goes around to each cubicle in the morning to say hello to everyone. She does not get scolded for using company time to talk to co-workers. In the afternoon, Jayson does the same thing as Shavon. He is not scolded, either. Therefore, you note that this routine behavior is a norm for both Shavon and Jayson. They exhibit the behavior and are not punished.

When a person is scolded or ignored when exhibiting a behavior, you can infer that the person has broken a norm. Suppose that Juan doesn't talk to Shavon or Jayson when they make their cubicle rounds. Everyone else is glad to take a moment to talk to them except Juan. Co-workers begin to ignore Juan for being unwilling to participate in this cohesiveness-building behavior. Therefore, the norm is to talk to Shavon and Jayson. Evidence of this is the "punishment" of Juan for not talking to them.

8c

Applying Concepts
DEVELOPING SKILLS | Identifying Group Norms

Consider the group on your list in which your membership is most important. List two norms of that group. How do you know that they are norms?

Building Cohesiveness

Effective groups often are those in which group members work well together and identify with group goals. **Cohesiveness** describes the bonds among group members that provide a sense of togetherness. Group cohesiveness is based on the extent to which group members accept the group's goals as their own. If a group member is not interested in the project, he or she is not going to be excited about meeting and working. Such apathy could cause group cohesiveness to decrease. A group's level of cohesiveness can influence the happiness of group members and the effectiveness of the group's output.

Highly cohesive groups. Cohesive groups share positive characteristics that help them work effectively.

- **A sense of purpose.** The primary characteristic of a highly cohesive group is that the group has formed a strong sense of the purpose. The members share a commitment to the group's goals.
- **Informality.** Groups with higher levels of cohesiveness have more uninhibited group meetings. The members like each other and, therefore, can speak their minds openly and get away with teasing each other.
- **Willingness to help.** Members of highly cohesive groups are willing to help each other complete tasks.

Less cohesive groups. Less cohesive groups also share characteristics that make them less effective.

- **Politeness and apathy.** Groups with lower levels of cohesiveness exhibit more politeness and apathy. Remember that if the group does not take care of socioemotional concerns at the outset, then the group will be mired in politeness for the remainder of the group's existence. This also constrains the cohesiveness. If you are not comfortable with your group members, you will likely not feel as close to them. And, given that the group hasn't dealt with socioemotional concerns, there are weak bonds of togetherness.
- **Low socioemotional concerns.** Less cohesive groups include members who want to get the meeting over with quickly. The meetings focus on task concerns with little or no mention of socioemotional concerns. If members do talk about non-task concerns, they tend to choose safe topics, like the weather.
- **Little disagreement.** Members of less cohesive groups are less likely to disagree or argue. Why do you think that is the case? Consider the dynamics of the group. First, the group members are still stuck in the over-politeness of the formation phase. Therefore, the politeness can prevent arguments or disagreements. Second, if your group members do not want to be there, do you think they would disagree or cause an argument that might *prolong* the meeting? That's not likely. Blindly agreeing with whatever anyone says will get you home quicker.

How do you build and maintain cohesiveness?

- **Get to know group members at the first meeting.** Spending time getting to know each other will increase cohesiveness and reduce tension among group members.

- **Involve all group members.** During meetings, be sure to solicit the input of all group members. When people feel as though they are a part of the group process, they feel more connected to the group and produce quality work.

- **Allow group members to speak freely and openly.** Defensiveness in the group can stifle cohesiveness by damaging positive relationships between group members. When group members can be open-minded and considerate of one another's ideas and opinions, group cohesiveness will be positively affected.

- **Spend time before and after a meeting talking about non-group-related topics.** Engaging in conversations about non-group-related topics enhances your connections with other group members, thus increasing cohesiveness.

- **Make the group's goals your own goals.** When group members are invested in positive goal attainment, they are more likely to enjoy working in the group. This creates cohesiveness among members.

Cultural CONNECTIONS | Karaoke Builds Cohesiveness

In previous chapters, we have discussed differences between individualist and collectivist cultures. You may recall that the United States is considered an individualist culture because of its emphasis on competition and personal achievements. On the other side, Japan is considered a collectivist culture because of its emphasis on group achievement, which the Japanese believe is more important than individual achievements.

One aspect of the Japanese culture that illustrates their collectivist nature is the number and popularity of karaoke bars operating in Japan. Business associates are known to frequent karaoke bars after work as a means of releasing stress from work and enhancing group cohesiveness.

The karaoke bar enables group members to focus on socioemotional concerns and increases the personal ties among group members.

Application

Suppose that managers in U.S. companies decided to "encourage" workers to congregate after work at a karaoke bar. How would the workers react? If you have an office of 50 workers at a U.S. company, how many do you think would show up at the karaoke bar?

In light of the lack of co-worker karaoke, how do workers in U.S. companies create cohesiveness?

Establishing Group Norms and Building Group Cohesiveness

Of your list of groups, label each group as highly cohesive, moderately cohesive, or less cohesive. What about each group makes you label it as high, moderate or low in cohesiveness?

Regarding the groups that are less cohesive, what do you think caused the low cohesion? What could have been done differently to make the group more cohesive? Is there anything that can be done now, if the group still exists?

Regarding the highly cohesive groups, what created the high cohesion? Identify the behaviors or actions of the group that make it so cohesive.

Positive and Negative Effects of Group Conflict

In any group environment there is bound to be conflict among the group members.

8c

Positive effects of conflict. People tend to think of conflict in any context as a negative event. However, conflict in groups can be quite beneficial to the group's ability to reach its goals.

- **Conflict can lead to more openness.** Conflict can provide a way for the group to argue openly about a proposed solution to a problem or decision to handle a situation. The arguments should focus on the task and not on the person. In other words, provide constructive criticism of the idea instead of insulting or provoking the person suggesting it.

- **Conflict can stimulate group involvement.** Group conflict can stimulate involvement of group members in the discussion. When called to provide input in a conflict situation, group members become immersed in the conversation and are actively involved in the issue.

- **Conflict can enhance group cohesiveness.** Overcoming a negative environment created by conflict and coming to a mutually acceptable decision can increase group cohesiveness as members see the outcomes of their group participation.

Negative effects of conflict. As you might expect, there are also potential negative effects of group conflict.

- **Conflict can produce negative feelings.** Just as in interpersonal conflict, group conflict can produce negative feelings among members. When task conflicts become personal insults, relationships among members can be damaged irreparably.

- **Conflict can decrease group cohesiveness.** If the conflict lasts too long and turns too personal, conflict can decrease group cohesiveness. If several members no longer feel comfortable in group meetings, the feelings of togetherness are likely to suffer.

- **Conflict can lead to group dissolution.** Some groups are unable to handle the effects of the conflict. As a result, the group dissolves. The dissolution might occur when several group members drop the course they are enrolled in, or when employees quit in order to get away from the group.

EYEONETHICS | Trust in the Workplace

John and his group worked hard creating a new promotion package for his company's latest product launch. The group met with their boss, Susan, and she gave them exceptional compliments for their work. However, when they had a meeting with the company executives to present the promotion package, Susan started the presentation by claiming that *she* created the idea for the new promotion package. She knew that John's group was responsible for the idea.

According to an article by Marshall Loeb (December 2006), a survey by Lore International discovered that employees are more interested in trust and honesty in their co-workers than they are interested in being friends with their co-workers. Clearly Susan is not trustworthy. The survey also revealed that poor interpersonal communication skills can hinder success in the workplace.

As you can imagine, John and his group were quite angry as they sat there listening to Susan take all the credit for *their* hard work.

Application

What should John's group do? Is there an ethical way to respond in this type of situation? Has Susan damaged the cohesiveness of John's group? Would such a situation increase or decrease the cohesion in John's group? Can John's group respond in a way that would change the cohesiveness of the group? How should they respond?

8d Distinguishing Between Problem Solving and Decision Making

Some people use "problem solving" and "decision making" interchangeably when discussing group work. However, there is a slight distinction between the two processes.

Decision making is the process of choosing among options that already exist. One of the most important reasons we form groups is to make decisions. When several people work on something together, they can make more creative decisions.

On the other hand, **problem solving** is a multistep process used by a group to create a plan to move from an undesirable state to a predetermined goal. When a group engages in problem solving, the group members may make many decisions in creating a solution. Therefore, one distinction between the two concepts is that decision making is a component of problem solving. A second distinction is that problem solving involves the creation of solutions while decision making involves deciding between options that already exist.

8e Effective Group Problem Solving

Problem solving is a bit more structured and complex than decision making. In fact, as stated earlier, decision making is often a component of problem solving.

Understanding the Process of Problem Solving

When a group is faced with the need to create an effective solution to a problem, group members should proceed with the following aspects of a problem in mind.

- **A problem represents** *an undesirable present situation.* When a group meets to solve a problem, the group members must be able to identify the undesirable aspect(s) of the current situation.

- **When a problem is identified, the group should specify** *a goal for eliminating the undesirable present situation.* The goal is the desired situation that will eliminate the undesirable one. The group should identify that goal.

- **The group should** *identify obstacles to reaching the goal.* An obstacle is anything that impedes creating or implementing a solution. Obstacles can include financial constraints, lack of necessary skills, and lack of public support.

Dewey's Problem Solving Model

In his celebrated book *How We Think*, published in 1910, John Dewey argued that decision making should be a logical, orderly process. His "Steps to Reflective Thinking" have provided one of the most useful, and we think one of the best, approaches to problem solving. Authors and theorists differ in their adaptations of the reflective thinking model, organizing it around five, six, or seven steps. We prefer a seven-step approach.

It is important that you go through these steps chronologically and not jump ahead in your discussion. Solutions are best discussed and evaluated only after a problem is thoroughly defined and analyzed. Keep in mind that some problems will require research and work that can take weeks or months outside of meetings for each of these steps.

Step One: Define the problem. Before you can solve a problem, you must first define it. By defining the key terms of the problem, group members decide how they will focus the topic, enabling them to keep on track and to avoid extraneous discussion. Suppose your college asks you to be part of a student advisory committee to address the issue "What can be done to alleviate the lack of parking on campus?" To answer the question, members must agree on what constitutes "lack of parking." Are there too few parking spaces? Is the problem how the spaces are designated—for example, is there adequate parking for faculty, but not for students? Is the problem not the number of spaces, but the condition of the parking lots? How your group defines the problem determines, to a large extent, how you will solve it. If you have determined that there is no problem with the condition of the lots or the number of spaces for faculty, you can safely delete these considerations from your discussion agenda.

Step Two: Analyze the problem. In analyzing any problem, a group looks at both its symptoms and causes. We gauge the severity of a problem by examining its *symptoms*. For example, the group needs to know not only the approximate number of students unable to find parking spaces, but also why it is detrimental. For instance students may be late for class or avoid using campus resources; or the students may fear for their safety walking to dimly lit and distant parking spaces. These symptoms point to the magnitude of the problem. Certainly, some symptoms are more serious than others, and group members must identify those needing immediate action.

However, the group is still not ready to propose remedies. The group must now consider the *causes* of the problem. By examining how a difficulty developed, a group may find its solution. The parking problem may stem from a variety of causes, including increased enrollment, inadequate use of distant parking lots, and some parking spaces earmarked for faculty and administrators.

Step Three: Determine the criteria for the optimal solution. Decision-making criteria are the standards we use to judge the merits of the proposed solutions. It is wise to state these criteria before discussing the solutions. Why select an action plan only to discover later that sufficient funding is unavailable? The group studying campus parking worked to avoid this pitfall. Some of the criteria they considered were as follows:

Criteria	Explanation
Economics	The proposal should be cost effective.
Aesthetics	The proposal should not spoil the beauty of the campus.
Growth	The proposal should account for future increases in enrollment.
Security	Students should feel safe as they go to and from parking lots.

The group could also have considered ranking parking privileges according to student seniority or giving students parking status equal to faculty.

Step Four: Propose solutions. Only after completing the first three steps is the group ready to propose solutions. This is essentially a brainstorming step with emphasis on the quantity, not quality, of suggestions. At this stage, the group should not worry about evaluating any suggested solutions, no matter how farfetched they may seem. This group's brainstorming list included the following:

Build a multistory parking lot in the center of campus

Construct parking lots near the edge of campus

Light and patrol lots in the evening

Initiate bus service between apartment complexes and the campus

Encourage students to carpool or to ride bicycles to campus

Step Five: Evaluate proposed solutions. Now the group is ready to evaluate each proposed solution using the criteria listed in the third step. First, the group considers the advantages of the proposed solution, and then they assess its disadvantages. For instance the centrally located, high-rise parking garage may not be cost effective and may intrude on the beauty of the campus, but it may use valuable land efficiently and limit the extent of late-night walking.

Step Six: Select a solution. After evaluating each proposed solution, you and your fellow group members should have a good idea of those solutions to exclude from consideration and those to retain. You will then weigh the merits and deficiencies of each. Your final solution may be a combination of several of the proposed remedies. For example, the group working on the campus parking problem could issue a final report advocating a two-phase solution: short-range and long-range goals. A short-range approach may involve converting a little-used athletic practice field to a parking facility, creating more bicycle parking areas, and encouraging carpools. The proposal for the long range could involve building a well-lit multistory parking facility, not in the middle of campus, but near the athletic complex, to be used during the week for general student parking and on weekends for athletic and entertainment events.

Step Seven: Suggest strategies for implementing the solution.

Once the small group has worked out a solution, members would normally submit their recommendations to another body for approval, action, and implementation. Sometimes, however, decision makers should not only select feasible and effective solutions, but also show how they can be implemented. How would the small group incorporate suggestions for implementing its solution? Members would probably recommend coordinating their plan with the long-range master plan for the college. Other administrators would have to be included. The group would probably also suggest a timetable detailing short- and long-range projects and might also identify possible funding sources.

In summary, the reflective thinking model enables a group to define a problem, analyze it, determine the criteria for a good solution, propose solutions, evaluate solutions, select a solution, and suggest ways to implement it. Decisions made by following this process are generally effective, and group members are satisfied with their work. Not only can this model benefit groups in business, government, education, and other organizations, it can also improve your individual decision making.

8e

Applying Concepts
DEVELOPING SKILLS

Using the Reflective Thinking Model

Consider the steps in the reflective thinking model. Can you identify any situations in which using an abbreviated version of the model might be more appropriate? Which steps would be more expendable in those situations?

8f Effective Group Decision Making

Groups need to have a plan when it comes to decision making, and it should include an organized and thoughtful discussion of the issue(s). There are several principles of effective group decision making. If your group recognizes the importance of these principles and implements them into its decision-making process, the group's decision will be more effective.

Group decision making is a shared responsibility. Group decision making requires the active participation of *all* members performing mutually reinforcing responsibilities. The presence of a group leader does not necessarily establish a leader-follower association or even an active-passive association. The relationship is usually better represented as a partnership.

Group decision making requires a clear understanding of goals. Every group has a goal. Sometimes that goal is predetermined. In your career, you may be part of a small group having the task of studying specific job-related problems and proposing workable solutions. In this instance, the group has a clear statement of its objective. In other situations, the goal of your group may be less clear. If that is the case, you will have to clarify, specify, or even determine your goals.

Group decision making benefits from a clear but flexible agenda. Every group needs a plan of action. Because a group's process affects its product, it is vital that members spend sufficient time generating an action plan. The best plan, or agenda, is one not dictated by the leader, but rather one developed by both the leader and the members of the group.

A group's agenda should be both specific and flexible. Group participants must know what is expected of them and how they will go about accomplishing the task at hand. Groups also need to be flexible as they pursue their goals. Unexpected obstacles may require revising the agenda. The group needs a backup plan.

Group decision making is enhanced by open communication. If all members of a group think alike, there would be no need for the group. One person could simply make the decision. Diversity encourages alternative perspectives. Both the group leader and individual members should protect and encourage the expression of minority views.

Groups should avoid groupthink, a term coined by Irving Janis (1982). **Groupthink** is a phenomenon that limits open communication and adversely

8f

affects the quality of decision making when group members fail to exercise independent judgment. Groupthink occurs when group members come to care more about conforming to the group and "not making waves" than they do about exercising the critical evaluation necessary to weed out bad ideas.

Group decision making requires adequate information. Access to information that is sufficient and relevant is extremely important. A group suffers if its information is based on the research of only one or two of its members. To avoid this problem, a group should follow a few simple steps.

1. The leader should provide essential information to the group as a starting point.

2. Each member of the group should contribute critical knowledge to the group.

3. The group should divide the gathering of information in a way that is efficient and yet provides some overlap.

Applying Concepts
DEVELOPING SKILLS

Identifying Decision Making Principles in Your Groups

Make a list of the various groups to which you belong or have belonged. Keep in mind that your previous group experiences are not limited to formal work groups or class-assigned groups; they may include family, clubs, and organizations (such as church groups, fraternities and sororities, honor groups, and professional groups). From your list, identify a situation in which your group engaged in decision making. Which of the principles listed in this section are you able to identify in that decision-making process? Have you ever been in a group that fell victim to groupthink? If so, what were the causes for and results of the groupthink?

Identifying Stages of Group Decision Making

Suppose you are in a group that has become focused on arguing about potential outcomes in the decision-making process. Each person has his or her own idea of how to decide on an option. You are getting nervous because you cannot see how the conflict is productive. In order to understand better the dynamics of group communication and decision making, it is important to examine the stages of group decision making.

Orientation. In the first stage, **orientation**, group members familiarize themselves with the task. This is similar to the formation phase of group development in that group members spend some time getting to know each other in addition to learning about their task.

Conflict. As they begin discussing the situation and suggesting solutions, the group members reach the **conflict stage**. In this phase, conflict is not necessarily negative. Conflict can produce better results as group members provide constructive criticism regarding proposed solutions. Group members should discuss openly the issue and the potential solutions to avoid groupthink.

Decision emergence. In the next stage, **decision emergence**, the group members begin to formulate a solution to the situation. At this point, they are able to move toward a decision. The decision is solidified and agreed upon in this stage.

Reinforcement. Finally, the **reinforcement stage** is the aftermath of the group; the group members reinforce their ability to come to a decision and to reach their primary goal. Group members leave with a positive feeling of accomplishment.

Unless under time pressure, most groups will exhibit these four stages of group decision making. However, the amount of time spent in each phase will depend on the nature of the situation being discussed and the composition of the group (experiences, expertise, and so forth).

Exploring Decision-Making Methods

There are a number of ways groups can come to a decision. These methods range from acceptance of the decision by everyone to acceptance by only a few (or one) group members.

Consensus. **Consensus** occurs when group members are willing to support a given decision or solution. Although, the purest form of consensus exists when there is unequivocal and unanimous support for the decision, unanimity is not necessary for consensus. Members may support a decision even though it is not their first choice. But, they accept that the decision is the best one possible.

An advantage of consensus is that the decision can be considered high quality because all members were in agreement. There is also a high level of group member commitment to and satisfaction with the outcome. Can you think of a disadvantage to consensus agreement? It is quite time consuming to get every member of the group to agree with one decision or solution. Additionally, the group can experience a lot of frustration as they attempt to gain consensus agreement. If you know that your group must come to a consensus agreement on the outcome or solution, then the group would be well-served to spend additional time in the brainstorming stage to come up with all possible solutions. The more solutions generated, the more likely the group will find a solution for which everyone can agree.

Majority rule. **Majority rule** occurs when the group votes and the solution chosen by the largest number of group members is suggested to be implemented. An advantage of majority rule is that it is less time consuming than a consensus vote. If there are only a couple of members who are against a solution, then the group can move on if the majority of the group is for the solution. A disadvantage of majority rule is that members who represent the minority vote may be disgruntled with the group and/or the solution chosen.

Minority rule. The opposite of majority rule is **minority rule**, in which a small number of group members make decisions for the whole group. This is most common in committee work in which a few members work on a particular project. For example, when a company has an annual company picnic, the entire employee base of the company is not in on the decision making regarding the planning of the picnic. Instead, a small group of employees is likely in charge of finding a date, location, and so forth. An advantage of minority rule, as you can see from this example, is that you do not have to call the entire group or committee (or all company employees) to a meeting. A disadvantage is that having only a few members make decisions can stifle creativity.

Expert opinion. There are two decision-making methods that involve only one person: expert opinion and authority rule. **Expert opinion** occurs when someone who is considered an expert on the topic makes the decision for the group. This is beneficial in a group in which there is little time to educate the group members about the intricacies of the situation. For example, in many crisis situations, an expert is identified to make decisions quickly and thoughtfully. If you put a group of people in this same situation, they may have a hard time efficiently creating a satisfactory decision. A disadvantage of expert opinion is similar to the disadvantage of minority rule—too little input in the decision or solution can lead to a flawed outcome.

Authority rule. Lastly, there is **authority rule** in which a decision is made by the group leader rather than the entire or majority of the group. Similar to expert opinion, authority rule allows a decision to be made quickly. Another benefit is that authority rule can prevent an unnecessary meeting, especially if the decision is one that does not require a group vote. A disadvantage of authority rule is that the decision made by the leader may not be considered satisfactory and, thus, is not accepted by the group.

CHOOSING THE BEST DECISION MAKING METHOD

Consensus	Majority Rule	Minority Rule	Expert Opinion	Authority Rule
How many people must be involved in making the decision?				
If, in order to remain motivated, all of the group members need to be in favor of a decision to make it successful, then *consensus* is best.	When only a majority of group members need to agree, you can use *majority rule*.	If the situation arises in which a small number of group members can make a decision, such as a committee, then you can use *minority rule*.	If the situation arises in which a trusted expert can make a decision for the group, then you can use *expert opinion*.	In situations in where the group leader can make a decision so that the entire group need not meet, he or she can handle such decisions, thus using *authority rule*.
How quickly does the decision need to be made?				
If a decision needs to be made quickly, consensus may not be appropriate.	If the group members must participate in the decision making, then *majority rule* may be better than consensus.	If the decision needs to be made quickly, but the leader is unavailable or delegates the decision to group members, then *minority rule* can be used.	If the decision needs to be made quickly, but the leader is unavailable or delegates the decision to group members, then *expert opinion* can be used.	If the decision needs to be made quickly and the issue is simple and does not require others to participate, then *authority rule* can be used.

8f

Applying Concepts
DEVELOPING SKILLS

Examining Group Decision Making and Choosing the Best Method

Suppose that you are asked to participate in a group that is charged with determining the most effective security plan for your campus. Your group consists of three undergraduate students and three professors—all from your college. Three options have been presented to your group: the installation of security cameras at the entrances of all campus buildings and dorms, metal detectors at the entrances of all campus buildings and dorms, and randomly placed security cameras (not necessarily focused just on the entrances of buildings).

How would the principles of decision making affect the way that the group should proceed? How would you envision the group moving through the stages of group decision making? Which of the decision-making methods would be most appropriate for this type of decision?

Competence SUMMARY

In this chapter, you have learned the following concepts. Check to be sure you have achieved each of the communication competencies.

8a Introduction to Group Communication

8b Identifying Types of Groups

- To be classified as a group, the members must possess interdependent goals, typically have a time frame for existence, and usually have an assigned or assumed leader.

- Effective group communication is important to organizations. It also serves several personal needs, which is a reason that we join groups.

- Groups can be classified as primary and secondary.

Competence. Can I identify the needs that I could have fulfilled by my inclusion in groups? Can I distinguish between the types of groups that exist?

8c Understanding Group Culture

- Group cultures are never static. The norms, roles, cohesiveness, and rules and patterns of interaction can change and adapt through communication.

- One way to examine group communication is to look at the phases of group development—formation phase and production phase. In the formation phase, group members are concerned with socioemotional concerns, or getting to know each other. In the production phase, the group's attention turns to task concerns, or their assigned task(s).

- At the outset, a group should set goals. Goals are objectives that the group strives to achieve. Goals can be categorized as task, personal, achievement, and maintenance.

- Groups develop norms over time. Norms are informal rules that dictate appropriate behavior and role responsibilities within the group.

- Every group has its own group culture. Group culture is the personality and beliefs of the group. The group culture is determined by roles, norms, cohesiveness, rules that guide interactions, and patterns of interaction.

- Group cohesiveness is the bonds among group members that provide a sense of togetherness. Cohesiveness is based on the extent to which individual group members accept the group's goals as their own.

- Conflict can prevent groupthink or ineffective problem solving, stimulate the involvement of group members, and enhance group cohesiveness. On the other hand, conflict can produce negative feelings among group members, decrease group cohesiveness (if the conflict drags on), and dissolve the group.

Competence. Do I know how groups progress through phases of development? Can I help my group set attainable goals? Can I explain how cohesiveness affects a group? Could I identify the positive and negative outcomes of group conflict?

8d Distinguishing Between Problem Solving and Decision Making

- Decision making is the process of choosing among options that already exist.

- Problem solving involves a group using a multistep procedure to create a plan to move from an undesired state to a predetermined goal.

Competence. Do I understand the difference between decision making and problem solving?

8e Effective Group Problem Solving

- Groups should investigate whether any restrictions might be imposed on their ability to create a solution to a problem. Restrictions could include task difficulty, multiple solutions, intrinsic interest, cooperative requirements, familiarity with the population, technical requirements, and freedom.

- Dewey's reflective thinking model outlines seven steps to effective problem solving: define the problem, analyze the problem, determine criteria for the optimal solution, propose solutions, evaluate the proposed solutions, select a solution, and suggest strategies for implementing the solution.

Competence. Do I know the restrictions that might exist when creating a solution to a problem? Can I explain the seven-step process of effective problem solving?

8f Effective Group Decision Making

- Decision making is a component of problem solving.

- Decision making is a shared responsibility that requires a clear understanding of group goals, a clear but flexible agenda, open communication, and adequate information.

- Groups make decisions in four stages: orientation, conflict, decision emergence, and reinforcement stages.

- There are many ways a group can come to a decision—consensus, majority rule, minority rule, expert opinion, and authority rule.

Competence. Can I identify the four stages of decision making? Can I explain the different ways that groups can come to a decision?

Review Questions

1. What are the two types of groups? Give one example of each of those types.
2. Explain group culture.
3. Discuss the creation of goals and include in your answer the four different types of goals.
4. What is a group norm? Provide an example of a possible group norm.
5. How do highly cohesive groups differ from groups low in cohesiveness?
6. List the positive and negative effects of conflict in groups.
7. What is the difference between problem solving and decision making?
8. List three characteristics of problems that groups should consider when engaging in problem solving.
9. Explain the difference between consensus and majority rule.

Discussion Questions

1. What are some ways in which you could change a group's culture?
2. Are there situations in which a group might be more productive with low cohesiveness? Explain your answer.
3. How does group conflict differ from interpersonal conflict?
4. Can a group be successful without going through all of the phases of group decision making? Why or why not?

Key Terms

achievement goal *p. 187*

authority rule *p. 202*

cohesiveness *p. 189*

conflict stage *p. 200*

consensus *p. 200*

decision emergence *p. 200*

decision making *p. 194*

expert opinion *p. 201*

formation phase *p. 186*

general norms *p. 188*

goal *p. 186*

group communication *p. 181*

group culture *p. 185*

groupthink *p. 198*

maintenance goal *p. 187*

majority rule *p. 201*

minority rule *p. 201*

norms *p. 188*

orientation *p. 200*

personal goal *p. 187*

primary groups *p. 184*

problem solving *p. 194*

production phase *p. 186*

reinforcement-stage *p. 200*

role norms *p. 188*

secondary groups *p. 184*

task *p. 187*

Managing Group Communication Apprehension

In previous modules, we have talked about communication apprehension (CA) in general (a feeling of anxiety about interacting with others). A general anxiety in all communication settings is called **trait apprehension**.

We have also previously identified two other types of communication apprehension: situation-specific and context-specific apprehension. We discussed situation-specific and context-specific apprehension in terms of interpersonal communication settings.

Another type of communication apprehension is called **audience-specific apprehension**. People who experience this type of CA experience anxiety depending on the audience involved in the setting. You might find that being in class-related groups with peers makes you anxious; someone else may be more anxious in groups of peers in the workplace.

EFFECTS OF GROUP MEMBER COMMUNICATION APPREHENSION ON GROUPS

Several researchers have conducted studies to determine how group members who have high group CA influence groups. McCroskey and Richmond (1988) suggest that members who have high group CA can be more detrimental to a group than high-CA people in other contexts.

Group members with high CA tend to participate less in group interactions (Sorensen & McCroskey, 1977). However, not all high-CA people respond to anxiety through shyness. Some group members will participate in group meetings by making comments that are off-topic (McCroskey & Wright, 1971), with the alleged purpose of creating an impression that they are not able to be productive members of the group.

Jensen and Chilberg (1991) summarized findings regarding high-CA group members. High-CA members are less likely to provide information or to seek information in group meetings. McCroskey and Richmond (1988) noted that high-CA group members make more irrelevant comments during group meetings.

High-CA members are more likely to engage in task-oriented discussions and less likely to engage in socially oriented discussions. Given the characteristics that we have already attributed to high-CA group members, the fact that they are less likely to participate in socially oriented discussions should not be surprising. The high-CA member is concerned with completing the tasks of the group in order to end association with the group. Thus, the high-CA member is more likely to partake in task-oriented discussions to move the group toward its end goal.

Despite their desire to engage in task-oriented discussion rather than socially oriented discussion, high-CA group members are not well suited for brainstorming. Their social reticence prevents them from engaging in the brainstorming process. If your group has a member who is high CA, Jablin (1981) recommends that the group use brainstorming techniques that require individual list-making first followed by group list-making.

According to McCroskey and Richmond (1988), high-CA group members are less likely to express strong agreement with other group member(s).

INFLUENCE OF LEADERSHIP ON GROUP MEMBER COMMUNICATION APPREHENSION

According to Bass (1981), leaders of a group serve two functions: initiation of task structure and consideration behaviors. Initiation of task structure involves the ability of the leader to keep the group on task. Consideration behaviors are those used by the leader to encourage group members as they work on their task, but also to encourage a healthy socioemotional group environment.

McCroskey (1982) reported factors that are thought to be associated with high communication apprehension: novelty, subordinate status, and degree of evaluation. Hawkins and Stewart (1990) combined Bass's two leader functions with McCroskey's factors contributing to high CA to see how leader functions serve to reduce or enhance group member communication apprehension.

Novelty

Novelty, or the uniqueness of the task or situation, can raise anyone's anxiety level. There is always some measure of uncertainty present when people face a task or situation that is unfamiliar. Once the task requirements become familiar to a group, apprehension created by novelty will be reduced. According to Hawkins and Stewart (1990), leaders who promote task structure by imposing guidelines and providing a vision for how the task will be accomplished will be able to reduce group member apprehension stemming from novelty of the task or situation.

Subordinate Status

Subordinate status relates to how group members (especially the leader) treat each other. Do your group members communicate with you as if you are an equal? Does one person in the group exert control by talking down to the other group members? You can also put yourself in a subordinate role by feeling as if you are not as competent or intelligent as your group members. If you are putting yourself in the subordinate role, then you need to re-examine your personal beliefs and picture yourself as a valuable group member. Every member of the group is valuable. Leaders who exhibit high levels of consideration encourage group members and reinforce the value of each member's contribution to the group.

Degree of Evaluation

Finally, the degree of evaluation involves how your leader and fellow group members judge your contributions. This may be a more prominent reason for a person to experience group communication apprehension. If someone evaluates your contribution (either a verbal contribution of an idea or a completed task assignment) negatively, you receive that negative evaluation in front of others. Such a situation can be much more intimidating than if your boss negatively evaluated you in a private meeting. As suggested above, you should consider constructive criticism to be positive feedback. You can learn from constructive criticism, which is often the point of the group work in the first place. A group leader who exhibits high consideration behaviors and high task structure can help to guide group members in their individual achievements with less threat of negative evaluation.

In summary, Hawkins and Stewart (1990) determined that leaders who can balance initiation of task structure with consideration behaviors will be most productive in reducing communication apprehension among their group members. Above all, McCroskey (1982) noted that over time group member communication apprehension will dissipate as a result of continued interactions with group members.

MANAGING GROUP COMMUNICATION APPREHENSION

Following are 4 practical tips that can help you manage your group communication apprehension.

Practicing for Success

Systematic desensitization is a method in which you engage in the activity that creates anxiety until you become less anxious in situations that involve that activity. For example, you could engage in small group activities to help lessen your group apprehension. Your instructor may provide several opportunities throughout the course for you to work on small activities with a group of classmates. Those activities are designed to help you learn group communication concepts, but also to make you more comfortable in a group setting.

Understanding the Group Process

By learning how communication creates and sustains a group, you may find some comfort in knowing that group communication is the foundation of any group. For a group to be successful, members must contribute to the task output and the socioemotional output of the group. Your contributions toward both are an integral component in the group process. Therefore, if your group communication apprehension originates

from thoughts that you have nothing to contribute to a group, you are wrong. You are just as important to your group as any other member.

Enhancing Your Communication Competence

Throughout this textbook, we have provided numerous opportunities to test your communication skills and work toward enhancing your communication competence. Competent communicators are able to successfully navigate communication interactions regardless of context. This does not mean that competent communicators are always successful, but rather, they are confident in their ability to communicate effectively, and therefore feel less communication apprehension.

Being Prepared

Some people exhibit situational apprehension in groups when they are not prepared for meetings. One way to ease your group communication apprehension is to be prepared for each meeting. If you were given a task, be sure to complete it prior to the meeting. Having to tell a group that you failed to accomplish the assigned task can make anyone apprehensive. An easy way to alleviate one form of apprehension is simple: be prepared!

Applying Concepts
DEVELOPING SKILLS

Overcoming Group Communication Anxiety

Suppose that you have a group member who has high group communication apprehension. You are involved in a group project for your class that requires every member of the group to participate in the delivery of the presentation. Based on the techniques you learned in this module, how would you help that group member overcome his or her anxiety?

MANAGING YOUR GROUP COMMUNICATION APPREHENISION

Practicing for Success	Systematic desensitization allows you to engage in short activities in groups to reduce your anxiety over time.
Understanding the Group Process	Knowing how a group functions and the value of each group member and his or her contributions should reduce apprehension caused by feelings of inadequacy.
Enhancing Your Communication Competence	Learning how to communicate more competently can give you more confidence in any communication setting, including small group interactions.
Be Prepared	Accomplish individual tasks on time and come to meetings prepared to discuss agenda items.

KEY TERMS

audience-specific
  apprehension *p. 207*

systematic desensitization *p. 209*
trait apprehension *p. 207*

Working Effectively in Groups

In this chapter, you will learn about the roles of group members, the role of the leader, how to run effective meetings, and the use of power by group members. Your communication competence will be enhanced by understanding:

- how being an effective group member can enable your group to be successful;
- the responsibilities to a group as a leader and as a group member;
- ways to make a meeting productive (as a group member or as the leader) so that everyone is more interested in attending the meetings;
- why some power bases are met with compliance while others are met with resistance.

9a Being an Effective Group Member

Until now, we have been focusing on identifying and understanding the functions of groups and group communication. Now we will shift the focus to the people in the group. Each group member takes on a role within the group. A **role** is a set of behaviors that serve a particular function within a group. Roles are determined by an individual's personality traits, abilities, and communication competence, but roles are also dependent on the needs of the group and the traits and abilities of the other group members.

When the group is forming, roles emerge. As members get to know each other and begin discussing their goal(s), behaviors enacted by the group members shape the roles each group member will later assume. Therefore, roles develop through the interaction among group members.

Task Functions

Roles are developed through behaviors. Thus we will identify three functions of behaviors in group interaction. Some behaviors serve a **task function** and affect the task output of the group. *Summarizing* decisions made or task assignments is a behavior that serves a task function. Another function is *information giving*, offering facts and research relevant to the group's task.

Summarizing. "Okay, we have decided that Matt is going to find some newspaper articles about recycling on campus and Susan is going to interview the facility management folks to find out how much less trash would be produced with a campus recycling program."

Information giving. "We have a recycling program in my hometown. Every house and apartment gets three blue plastic boxes: one for glass, one for plastic, and one for cans. The fact that the town picks up the recycling once a week really encourages people to recycle."

Maintenance Functions

Behaviors that serve a **maintenance function** are those that influence the interpersonal relationships among group members and the overall climate of the group. *Tension-relieving* behaviors serve to decrease any negativity or aggravation in the group. Telling jokes is a tension-relieving behavior. *Gatekeeping* is another function that allows a group member to make sure every group member has a chance to speak.

Tension-relieving behavior. "This discussion is lasting a little longer than expected and everyone is getting cranky. Let's take a break for a few minutes."

Gatekeeping. "Sally, you have been trying to get in your opinion. Was there something you wanted to add to the discussion?"

Task and maintenance behaviors are beneficial for the group. Both of them enable the group to work toward its goal(s) and to function effectively.

Self-centered Functions

Self-centered functions often represent a hidden agenda on the part of the person exhibiting the behavior. Self-centered behaviors alleviate one group member's personal unmet needs at the expense of the entire group. Three types of self-centered behaviors are withdrawing, blocking, and status and recognition seeking.

Withdrawing. Withdrawing from a group occurs verbally and/or nonverbally. Verbally withdrawing occurs when a person ceases to contribute to the discussion. Nonverbal withdrawal cues can include leaning back or slouching in a chair, scowling, and not maintaining eye contact with other group members. You are likely to see withdrawing behaviors when conflict arises in the group. Some people prefer to avoid confrontation, and, thus, will withdraw from the interaction to avoid the conflict.

Blocking. Blocking occurs when a group member continues to raise objections with the purpose of preventing the group from progressing in its task completion. Blockers are not devil's advocates. A devil's advocate raises a legitimate, potential problem in order for the group to anticipate glitches in its plans.

Status and recognition seeking. The third self-centered function is status and recognition seeking. A person who needs to feel important might boast about accomplishments, such as a recent test score. The person might also talk about a close mentoring relationship with the professor. These statements divert attention from the group's topic to the self-centered group member.

Of course, it is possible that a person's behavior can have both task and maintenance functions. Consider the following example. Can you identify the functions?

> We have heard from Mark, Susan, and Ryan who are in favor of pursuing the goal of getting a dorm recycling program started. However, we haven't heard from Sally. Sally, are you in favor of this idea?

In this statement, the speaker is summarizing the proceedings of the meeting thus far (a task function), including the fact that Sally has not yet spoken. Therefore, the speaker uses gatekeeping behavior to be sure that Sally's opinion is heard.

It is also possible that, at first, a person's behavior could be labeled as a task or maintenance function but later be interpreted as a self-centered function. Suppose that one group member is an information giver in the first meeting. You might leave that meeting thinking that the person has provided a lot of valuable information. In subsequent meetings, the same group member continues the information-giving behavior, but doesn't allow other group members the opportunity to talk. Therefore, what was once considered a positive task behavior is now seen as a negative blocking or status/recognition-seeking behavior.

The Responsibilities of Group Members

Often group members assume that only the group leader has responsibilities within the group. In fact, group members also have important responsibilities. Whether your group is a self-directed group or a body of members with a traditional leader, the ideal leader-member relationship is not an active-passive partnership. To enhance the quality of the group's product, all members must participate actively. What do group members do? If you reflect on our example of the group tackling the campus parking problem, you can see how these group members handled their responsibilities.

Productive group members undertake five key responsibilities.

Inform the group. Group members should enlarge the information base on which decisions are made and action is taken. A decision is only as good as the information on which it is based. If the group does not know all the causes of a problem, for example, its proposed solution may not solve it. The greater the number of possible solutions a group considers, the greater its chance of selecting the best one.

You enlarge the group's information base in two ways.

- **Contributing knowledge.** You contribute what you already know about the issue being discussed. Hearsay information is worth mentioning at this stage, as long as you acknowledge that it is something you have heard but cannot prove. Another member may be able to confirm or refute it, or it can be put on the agenda for further research. It is important to dispel popular misconceptions so that they do not contaminate the decision-making process.

- **Contributing information.** Group members contribute to a group's understanding of a topic by gathering additional relevant information. Ideas surfacing during a group meeting may help shape the agenda for the next meeting. You may hear ideas that you want to explore further. You may need to check out facts before the group can clarify the dimensions of a problem or adopt a particular plan of action. The research and thought you give to a topic before a meeting will make a meeting itself more efficient and productive.

Advocate personal beliefs. Group members should not only provide information to help make decisions, but they also should use that data to develop positions on the issues being discussed. Participants should be willing to state and defend their opinions. A good participant is open-minded, though—willing to offer ideas and then revise or retract them as additional facts and expert opinion surface. Your opinions may change as they are challenged throughout the discussion.

Question other participants. Effective participants not only give but also seek information and opinions. Knowing how and when to ask an appropriate question is an important skill. As one advertisement claims, "When you ask better questions, you tend to come up with better answers." Asking effective questions requires active listening, sensitivity to the feelings of others, and a desire to learn. Group members should seek clarification of ideas they do not understand and encourage others to explain, defend, and extend their ideas.

Evaluate ideas and proposals. Too often we either accept what we hear at face value or remain silent even though we disagree with what is said. Yet challenging facts, opinions, and proposals benefits the quality of discussion. It is the group's obligation to evoke a range of positions on the issue being discussed and then separate the good ideas from the bad. Each idea should be discussed thoroughly and analyzed critically. A decision based on incorrect information or faulty reasoning may be ineffective or even counterproductive. Thus, all group members are obligated to evaluate the contributions of others and to submit their own positions to rigorous testing. This is sometimes difficult to do. Yet participants should not be defensive about their ideas, but instead be open to constructive criticism.

Support and monitor other group members. A group is a collection of individuals having different personalities. Some may be less assertive than others and may have fragile egos. Reluctant to express their ideas because they fear criticism, they may cause the group to lose important information and to rush into a decision. They may even foster the groupthink we discussed earlier. In addition to providing support for reticent individuals, members should also take note of possible dysfunctional, self-oriented behaviors that impede the group's progress.

Ronald Adler and Jeanne Elmhorst (1999) describe some of these roles and behaviors:

- The *blocker*. Prevents progress by constantly raising objections.
- The *attacker*. Aggressively questions the competence or motives of others.
- The *recognition seeker*. Repeatedly and unnecessarily calls attention to self by relating irrelevant experiences, boasting, and seeking sympathy.
- The *joker*. Engages in joking behavior in excess of tension-relieving needs, distracting others.
- The *withdrawer*. Refuses to take a stand on social or task issues; covers up feelings; does not respond to others' comments.

The climate of the group should encourage openness and acceptance. It is the job of both the leader and the group members to create and reinforce this climate.

Applying Concepts
DEVELOPING SKILLS

Identifying Group Member Roles in Your Group

Think of a group to which you currently belong or previously belonged. List the first names of all of the members (or those with whom you are closest). What role does each person play in the group? How does each role influence the communication and productivity of your group? Is there a group member who exhibits a disruptive role? What might you do to make that role more productive?

9b Being an Effective Group Leader

A **leader** influences people and their behaviors. Group leaders can be assigned or assumed. **Assigned leaders** are appointed by someone outside of the group. Your boss or your professor might assign someone to be the leader of your group. **Assumed leaders** are those who emerge from the communication within the group. Also known as emergent leaders, assumed leaders often experience more respect and compliance from the group members because they chose their leader rather than having one imposed on them.

Leadership involves communication that modifies or influences the behaviors of others in order to accomplish a common group goal. By incorporating the accomplishment of a goal in the definition of leadership, we are excluding from the definition any group member who attempts to influence one member in hopes of sabotaging the group.

Why is leadership important? Leadership can be an important component of group success. An effective leader can influence group members to want to succeed in attaining the group goal. For the individual, leadership can provide a boost of self-esteem, especially if the group is successful. Leadership provides an opportunity to enhance personal communication competence.

Applying Concepts DEVELOPING SKILLS | Identifying Leadership Characteristics

Construct a brief list of the characteristics that you would attribute to a good leader. What characteristics did you include? Refer to your list as you read about the different approaches to leadership.

Approaches to Leadership

Over time, many approaches to leading a group have evolved. Initially, there was a belief that leaders were born and, thus, had certain similar characteristics. However, there is no one best way to lead a group. Leadership approaches can vary depending on the situation. You'll see some examples of that below.

Trait approach. When researchers started examining leadership, they began by considering the physical and psychological traits of leaders, or the **trait approach** to leadership. The trait approach suggests that all leaders possess similar traits that enable them to be effective leaders, such as height, attractiveness, and gender in addition to psychological traits of high intelligence and communication competence. In other words, leaders are born, not made.

Can you identify effective leaders who are not tall, attractive males? That is precisely the problem with the trait approach. Physical traits are not indicative of leadership abilities. Napoleon was a notoriously short man who was an effective leader. Many considered President Abraham Lincoln to be a very unattractive man. Yet political scholars often rank him among the top presidents in U.S. history.

Style approach. Because researchers could identify many effective leaders who did not exhibit the necessary traits found in the trait approach, they needed a new means of identifying effective leaders. The **style approach** examines whether the leader could choose a way of communicating (or a style) that would increase effectiveness. Three management styles were identified: authoritarian, democratic, and laissez-faire. The three styles vary in terms of how much supervision the leader takes in the group.

- **Authoritarian style.** In the *authoritarian style*, leaders maintain strict control over group members. They use the power of their position (the fact that they are the legitimate leader) to persuade group members to obey them. Because they are the legitimate leader of the group, they have the power to reward group members if they obey, and punish group members if they do not.

- **Democratic style.** *Democratic style* includes leaders who maintain some control within the group, but allow group members to contribute to the group's decisions. The democratic leader guides, rather than controls, the group. This style tends to be more popular among groups who don't want a pushy authoritarian leader or who need more structure than is found in the laissez-faire style.

- **Laissez-faire style.** The *laissez-faire style* is one in which the leader maintains a "hands-off" attitude toward the group. The group members have a high degree of autonomy and self-rule. The leader is often just a figurehead who merely serves as a leader in name only. However, the laissez-faire leader is available to answer questions from group members.

Situational approach. From this approach, researchers began to question whether effective leadership was based not on communication styles, but on situational conditions. The **situational (or contingency) approach** suggests that the best leadership style depends on the nature of the situation.

Authoritarian style is most appropriate and effective for groups (a) in stressful environments; (b) if there are many tasks that must be completed in a short amount of time; and (c) when group members have little knowledge of the subject and little motivation to work toward group goals.

9b

Democratic style is more productive in nonstressful situations, and when there is time to have meetings, discuss necessary tasks and issues, and come to some decisions.

Laissez-faire style is best for groups comprised of equally competent and independent group members who are motivated to work toward group goals.

Functional approach. The **functional approach** is one that emphasizes emergent leadership. But, rather than one leader emerging to lead the group from task decisions to successful goal attainment, a different leader emerges as the group moves from task to task.

The functional approach is based on two assumptions.

- **Different functions will be needed.** At different points in the group's existence, different functions will be needed, such as inspiring or initiating the group. Some group members may be more suitable than other group members to enact certain behavioral functions.
- **Different people can perform these functions.** Any group member can perform necessary behavioral functions—not just the leader.

Applying Concepts
DEVELOPING SKILLS

9b

Examining Leaders and Their Approaches to Leadership

Consider the leader of the group that you have been discussing in the applications in this chapter. What leadership approach does/did that person exhibit? What characteristics does that leader have that exemplify that approach? Is/was the person an effective leader? Why or why not?

The Responsibilities of Group Leaders

When individuals complain about the lack of cohesiveness and productivity of their group, much of their criticism is often directed toward the group's leader. Just as effective leadership depends on effective membership, so does effective membership depend on effective leadership. Leaders have certain responsibilities that, if fulfilled, will help the group meet its goal.

Plan the meeting. The leader's primary responsibility is planning an agenda. This does not mean dictating the agenda; rather, the leader offers suggestions and solicits group input into the process. Planning a meeting ensures that group members address important issues.

Create an agenda. An **agenda** is a pre-set plan for members to follow during a meeting. Agendas should include several components. There should be a stated purpose for the meeting and a date and location for the meeting. Give group members plenty of advanced notice about the meeting in order to avoid poor attendance. Providing beginning and ending times for the meeting helps move the group members along in order to get through all the agenda items. A list of topics for discussion comprises the body of the agenda.

Many agendas end with **minutes** (summary statements about items of discussion) from the previous meeting. These are appropriate if there needs to be an official record of what is discussed in meetings. Finally, the agenda should conclude with "announcements" that members can make about any of the tasks at hand.

Conduct the meeting. It is important to start the meeting on time. If the group members sit around and wait for late members, the group is reinforcing negative behavior (not to mention the disrespect that the late member is showing toward members who arrive on time). The late-comers will eventually see the importance of arriving on time so as not to miss important meeting information.

- **Orient the group.** How a meeting begins is extremely important in setting expectations that affect group climate and productivity. A leader may want to begin a meeting with some brief opening remarks to orient the group to its mission and the process it will follow.

    For some groups that you will lead, it will not always be appropriate or even desirable to begin a meeting with a structured speech. Still, leaders should try to accomplish several objectives early in the group's important first meeting. Your opening speech should:

    > Stress the importance of the task

    > Secure agreement on the process the group will follow

    > Encourage interaction among members

    > Set an expectation of high productivity

- **Involve all members in the discussion.** A leader must make certain that participation among group members is balanced. A person who speaks too much is as much a problem as one who speaks too little. In either case, the potential base of information and opinion is narrowed. Leaders can encourage more thoughtful and balanced discussion by asking members to think about a particular issue, problem, or solution prior to the discussion and then asking each member to share ideas with the group before discussing each. This strategy often promotes a more thoughtful analysis of the topic and encourages each member to participate in the discussion. Remember our position that all members share the responsibility of group leadership. If someone is not contributing to the discussion, any member of the group can ask the silent person for an opinion.

- **Encourage openness and critical evaluation.** After the group has shared information and ideas, the leader must guide the group in evaluating them. The leader may do this by directing probing questions to specific individuals or to the group as a whole. Here are several ways in which a leader can achieve and maintain a climate of free and honest communication:

> Be sensitive to the nonverbal communication of participants.
>
> Encourage group members to verbalize both their reluctance and their excitement about the ideas other members are expressing.
>
> Keep criticism focused on ideas, rather than on personalities.

- **Keep the group on target.** Effective leaders keep their sights on the group's task while realizing the importance of the *social dimension*, or concerns about the personal relationships among group members. There is nothing wrong with group members becoming friendly and socializing. This added dimension can strengthen your group. However, when social functions begin to impede work on the task, the group leader must "round up the strays" and redirect the entire group to its next goal.

- **Introduce new ideas and topics.** If the leader perceives that the conversation is winding down, he or she can:

> *Initiate new topics for research and talk.* This strategy helps when a lapse in conversation is caused by the group's lack of focus or lack of motivation.
>
> *Be willing to move on to the next phase of group work.* This strategy is most effective if the lapse in the group's progress signals that research and discussion have been exhausted.

- **Summarize the discussion.** A leader should provide the group periodic reviews of what has been decided and what remains to be decided. These summaries keep members focused on the group's task, and should occur during at least three phases in the group meeting: the beginning of the meeting, after each agenda item, and in concluding the meeting.

Do not let a meeting run late because of an inability to end a discussion. If your group has reached the ending time for the meeting, it is important to schedule another meeting to continue the discussion. Keeping members later than the stated ending time can cause members to skip meetings or stifle involvement out of frustration.

Evaluating a Leader's Ability to Plan and Conduct a Successful Meeting

Using the same leader as in the last application, evaluate that leader's effectiveness in planning and conducting a meeting. What could the leader have done differently to create a more effective meeting? What could the group members have done differently to enable the group to have had a more productive meeting? If the meetings were as productive as possible, what traits of the leader and group members led to that successful meeting?

EYE**ON**ETHICS

Leader and Member Responses When Groups Fail

An anonymous benefactor has contributed funds to sponsor a Career Day on Emily's campus. The president of the Student Government Association appoints Emily, a first-year student, to chair a committee charged with drafting a detailed proposal for Career Day activities. Despite Emily's efforts to encourage open discussion and to distribute the workload, two of the five committee members have contributed little. Kate, a junior, opposes most of the ideas offered by others, seldom volunteers any concrete suggestions of her own, and often wants to discuss issues unrelated to the committee's task. Gary, a senior, seldom attends meetings, and when Emily asks for his input, he usually shrugs and says, "Whatever you decide is fine with me." After three unproductive meetings with all five members present, Emily is concerned that the committee may not meet its deadline for the report. She decides to call a private meeting with the other two productive members and draft the report. They finish it in a few hours and then present it to the full committee at the next meeting, allowing all the members to discuss and vote on it.

Application

Is Emily's strategy an ethical one for a committee chair? When a group is not functioning effectively, should the leader do everything possible to ensure that all members participate in the decision-making process, or is it more important to ensure that the group take action, even if it means giving more power to selected members? What responsibility do the members have to ensure equal participation?

9c Using Group Meeting Times Effectively

One complaint about group work is the need to hold and attend group meetings. Meetings define the group. Earlier in this chapter, you learned about the responsibilities of the group leader in planning and conducting a group meeting. In this section, you will learn about how *all* group members can contribute to effective and efficient meetings.

Why do you need to have group meetings? The group meeting reinforces group goals and the tasks that need to be accomplished to meet those goals. By meeting face-to-face, members show a commitment to achieving group objectives and can share their successes as they complete necessary tasks.

Reasons for Unproductive Meetings

As you may recall from Chapter 8, professionals lose an estimated 31 hours a month—nearly four workdays—in unproductive meetings (SMART Technologies, ULC, 2004). What could be the cause or causes of unproductive meetings?

No expressed purpose for the meeting. One handy tip is that if the agenda of the meeting can be handled in a memo, you should send a memo instead of holding a meeting. Make the purpose of the meeting clear to the group members.

Unstated agenda items. If members are not clear about what is to be accomplished during a meeting, then there is nothing that keeps them focused on the important tasks. Therefore, providing group members with a meeting agenda allows groups to see what items need to be addressed, and it helps members stay on task and move through the agenda items efficiently.

Meetings that run too long. Long meetings are typically considered unproductive and can be attributed to a number of causes. For example, if there is no agenda, members may just talk about anything regarding the group goals rather than working on specific items that need attention.

Too much social time. Socializing adds a lot of extra time to a meeting. However, do keep in mind that socializing during a meeting is important if kept under control. Socializing can help increase cohesiveness, but time for socializing should be built into the agenda.

Meeting agendas can keep the group focused on the tasks that need to be discussed, and thus keep the meeting within the specified time limit.

The task dimension includes concerns about the work that the group must accomplish, and it should be the primary focus of the group meeting.

Creating an Environment for a Productive Meeting

There are several things that group members can do to create an environment that is conducive to productive, efficient, and effective meetings.

Stick to the agenda. Focus on agenda items and listen carefully to each other. Do not text message, email, or instant message during the group meeting.

Keep members on track. Use nonverbal communication, or even verbally ask members, to make sure that everyone understands what is being discussed. When everyone in the group understands the group goals and the tasks necessary to attain those goals, the group can move more swiftly toward attaining those goals.

Seek needed information. Recognize when the group needs more information to consider an agenda item. The group might determine that it needs more information about an issue before discussions can proceed. Therefore, the discussion should be included on the agenda for the next meeting.

Seek expert help. Postpone discussions that require the expertise of an absent group member. There are times when someone is unable to attend a group meeting. When an agenda item requires the expertise of the absent group member, the group should end the discussion and include that item on the agenda for the next meeting.

Allow enough time. Recognize when your group needs more time to contemplate an agenda item. Your group might also find that the topic is one that requires more thoughtful contemplation and is not easily voted on or decided. Therefore, group members can suspend their discussion until the next meeting when they will have had time to ponder the issue and/or discuss the issue with other colleagues.

Delegate a task to a couple of group members. Sometimes an agenda item is one that can be considered and decided by a couple of the group members rather than the entire group. If that is appropriate, then there is no need to waste meeting time on that item.

While the leader is primarily responsible for planning and conducting the meeting, remember that *every* group member is responsible for the success or failure of a group meeting. You and your fellow group members can help the leader keep the discussion focused on tasks and, when appropriate, limit the social talk.

Concluding the Meeting

When the meeting is finished, group members can resume their social talk. At this point, the group members are on their own time schedules and can work with another group member on a task or schedule a meeting together to do additional research. The conclusion of the meeting is an important time for enhancing cohesiveness because social talk can resume and group members can schedule meetings with each other to continue working on various tasks.

One final note about group meetings is that absent group members are responsible for finding out what they missed in the meeting. Group members understand when a circumstance arises that prevents you from attending a meeting. However, you need to be an active participant in the group by taking responsibility for catching up on information discussed in order to arrive at the next meeting prepared to be a productive member.

9d

Applying Concepts
DEVELOPING SKILLS

How Would You Make a Meeting More Productive?

What do you consider to be the three worst things about meetings? Given the suggestions listed above, what could you do differently in a meeting to avoid those three things?

9d Power and Group Communication

Power is the ability to influence the behavior of others. Power is not the sole property of a leader, but rather can be possessed by any and every group member. Through communication, leaders and followers create a relationship based on power.

Power Bases

According to French and Raven (1960), there are five bases of power: legitimate, reward, coercive, referent, and expert. Later, a sixth power base, information power, was added to their list.

Legitimate power. **Legitimate power** is based on the authority or title held by the person. For example, police officers have legitimate power as do professors. Legitimate leaders have the ability to request certain behaviors of you, and because of their position-based authority, you are required to comply.

Reward power. A second type of power is **reward power**, which is based on a person's ability to reward your compliance. Rewards can be tangible (such as money and compliments) or intangible (such as esteem and companionship). You may be more likely to comply with a request from someone who can reward your behavior. For example, you might work overtime for a month because your boss has the ability to reward you with a raise and/or a promotion.

Coercive power. People who possess reward power are also likely to possess **coercive power**, or the ability to persuade by punishing or threatening someone. One aspect of coercive power is the ability to withhold rewards as a means of punishment. For example, your boss might tell you that if you do not work overtime this week, he or she will fire you. Leaders who use coercive power are often not held in high esteem by group members. Threats and punishment breed resentment and rebellion, which are not productive group behaviors.

Referent power. **Referent power** is based on the attraction or likeability of a person as perceived by group members. For example, a person who is well-liked and admired possesses referent power. As such, group members might comply with the requests of the person with referent power in order to increase the potential reciprocated attraction.

Expert power and information power. A fifth power base is **expert power**, which is based on a person's vast knowledge of a subject. Expert power is often talent-based or education-based. Expert power is different from **information power**, which is the ability of a group member to influence others because of the information they possess. A person with information power may have access to data or research that is not accessible to everyone else. For example, one group member may be an engineering major who can discuss the dynamics of building a parking garage. That person has expert power because she or he possesses vast knowledge on the topic. Another group member may have written a paper in the past regarding the design of college campuses. Therefore, he or she has information power—possessing information that group members can use.

Source of Power

Often a person who holds legitimate power also has reward and coercive power because of the nature of the authority or title held by the person. These three power bases are external to the person who holds the power. In other words, they are based on *extrinsic* factors, or traits external to the person, such as the position that the person holds at the time, rather than an intrinsic trait of the person.

Referent, expert, and information power stem from *intrinsic* traits, or traits that reside within the person based on personality or knowledge factors. Despite the distinction between extrinsic and intrinsic power bases, it is possible for a person to possess both. For example, a legitimate leader may possess legitimate, reward, coercive, referent, and expert power. The more power bases from which a person can influence others, the greater the likelihood that the person can dominate the group.

Applying Concepts DEVELOPING SKILLS | **Identifying Power Bases**

Which power bases do you typically use when persuading others? In previous groups to which you belonged, what power bases did the leaders use with group members? What were the effects of your use of power bases and the leaders' use of power bases? In other words, was there resistant compliance or was there whole-hearted compliance?

9d

POWER BASES AND COMPLIANCE

Power Base	Source of Power	Compliance
Legitimate	Position – Extrinsic	Resistance*
Reward	Position – Extrinsic	Resistance*
Coercive	Position – Extrinsic	Resistance*
Referent	Person – Intrinsic	Compliance
Expert	Person – Intrinsic	Compliance
Information	Person – Intrinsic	Compliance

*When someone uses a power base that originates in the position that he or she holds, group members comply but can be resistant. In other words, the group members feel as though they have to comply with the power wielder because that person has a stated position that justifies the use that source of power. For example, you might comply with your boss's requests because of that superior-subordinate position. The same is true for a group leader.

However, when the power base resides within a person (i.e., someone you like and/or respect), you willingly comply as a result of your positive feelings toward the power wielder. For example, suppose you have a group member who is intelligent and friendly. When someone asks you to take notes at a meeting that he or she will have to miss, you gladly help out (comply) because of your positive feelings toward that person.

Cultural CONNECTIONS | Power Distance and Organizational Participation

One characteristic of culture is called power distance. Geertz Hofstede (2001) wrote about power distance. **Power distance** refers to the degree to which members of a culture accept unequal distributions of power. In high-power-distance cultures, members accept hierarchical distinctions between those with much power and those with little power. Members accept decisions made by authority figures. High-power-distance cultures include Arab countries and India. Indian culture considers it inappropriate for men and women to walk side by side. The male walks a couple of paces ahead of the woman.

Low-power-distance cultures seek equal distribution of power and members question authority. Australia, Israel, and the United States are considered low-power-distance cultures. In these cultures, power is used for legitimate purposes rather than to punish/coerce as in high-power-distance cultures.

Organizations that operate in high-power-distance cultures tend to prefer an authoritarian style of leadership because of the perceived unequal distributions of power. The members of such organizations expect to be closely supervised.

In low-power-distance cultures, a democratic style of leadership is preferred. As such, subordinates expect to have a higher degree of autonomy and independence in the workplace.

Problems arise when members of a high-power-distance culture interact with members of a low-power-distance culture. For example, students from high-power-distance cultures who study in a low-power-distance culture have difficulty adjusting to a lack of supervision and delegation. When students from low-power-distance cultures study in a high-power-culture, they often have difficulty handling the strict supervision and inability to question professors.

Application

In what way(s) might power distance affect group decision making? In what way(s) might power distance affect group problem solving?

9d

Competence SUMMARY

In this chapter, you have learned the following concepts. Check to be sure you have achieved each of the communication competencies.

9a Being an Effective Group Member

- A role is a set of behaviors that serves a particular function within a group. Roles emerge during the formation phase of group development.
- Roles serve task functions, maintenance functions, and self-centered functions.
- Productive group members inform the group, advocate personal beliefs, question other participants, evaluate ideas and proposals, and support and monitor other group members.

Competence. Can I distinguish between task functions and maintenance functions associated with different roles in the group? Do I know how to be an effective, productive group member?

9b Being an Effective Group Leader

- Leaders influence people and their behaviors. They can be assigned by someone outside of the group or emerge among other group members as the leader.

- There are several approaches to leadership: trait, style, contingency, and functional. Trait approach is outdated and has been shown to be inaccurate. The other three approaches are still commonly associated with group leaders.

- Leaders are responsible for conducting group meetings, which includes creating and distributing a meeting agenda.

Competence. Do I know the difference between assigned and assumed leaders? Could I recognize the different leadership styles of several leaders? Do I know how to create an agenda and conduct a meeting?

9c Using Group Meeting Times Effectively

- Meetings can be unproductive if they have no purpose, they run too long, or too much time is spent socializing.

- Members can create an environment for a productive meeting by focusing on agenda items, recognizing the need for more time to research information, contemplating an issue, and consulting an absent group members.

Competence. Can I identify reasons why some meetings are unproductive? Do I know my responsibilities as a group member to enable my group to have a productive meeting?

9d Power and Group Communication

- There are six bases of power from which group members draw to exert influence on group members: referent, legitimate, reward, coercive, expert, and information.

- Power bases differ with regard to whether the power is extrinsic (based on a person's assigned position) or intrinsic (based on a person's knowledge and affinity).

- Power bases that draw from extrinsic characteristics are often met with resistance. Power bases that draw from intrinsic characteristics are often met with compliance.

Competence. Can I list and explain the six power bases? Do I know why some power bases are extrinsic and others are intrinsic? Could I explain why extrinsic power bases are met with resistance and intrinsic power bases are met with compliance?

Review Questions

1. How do roles differ with regard to task function, maintenance function, and self-centered function?
2. Name one task role, one maintenance role, and one self-centered role.
3. Distinguish between the style approach, contingency approach, and functional approach to leadership. How are they similar and how are they different?
4. What are the primary causes of unproductive meetings?
5. Explain the six power bases.

Discussion Questions

1. Of the list of the responsibilities of a group member, what do you consider to be the two or three most important responsibilities? Why do you think those are more important than the others?
2. Of the list of the responsibilities of a group leader, what do you consider to be the two or three most important responsibilities? Why do you think those are more important than the others?
3. The leader is the most important group member. Refute or defend this statement.

Key Terms

agenda *p. 220*

assigned leader *p. 217*

assumed leader *p. 217*

coercive power *p. 226*

expert power *p. 226*

functional approach *p. 219*

information power *p. 226*

leader *p. 217*

leadership *p. 217*

legitimate power *p. 226*

maintenance functions *p. 213*

minutes *p. 220*

power *p. 225*

power distance *p. 228*

referent power *p. 226*

reward power *p. 226*

role *p. 212*

self-centered functions *p. 213*

situational (or contingency) approach *p. 218*

style approach *p. 218*

task function *p. 212*

trait approach *p. 217*

Public Speaking

Public speaking can benefit you personally in three ways:

- **Public speaking can help you acquire skills important to your success in college.**

- **Public speaking can help you to become more knowledgeable.**

- **Public speaking can help build confidence that you can apply to many aspects of your life.**

Mastering public speaking requires practice, but your efforts will bring you these three personal rewards.

Frequently asked questions

How can I choose an interesting topic that my audience will enjoy listening to? (See Chapter 10, page 241)

I've never spoken before an audience. How will I ever keep my voice from quivering and my stomach from being tied up in knots? (See Module G, page 253)

Where can I find appropriate information to support my speech? (See Chapter 11, page 256)

Now that I have lots of information, how can I bring it together into an understandable format? (See Chapter 12, page 282)

How can I present my message in an effective way? (See Chapter 13, page 317)

What tips can help me present an effective informative speech? (See Chapter 14, page 341)

How can I persuade my audience to share my passion about my topic? (See Chapter 15, page 363)

Help! I've just been invited to give the toast at my brother's wedding. (See Module I, page 392)

I'm participating in a group presentation for my biology class. How should we proceed? (See Module J, page 396)

CONTENTS

PART FOUR Public Speaking

THE SPEECH-MAKING PROCESS

ANALYZING YOUR AUDIENCE (CHAPTER 10)

Prepare a speech that can be targeted to meet the needs of *your* audience.

GENERATING YOUR TOPIC (CHAPTER 10)

Consider topics that interest you or your listeners, that suit the occasion, and those you encounter in the course of your research.

RESEARCHING YOUR SPEECH TOPIC (CHAPTER 11)

Once you have chosen your topic, research helps you focus it and determine your specific purpose.

SUPPORTING YOUR SPEECH (CHAPTER 11)

Supporting materials give your ideas clarity, vividness, and credibility to make the audience understand, remember, and believe what you say.

ORGANIZING YOUR IDEAS (CHAPTER 12)

Clear organization arranges ideas so that your listeners can remember them. It also maximizes your information so that listeners have more than one chance to "get" your point.

OUTLINING YOUR SPEECH (CHAPTER 12)

Outlining your speech is the preliminary written work necessary to foster clear organization of your oral message. When you outline, you organize and reorganize material, into a pattern that is easy to recognize and remember.

DELIVERING YOUR SPEECH (CHAPTER 13)

Your manner of presenting a speech—through your unique voice, body, and language—forms your style of delivery. *What* you say is your speech content and *how* you say it is your delivery.

general attitudes: *favorable*, *unfavorable*, or *neutral*. They can be slightly, moderately, or strongly favorable or unfavorable toward your topic, and you should try to determine this level of intensity. A speech for listeners who only slightly oppose your position that the Amber Alert system is a desirable way of apprehending suspected criminals will be different from a speech for listeners who strongly oppose it.

- **Favorable audiences.** A **voluntary audience** has assembled of its own free will and it usually has a favorable attitude toward the speaker. Most adults who attend a worship service or a political rally are there voluntarily. Similarly, you may be taking this class as an elective, just because you believe it will benefit you. The audience's positive feelings about the speaker may allow the speaker to have a greater impact on the audience.

- **Unfavorable audiences.** A **captive audience** feels required to be present and may have an unfavorable attitude toward the speaker. Chances are that you have been part of a captive audience at many school assemblies during your education. You may attend a speech given by someone visiting your campus because you are required to do so for this or some other course.

  Your reasons for attending a speech or a presentation may have a significant effect on your disposition as you listen. The speaker will need to overcome your unfavorable attitude in order to have a positive impact on the audience.

- **Neutral audiences.** If you sense that some of your listeners are *neutral* toward your topic, you should try to uncover the reasons for their neutrality because it will affect your message. Some may be *uninterested* in your topic, and you will want to convince these listeners of its importance. Other listeners may be *uninformed* about your topic, and your strategy here should be to introduce your listeners to the data they need to understand and believe your ideas.

  Still other listeners may simply be *undecided* about your topic. They may be interested and informed, aware of the pros and cons of your position. However, they may not have decided which position they support. Your strategy in this instance should be to bolster your arguments and point out weaknesses in the opposition's case.

Of course every audience member is different, but because they are gathered to hear the speech, they probably share some attitudes; your goal will be to determine the prominent attitudes and target your speech toward them. The more you know about your audience's disposition, the easier it will become to speak effectively to an audience, no matter what their disposition.

Applying Concepts
DEVELOPING SKILLS | Determining Audience Dispositions

If you sense that your audience is neutral toward your topic, what information will you attempt to uncover to find out why? How about if they are favorable or unfavorable?

Size of audience. The greater the number of people involved in speech communication, the less chance there is for verbal interaction between the speaker and individual listeners. As the audience grows larger, the speaker will have to use greater volume and larger gestures. The language of the speech may become more formal, especially if the speaker knows that the speech will be published or videotaped.

Occasion. The reason for the speaking event is a critical factor in determining what type of audience you will be facing. You need to ask yourself (and maybe even some members of the group), "Why is this audience gathering? What special circumstances bring them together?" Occasions can be formal or informal, serious or fun, planned or spontaneous, closed to the public or open to all.

Physical environment. Every physical environment or setting contains unique obstacles to communication. It makes good sense to practice a speech in the room where you will speak. If this is not possible, you should always try to find out something about the physical location where you will be speaking.

The size of the room itself may impede communication. You may be speaking to a large audience through an inadequate or defective public address system. You may be speaking as some audience members finish a meal.

Time. As you develop your speech, you should consider the time of day when you will deliver your speech. If you had your choice, would you rather take a college class at 9:00 a.m. or 1:00 p.m.? Both students and faculty seem to agree that classes at 1:00 p.m. are particularly difficult to attend and to teach because everyone's energy seems low. Where your speech is placed in a program may also affect how your audience receives it. If you follow several other speakers, you may need to work harder at getting and keeping the attention of your listeners.

Applying Concepts
DEVELOPING SKILLS

Your Comfort Zone and Speaking Situations

Describe your public speaking comfort zone with regard to audience size, occasion, physical environment, and time. In other words, what size audience are you most comfortable speaking to? Is there a particular time of day that you feel is your best time to speak in front of an audience?

How will you adapt to a speaking situation that does not fall within your comfort zone?

Understand the Diversity of Your Audience

Your first step as a speaker is to discover and evaluate as many specific characteristics of your audience as possible—including both demographic and psychographic characteristics. Let's consider more closely how this process works.

Examining audience demographics. Demographics is the term for the descriptive characteristics of your audience, including age, sex, education, and group membership. Depending on your choice of speech topic, other demographics to explore include religion, ethnicity, and economic status. Demographic analysis helps you tailor a message to a specific audience. You will never know everything about your listeners, and so you will make generalizations from the information you do know. But, be careful not to turn these generalizations into stereotypes about audience members. This will undermine your speech-making efforts.

- **Age.** Your communication class may include first-year college students, people returning to college to change careers, and others pursuing interests after retirement. People who are 18 to 20 years old today relate to Watergate and the U.S. boycott of the 1980 Summer Olympics only as important topics of history. While they may be eager to learn more about those topics, they may not understand most casual references to them.

- **Sex.** Some students fall into the trap of stereotyping when they consider the sex of their audience. What seems to be sensitivity to sex turns out to be disguised sexism: "I'm going to inform you girls about the rules of football so you won't drive your boyfriends crazy with silly questions while they're trying to watch the game." Or "This recipe is so easy that even you guys should be able to fix it and avoid starving."

    Virtually every topic is or can be made relevant to both sexes. If you are speaking to a group consisting of both men and women, focus on ways to make your topic relevant to everyone in the room. Approach any topic in such a way that everyone can get something out of it.

- **Education.** The educational level of your audience affects not only what subjects you can choose, but also how you approach those particular subjects. If you have the opportunity, find out not only what your audience knows about a potential speech topic, but also whether audience members have experience relevant to that topic.

- **Group membership.** If you are speaking to an organization—local, regional, or national—your audience analysis will require you to research the nature of that group as thoroughly as you can. You may be speaking to a charity group or a political group. You could be pitching a new product to a group of potential clients. How you develop your speech will reflect assumptions you have made about your audience. You can presume that audience members who belong to the Sierra Club, Greenpeace, or the Nature Conservancy have environmental concerns. Yet some of those groups have diverse goals and different methods of achieving them.

Applying Concepts
DEVELOPING SKILLS

Assessing the Demographics of Your Classmates

Prepare an audience profile of your class using the demographic characteristics discussed or mentioned in this chapter. After your analysis is done, answer the following questions: Which categories were easiest to determine? Which required more guesswork? Which characteristics do you think will be more important for most speeches given in this class?

Analyzing audience psychographics. Psychographics is a term for psychological characteristics of the audience such as values, beliefs, attitudes, and behaviors. These elements help us understand how our listeners think, feel, and behave. If you look at Figure 10.1 you will see that, typically, our behavior is shaped by our attitudes, which are based on our beliefs, which are validated by our values. To understand better the interaction among these elements, we will look at each layer of the onion, beginning with values and moving outward.

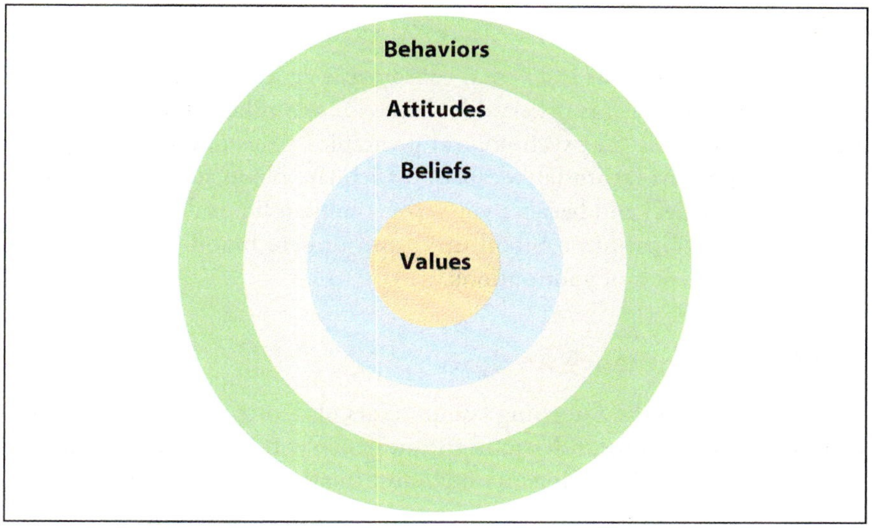

10b

Behaviors

Attitudes

Beliefs

Values

Figure 10.1
Levels of Influence

Values. A **value** expresses a judgment of what is desirable or undesirable, right or wrong, and is usually stated in the form of a word or phrase. For example, most of us probably share the values of equality, freedom, honesty, fairness, and justice. These values compose the principles or standards we use to judge and develop our beliefs, attitudes, and behaviors.

You can see from Figure 10.1 that our values are at our core. They are most resistant to change. While our actions may not always be consistent with our values, those standards nevertheless guide what we believe and how we act.

Beliefs. A **belief** is something you accept as true, and it is usually stated as a declarative sentence. We probably do not think about many of our beliefs because they are seldom challenged: Observing speed limits saves lives, or sexual abuse is psychologically harmful to children are both examples of a belief.

Sometimes an audience holds a belief that is not true, and your first goal as a speaker is to correct that belief. For instance, someone may believe that, at a public college or university, students "pay" the instructors to teach. However, the state taxpayers are paying the majority of the public college or university expenses.

Attitudes. An **attitude** is an expression of approval or disapproval. They are our likes and dislikes. A statement of an attitude makes a judgment about the desirability of an individual, object, idea, or action. Examples of statements of attitude include the following: I oppose further tuition increases; I prefer classical music to jazz. Attitudes usually evolve from our values and beliefs.

Behaviors. A **behavior** is an overt, observable action; in other words, it is how we act. Because it is observable, behavior is unlike values, beliefs, and attitudes, which are all psychological principles. You may feel that giving blood is important (attitude) because an adequate blood supply is necessary to save lives (belief) and because you respect human life (value). Your behavior as you participate in a blood drive and donate blood is a logical and observable extension of your outlook.

Conduct an Audience Analysis

If you understand the foregoing components of demographics and psychographics, you begin to understand the audience you intend to inform, persuade, or entertain. How do you obtain information about your audience?

Use your powers of observation and deduction. You can observe some demographic factors directly. You can make educated guesses about people's values, beliefs, and attitudes by observing their behaviors.

Conduct interviews or administer questionnaires. If you are unable to learn enough about your audience through your powers of observation, you have other options. You can conduct interviews or questionnaires which may be informal or, if you have the time and resources, formal. You could interview classmates informally during conversation before or after class. Questionnaires administered during class may be as simple as asking for a show of hands to answer a question ("How many of you have broadband Internet access?") or as formal as asking classmates to answer a written questionnaire.

Figure 10.2 provides a sample audience questionnaire that you can use as a model for how you can construct a questionnaire. Notice that it contains

Figure 10.2
Sample Audience Questionnaire

Please take a few minutes to answer the following questions. The information gathered will be used to assist me in preparing for my persuasive speech. To maintain anonymity, do not include your name. Thank you for your assistance.

1. Please indicate your sex.   ☐ Female   ☐ Male

2. Do you live on or off campus?   ☐ On campus   ☐ Off campus

3. How would you describe your current state of health? (Circle your answer.)
   Very Unhealthy   Unhealthy   Neutral   Healthy   Very Healthy

4. How would you describe your eating habits? (Circle your answer.)
   Very Unhealthy   Unhealthy   Neutral   Healthy   Very Healthy

5. I believe that eating animals is unethical. (Circle your answer.)
   Strongly Disagree   Disagree   Neutral   Agree   Strongly Agree

6. Would you consider changing your eating habits if it would improve your health?
   ☐ Yes   ☐ Maybe   ☐ No

7. A vegetarian diet is a healthy diet.
   ☐ Agree   ☐ Neutral   ☐ Disagree

8. Are you a vegetarian?
   ☐ Yes   ☐ No

9. What do you think are the benefits of a vegetarian diet? (Please explain your answer.)

10. What do you think are the drawbacks of a vegetarian diet? (Please explain your answer.)

10b

both *closed questions*, those respondents answer based on a finite set of responses, and *open questions*, those inviting respondents to answer in their own words.

Apply the Results to Your Speech

Once you have collected your formal and/or informal information, you will be in a better position to determine your listeners' needs or what motivates them.

- Keep in mind that your understanding of the audience will never be complete. You may have to make educated guesses based on incomplete data.
- Remember, too, that some information you may collect will be irrelevant to your speech topic.
- Finally, you must remind yourself that your audience is not a uniform mass, but a collection of individuals with varying experiences, values, beliefs, attitudes, behaviors, and personalities.

When you have the results of your audience analysis, you do not necessarily have to choose a speech topic that most closely mirrors their interests and attitudes. How then are the audience analysis results useful for your speech?

Formulate an effective introduction. In the introduction of your speech, you should state how your speech topic relates to your audience (which we will discuss more completely in chapter 11). In other words, why should they listen to your speech?

10b

Adapting Your Message to Different Learning Styles

If you value your listeners and want to communicate successfully, then you must consider their diversity and view public speaking as an audience-centered activity. You can accomplish this in three ways.

- **Recognize your own place as part of the audience.** You must be ready to admit that you are only one part of the total audience, a fact that should make you want to learn as much as possible about the other parts.

- **Respect your listeners.** Respect and care for the audience means wanting to enhance their knowledge and understanding by providing interesting or useful information. To do this, you must recognize and appreciate their beliefs, values, and behaviors.

- **Recognize and act on audience feedback.** This feedback can be verbal and nonverbal. Speakers who are attuned to their audience members will try to discover and cultivate interests their listeners already have, as well as challenge them with new, useful topics.

Competent public speakers consider the diversity of their audiences and use appropriate channels to communicate with as many of them as possible. Your audience may consist of visual or auditory learners. Visual learners need to have visual reinforcement of a message in order to remember it. For example, incorporating visual aids can assist visual learners in recollecting the main points of your speech. Auditory learners can learn best by listening. In order to reach the auditory learners in your audience, you should use inflection, enunciation, appropriate volume, and pauses to avoid a monotonous tone that your audience will tune out shortly after you begin your speech.

Application

What other methods of visual and auditory reinforcement could you add to your speech? How would you adapt your delivery style if you had a classmate who is blind or a classmate who is deaf?

Use appropriate language. You can also use your audience analysis results to determine the language that you use in your speech. How well-educated are your audience members? Are there particular words or phrases that may be offensive to them?

Be aware of the audience's disposition. We discussed earlier in this chapter that knowing the audience's disposition can help you to construct your arguments to best suit their attitudes and their knowledge about you and your speech topic.

10c Choosing and Narrowing Your Speech Topic

After you have completed this course, most of the speeches you deliver will be on topics related to your career or the activities and causes that involve you. In this course, however, your speech topics can be far more wide

CHOOSING AN EXCELLENT SPEECH TOPIC INVOLVES SEVERAL STEPS
(1) Generate a list of ideas for possible topic
(2) Select a topic
(3) Focus the topic
(4) Determine your general purpose
(5) Formulate your specific purpose
(6) Word your thesis statement

ranging. Selecting a topic that reflects your own interests, those of your audience, and that suits the speaking occasion provides your first opportunity to exercise your creativity and to make the speech uniquely yours.

Generate a List of Ideas for Possible Topics

The first step in the process of selecting a speech topic is brainstorming. **Brainstorming** involves creating a list of all of the ideas that come to your mind without evaluating or censoring any of them.

Too often, a speaker spends insufficient time generating a list of potential topics. As a rule, the larger your list of possible topics, the better the topic you will finally select. Remember, do not evaluate or criticize your list as you brainstorm.

You can make your brainstorming more effective by asking and answering four questions:

1. What topics interest *you*?
2. What topics interest *your listeners*?
3. What topics develop from *the occasion*?
4. What topics develop from *your research*?

Your answers will help you devise a list of many topics from which you can then select the most appropriate.

10c

Figure 10.3
Brainstorming

What topics interest *you*?

_____

_____

_____

What topics develop from *the occasion*?

_____

_____

_____

Brainstorming

What topics interest *your listeners*?

_____

_____

_____

What topics develop from *your research*?

_____

_____

_____

Look to yourself for topics. *Self-generated topics* come from you—your memory, your interests, and your experiences. Use what you know as a starting point in your topic selection process. Don't worry that you don't know enough about each topic at this stage to construct a speech. Research will help you later in focusing, developing, and supporting your topic.

Because these topics come from *your* knowledge, experience, and interests, your commitment to them is usually strong. Your interest and knowledge will motivate you in preparing your speech, and your enthusiasm for your topic will enliven and enhance your speech delivery.

Be aware of potential problems associated with self-generated topics. For instance, if your topic is technical, be especially attentive to the language you choose to convey your meaning. Second, do not become too involved with your topic to the point that you are no longer objective about it. And third, be aware of the fact that your audience might not share your enthusiasm for your topic. But if you work hard at it, you can make them interested.

10c

Applying Concepts
DEVELOPING SKILLS

Choosing a Topic Based on Your Interests and Experiences

Brainstorm ideas that could make good speech topics based on your own interests and experiences. Be sure to come up with at least five different *original* topics.

Look to your classmates for topics. Pursuing *audience-generated topics* is a second way of triggering speech subjects. What topics interest or seem important to your listeners? Articles in your campus or local paper or letters to the editor may suggest issues of concern. Use the audience analysis strategies detailed earlier in this chapter to help you understand their needs and generate topics that will be effective and appropriate.

Applying Concepts
DEVELOPING SKILLS | **Ask Your Classmates About Their Interests**

Interview three of your classmates. Ask them to tell you about their interests and experiences. Generate a list of at least five different *original* topics from your interviews that are not the same as the topics you listed in the last Applying Concepts activity.

Choose timely topics. *Occasion-generated topics* constitute a third source of speech subjects. When and where a speech is given may guide you in selecting a topic. A speech on setting goals may benefit your classmates more at the beginning of the term, whereas a speech on stress management may have more impact preceding midterm or final exams.

Online reference works can greatly aid your search for occasion-generated topics. We accessed the AnyDay-in-History page (http://www.scopesys.com/anyday) and typed "October 11." We generated lists of 101 individuals who were born or died on this day and events that occurred. Many of these entries could make or lead you to excellent speech topics. You could discuss the life and contributions of explorer Meriwether Lewis or actor and director Orson Welles, or the premiere of *Saturday Night Live* in 1975.

Applying Concepts
DEVELOPING SKILLS | **Explore Timely Topics**

What events are coming up in the next two months that you could incorporate into a speech topic? Consider religious events, holidays, and arts or sporting events as a few of the events that you may not normally think about. Create a list of at least five different *original* topics based on upcoming events.

Research topics. *Research-generated topics*, a fourth strategy for sparking speech ideas, require you to explore a variety of sources. You could browse through magazines or journals in the current periodical section of your library or at a local newsstand. Bookstores are convenient places to discover speech topics because the books are grouped by general subject area and are arranged to catch your eye.

You could look at new Web sites to generate a list of possible speech topics. Be sure to access all types of "news," including science, health, world news, and technology. Each area could provide you with one word that sparks an idea for a speech topic.

Applying Concepts
DEVELOPING SKILLS

Finding Topics Through Research

Go to the periodicals section of your school or local library. Find the periodicals that contain topics of interest to you (e.g., *Discover* magazine, *People* magazine, or *Racer* magazine). Generate a list of five different, *original* topics that you haven't used in previous applications based on your research.

Select a Topic

It is important that you use all four of these strategies to generate possible speech topics. If you end your topic-generation process too quickly, you limit your options. If you have completed the four previous "Applying Concepts" activities, you should now have a substantive list of self-, audience-, occasion-, and research-generated topics, which gives you maximum flexibility in selecting one topic. Be sure to consider how accessible the information is for your speech topic since you will have to conduct research in order to develop the body of your speech.

10c

Focus Your Topic

Even though we have heard students speak on topics that were too narrow, this is rare. More commonly, students tackle topics that are too broad, leaving too little time to develop their ideas. Narrowing the scope of your inquiry gives direction to your research and allows you sufficient time to support the specific ideas you will present to your audience.

Subdivide your topic. When you decide on a topic area, determine some of its divisions, or subtopics. The subject of "loneliness," for example, could focus on any of the following topics: the causes of loneliness, loneliness and the elderly, characteristics of the lonely person, or strategies for coping with loneliness. You could never discuss all these topics meaningfully in a short speech.

Do more research. Another way to narrow your topic is through research. The more you read about your topic, the more you will likely discover its many aspects. Some may be too narrow for a complete speech, but others may be suitable for an entire speech or may be combined to form a speech.

Suppose that for a 5-to-7-minute informative speech assignment, Rob developed three main points in the body of his speech on baseball:

    I. The history of baseball

    II. How the game is played

    III. The uniform and equipment used

You probably noticed that each of his main points is too broad. Rob's problem was that he needed to focus his topic further. One possibility for Rob was to concentrate on the history of baseball and maybe focus on a specific era that interested him. Each of these topics would probably have interested and informed Rob's listeners, regardless of their fondness for baseball.

Baseball during the Civil War

The all-black leagues operating from the 1920s until the integration of baseball during the 1950s

The All-American Girls Professional Baseball League formed during World War II when many professional baseball players were being drafted

---

Applying Concepts
DEVELOPING SKILLS

Focusing Your Topic

Choose your favorite of the five topics you created in the previous application, and focus that topic.

- Does your topic need to be subdivided?
- Will you need to do more research to find more details on a narrower aspect of your topic?
- What aspect of your topic could be the main point of your speech?

Determine Your General Purpose

The general purpose of your speech defines your relationship with the audience. The **general purpose** is one of the following: to inform, to persuade, or to entertain.

Speeches to inform. A **speech to inform** has as its objective to impart knowledge to an audience. You convey this information in an objective and unbiased manner. Your goal is not to alter the listeners' attitudes or behaviors, but to facilitate their understanding of your subject and their ability to retain this new information. We discuss the speech to inform in greater detail in chapter 14.

Speeches to persuade. A **speech to persuade** seeks to influence either beliefs or actions. The former, sometimes called a speech to convince, focuses on audience beliefs and attitudes. A speech designed to persuade audience members to embrace a belief stops short of advocating specific action. A speaker may argue, for example, that polygraph testing is unreliable without suggesting a plan of action.

A speech designed to persuade to action attempts to change not only the listeners' beliefs and attitudes but also their behavior. Such a speech could move the audience to boycott a controversial art exhibit or to contribute money to a charity. In either case, the speaker's goal would be first to intensify or alter the audience's beliefs and then to show how easy and beneficial taking action could be. We discuss the speech to persuade in chapter 15.

Speeches to entertain. A **speech to entertain** is designed to make a point through the creative, organized use of humorous supporting materials. It differs from *speaking to entertain*, a general phrase covering several types of speaking. Speaking to entertain includes humorous monologues, stand-up comedy routines, and storytelling, for example. When you tell your friends jokes or recount a humorous anecdote, you are trying to entertain them. You are probably not trying to develop a key point in an organized, methodical way.

A speech to entertain is more formal than simply speaking to entertain because it is more highly organized and its development is more detailed. Speeches to entertain are often delivered on occasions when people are in a festive mood, such as after a banquet or as part of an awards ceremony. We discuss the speech to entertain in more detail in Module J.

Formulate Your Specific Purpose

Broadly speaking, a speech may have one of three general purposes: to inform, to persuade, or to entertain; the specific purpose is more descriptive. A **specific purpose** statement includes three parts: the general purpose, the audience, and the goal.

- **Begin with the general purpose of the speech.** It should be stated as an infinitive, such as "To convince" or "To inform."
- **Name the individuals to whom the speech is addressed.** This is usually phrased simply as "the audience" or "my listeners."

- **State what you want your speech to accomplish.** What should the audience know, believe, or do as a result of your speech? For instance, you may want to establish the belief that alcoholism is hereditary. Your complete specific purpose statement might be:

  - To convince the audience that alcoholism is hereditary.

Other examples of specific purpose statements:

  - To inform the audience about various spring break opportunities.
  - To convince the audience that homelessness is a problem that can be solved.
  - To move the audience to spend their spring break building a house for Habitat for Humanity.

Applying Concepts **DEVELOPING SKILLS** | **Practice Formulating Your Specific Purpose**

Using the following topic areas, narrow each subject and write a specific purpose statement for an informative speech and a persuasive speech on each topic.

a. Attractiveness
b. Class attendance
c. Credit cards
d. Diet and nutrition

10c

Word Your Thesis Statement

A **thesis statement** is a one-sentence synopsis that presents the central idea of the speech. It refines and clarifies the specific purpose by summing up the main points you will make in the speech.

Although a thesis statement is designed to keep you focused, it may change as you continue to work on and develop your speech. As you begin to develop your key ideas, you will be able to determine whether you can support your thesis statement.

The following example illustrates how you can narrow a topic's focus from a general area to the speech's thesis statement.

Topic Area: Eradicated childhood infectious illnesses

Topic: The return of eradicated childhood infectious illnesses

General Purpose: To inform

Specific Purpose: To inform the audience about the return of three childhood infectious illnesses (measles, mumps, and whooping cough) that were thought to have been eradicated

Given this topic and purpose, let's examine an ineffective thesis statement and then a more effective thesis statement.

Ineffective Thesis Statement: You could get sick with some illness that you thought was gone.

Why is this an ineffective thesis statement? What are the main points of this speech? The thesis statement does not state the main points of the speech. How will you know what you will need to research? How will you organize the main points of your speech? Having an effective thesis statement organizes your speech and simplifies the research process.

Effective Thesis Statement: In order to understand the current state of three childhood illnesses, we will examine their history, their re-emergence, and the actions being taken to treat new cases of these illnesses.

This thesis statement helps you to narrow your research to information pertaining to three specific childhood illnesses (measles, mumps, and whooping cough). Its three clearly stated main points will help you organize and develop your speech when you begin to research your topic.

Now look at the following example of a persuasive speech topic development.

Topic Area: Police oversight

Topic: Mandatory videotaping of police

General Purpose: To persuade

Specific Purpose: To persuade the audience that all police actions in police stations should be videotaped

10c

With this persuasive speech topic, compare the following ineffective and effective thesis statement. Why would the second be more useful to you as you research and organize your speech?

Ineffective Thesis Statement: Police stations should have security cameras in every room to protect the rights of detainees.

The thesis statement is ineffective because it does not indicate the main points of the speech that will help support the argument that security cameras are needed in all police stations.

Effective Thesis Statement: Videotaping all police actions in police stations will deter police misconduct, discourage false charges of police misconduct, and restore public confidence in police work.

This thesis statement lists the main points of the argument so that the speaker knows how to focus his or her research, and how to construct the speech after completing the research process.

WORKING TOWARD A THESIS STATEMENT

GENERAL PURPOSE	SPECIFIC PURPOSE	THESIS STATEMENT	WORKING THESIS
One of three purposes: • To inform • To persuade • To entertain	Three parts: • General purpose • The audience • The goal	One-sentence synopsis of your speech	A statement based on your current research that summarizes what you will say in your speech

---

Applying Concepts
DEVELOPING SKILLS

Writing a Thesis Statement

Using the topic that you focused in the last activity, write a thesis statement. Though you have likely not conducted much research on your topic at this point, do you anticipate changing your thesis statement after you research the topic?

10c

EYEONETHICS | Sensitive Speech Topics

A colleague of ours had a long and distinguished career teaching communication. After class one day, she returned to her office visibly upset. When questioned by her colleagues, she said one of her students had announced in his speech introduction that his purpose was to teach the class how to make a lethal poison using ingredients people already had in their homes or could easily buy. "Moreover," she said, "to stress the significance of the topic, he assured us that this substance would kill any living animal, certainly even the heaviest human being."

Application

What ethical considerations should the student have considered when constructing his speech? How could audience analysis have better informed his speech topic?

Competence SUMMARY

In this chapter, you have learned the following concepts to increase your communication competence.

10a Overview of the Speaking Process

- The speech-making process includes seven major steps that will be covered in the remaining chapters of this book: analyzing the audience, generating a topic, researching your topic, providing support, organizing your ideas, outlining your speech, and delivering your speech.

Competence. Approaching the overall speaking process with confidence will start you on the journey to becoming a confident, competent speaker.

10b Analyzing Your Audience

- Audience disposition describes how the listeners are inclined to react to a speaker and his or her ideas.
- It is important to understand both the demographic and psychographic aspects of your diverse audience.
- When choosing a speech topic, consider the size of the audience, the occasion, the physical environment, and the time of day and day of the week in which your speech will occur.
- You should use your audience analysis results to determine how best to relate your topic to your audience in your speech introduction.

Competence. Understanding the interests of your audience members will enhance your speech and increase your likelihood of delivering a successful speech. Competent communicators seek information about their audience and use that information to maximize their speech impact.

10c Choosing and Narrowing Your Speech Topic

- Brainstorming for topic ideas is an effective first step in choosing an idea.
- Topic ideas can come from your personal experiences, your audience's interests, the nature of the occasion, and your research.
- It is important to focus your topic through research, so that the speech isn't too long and undeveloped.

- A general purpose states the overall purpose of the speech: to inform, to persuade, or to entertain. The specific purpose expands the general purpose by adding the audience and details about the main points the speech will cover.
- A thesis statement is one sentence that contains a synopsis of the speech, and it is designed to help you stay focused on what you should research for the content of your speech.

Competence. When your speech topic is focused and fits the purpose of the speech occasion, you can be more effective at meeting the objective of the speech.

Review Questions

1. What are the major steps in the process of speech making?
2. Describe several ways you can find out about your audience and create a speech that will meet their needs.
3. What are the benefits of having a thesis statement prior to beginning the speech-writing process?

Discussion Questions

1. How do perceptions influence audience analysis?
2. Select several topics that on first glance appear to be of interest primarily to people of one particular age, group, gender, economic status, etc.—for example, the Lamaze method of childbirth, sports and male bonding, or expensive wines. Discuss how speakers could justify these topics as important to a broader audience.
3. Explain the differences between a specific purpose and a thesis statement.

Key Terms

attitude *p. 238*

audience disposition *p. 232*

behavior *p. 238*

belief *p. 238*

brainstorming *p. 242*

captive audience *p. 234*

demographics *p. 236*

general purpose *p. 246*

psychographics *p. 237*

specific purpose *p. 247*

speech to entertain *p. 247*

speech to inform *p. 246*

speech to persuade *p. 247*

thesis statement *p. 248*

value *p. 238*

voluntary audience *p. 234*

Managing Speaker Apprehension

One form of communication apprehension, public speaking anxiety, affects even people with a great deal of public speaking experience. Perhaps you have experienced public speaking anxiety, too. Many students delay taking a public speaking course because of their anxiety. But with the tips to control your nervousness provided here, you should be able to deliver your speeches confidently and successfully.

James McCroskey has studied the anxieties of public speaking extensively. His data, collected from several thousand students, confirm that public speaking generates greater apprehension than other forms of communication. Nearly three-fourths of college students fall into the "moderately high anxiety" to "high anxiety" range! McCroskey and coauthor Virginia Richmond conclude: "What this suggests, then, is that it is 'normal' to experience a fairly high degree of anxiety about public speaking. Most people do. If you are highly anxious about public speaking, then you are 'normal.'"

CONTROL YOUR NERVOUSNESS

Your goal should not be to eliminate nervousness. Nervousness is natural, and attempting to eliminate it is unrealistic. Most experienced, successful public speakers still get nervous before they speak.

Some nervousness can actually benefit a speaker. Nervousness is energy, and it shows that you care about performing well. Use that nervous energy to enliven your delivery and to give your ideas impact. Instead of nervously tapping your fingers on the lectern, for example, you can gesture.

Your goal, then, is to control and channel your nervousness.

FOCUS ON YOUR SPEECH, NOT YOURSELF

Keep in mind the adage that it always looks worse from the inside. Because you feel nervous, you focus on your anxiety, exaggerate it, and become more nervous. Remember, though, your audience cannot see your internal state! Many times students have lamented their nervousness after concluding a speech, only to learn that classmates envied them for being so calm and free from stage fright.

KNOW YOUR SPEECH

You certainly do not need to memorize the entire speech. Yet, if you are well prepared, you should have memorized the outline of major points for your speech and the order in which you want to present them. If you forget your notes, or drop them on the way to the lectern and cannot get them back into proper order, you should still be able to deliver the speech. (Take a minute to number your note cards and have one less worry.)

VIEW SPEECH MAKING POSITIVELY

One method for reducing communication anxiety is called **cognitive restructuring**. This approach recognizes that nervousness is, in part, caused by illogical beliefs. If speakers can restructure their thinking and focus on positive rather than negative self-statements, they reduce their anxiety. Cognitive restructuring involves two steps. First, you identify your negative self-statements ("Everyone will laugh at me when I give my speech"). Second, you replace the negative thoughts with positive ones ("My audience understands what it's like to be nervous and will support my speaking efforts").

Public speakers can also use **visualization** to reduce their nervousness and improve their performance. You can lower speech anxiety if you visualize yourself delivering an effective—not a perfect—presentation. Imagine yourself in the room where you will be delivering your speech. Visualize yourself standing in front of the audience speaking clearly and confidently. Picture the audience smiling back at you as they listen attentively to you. As part of your visualization, imagine the audience clapping appreciatively at the conclusion of your speech.

PRACTICE YOUR DELIVERY

Mental rehearsal is no substitute for oral and physical practice. Merely thinking about what you plan to say will never adequately ready you to deliver a prepared speech. Speech making is an active process. You gain a heightened knowledge of what you plan to say, as well as increased confidence in your abilities, just by practicing your speech out loud.

Most of your practice will probably be done in seclusion. Practice any way that will help you, being sure to stand as you rehearse. Visualize your audience, and gesture to them as you hope to when giving the speech. You may even want to record and listen to or watch your speech if you have access to that equipment. Give yourself the opportunity to stop for intensive practice of rough spots in your speech. Just make sure that you also practice the speech from beginning to end without stopping.

As valuable as solitary practice is, you should also try your speech out on at least a few listeners, if at all possible. Enlist roommates and friends to listen to your speech and help you time it. The presence of listeners should make it easier to practice the nonverbal aspects of your speech including how you walk to the speaking location and the way you will leave it after finishing your speech. Your rehearsal audience can tell you if there are parts of your speech that are too complex and hard to grasp.

MANAGING SPEAKER APPREHENSION		
VISUALIZE	**PRACTICE**	**REVIEW**
▪ Remember that nervousness is normal. ▪ Visualize yourself giving a successful speech.	▪ Believe in your topic. ▪ Know your speech. ▪ Practice your delivery.	▪ Ask yourself several key questions. ▪ Among them should be how you think you did, how your audience reacted to your speech, and whether/how techniques you used to reduce your nervousness were successful.

REVIEW YOUR PERFORMANCE

After each speech, assess your performance. Don't be too critical as you evaluate your performance. You will do some things well, and this should build your confidence. Other aspects of your speech you can improve, and you should work on these.

Ask yourself the following questions after your speech:

- How did I react when I walked to the front of the room to speak?

- Did I remember what I planned to say?

- Did I have trouble finding my place in my notes?

- What techniques did I try in my speech that worked? What didn't work?

- Did I get less or more nervous as the speech progressed?

- How did the audience respond to my speech? What did their nonverbal communication convey as I delivered my speech?

Applying Concepts
DEVELOPING SKILLS

Capitalize on Your Strengths

Make a list of your strengths and weaknesses as a speaker. How might you capitalize on your strengths when delivering speeches? In what ways can you improve your weaknesses to enhance your speeches?

Researching Your Speech Topic and Supporting Your Speech

In this chapter, you will learn about how to conduct research on your speech topic by collecting information and how to use that information as evidence to support your speech topic. Your communication competence will be enhanced by understanding:

- how to implement the five-step sequence for conducting research;
- where to locate credible resources for your speech;
- how to include useful supporting statements in your speech;
- why you need to cite sources in your speech.

11a Researching Your Topic

In the previous chapter, we discussed how to select a topic. Here we consider the second step in the speech-making process: how to research a topic. **Research** is the process of gathering evidence and arguments you will need to understand, develop, and explain your subject.

Although we are covering research techniques in this chapter, remember research should occur throughout the speech construction process. Once you have chosen your topic, additional research helps you focus it and determine your specific purpose. How much research is enough for a classroom speech? Your instructor may specify a minimum number of sources you are to cite during your speech. Does that mean your research is finished when you reach that magic number? Not necessarily. In short, research your topic until you have enough authoritative evidence to make an informative or persuasive statement to your listeners.

We'll break the research process into a five-step sequence that can help you see the big picture and assist you in generating excellent ideas and supporting material, regardless of your speech topic. First, we'll look more closely at each step of this sequence.

Assess Your Personal Knowledge

The first question you should ask and answer is, "What do I already know that will help me develop my topic?" Use your personal knowledge as a starting point for researching your topic. For example, a student who assisted her father in administering polygraph tests chose as her speech topic the use and misuse of lie detectors because she already had an understanding of the equipment and processes used. For other students, personal knowledge will be more general and they will need to rely more fully on research.

11a

THE FIVE-STEP RESEARCH SEQUENCE

1. **Assess your personal knowledge of the topic.**

   Begin by making a list of what you already know about your topic, including things you have read, heard, observed, or experienced about your topic.

2. **Develop your research plan.**

   Ask yourself several questions:
   - What information do I need?
   - Where am I most likely to find it?
   - How can I obtain this information?
   - What time constraints affect my research options?

3. **Collect your information.**

   In today's technical environment, you will likely be able to find what you need from a variety of online sources:
   - Academic search engines
   - Databases
   - Podcasts

   Don't forget to check your local or college library for sources that may not be available online:
   - Magazines and journals
   - Newspapers
   - Government documents
   - Books

4. **Record your information.**

   You'll need to be sure you have the information at your fingertips when you start assembling your speech.
   - Evaluate online sources for reliability.
   - Email electronic sources to yourself.
   - Make detailed notes on library sources.
   - Avoid plagiarism by putting information into your own words and recording the sources.

5. **Conclude your search.**

   Consult your research plan and fill in any gaps that remain.

11a

Applying Concepts
DEVELOPING SKILLS

Assess Your Personal Knowledge of Your Topic

Think about the next speech you are working on for this course. As a starting point, ask yourself what you already know about your topic and make a list of everything that comes to mind regarding the topic.

Develop Your Research Plan

A clearly worded thesis statement (a concise statement of the purpose of your speech and the main points you will make to support it) can help you determine your research plan.

Let's use the sample thesis statement from chapter 10 to show how you can develop your research plan:

> In order to understand the current state of three childhood illnesses, we will examine their history, their re-emergence, and the actions being taken to treat new cases of these illnesses.

Begin by answering several questions:

1. **What information do I need?** Identify what information you need to focus your purpose and back up all of your points. For our example, we will need to find information about the history of measles, mumps, and whooping cough, the re-emergence of these illnesses, and plans to treat cases of the illnesses.

2. **Where am I most likely to find it?** We will want to seek sources that discuss childhood infectious illnesses that scientists considered eradicated. Sources can be found online or in your college library (or local library).

3. **How can I obtain this information?** In our example, medical journals would be too technical and contain too much jargon for a non-tech-savvy, general audience. Instead, we could consider science periodicals, such as *Discover, Scientific American*, or health Web sites like WebMD. If your topic is currently part of the national or international news, you should go to news sources, such as online news Web sites (e.g., cnn.com or nytimes.com).

4. **How will time constraints affect my research options?** If your topic requires information that is obtainable through online sources or references that are available in your library, you will need to consider whether you can access the needed sources before you are scheduled to present your speech in class. If they are not readily available, you will likely want to change your topic.

Applying Concepts **DEVELOPING SKILLS**	Develop Your Research Plan

Now work through the planning process for your own project. Write out your research plan for your topic by answering the four questions listed above.

Collect Your Information

For most topics, there is probably more information than you can locate and read in the time allotted for your research. How do you search for and find useful information for your speech?

Online sources. Today much research takes place online in an information landscape that continues to undergo revolutionary changes. Changes will no doubt occur between the time we write this and the time you use it, but we have taken great effort to provide accurate information about electronic sources in this chapter.

- **Search engines.** Choose an academic search engine that filters the extraneous information from the essential information.

  Here are a few academic search engines and their addresses:

Academic Info	www.academicinfo.net
Galaxy	www.galaxy.com
Librarians' Internet Index	www.lii.org
Intute	www.intute.ac.uk/

  Academic search engines provide more focused and higher-quality information than what you are likely to gather using a general, commercial search tool.

- **The invisible Web**. Locate information more difficult to find by using what is sometimes called the invisible Web.

  These rich databases of public, government, corporate, and private information contain more information than what you can find using conventional search engines. If you are interested in exploring the invisible Web, check out the following portals:

  CompletePlanet http://aip.completeplanet.com "70,000 searchable databases and specialty search engines."

  Invisible-Web www.invisible-web.net "Select a category to drill-down through the database."

  ProFusion www.profusion.com "Access hundreds of specialized vertical search engines."

- **Podcasts.** Look at podcasts for important information about your topic. One of the newest channels for information dissemination is the **podcast**, which is a previously recorded and sometimes scripted speech, message, or radio or television broadcast. Users can access podcasts through iTunes, company Web sites, and media Web sites, and download

EVALUATING ELECTRONIC INFORMATION

Because many Web sites you access have never been edited, fact-checked, or reviewed, you are responsible for checking the reliability and validity of the sources you use. Before you use the information you find, ask yourself these basic questions:

Purpose and Audience

- What is the purpose of this site?
- What type of site is it?
- Is there an institution, agency, or organization identified as sponsoring the site?
- Who is the author's apparent audience, as reflected by the vocabulary, writing style, and point of view?

Expertise

- Is the author, compiler, or Web master identified?
- Does the author have apparent expertise on the subject? Are the authors' or compilers' credentials provided?
- If the site is a compilation, are sources and authors of individual works identified?
- Is the site linked to another site that you already trust or value?
- Are sources or viewpoints missing that you would expect to be present?
- What does this page offer that you could not find elsewhere?

Objectivity

- Does the author's affiliation with, or the site's sponsorship of, an organization, institution, or agency suggest a bias?
- Are opposing views represented or acknowledged?
- Are editorial comments or opinions clearly distinguished from facts?

11a

Accuracy

- Can you corroborate the facts using either other Internet sources or library resources?
- Have you found misspellings and grammar mistakes?
- Does the author solicit corrections or updates by email?

Timeliness

- Can you tell when the site was created or updated?

Source: We adapted this list from Fenton & Reposa (1998); Library Tutorial (2005); Grassian (2006); and Stanger (2008).

them to any MP3 player. The first podcasts were developed by media outlets to allow viewers and listeners access to broadcasts that they may have missed or would like to review.

Currently, companies are using podcasts to communicate with board members and customers. Colleges and universities are using podcasts for recruiting students. Podcasts can provide you with a unique source for useful information about your speech topic.

FINDING PODCASTS

Directory of podcasts available for download:

- podcast.com
- podcastalley.com
- podcastbunker.com
- podcastpickle.com

Specific interest podcasts (a *small* selection):

- ScientificAmerican.com/podcast—podcasts related to scientific information provided by *Scientific American* periodical
- reuters.com/tools/podcasts/video—podcasts containing the latest news, entertainment, and business information
- podcasts.military.com—podcasts of interest to the military community and those with interests in military, sponsored by a support organization for military families

11a

Library Sources. Your college, university, or local public library online catalog is an excellent resource that can point you in the direction of their holdings. But keep in mind that not every publication has been made available electronically. You may have to go to the library to retrieve the original hard copy.

- **Magazines and journals.** With more than 190,000 magazines from which to choose, how do you keep from being overwhelmed with information?

  Use an index to help you filter useful information from extraneous information. Many standard indexes are now available online to guide you as you focus your search even more.

  Full-text databases give you access to articles in hundreds or even thousands of periodicals and scholarly journals. You can then print useful articles or email them to another address.

Find the online versions of particular magazines and journals you think might be helpful. Some magazines provide full-text copies of current issues, along with searchable archives; others give you only sample articles.

Find the hard copies.

Remember that the periodicals and journals you find may be highly specialized, containing jargon and technical language familiar only to people in that field. Even if you easily understand these articles, you may have to simplify the language and ideas for your audience.

LIBRARY SOURCES

- Magazines and journals
- Newspapers
- Government documents
- books

Your local reference librarian can acquaint you with the library's holdings and help make your search more efficient.

- **Newspapers.** Newspapers offer abundant information—local, national, or international in scope. How do you find the articles about your speech topic?

  Powerful databases such as LexisNexis Academic contain full-text newspaper articles, in addition to other sources.

  Most newspapers now have sites on the Internet and provide indexes to their own archives. If you have selected a localized topic, you may want to research specific newspapers directly.

  If you're unsure about newspaper titles, Newslink (http://newslink.org) lets you browse lists of newspapers. You can search for newspapers by U.S. state, as well as world newspapers by continent or country, and click on links to specific papers.

  Some newspapers allow free access to archived articles for only a certain period of time; you may have to pay to read or print older articles.

- **Government documents.** The most prolific publisher in the United States is the federal government. Online you can find presidential speeches, pending legislation, and contact information for senators and representatives. What documents are available?

Almost every federal agency has a Web site. You can search for the one that is most likely to store information about your speech topic.

Several government databases are searchable by keyword. Among the more popular databases are LexisNexis Government Periodicals Index, Federal Register Online, and MarciveWeb DOCS.

Some Web addresses allow you to access virtually any area of government. The Library of Congress maintains THOMAS: Legislative Information on the Internet at: http://thomas.loc.gov. The Government Printing Office maintains a two-page list of links to government information products at www.access.gpo.gov.

- **Books.** Books, of course, are excellent sources of information, but there are advantages and disadvantages.

  Advantages. They are longer than magazine and newspaper articles. Therefore, books allow authors to discuss topics in greater depth. They often provide a bibliography of sources consulted.

  Disadvantages. They may not be as current as magazines. Magazines provide more up-to-date information because they are published more frequently. Unless you access the book online, a book may also not be as accessible. Magazine articles are concise sources of information; thus you can find information more quickly in them than in a book.

  Despite these limitations, books can be an integral part of your research plan.

11a

Applying Concepts DEVELOPING SKILLS | Collect Your Information

Which of the resources discussed would be useful for your research efforts? Which resources are not likely to contain information about your topic? Using your research plan, identify the specific sources you will be using and locate the electronic or hard copy versions.

Record Your Information

Thanks to the Internet, you can often access an entire article electronically and email it to your own account. Therefore, you have the ability to read the article more diligently later as you write your speech. However, if not all of the information you seek is available electronically, then you will need to take notes.

Taking notes. When you are taking notes from a source, be sure to decide whether you want to write down word for word content from the source (with the intention of putting information into your own words later) or if you are going to summarize the article in your own words in your notes. You do not want to unintentionally include information from a source word for word in your speech, and thus commit plagiarism.

A good habit when taking notes is to first write down the source's bibliographic information. That way you will always know where the information came from, and can cite the source during your speech.

Avoiding plagiarism. **Plagiarism** is "the false assumption of authorship: the wrongful act of taking the product of another person's mind, and presenting it as one's own" (Lindey, 1952). Plagiarism can involve the unauthorized use of another person's written work, art, and music. Plagiarism is such a serious offense that in most colleges and universities it is grounds for failing the course or dismissal from the school.

Plagiarism applies to more than simply copying of another's *words*. It is possible to plagiarize another's *ideas* and *organization* of material. For example, if you presented a speech organized around the five stages of dying (denial, anger, bargaining, depression, and acceptance) and did not give credit to Elisabeth Kübler-Ross, you would be guilty of plagiarism. On the other hand, if your speech analyzed the political and economic implications of a pending piece of legislation, you would probably not be guilty of plagiarism. Kübler-Ross published her stage model in her book *On Death and Dying*, whereas the second example relies on a commonly accepted pattern of analyzing public policy initiatives. As you can see, the line between legitimate appropriation of material and plagiarism can be unclear. As a speaker, you must always be on guard to credit the source of your ideas and their structure.

Widespread use of the Internet for research may be blurring the distinction between *intentional* and *unintentional* plagiarism. Web site content and design changes from day to day and, together with the ease of browsing numerous sites in a short period of time, lets readers pick up phrases, ideas, or even organizational patterns almost subconsciously. If a researcher has not recorded URLs for key sites, retracing steps and finding those sites again may be difficult. Unintentional plagiarism may be committed due to ignorance or sloppy research methods, but the effect is still the same: one person is taking credit for the work of another.

Unintentional plagiarism sometimes occurs because of a common misperception that by simply changing a few words of another's writing you have paraphrased the statement and need not cite it. Let's look at an example.

STATEMENT BY CAROLYN KLEINER BUTLER

Black-only baseball squads had existed since before the Civil War, but there was no organized competition until former pitcher Rube Foster helped form the Negro National League in 1920, which was relaunched in 1933 and joined by the Negro American League in 1937.

Speaker's plagiarism (through paraphrasing) of Carolyn Kleiner Butler

African American baseball teams are older than most of us imagine. And African Americans made a strong impression quickly once baseball was integrated. Though there were black-only baseball squads even before the Civil War, they hadn't competed in an organized way until the formation of the Negro National League in 1920. By 1937 the Negro American League was also operating.

Speaker's appropriate citation of Carolyn Kleiner Butler

African American baseball teams are older than most of us imagine. And African Americans made a strong impression quickly once baseball was integrated. Carolyn Kleiner Butler, a contributing editor for *U.S. News & World Report* and a frequent contributor to *Smithsonian Magazine*, notes that though there were black-only baseball squads even before the Civil War, they hadn't competed in an organized way until the formation of the Negro National League in 1920. In her article in the April 2005 issue of *Smithsonian Magazine*, Butler notes that by 1937 the Negro American League was also operating.

Notice that the appropriate citation above not only tells the listener something about Butler's credentials, but also explains exactly where her words appeared. With that information, any listener wanting to read the entire article could find it quickly.

11a

Applying Concepts
DEVELOPING SKILLS | **Recording Your Information**

How do you record information (that is, take notes) from a source? What additional steps will you take to ensure that you are not plagiarizing your sources for your next speech?

Conclude Your Search

Your research plan can help you determine whether you have found support for all of the points you plan to make in your speech or if gaps remain. Your goal is to support your ideas with the most compelling evidence and arguments you can find.

An important part of effective research is knowing when to stop accumulating materials and when to start using them. When you stop finding useful resources or when the resources you are finding are replicating what you already have, then you should stop conducting research and start developing your speech. If you encounter a problem or question you cannot answer, you can always go back to search for a specific piece of information.

Applying Concepts
DEVELOPING SKILLS

Concluding Your Speech

Consult your research plan to make sure you have found support for all of the points you plan to make in your speech. If gaps remain, target your search to fill in the unanswered questions. If you have more sources than you can use, prioritize them to produce the most effective speech.

Cultural CONNECTIONS

Restricted Access to Information on the Internet

According to Techweb (2009), the number of Internet users in China had reached 300 million in 2008, which is double the number of users reported in 2006. That means that 22.6% of the Chinese population are Internet users, which now exceeds the global percentage (21.9%) of Internet users.

A U.S. State Department report on human rights released in March 2007 says there are tens of thousands of people who monitor the Internet in China (Lemon, 2007). The human rights report also noted that the Chinese government is using domestic and international companies to help restrict access that the Chinese have to the Internet. Yahoo and Google have been criticized for complying with censorship requests by the Chinese government (*Information Week*, 2006). For example, Yahoo and Google censor search results for "Tiananmen" and "Dalai Lama" (Coonan, 2009). At the 20th anniversary of the Tiananmen Square crackdown in June 2009, the Chinese government blocked access to YouTube, Twitter, and Flikr (*The New Zealand Herald*, 2009).

According to a Freedom House report released on April 1, 2009, Cuba has the strictest Internet access with the Castro regime controlling almost every aspect of the Internet (BBC Monitoring Worldwide Media, 2009). Iran and Tunisia were also reported as "Not Free" by Freedom House. Other countries (many Islamic countries) block users from accessing information about certain topics, such as alcohol, drug, sex, gay and lesbian issues, and gambling Web sites (Quirk, 2006).

Application

How would restricted access to information, such as government documents and news sources, affect your ability to create an effective speech?

11a

11b Supporting Your Speech

Your goal is to present a clear, memorable, and believable message to your audience. Effective supporting materials help you anchor your ideas in the minds of your listeners. As you look over the bits of information gathered from your research, think about how they can help you support the message you are giving. What types of support will be useful for your speech?

CONSIDER THE PURPOSES OF YOUR SUPPORTING MATERIAL	CONSIDER THE TYPES OF MATERIAL AVAILABLE FOR YOUR TOPIC	EVALUATE THE VALIDITY AND STRENGTH OF YOUR SUPPORT
Clarity • Make sure your message is clear and understandable. **Vividness** • Use vivid support that will help your listeners remember your message. **Credibility** • Effective support for your message can help establish your credibility and make your listeners more likely to believe what you say.	The form that each piece of your support will take should vary depending on the subject matter and its purpose. • Use *examples* as specific illustrations. • Use *narration* or storytelling as a vivid way to present your message. • Use *comparison* to show how your message is similar to what your audience already knows. • Use *contrast* to show how your message is different from what your audience already knows. • *Statistics* allow you to report on large amounts of information. • *Testimony* allows you to present the ideas of others.	Carefully consider the *evidence,* or proof, that you present and be sure it is both valid and sufficient to prove your points. Remember that effective listeners will also be carefully evaluating the validity and strength of your speech. • Is the evidence quoted in context? • Is the source of the evidence an expert? • Is the source of the evidence unbiased? • Is the evidence relevant to the point being made? • Is the evidence specific? • Is the evidence sufficient to prove the point? • Is the evidence timely?

Consider the Purposes of Your Supporting Materials

Supporting materials in a speech serve a variety of purposes. They help give your ideas clarity, vividness, and credibility. If the supporting materials in your speech make the audience understand, remember and believe what you say, you have done a good job selecting them.

Clarity. **Clarity** refers to the exactness of a message. As a speaker, your first goal is to communicate clearly. You can establish clarity by explaining your idea so that listeners *understand* it. Use vocabulary that is familiar to your audience. Clear supporting materials help listeners better understand your ideas.

Vividness. **Vivid** supporting materials are striking, graphic, intense, and memorable. You establish vividness by presenting your idea so that listeners will *remember* it. A major purpose of supporting materials, then, is to help your audience remember the key points in your speech.

Suppose that someone wanted to compare the number of deaths resulting from the terrorist attacks on the World Trade Center in New York City in September 2001 with the bombing of the Murrah Federal Building in Oklahoma City in April 1995.

Which of the following statements makes a stronger impression?

Considerably more people died in the New York City terrorist attacks than in Oklahoma City.

or

At the anniversary of the Oklahoma City blast, people traditionally stand in silence one second for each victim—168 seconds, or nearly three minutes, which feels excruciating. To do the same in New York City would take almost an hour and a half (Ripley, 2001).

The first comment is something that Amanda Ripley, social issues commentator for *Time* magazine, could have said. The second is what she actually wrote to demonstrate the enormity of the loss in New York City. Which statement do you think is more vivid and memorable? Most people would choose the second statement. The first remark is general and the second is specific.

Credibility. **Credibility** refers to the dependability or believability of a speaker or that speaker's sources. You establish credibility by presenting the idea so that listeners *believe* it. Your main points will be more credible if you present evidence that these ideas are shared by several experts.

For example, you see the headline "Scientists Discover Microbial Life on Mars." Would it make a difference whether you saw this on the cover of *Scientific American* or the *National Enquirer*? A scientific article reviewed and selected for publication by a panel of experts is significantly more believable than an article from any weekly tabloid.

Considering the Purposes of Your Supporting Material

Find a speech on You Tube or a Web site of your choice. Assess the speaker's use of clarity, vividness, and credibility. How well do you think it suits the speaker's purposes?

Consider the Types of Material Available for Your Topic

To help you achieve clarity, vividness, and credibility in your speaking, consider the types of supporting material available to you. Keep in mind that there is no one best type of support for ideas. Select what is most appropriate to your topic, your audience, and yourself.

Examples. An **example** is a specific illustration of a category of people, places, objects, actions, experiences, or conditions. In other words, examples are specimens or representations of a general group.

- **Actual examples.** An actual example is real or true. Measles, mumps, and chicken pox are examples of common childhood illnesses. *Schindler's List*, *Saving Private Ryan*, and *Indiana Jones and the Kingdom of the Crystal Skull* are examples of Steven Spielberg movies.
- **Hypothetical examples.** A hypothetical example, on the other hand, is imaginary or fictitious. A speaker often signals hypothetical examples with phrases such as "Suppose that," "Imagine yourself," or "What if." Hypothetical examples clarify and vivify the point you are making, but they do not prove the point.

Narration **Narration** is storytelling, the process of describing an action or series of occurrences.

As a participant in the events, the story you tell about that event is called a *personal narrative*. Personal narratives can be rich and interesting supporting materials because we tend to believe the accounts of people who have experienced events firsthand.

When you speak from the point of view of a witness and use the pronouns *he*, *she*, or *they*, you are telling a *third-person narrative*.

Comparison. **Comparison** is the process of depicting one item—person, place, object, or concept—by pointing out its similarities to another, more familiar item.

A *literal comparison* associates items that share actual similarities. Bill Gates used the following literal comparison in a 2005 speech critiquing contemporary high school education:

> Training the workforce of tomorrow with the high schools of today is like trying to teach kids about today's computers on a 50-year-old mainframe. It's the wrong tool for the times. Our high schools were designed fifty years ago to met the needs of another age. Until we design them to meet the needs of the 21st century, we will keep limiting—even ruining—the lives of millions of Americans every year.

When you draw a *figurative comparison*, you associate two items that do not necessarily share any actual similarities. The purpose of figurative comparisons is to surprise the listener into seeing or considering one person, place, object, or concept in a new way.

One student, describing the density of a neutron star, quoted from *Sky & Telescope* magazine that "your bathroom sink could hold the Great Lakes if the water were compressed to the density of a neutron star."

Contrast. **Contrast** links two items by showing their differences.

A *literal contrast* distinguishes items that do share some similarities. In a persuasive speech on the dangers of over-exposure to the sun, our student Patricia effectively used the following literal contrast:

> Sunblocks are either chemical or physical. Oils, lotions, and creams that claim a certain SPF factor all contain chemical blocks. On the other hand, zinc oxide, the white or clay-looking material you see some people wearing, usually on their noses, is a physical block.

A *figurative contrast*, on the other hand, distinguishes items that share no similarities. You can use comparison and contrast together in your speech. If you clarify a term by showing how it is similar to something the audience knows, you can often make the term even clearer by showing how it differs from something the audience also knows.

Statistics. **Statistics** are collections of numerical data. Used appropriately, statistics, too, can make your ideas clear and vivid, increase your credibility, and prove your point. We place a great deal of trust in statistics that we feel have been accurately gathered and interpreted.

When you use statistics in your speech, you can demonstrate trends or compare a situation today with one in the past. Used inappropriately, however, statistics may baffle or even bore your audience. The following five suggestions should guide you in presenting statistical material.

11b

1. **Do not rely exclusively on statistics.** If statistics are your only form of supporting material, your audience will likely feel bombarded by numbers and possibly become confused. Remember, your listening audience has only one chance to hear and assimilate your statistics. Use statistics judiciously and in combination with other forms of support. A few key statistics combined with examples can be quite powerful.

2. **Round off statistics.** The statistic of $1,497,568.42 should be stated as "a million and a half dollars." Rounding off statistics for your listeners is neither deceptive nor unethical. Instead, it reflects your concern for helping your audience understand and retain key statistical information.

3. **Use units of measure that are familiar to your audience.** In her speech on London tourist attractions, Veronica described the London Eye as being "135 meters high—equivalent to 64 red telephone boxes stacked on top of one another" (*London Eye*, 2009). If she had stopped there, listeners unfamiliar with the metric system or with British phone boxes would have had only a vague idea of the height Veronica was describing. However, she wisely converted meters to feet, adding that the London Eye is 443 feet tall.

   Six hundred renminbi would probably have been a meaningless figure to most of her listeners. Kim helped her audience to understand the statistic by translating it to U.S. dollars and by indicating how it compared with other salaries in the region.

4. **Use presentational aids to represent or clarify relationships among statistics.** When you have multiple statistics to present to an audience, such as a comparison of countries by GDP, you should use a presentational aid. Listeners will be able to see the statistics and comprehend them more easily than if you just state the statistics in your speech.

5. **Stress the impact of large numbers.** Use repetition to help your audience understand and remember the enormity of the statistics.

USING STATISTICS APPROPRIATELY

Do not rely exclusively on statistics.
Round off statistics.
Use units of measurement that are familiar to your audience.
Use presentational aids to represent or clarify relationships among statistics.
Stress the impact of large numbers.

11b

Testimony. **Testimony**, sometimes called quotation, is a method in which you quote or paraphrase the words and ideas of others.

In his speech, "Ribbons: Function or Fashion," Tony Martinet discussed how awareness ribbons can inform and connect communities. To give his ideas credibility, he used the testimony of a communication professor.

> Dr. Judith Trent, a communication professor at the University of Cincinnati, states in the *Cincinnati Enquirer* of September 18, 2001, that wearing a ribbon, "shows you're a part of something that's larger than yourself. It helps to unify and support the cause. It's a public signal about a private thought." By wearing ribbons, people can easily give support and find comfort in people around them.

Tony clearly identified his source and quoted her directly, trusting her credibility and her words to persuade his listeners. Testimony relies largely on the reputation of the source being quoted or paraphrased.

As a speaker, you use personal testimony when you support your ideas with your own experiences and observations.

EYEONETHICS | The Privacy of Public Information

Jeanine was researching a speech on the problem of child sexual abuse. While she was searching the Internet, she discovered a series of forums devoted to this topic, including a newsgroup, a listserv, and a live chat group. She found thought-provoking and useful discussions in the newsgroup and listserv, but the chat discussions were the most intimate and revealing. There, sexual abuse survivors described their memories of actual incidents and talked about how the trauma affected their adult lives.

Jeanine took notes on some of the most remarkable stories and decided to recount one in her speech, to add drama.

Application

Is this a legitimate way for Jeanine to use her research? Should stories told on the Internet be considered public property, available for anyone to write or speak about? Should Jeanine try to find out whether the speaker would feel comfortable about having the story repeated in a speech? Should she try to verify that the story is true?

11b

Considering the Types of Material Available for Your Topic

Which type of material will be most effective in conveying information to your audience about your speech topic? Which of the types of material do you find most compelling when you are listening to a speech? What makes some types of material more effective than others?

Evaluate the Validity and Strength of Your Support

Speakers should choose supporting materials carefully and ethically. The positions you develop in your speech will be only as strong as the evidence supporting them. Seven guidelines will help you evaluate the validity and strength of your supporting materials as well as evidence you hear others present in their speeches.

Is the evidence quoted in context? Evidence is quoted *in context* if it accurately reflects the source's statement of the topic. Evidence is quoted *out of context* if it distorts the source's position on the topic. For example, suppose Joyce was preparing a speech on the topic of hate crimes on campus. She has read in the campus paper the following statement by the president of her college:

> We've been fortunate that our campus has been relatively free of bias-motivated crimes. In fact, last year, only two such incidents were reported—the lowest figure in the past five years. Yet, no matter how small the number is, any hate crime constitutes a serious problem on this campus. We will not be satisfied until our campus is completely free from all bias-motivated intimidation.

Now, suppose Joyce used the following statement to support her position that hate crimes are prevalent on campus:

> We need to be concerned about a widespread and growing problem on our campus: the prevalence of hate crimes. Just this past week, for example, our president argued that hate crimes constitute, and I quote, "a serious problem on this campus."

The president did say those words, but Joyce failed to mention the president's position that hate crimes on campus are few and decreasing.

11b

By omitting this fact, she has distorted the president's message. Joyce presented the evidence out of context. The evidence you cite in your speech should accurately represent each source's position on the topic.

Is the source of the evidence an expert? An *expert* is a person qualified to speak on a particular topic. We trust the opinions and observations of others based on their position, education, training, or experience. As a speaker, select the most qualified sources to support your position.

Is the source of the evidence unbiased? When individuals have a vested interest in a product, a service, or an issue, they are often less objective. You expect representatives of political parties, special-interest groups, and labor unions to make statements advancing their interests.

Is the evidence relevant to the point being made? Both speakers and listeners often fail to apply this guideline in evaluating evidence. A speaker who contends that amateur boxing is dangerous but presents only evidence of injuries to professional boxers has clearly violated the relevance criterion. As you construct your speech, identify your key points and make certain your evidence relates specifically to them.

Is the evidence specific? Which of the following statements is more informative?

> The new convention center will increase tourism a lot.
> The new convention center will increase tourism by 40 percent.

What does "a lot" mean in the first statement? Twenty percent? Fifty percent? We don't know. The second statement is more precise. Therefore, we are better able to assess the impact of the new convention center. Words such as *lots*, *many*, *numerous*, and *very* are vague. When possible, replace them with more specific words or phrases.

Is the evidence sufficient to prove the point? In her speech on rap music, Lea played excerpts from two rap songs, one song she characterized as anti-woman and the other as anti-police. She encouraged her listeners to boycott rap music because "it demeans women and law enforcement officers." Lea did not apply this sixth guideline to her evidence. Two examples do not justify a blanket indictment of rap music. When considering the guideline of sufficiency, ask yourself, "Is there enough evidence to prove the point?"

Is the evidence timely? The timeliness of information is especially important if you are speaking about constantly changing issues, conditions, or events. What you read today may already be dated by the time you give your speech.

11b

Some speech topics, however, are timeless. If you deliver a speech on the ancient Olympic Games, your most authoritative sources may be history textbooks. If, however, your topic concerns current drug-testing procedures in Olympic competition, it would be vital for you to use the most recent sources of the best quality you can find. The date of your evidence must be appropriate to your specific argument.

Applying Concepts
DEVELOPING SKILLS

Evaluating the Validity and Strength of Your Support

When is it okay to use sources that are more than 5 years old? Is there more recent information about your speech topic or are you likely going to have to go back several decades or centuries to find relevant sources? As you finish evaluating your supporting material, ask yourself this: Do I have a sufficient amount of material that has been published in the past 5 years?

Competence SUMMARY

In this chapter, you have learned the following concepts. Check to be sure you have achieved each of the communication competencies.

11a Researching Your Topic

- Research is important when you are looking for credible information to add as supporting material in your speech.
- Creating and following a research plan will enable you to find information more quickly and easily.
- There are various resources that you can examine as you research your speech topic: magazines and journals, newspapers, government documents, and books.

Competence. Can I find the most current information about my speech topic? Do I know how to incorporate it into my speech so that I can be a more credible speaker?

11b Supporting Your Speech

- Your audience will be more likely to believe and understand your message if you use supporting material. Supporting materials give your message clarity, vividness, and credibility.

- To achieve clarity, vividness, and credibility in your speaking, you can use any of the types of supporting material available to you: examples, narration, comparison, contrast, statistics, and testimony. Select what is most appropriate to your topic, your audience, and yourself.

Competence. Can I explain the different types of supporting material that I could choose to enhance my message? Do I understand the importance of supporting material in helping the audience understand my topic?

Review Questions

1. With regard to conducting research, what does it mean to assess your personal knowledge?
2. What questions do you need to answer as you create a research plan?
3. How do you know when to stop conducting research?
4. What are the three purposes of supporting material?
5. What is a hypothetical example?
6. What are narratives and how are they used in a speech?
7. Give an example of a literal comparison and a figurative comparison.
8. What is the difference between a comparison and a contrast?
9. Name three of the rules regarding the use of statistics in your speech.

Discussion Questions

1. Can a speech be effective if it lacks clarity, vividness, and/or credibility? Is there one of the three that is less important that the others?
2. Are statistics often misused by the news media? Defend your answer.
3. Suppose that you are going to give a speech about saving the rainforests. Which of the types of supporting material would be most effective to persuade the audience to take action?

Key Terms

clarity *p. 268*

comparison *p. 270*

contrast *p. 271*

credibility *p. 269*

example *p. 270*

narration *p. 270*

plagiarism *p. 265*

podcast *p. 260*

research *p. 257*

statistics *p. 271*

testimony *p. 273*

vivid *p. 269*

Interviewing

In chapter 11, you learned how to conduct research to find credible information for your speech. The research sources that you were directed to investigate in that chapter are called *secondary sources* because they report research conducted by other people.

In this module, you will learn how to conduct *primary research*—meaning that you collect information firsthand by asking other people to give you their experiences and expertise regarding your topic. Interviews are one form of primary research that can provide you with valuable information about your topic.

ADVANTAGES OF INTERVIEWS

Depending on your purpose, an interview may be the best source of firsthand information. Today you can interview people by email, instant messaging, or in electronic chat rooms, as well as by telephone or in person. The personal interview can aid you in four ways.

- **If published sources are inaccessible, the personal interview may be your only option.** The topic you have chosen may be so novel that sufficient information is not yet in print or online. Your topic may also be so localized as to receive little or no coverage by area media.

- **Interviews permit you to adapt your topic to your specific audience.** Take, for example, the topic of recycling. If you interview the director of your school's physical plant to find out how much trash custodians collect and dispose of

each day, you can give your speech a personal touch. You could take your speech one step further by figuring out how much your college could contribute to resource conservation. This shows your audience how this topic affects them directly. You will grab their attention.

- **Personal interviews provide opportunities for you to secure expert evaluation of your research and suggestions for further research.** The experts you interview may challenge some of your assumptions or data. If this happens, encourage their feedback and don't get defensive. Knowing all the angles can only help you give a more thoughtful speech. Near the end of your interview, ask your interviewee to suggest additional sources that will help you better research and understand your topic.

- **Personal interviews can enhance your image as a speaker.** Listeners are usually impressed that you went beyond library or online research in preparing your message.

PREPARING FOR THE INTERVIEW

Once you decide to conduct a personal interview, you must take several steps in preparation.

PREPARING FOR THE INTERVIEW
Determine whom you want to interview
Decide the format for the interview
Schedule the interview
Research the person to be interviewed
Prepare a list of questions

Determine Whom You Want to Interview

Your interviewee should be someone who is both knowledgeable on the topic and willing to speak with you.

Decide on the Format for the Interview

Will you conduct it face to face, by phone, or online? The answer will depend on the several factors.

- **Face to face.** A face-to-face interview may give you the most information. People tend to open up more when they interact verbally and non-verbally. As a face-to-face interviewer, you can both listen to what the interviewee says and observe the nonverbal messages.

- **Telephone.** An interview over the phone is another possibility when you cannot travel to the expert.

- **Email.** Conducting an interview by email or computer chat room has both advantages and disadvantages. The email interview is time consuming because you must prepare a set of questions, send it to the interviewee, and wait for a response. It has the added disadvantage of not allowing for immediate follow-up questions. If something needs clarification, you must email another question. An interview in a chat room or by instant messaging eliminates this time lag. However, the email interview often results in more thoughtful and better-worded responses than face-to-face, telephone, or chat room interviews.

Schedule the Interview

When requesting an interview, identify yourself and the topic on which you seek information. Let the person know how you intend to use that information, the amount of time needed for the interview, and any special recording procedures you plan to use. Some people may object to being quoted or to having their comments recorded. If this is the case, it is best to find that out ahead of time rather than at the interview. You are likely to discover that most people you seek to interview are flattered that you selected them as experts and are therefore happy to cooperate.

Research the Person to Be Interviewed

Obviously, your selection of the interviewee suggests that you already know something about him or her. In addition, read any articles the interviewee has published on your topic before the interview. This enables you to conduct the interview efficiently. You won't ask questions that the person has already answered in print, and your prior reading may prompt some specific questions on points you would like clarified. Also, your research will show that you are prepared. The interviewee will take you and the interview seriously.

Prepare a List of Questions

Always have more questions than you think you will be able to ask, just in case you are mistaken. Mark those that are most important to your research, and ask them first. You may want to ask some closed and some open questions, as Joel did when he interviewed a professor of recreation for his speech on how American adults spend their leisure time.

Closed questions are those that can be answered with a yes, a no, or a short answer. For example, Joel asked, "Do American adults have more time for leisure activities today than they did a generation ago?" and "How many hours per week does the typical adult spend watching TV?" The first question can be answered by a yes or a no; the second, with a specific figure.

Open questions invite longer answers and can produce a great deal of information. Joel asked this open question: "How do American adults typically spend their leisure time?" When you ask open questions, sit back and prepare to listen for a while! The less time you have for the interview, the fewer open questions you should ask. Open questions can sometimes result in rambling responses. At times, the interviewee's rambling will trigger questions you would not have thought of otherwise. Joel was surprised to learn that American adults spend approximately two hours a week in adult education, a venture he had not included on his initial list of adult leisure activities. When you and the interviewee have plenty of time, and particularly if you are recording the interview, open questions can provide the richest information.

CONDUCTING THE INTERVIEW

The face-to-face interview is an excellent opportunity to practice your interpersonal communication skills. Specifically, you should follow these guidelines.

Opening the Interview

Introduce yourself when you arrive and thank the person for giving you time. Restate the purpose of the interview before you begin asking questions.

Maintaining the Interview

Conduct the interview in a professional manner. For instance, if you interview the president of the local savings and loan, don't show up in cut-off jeans, sandals, and your favorite flannel shirt. Make sure you arrive appropriately dressed. Be ready and able to set up and handle any recording equipment with a minimum of distractions.

Try to relax the interviewee and establish a professional atmosphere. Make sure you pose questions that are clear and direct, and when your interviewee answers, listen actively. Take notes efficiently and follow up when necessary.

You should control the interview without appearing to be pushy or abrupt and make sure you do not overstay the amount of time you asked for when you scheduled the interview.

Concluding the Interview

Thank the person again for the interview when you have finished, shake hands, and leave on schedule.

FOLLOWING UP ON THE INTERVIEW

After the interview, review your notes or listen to your recording. Do this as soon as possible, while your memory is still fresh. If you are unclear about something that was said, do not use that information in your speech. You could call your interviewee to clarify the point if you think it will be important to the audience's understanding of the topic.

As a matter of courtesy, you should write to the people you interviewed, thanking them for the time and help they gave you. You may even want to send them a copy of your finished speech if it is in a manuscript form.

KEY TERMS

closed questions *p. 280*
open questions *p. 280*

Organizing and Outlining Your Speech

Your communication competence will be enhanced by understanding:

- why an organizational pattern for structuring your speech enhances your credibility as a speaker;
- how developing the key ideas in your speech can help your audience understand your topic;
- how an effective introduction and conclusion for your speech can create audience interest in your topic;
- how to properly construct an outline for your speech so that your audience understands your purpose.

12a Organizing the Body of Your Speech

Clear organization arranges ideas so that your listeners can remember them. It also maximizes your information so that listeners have more than one chance to "get" your point.

Although you deliver it *after* the introduction, organize the body of your speech first, because in order to "tell us what you are going to tell us," you must first determine what to tell us. In constructing the body of a speech, your best strategy is to divide the speech into key ideas, and then develop each idea.

If your research is productive, you'll gather more information than you can use in your speech. Deciding what is relevant, irrelevant, or missing from your research requires you to examine items of information and the relationships among them. You will combine and restructure the different pieces of information and arrange your information so that you can present it effectively, in a way your listeners can understand.

In the body of the speech, you develop your key ideas according to a specific organizational pattern. Public speakers employ a wide variety of organizational structures. Here you will learn several commonly used patterns.

Keep in mind as you consider these patterns that no pattern is best. To be effective, you must select a structure that accomplishes the purpose of your speech. In other words, fit the organization to your topic, rather than your topic to the organization.

SIX TYPES OF ORGANIZATIONAL STRUCTURES

Structure	Description	Function
Topical	Organizes according to aspects, or subtopics, of the subject.	Informative or persuasive speeches
Chronological	Organizes according to a time sequence.	Informative or persuasive speeches
Spatial	Organizes according to physical proximity or geography.	Informative or persuasive speeches
Causal	Traces a condition or action from its causes to its effects, or from effects back to causes.	Informative or persuasive speeches
Pro-con	Presents both sides of an issue by explaining the arguments for a position and the arguments against.	Informative or persuasive speeches
Problem-solution	Establishes a compelling problem and then presents a convincing solution.	Persuasive speeches

Topical Division

The most common organizational pattern for public speeches is the topical division. The **topical division** organizes the speech according to aspects, or subtopics, of the subject. Here are examples of the topical pattern for an informative speech and for a persuasive speech.

SPECIFIC PURPOSE: To inform the audience on the types and tastes of coffee

Key Ideas:

I. Types of coffee
   A. Dark roasts
   B. Blends
   C. Decaffeinated
   D. Specialties

II. Tastes of coffee
   A. Acidity
   B. Body
   C. Flavor

12a

SPECIFIC PURPOSE: To persuade the audience to adopt a pet

Key Ideas:

   I. Caring for a pet reduces anxiety and stress.

  II. Caring for a pet increases exercise and physical health.

 III. Caring for a pet decreases loneliness and depression.

As these examples suggest, topical organization is particularly appropriate as a method of narrowing broad topics, which may explain its widespread use. The topical pattern is also attractive because it lets you select subtopics to match your own interests and the interests and needs of your audience.

Chronological Division

The **chronological division** pattern organizes a speech according to a time sequence. Topics that begin with phrases such as "the steps to" or "the history of" are especially appropriate to this organization. The following ideas are developed chronologically:

SPECIFIC PURPOSE: To inform the audience of Elisabeth Kübler-Ross's five stages of dying

Key Ideas:

   I. Denial

  II. Anger

 III. Bargaining

 IV. Depression

  V. Acceptance

SPECIFIC PURPOSE: To inform the audience about the history of garage rock

Key Ideas:

   I. The 1960s: The British Invasion Inspiration

  II. The 1980s: The Garage Band Revival

 III. Today: The Neo-Garage Movement

Chronological organization is especially appropriate if you are explaining procedures or processes. For the speech on coffee, used earlier as an example of topical organization, the speaker could have organized her ideas chronologically if her main points were (1) selecting the coffee, (2) grinding the coffee, (3) brewing the coffee, (4) serving the coffee, and (5) storing used coffee.

Spatial Division

You use **spatial division** when your main points are organized according to their physical proximity or geography. This pattern is appropriate for a speech discussing the parts of an object or a place. Examples of spatial division are the following:

SPECIFIC PURPOSE: To inform the audience about the halls and palaces of the Forbidden City in Beijing, China

Key Ideas:

  I. The Halls of Harmony

  II. The Palace of Heavenly Purity

  III. The Palace of Earthly Tranquility

  IV. The Hall of the Cultivation of the Mind

SPECIFIC PURPOSE: To inform the audience of the parts of the U.S. National Holocaust Memorial Museum

Key Ideas:

  I. Four classrooms, two auditoriums, and two galleries for temporary exhibits occupy the lower level.

  II. The permanent exhibit occupies four floors of the main building.

  III. The library and archives of the U.S. Holocaust Research Institute occupy the fourth floor.

Causal Division

When you want to trace a condition or action from its causes to its effects, or from effects back to causes, you would use **causal division.** The following speech outline illustrates the causal pattern:

SPECIFIC PURPOSE: To inform the audience about the effects and causes of sports-victory riots

Key Ideas:

  I. Effects

    A. Death and injuries

    B. Vandalism

    C. Law enforcement costs

II. Causes
   A. The competitive nature of sports
   B. Mob psychology
   C. Unfavorable economic conditions
   D. Inadequate police presence

Because the causal pattern may be used any time a speaker attributes causes for a particular condition, it is suitable for persuasive as well as informative speeches. A speaker could attempt to prove that certain prescription drugs are, in part, responsible for violent behavior among those who use them; or that new antibiotic-resistant bacteria are increasing infections once thought to be under control. The causal pattern would work well for speeches on any of these topics.

Pro-con Division

The **pro-con division** presents both sides of an issue by explaining the arguments for a position and the arguments against. Because it is balanced in perspective, this pattern is more appropriate for an informative speech than for a persuasive one. After discussing each side of the issue, however, you could choose to defend the stronger position. In this case, your division becomes *pro-con-assessment*, a pattern appropriate for a speech to persuade. The following outline demonstrates a pro-con analysis of a controversial issue:

SPECIFIC PURPOSE: To inform the audience of the arguments for and against an increase in the minimum wage.

Key Ideas:

I. Increasing the minimum wage would be beneficial.
   A. The number of poor would decrease.
   B. The number of people on welfare would decrease.
   C. The concept of social justice would be affirmed.

II. Increasing the minimum wage would be harmful.
   A. Unemployment would increase.
   B. Inflation would increase.
   C. Business bankruptcies would increase.

An advantage of the pro-con pattern is that it sets an issue in its broader context and provides balance and objectivity. A disadvantage is the time required to discuss both sides of an issue in sufficient detail. Therefore, you will probably want to use this strategy only in one of your longer speeches for this class. If you do not devote sufficient time to each idea, a pro-con or pro-con-assessment development may seem simplistic or superficial to your audience.

12a

Problem-Solution Division

In **problem-solution division** the order of the ideas is pre-determined: You first establish a compelling problem and then present a convincing solution. Because you advocate a plan of action, this pattern is by nature persuasive.

Speeches that call for a law or some action often use a problem-solution format, as in the next example:

SPECIFIC PURPOSE: To persuade the audience to support reform of our national park system.

Key Ideas:

I. Our national parks are threatened.
    A. Political influence is a threat.
    B. Environmental pollution is a threat.
    C. Inadequate staffing is a threat.

II. Our national parks can be saved.
    A. The National Park Service should have greater independence.
    B. Environmental laws should be stricter.
    C. Funding should be increased.

A common alternative to the problem-solution division is to divide the speech into a discussion of problems, causes, and solutions. Notice how Matt used this approach:

SPECIFIC PURPOSE: To persuade the audience that involuntary psychiatric commitment laws should be reformed.

Key Ideas:

I. The problems caused by involuntary commitment laws are serious.
    A. Many are potential victims of being wrongfully committed.
        1. The elderly are especially at risk.
        2. The poor are at risk.
        3. All of us are at risk.
    B. Victims face physical and financial dangers.

II. Two factors perpetuate these problems.
    A. Medicare policies indirectly encourage hospitals to commit patients regardless of their actual health.
    B. Involuntary commitment laws are too vague.

III. To remedy this problem, we must act on three levels.
    A. The federal government must reform involuntary commitment procedures.
    B. The psychiatric industry must establish greater control over mental hospitals.
    C. We, as individuals, must take action as well (Whitley, 1997).

12a

Choosing Among the Organizational Divisions

Select a topic appropriate for an informative or a persuasive speech in this class. Brainstorm several key ideas and an appropriate organizational pattern for the body of your speech. Which organizational pattern did you choose?

12b Developing Your Key Ideas

Assume that your speech is divided into the key ideas using the most appropriate pattern to organize them. Now you need to develop each main point. Obviously, the number of main points you can develop in a speech depends on the time you have been allocated to speak, the complexity of the topic, and the audience's level of education and knowledge of the subject. There is no fixed rule, but most speech instructors recommend that you develop at least two but not more than five main points. Many speakers find that a three-point structure works best.

Regardless of the number of points you select, your responsibility is to explain and support each one sufficiently. The organizational strategy we suggest is one we call the "4 S's." Your listeners will better comprehend and remember your speech if you *signpost*, *state*, *support*, and *summarize* each idea.

Signposting the Idea

One organizational cue you can use is signposting. A **signpost** is a word such as *initially*, *first*, *second*, and *finally*. Just as a highway signpost tells travelers where they are in their journey, so a signpost in a speech tells the audience where they are in the speaker's message. Signposts help listeners follow your organizational pattern and increase the likelihood that they will remember your key ideas. For example, "A second component of the application process . . ." The phrase "second component" signals to your audience that you are moving to the next main point of your speech.

Stating the Idea

Each major idea needs to be worded precisely and with impact. In her persuasive speech, Esperanza argued the benefits of a multicultural college experience. Her specific purpose was to persuade the audience that ethnic studies (ES) courses should be required for all students. Using a topical organization, Esperanza presented three reasons to support her proposal.

12b

Before we tell you how she actually worded those ideas, let's take a look at how a less experienced student might have stated them:

1. ES courses promote cultural awareness.
2. I would like to discuss ES courses and what research and expert opinion say about the way they affect conflict that may be ethnic or racial.
3. Third, social skills.

Do these points seem related to each other? Are they easy to remember? No, they're a mess! To avoid clutter, keep the following suggestions in mind when wording your key ideas.

1. **Main headings should clearly state the point you will develop.** The first statement ("ES courses promote cultural awareness") does that; the others do not.

2. **Main headings should usually be worded as complete sentences.** Think of the main heading as a statement that you will prove with your supporting materials. Listeners would probably remember the wording of statement 1 in the previous list. As a result, they would remember the point of the speaker's evidence. That is not true of either the wordy second statement or the final fragment, "social skills."

3. **Main headings should be concise.** You want listeners to remember your key ideas. The first statement is easier to remember than the second. The third statement is the shortest, but it isn't a complete sentence. Remembering it doesn't help you understand the point the speaker made.

4. **Main ideas should be parallel to other main ideas.** Parallel wording gives your speech rhythm and repetition, which are two qualities that help listeners remember your points.

5. **Main ideas should summarize the speech.** When you state your main points, listeners should see how those points reflect your thesis statement and achieve your specific purpose.

Now let's see how Esperanza worded each of her key ideas:

SPECIFIC PURPOSE: To persuade the audience that ES courses should be required for all students

Key Ideas:

  I. ES courses promote cultural awareness.

  II. ES courses reduce ethnic and racial conflict.

  III. ES courses improve social skills.

12b

Each of these main headings clearly states a distinct point that Esperanza will argue. Each statement is a concise, complete sentence. All three sentences are grammatically parallel (promote, reduce, improve). Notice, too, that each of the three key ideas supports the purpose of her speech.

An alternative to introducing your key idea as a declarative sentence is to ask a question. Here is a speech that Elly created:

SPECIFIC PURPOSE: To persuade the audience that the United States should continue to fund the space station *Freedom*.

Key Ideas:

   I. What will we gain scientifically?

   II. What will we gain technologically?

   III. What will we gain economically?

Elly introduced each of these ideas with a signpost, for example:

A third question we must answer to determine the merits of the space station is: What do we have to gain economically?

She was then ready to answer that question using various types of supporting materials.

Supporting the Idea

This third S is the meat of the "4 S's." Once you have signposted and stated the idea, you must support it. Several categories of supporting materials are at your disposal, limited only by the amount of research you have done and by time limits on your speech. Some of those categories of supporting materials are examples, narration, comparisons, and statistics.

In her speech on Victorian homes, Jennifer combined specific language with visual aids to depict the different style of each room. For example, as part of her "support" for the first room, the parlor, she stated:

The parlor in Conglomeration House is done in the Rococo revival style, which is almost exclusively used in interior design. In their book *The Secret Lives of Victorian Homes*, Elan and Susan Zingman-Leith, who restore Victorian houses, give us this wonderful example of this style. [Jennifer showed an enlarged photograph.] Typical of the Rococo theme, the walls are painted white or a pastel color and are broken into pastels decorated with wooden molding or even artwork painted directly onto the wall. Around the windows and ceiling are intricately carved wooden details that are influenced by botanical or seashell designs. These are painted to match the color of the walls, but are heavily accented with gilt, or gold-colored paint.

Summarizing the Idea

A summary at the end of each major division helps wrap up the discussion and refocus attention on the key idea. These periodic summaries may be as brief as one sentence. Our students sometimes summarize a point by saying, "So I've told you a little about _____." What you say in these summaries within the body needs to be more substantial and more varied than that. An effective summary should reinforce the point you have just developed and also provide a note of closure for that key idea.

If you introduced your idea as a question, your summary should provide the answer. Remember, your point is lost if the audience remembers only your question; they must remember your answer. Elly summarized her point this way:

> So the answer to our third question is clear and convincing. What do we have to gain economically from continued funding of the space station? A brighter economic future for American workers, American communities, and the American economy.

Jennifer summarized her first key idea with the following statement:

> So the parlor gives us a wonderful example of the Rococo revival architectural style: very feminine, very ornate, and very French.

Such a summary not only clued her audience that she had finished discussing this first room, but also alerted them that they were about to move to the second room on the tour.

We believe that the use of the "4 S's" is fundamental to effective organization within the body of any speech. As you master the "4 S's" and gain confidence in public speaking, clear organization will become almost a reflex reaction performed without conscious effort. As your ability to organize ideas clearly becomes second nature, you will find that the structure of your thinking, writing, and speaking has greatly improved.

12b

Applying Concepts DEVELOPING SKILLS | Using the "4 S" Strategy

For this application, use the topic you chose for the previous Applying Concepts/Developing Skills box. Using the "4 S" strategy, develop one key point. Signpost and state the idea. Support it with at least two types of supporting materials, citing at least two quality sources.

12c Connecting Your Key Ideas with Transitions

A speech is composed of key ideas, and you have just seen how to develop each according to the "4 S" approach. Those key ideas form the building blocks of your speech. For your speech to hang together, however, you must connect those ideas.

A speaker moves from one idea to the next with the aid of a transition. A **transition** is a statement connecting one thought to another. Without transitions, the ideas of a speech are introduced abruptly. As a result, the speech lacks a smooth flow of ideas and sounds choppy.

A transition not only connects two ideas, but also indicates the nature of the connection between the ideas. Transitions are usually indicated by words or phrases near the beginning of a sentence that indicate how that sentence relates to the previous one. You will use some transitions *within* each of your main points to offer illustrations (*for example*), indicate place or position (*above*, *nearby*), or make concessions (*although*, *of course*). However, the transitions you use between the main points of your speech will indicate four basic types of connections: complementary, causal, contrasting, and chronological (Leggett, 1991; DiYanni, 2001).

Complementary Transition

A **complementary transition** adds one idea to another, thus reinforcing the major point of the speech. Typical transitional markers for complementary transitions include *also*, *and*, *in addition*, *just as important*, *likewise*, *next*, and *not only*.

The following example uses a complementary transition to reinforce the speaker's thesis.

> It is clear, then, that golf courses have sociological effects on communities where they are located. *Just as important*, however, are their environmental effects.

Causal Transition

A **causal transition** emphasizes a cause-and-effect relation between two ideas. Words and phrases that mark a causal relationship include *as a result*, *because*, *consequently*, and *therefore*.

In his speech, Victor documented problems resulting from excessive noise. As he shifted his focus from cause to effect, he used the following transition:

> We can see, then, that we live, work, and play in a noisy world. *An unfortunate result* of this clamor and cacophony is illustrated in my second point: Excessive noise harms interpersonal interaction.

Contrasting Transition

A **contrasting transition** shows how two ideas differ. These transitions often use markers such as *although*, *but*, *in contrast*, *in spite of*, *nevertheless*, *on the contrary*, and *on the other hand*.

In her tour of Conglomeration House, Jennifer moved her audience from her first to her second main idea with the following clear contrasting transition:

> *In sharp contrast* to the parlor is the library, the man's retreat in the home. This is the second room we will visit on our tour.

12d

Chronological Transition

A **chronological transition** shows the time relationships between ideas. Sample words and phrases to indicate a chronological transition include *after*, *as soon as*, *at last*, *at the same time*, *before*, *later*, and *while*.

Will informed his classmates on the SQ3R system of studying and remembering written material. He organized his five main points around five key words: *survey*, *question*, *read*, *recite*, and *review*. His transitions emphasized the natural sequence of these stages:

> *After* surveying, or overviewing, what you are about to read, you are ready for the second stage of the SQ3R system: to question.

A second example of a chronological transition is the following:

> If thorough preparation is the first step in a successful job interview, the *second* step is to arrive on time.

A good transition serves as a bridge, highlighting the idea you have just presented and preparing your listeners for the one to come. It smoothes the rough edges of the speech and enhances the cohesiveness of your ideas. Note, however, that transitions alone cannot impose order on a speech. The main ideas and their natural links must already exist before you can underscore their connections with transitions (DiYanni, p. 197).

Effective transitions require more than just inserting a word or phrase between two ideas. If you find yourself always using a single word such as *now*, *next*, or *okay* to introduce your ideas, you need to work on your transitions. Avoid using weak and pedestrian phrases as transitions, such as "Moving on to my next point" or "The next thing I would like to discuss." Instead, work on composing smooth, functional transition statements.

Applying Concepts **DEVELOPING SKILLS**	**Adding Transitions to Your Speech**
Using your outline from the previous application, after stating your internal summary, include a transition that guides listeners to your next key idea. Remember, you are developing just one compelling argument, so you should be able to deliver this point within two or three minutes.	

12d Organizing the Introduction of Your Speech

After you work on the body of your speech, you are ready to turn your attention to the introduction and conclusion. To get your speech off to a clear, interesting start, we'll discuss five objectives for an introduction and the ways to achieve them.

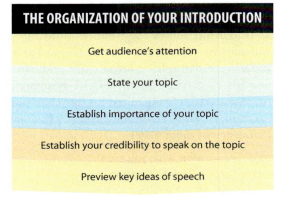

THE ORGANIZATION OF YOUR INTRODUCTION

Get audience's attention

State your topic

Establish importance of your topic

Establish your credibility to speak on the topic

Preview key ideas of speech

Get the Attention of Your Audience

Your first objective as a speaker is to secure the audience's attention. If you are fortunate enough to have a reputation as a powerful, captivating speaker, you may already have the attention of your listeners before you utter your first word. Most of us, however, have not yet achieved such reputations. Consequently, it is important to get the audience quickly involved in your speech. The strategy you select will depend on your personality, your purpose, your topic, your audience, and the occasion. Your options include the following five possible techniques for getting the audience's attention.

Question your audience. A speaker can get an audience involved with the speech through the use of questions, either rhetorical or direct. A **rhetorical question** stimulates thought but is not intended to elicit an overt response. For example, consider the following opening question:

> What would you do if you saw your best friend copying another student's answers during a test?

A question is rhetorical if it is designed to get the audience thinking about a topic.

A direct question seeks a public response. Audience members may be asked to respond vocally or physically. For example:

> How many people have worked as a volunteer for some charitable group within the last year?

Like the rhetorical question, a direct question gets the audience thinking about your topic. But the direct question has the additional advantage of getting your listeners physically involved in your speech and, consequently, making them more alert. When you ask a direct question and you want oral responses, you need to pause, look at your listeners, and give them sufficient

12d

time to respond. If you want your listeners to answer your direct question by a show of hands, raise your hand as you end the question.

You should use caution when using a question to get the audience's attention.

1. **Avoid asking embarrassing questions.** "How many of you are on scholastic probation?" "Has anyone ever spent a night in jail?" Common sense should tell you that most people would be reluctant to answer direct questions such as these.

2. **Don't use a question without first considering its usefulness to your speech.** Remember that asking a valid question that listeners answer either openly or to themselves gets them immediately involved and thinking about your speech topic. Just don't rely on a question because you have not developed or found a more creative attention-getter.

Arouse your audience's curiosity.   A lively way to engage the minds of your listeners is the technique of suspense. Get them wondering what is to come. Jake chose to keep his audience in suspense in his attention-getting step. Notice, also, how he incorporated rhetorical questions in his introduction to heighten his listeners' curiosity:

> A 76-year-old mother of four slices bread at her kitchen counter. In a moment, her life will be over—cut down by a culprit who has been lying quietly in wait for almost two decades. In a way, she's lucky. This culprit frequently strikes women far younger than she. But nevertheless, in a moment a family will begin to mourn. But who was this stealthy assassin? Some rare and untreatable virus? No. An incredibly patient serial killer? Uh-uh. The truth is this villain is not only far deadlier than both of these, but also the most preventable (Gruber, 2001).

Jake resolved the suspense when he introduced his topic: heart disease in women.

Stimulate your audience's imagination.   Another way to engage the minds of your listeners is to stimulate their imaginations. To do this, you must know what meanings they share, and this requires some good audience analysis on your part. Notice in the following example how Jennifer began her speech by relating a personal experience that many in her audience probably found familiar:

> The year was 1984. Saturday morning had finally arrived, and I was in my Strawberry Shortcake nightgown, complete with Strawberry Shortcake necklace and watch, humming along with the theme to *The Smurfs*. I can still hear it in my head. [She hums part of the show's theme song.] My sister sat beside me with her Optimus Prime Transformer in hand. My younger brother was quietly awaiting *Teenage Mutant Ninja Turtles* to come on. All was right with the world.

In the rest of her speech Jennifer discussed "retro toys" such as Transformers and Strawberry Shortcake and the reasons for their return to store shelves.

Promise your audience something beneficial.   We listen more carefully to messages that are in our self-interest. In Chapter 10, we recommended that you consider your listener's needs when you decide on a topic for your speech. If you can promise your audience something that meets one or more of their needs, you secure their attention very quickly. For example:

> I am about to give you information that can save you hundreds of dollars in income tax next April.

> OR

> The information I will give you in the next ten minutes will help you buy an excellent used car with complete confidence.

Savings and consumer confidence—the promises of these two attention-getters—are directly related to the interests of many audience members.

Amuse your audience.   The use of humor can be one of a speaker's most effective attention-getting strategies. Getting the audience to laugh with you makes them alert and relaxed. You can use humor to emphasize key ideas in your speech, to show a favorable self-image, or to defuse audience hostility. However, any humor you use should be tasteful and relevant to your topic or the speaking occasion. As a speaker, you must be able to make a smooth and logical transition between your humorous opening and your speech topic. Telling a joke or a funny story and then switching abruptly to a serious topic trivializes the topic and may offend your listeners.

Stacey encouraged her classmates to study a foreign language, introducing her classroom speech with the following attention-getting riddle:

> What do you call someone who is fluent in many languages? A polylingual. What do you call someone who is fluent in two languages? A bilingual. What do you call someone who is fluent in only one language? An American! This is a joke commonly told among the Japanese. Behind the apparent humor of this joke are some embarrassing truths.

Stacey combined humor and rhetorical questions to get her listeners' attention. She then discussed those "embarrassing truths" and the price we pay for speaking only one language.

Which type of attention-getter would be most effective for the topic you have
used for the Applying Concepts/Developing Skills boxes in this chapter? How
would you apply it to that speech topic?

State Your Topic

Once you have your audience's attention, state the topic or purpose of your
speech directly and succinctly. For an informative speech, your statement of
purpose typically takes the form of a *simple declarative sentence* and clearly
informs the audience of your topic:

> Today, I will show you how you can improve your study skills.

This second goal of a speech introduction is vitally important, even
though the actual statement of purpose will take only a few seconds for you
to say.

Establish the Importance of Your Topic

The third goal in organizing the introduction to your speech should be to
convince the listeners that the topic is important to them. You want to
motivate them to listen further. Do you remember the way Jake tapped his
listeners' curiosity before introducing his topic of heart disease in women?
He then *provided statistics and examples* to establish the importance of his
topic for the women and men in his audience:

> "[T]he truth," as stated in the *Pittsburgh Post Gazette* of December 12, 2000, "is that
> heart disease kills more women every year than all forms of cancer, chronic lung
> disease, pneumonia, diabetes, accidents, and AIDS combined." Whereas one in
> twenty-eight women will die of breast cancer, one in five will die of heart disease.
> And guys, before you take the next nine minutes to decide what you'll eat for
> lunch, ask yourself one question: What would my life be like if the women who
> make it meaningful are not there? Clearly, this is an issue that concerns us all
> (Gruber, 2001).

Establish Your Credibility to Speak on Your Topic

The fourth goal of a speech introduction is to establish your credibility to
speak on your topic. Establishing your qualifications to address your audience
on that topic begins in the introduction and should continue throughout the

12d

rest of your speech. *Introducing relevant supporting materials* and *citing their sources* are two ways to demonstrate that you have carefully researched and considered your topic.

You can also enhance your credibility by *drawing on your own experience* with your topic. Student speaker Humberto mentioned in the introduction of his speech on computer scams how he had once almost been victimized. In the final point of his speech body, he explained how he detected the fake money order he had received to pay for a boat he was selling.

Preview Your Key Ideas

A final objective in organizing your introduction is the **preview statement**, in which you "tell us what you're going to tell us." The preview, working like a map, shows a final destination and reveals how the speaker intends to get there. As a result, the audience can travel more easily through the body of the speech. A speaker addressing the issue of urban decay could preview her speech by listing the four topics to be covered in the body of the speech and preparing the audience to listen more intelligently:

> To better understand the scope of this problem, we must look at four measurable conditions: the unemployment rate, housing starts, the poverty level, and the crime rate.

Preview statements are usually from one to three sentences in length. Rarely do they need to be longer. The following examples are appropriately brief and specific in preparing the audience for the key ideas and the organizational pattern of the speech:

> Assuming that you have the necessary materials, the three steps to constructing a piece of stained glass are, first, selecting or creating a design; second, cutting the glass; and third, assembling and fixing the individual pieces.

> A person suffering from narcolepsy, then, experiences unexpected attacks of deep sleep. This little-known sleep disorder is better understood if we know its symptoms, its causes, and its treatment.

If you have written an effective thesis statement for your speech, you'll have no trouble constructing a preview statement as clear as these examples.

Applying Concepts **DEVELOPING SKILLS** | **Writing a Preview Statement**

Write a preview statement for your speech topic used in previous Applying Concepts Developing Skills boxes in this chapter.

Put It All Together

How does the introduction sound when all five of its functions are working together? Rosa showed that she knows how to develop a complete and effective introduction:

> According to an old Native American saying, every person dies three times. The first time is the moment your life ends. The second is when your body is lowered into the ground. The third is when there is no one around to remember you. I'm going to talk to you today about death, or rather the celebration of death.

Rosa arouses her listener's curiosity by beginning with a thought-provoking quotation, satisfying their curiosity by enumerating how someone dies three times, and continuing to arouse curiosity by arguing that death can be celebrated.

> This is a special celebration that comes from a Mexican tradition called *Dia de los Muertos*, or Day of the Dead. Now it may seem strange and morbid to speak of celebration and death in the same breath, but in the Mexican culture, death is embraced and worshipped just as much as life is.

Rosa satisfies the audience's curiosity by explaining how one culture celebrates death.

> After I give you a little background on *Dia de los Muertos*, I'll explain the different ways this holiday is celebrated and show you some of the traditional objects used in the celebration.

Rosa previews the ideas she will develop in the body of her speech.

Throughout her introduction, Rosa tried to establish her credibility to speak on the topic by demonstrating (1) preparation—she followed the steps of an introduction outlined in her textbook and (2) accuracy—she referred to history and quoted an old Native American saying.

If you achieve the five objectives we have outlined for a speech introduction, your audience should be attentive, know the purpose of your speech, be motivated to listen, trust your qualifications to speak on the topic, and know the major ideas you will discuss.

12e Organizing the Conclusion of Your Speech

Although it is often briefer than the introduction, your conclusion is vitally important to achieving your desired response. The conclusion is the last section your listeners hear and see and must be well planned and carefully organized. It will be easier to develop if you work to achieve three goals.

THE ORGANIZATION OF YOUR CONCLUSION

Summarize your key ideas

Activate audience response to your speech

Provide closure

Summarize Your Key Ideas

In the **summary statement**, you "tell us what you told us." Of all the steps in the process of organization, this should be the easiest to construct. You have already organized the body of the speech and, from it, constructed a preview statement. The summary parallels your preview. If your speech develops three key ideas, you reiterate them.

An excellent summary step, however, does more than just repeat your key ideas. It also shows how those ideas support the goal of your speech. Remember Stacey's humorous attention-getter to her speech encouraging her classmates to study a foreign language? In the speech, she discussed three harms from the nation's failure to promote bilingualism: "First, we lose economically . . . Second, we lose scholastically . . . Third, we lose culturally." Notice how Stacey reiterates and reinforces these points in the summary step of her conclusion:

> Clearly, these three points show us that by being monolingual we lose *economically*, *scholastically*, and *culturally*. Becoming proficient in another language and its culture may help us reduce our deficit and increase our competitiveness in world trade by recognizing possible problems in marketing campaigns. We will gain intellectually by increasing our vocabulary and expanding our minds. We will gain culturally by breaking barriers and possibly eliminating misunderstandings that occur as a result of being unfamiliar with another language, its people, and its culture.

The summary step gives the listener one last chance to hear and remember the main points of your presentation. Thus, the summary step reinforces the ideas of the speech and brings it to a logical conclusion.

Activate Audience Response

What do you want your audience to do with the information you have provided or the arguments you have proved? The second function of a speech conclusion is to activate an audience response by letting your listeners know whether you want them to accept, remember, use, believe, or act on the content of your speech. The conclusion is your last opportunity to ensure your audience's involvement. Some suggestions:

- Challenge them to remember and use what they learned.
- Remind them of the significance of not acting.
- Invigorate or animate your listeners about the subject.

This second function of a conclusion should certainly do something other than say, "I hope you enjoyed my speech." Consider the following example of an ineffective statement and an effective statement that is more useful to the audience.

> **Ineffective:** I hope you'll find what I've said about the film scores of Philip Glass useful.

> **Effective:** The next time you find your attention drawn to a movie's soundtrack because you like the music or feel that it could stand on its own, think about the painstaking process of matching sight and sound that an acclaimed composer like Philip Glass has to go through.

Provide Closure

An effective final statement ties the speech together and provides a strong note of closure. You should not have to tell your listeners that the speech is finished (as in "*That's it.*"). Your wording, as well as your delivery, should make this clear. The audience should know that you are about to finish, and they should have the feeling that you have said exactly as much as you need to say. Without resorting to saying, "In conclusion," or "To conclude," you should mark the end of your speech by

- slowing your speech rate;
- maintaining direct eye contact with your listeners; and
- pausing briefly before and after your final sentence.

Sometimes a speaker employs what is called a **circular conclusion**, in which the final statement echoes or refers to the attention-getting step of the introduction. Remember Jennifer, the grown-up Strawberry Shortcake who spoke about retro toys? At the end of her speech, she brought her listeners back to the familiar scene she had created at the start of her introduction:

> Toy comebacks seem to run in 20- to 30-year cycles; I wonder how many different Elmos there will be in 20 years. For now, on Saturday morning, the Disney Channel delights us with *The Wiggles*, *Stanley*, and the *Higgleytown Heroes*. The little girl in

12e

the Strawberry Shortcake nightgown is my four-year-old, Maddie. She and her baby sister hold their Care Bear dolls and sing along with the programs. Strawberry Shortcake still brings me joy, only now the joy comes from watching how happy Strawberry and her gang make my little girl.

Your final statement does not have to allude to your attention-getting step. Any of the specific techniques we discussed for gaining audience attention can help bring your speech to a strong, clear, psychologically satisfying conclusion. You can, for example, ask a question, even the same one you began with or a variation of it.

Through lively delivery, you could energize the audience to act on the information you have provided. In a speech presented on more formal occasions than a classroom assignment, you may end by complimenting and thanking the audience.

Applying Concepts
DEVELOPING SKILLS | Concluding Your Speech

What technique would you use to conclude your speech? Write a concluding statement for the speech topic you chose for the previous Applying Concepts/ Developing Skills boxes.

Put It All Together

All three functions of the conclusion are important. The summary step reinforces the *ideas* of the speech, while the final two functions reinforce the *impact* of the speech. Consider how Jake accomplished these three functions at the end of his persuasive speech. His use of words such as *we* and *ourselves* involved his listeners, and he used a circular conclusion, revealing the identity of the 76-year-old mother of four he mentioned in his attention-getting step:

> So today, we have learned about the problems of heart disease in women, traced its cause, and put forth some answers.

Jake restates his key ideas.

> As with anything, these solutions aren't perfect—and it's unlikely we'll be able to change society or stop this virulent disease in its tracks. We can, however, change ourselves. Through controlling risk on a personal level, lives will be saved. Not every life, but many.

12e

Jake requests audience action.

> And that 76-year-old mother of four? She was my grandmother. She died last August. But the tragedy was not in the years we have lost with her. It isn't even in the fact that those years could've been saved through different habits and greater understanding. The tragedy will only be if others do not learn from her example. Regret—that's the real tragedy (Gruber, 2001).

Jake provides closure.

In your speech *preparation*, you should prepare the body of your speech first. Speakers who begin preparing speeches by starting with the introduction often end up trying to fit the rest of their speech to the introduction. Some instructors recommend that you develop your introduction next and your conclusion last. Others suggest that you prepare your introduction last. Remember, there is no one correct way of constructing a speech. Select the method that works best for you.

EYEONETHICS | Chronemics and Public Speaking

As discussed in Chapter 5, *chronemics* is a nonverbal cue that indicates our use of time as a means of communication. In public speaking courses, you are likely to be given a time limit for each speech that you present in class. However, not every culture is restricted by time.

According to Edward T. Hall (1983), cultures can be described as monochronic or polychronic. The United States is a *monochronic culture* that is time-bound, meaning that speeches have time limits and meetings start at the time they were scheduled. Kenya is a *polychronic culture* in which time is abstract. As such, Kenyans give speeches that are not restricted by time limits, and ceremonies can last all day rather than contained within a particular time frame.

Kenyans are often called upon to speak at various ceremonies. In the United States, for instance, a best man's toast to the bride and groom typically lasts no more than 5 minutes. In Kenya, a speaker is expected to speak for as long as he deems necessary (it's less common for a woman to speak at any occasion). For Kenyans, it is more important to fully represent the occasion and acknowledge the importance of the occasion than it is to adhere to time restrictions. As Miller (2002) states, "Harmony is more important than whether or not an individual makes it to his next appointment" (p. 180).

Application

Suppose that you are in charge of an event at which your invited speaker is Kenyan. If the speaker continues to speak for half an hour after telling him that he had 15 minutes to speak, would it be ethical to stop his speech before he is finished? How would you handle such a situation?

12e

12f Outlining Your Speech

Outlining your speech is the preliminary written work necessary to foster clear organization of your oral message. When you outline, you organize and reorganize material into a pattern that is easy to recognize and remember.

FUNCTIONS OF OUTLINING

Tests the scope of the speaker's content
- Have you narrowed the topic sufficiently to cover your key ideas in some depth?
- Or are you trying to cover too much material, so that you will merely skim the surface of the subject, repeating things your audience already knows?

Tests the logical relation of parts
- Does one idea in the outline lead to the next in a meaningful way?
- Do the arguments or subtopics under each of your main points really develop that point?

Tests the relevance of supporting ideas
- Do the subpoints match the main point under which they are placed?

Checks the balance of the speech
- Do each of the main points contain approximately the same number of subpoints?

Serves as delivery notes
- Once your outline is completed, use it to create your keyword outline.

12f

Principles of Outlining

Correct outlines take one of two possible forms: the complete sentence outline and the key word or phrase outline. In a complete sentence outline, each item is a sentence; each item in a key word or phrase outline is a word or group of words. As you construct your outline, you will work more efficiently and produce a clearer outline if you follow a few rules, or principles.

Singularity.   Each number or letter in the outline should represent only *one* idea. A chief goal of outlining is to achieve a clear visual representation of the connections among parts of the speech. This is possible only if you separate the ideas. For example, suppose a speaker preparing a speech on color blindness has worded a key idea as "causes of and tests for color blindness." The phrase contains two distinct ideas, each requiring separate discussion and development. Instead, the speaker should divide the statement into two main points: "causes of color blindness" and "tests for color blindness."

Consistency. Second, main and subpoints in the outline should be represented by a consistent system of numbers and letters. Main ideas are typically represented by Roman numerals: I, II, III, and so forth. Label subpoints under the main points with indented capital letters: A, B, C, and so forth. Beneath those, identify your supporting points with indented Arabic numerals: 1, 2, 3, and so on. Identify ideas subordinate to those with indented lowercase letters: a, b, c, and so on. Using this notation system, the labeling and indentation of a typical outline would appear as follows:

I. Main point
   A. Subpoint
      1. Sub-subpoint
      2. Sub-subpoint
   B. Subpoint
      1. Sub-subpoint
      2. Sub-subpoint
         a. Sub-sub-subpoint
         b. Sub-sub-subpoint

II. Main point
   A. Subpoint
   B. Subpoint
      1. Sub-subpoint
      2. Sub-subpoint
   C. Subpoint

Adequacy. If any point has subpoints under it, there must be at least two subpoints. If you have a I, you must have a II. If you have an A, you must also have a B. (You may, of course, also have subpoints C, D, and E.) If you have a 1, you must also have a 2.

Uniformity. Each symbol (Roman numeral or letter) in a sentence outline should introduce a complete sentence. Each symbol in a word or phrase outline should introduce a word or phrase. Keep the form of the outline consistent. Sentences and phrases should be mixed only in your speaking outline.

Parallelism. Finally, main points throughout the outline should have parallel grammatical construction. For example, a key phrase outline of a speech on how to write a résumé begins with a first main point labeled "Things to

12f

include." The second point should be "Things to omit," rather than "Leaving out unnecessary information." The first point is worded as a noun phrase and, therefore, you must follow it with another noun phrase ("Things to omit"), rather than a predicate phrase ("Leaving out unnecessary information"). This does not mean that you must choose noun phrases over verb phrases, but rather that all points must match grammatically.

Stages of Outlining

If you have difficulty generating or discovering the main points for a speech topic you have chosen, don't worry; you are not alone. Let's trace that process of creating an outline.

The working outline. The first step in preparing an outline is to construct a **working outline**, a list of aspects of your chosen topic. Such a list may result from research you have already done or from some productive brainstorming. Once you have spent significant time researching the subject, you will notice topics that are repeated in different sources on the subject.

At this stage the term *outline* is very loose; the list of key ideas you are developing does not have any numbers or letters attached to it. That's fine, since these notes are for your benefit alone. This working outline is not so much a finished product as it is a record of the process you go through in thinking about a speech topic.

For example, Elvir Berbic began writing his informative speech using the following working outline:

SPECIFIC PURPOSE: To inform the audience about differences between three generations (Baby Boomers, Generation X, and Millenials)

Key Ideas:

    I. Baby Boomers

   II. Generation Xers

  III. Millenials

The formal outline. Your **formal outline** is a complete sentence outline reflecting the full content and organization of your speech. In its final form, it is the finished product of your research and planning for your speech. A stranger, picking up your formal outline, should be able to understand how you have organized and supported all your main points. If you keep that goal in mind, you should have no trouble deciding what to include. To save space, we'll show you the substructure under just his first main point. Here is Elvir's formal outline that he produced from his working outline.

Formal Outline

Speech Title:

What a Difference a Generation Makes

◄—— Elvir's simple title not only gets attention but also hints at his topic. To check the goals of the speech, Elvir then states his specific purpose and thesis.

Specific Purpose:

To inform the audience about differences between three generations (Baby Boomers, Generation X, and Millennials)

Thesis Statement:

Several key features influenced the three most recent generations: Baby Boomers, Generation X, and Millennials.

Introduction

We're living in an age when multiple generations are working side by side in the workplace. According to Zemke, Raines, and Filipczak, authors of the 2000 book *Generations at Work*, generational differences can create problems in the workplace. Everyone in this room may not be from the same generation. I'm a member of the Millennial generation, and I have read extensively about generational differences. Because all of you are part of one of the generations that I'll discuss today, I think you will find the information interesting, too.

◄—— Note that Elvir writes out the entire introduction, gaining audience attention by stating a fact related to his speech topic. He builds his credibility by mentioning that he's a Millennial, that he's read extensively about the subject of his speech, and he cites a source.

　　A generation is defined by historians Neil Howe & William Strauss in their book *Millennials Rising* written in 2000 as a "society-wide peer group," born over approximately the same time period, "who collectively possess a common persona" (p. 40). Each generation is characterized by defining historical events, such as 9/11, that happen in their formative years. These events shape the attitudes, beliefs, and values of a generation. The Vietnam War, the Space Shuttle Challenger explosion, and the Columbine shootings are defining moments for each of the three generations I will discuss. Drawing from Ron Zemke's insightful book, *Generations at Work*, today I'm going to explain several key features that characterize the three most recent generations: Baby Boomers, Generation X, and Millennials.

◄—— His introduction ends with a clear preview of the three main points Elvir plans to discuss.

　　The first generation is the Baby Boomer generation.

◄—— Signpost and statement

Body Outline

I. Baby Boomers were born between the years 1943 and 1960.
　A. There are several defining general characteristics of the Baby Boomers.
　　1. They are the first generation to work 60 hours a week.
　　2. Baby Boomers are often referred to as the "Me Generation" because they are focused on making themselves better. They go to the gym, get plastic surgery, and purchase self-help materials.

◄—— The outline's three main points match Elvir's thesis and preview statements. Each item in the outline is a complete sentence. Each level of the outline has at least two headings, and many subpoints are grammatically parallel.

12f

3. Boomers' interest in seeking an equal playing field for everyone make them actively involved in the fight for civil rights.

B. These general characteristics were born from the core values of Baby Boomers.
   1. In the workplace, Boomers value hard work and involvement. They are optimistic and team oriented.
   2. Both in and out of the workplace, they are concerned with personal gratification and personal growth.

C. Several other features of Boomers distinguish them from the other two generations.
   1. They buy whatever is trendy, including clothing, plastic surgery, and electronic gadgets.
   2. Boomers are the first generation to acquire credit card debt.
   3. They typically read magazines like *Business Week* and *People*.
   4. Their sense of humor is similar to that found in the print cartoon *Doonesbury*.

The Baby Boomer generation produced the next generation known as Generation X.   ← **Signpost and statement**

II. Generation X includes people born between 1960 and 1980.   ← **The second main point follows the pattern of the first main point. Similar subpoints are used to allow the audience to make parallels between Baby Boomers and Gen Xers.**
   A. The general characteristics of X'ers explain their behaviors.
      1. In the workplace, X'ers need feedback and flexibility, and they are not fond of close supervision in the workplace.
      2. X'ers came home from school each day to an empty house, making X'ers the first generation of "latch key" kids. As the first generation to see an increase in parental divorce, they are comfortable with change.
      3. X'ers work to live, not live to work. In a study published in 2002,   ← **Elvir cites another source within his speech.**
         researchers Smola and Sutton report that X'ers are less loyal to the company they work for and they place less importance on work life than Boomers.

   B. X'ers' core values mirror their general characteristics.
      1. They are self-reliant and pragmatic. X'ers witnessed the first Live Aid concert, which made them think globally given its emphasis on world hunger.
      2. As the first generation to grow up using computers, VCRs, and cable television, X'ers value technological literacy.

   C. Some of the other features of the X'ers further explain their generation.
      1. They began the trends of multiple piercings and tattoos. Unlike their Boomer parents, they prefer functional clothing and Japanese cars.
      2. They are cautious and conservative with their money.
      3. X'ers typically read magazines like *Spin* and *Wired* in addition to chat room dialogue.
      4. The print cartoon *Dilbert* appeals to their sense of humor.

While Generation X is characterized as self-reliant, the next generation, the Millenials, are much more dependent upon their parents.

Signpost and statement

III. Millennials were born between the years 1980 and 2000.
  A. The general characteristics of the Millennial are in stark contrast to the characteristics of their parents, the X'ers.
     1. Having absent parents, X'ers were determined to make sure their children knew they were loved. As a result, the Millennials are often over-protected by their parents, who keep the Millennial child's calendar full from morning to night.
     2. Millennials are more technologically savvy than any previous generation.
     3. What their parents think is important to Millennials; in fact, they think their parents are cool.
  B. The core values of the Millennials reflect their close relationships with their parents.
     1. They are optimistic, confident, and moral.
     2. They value civic duty, achievement, and diversity.
  C. Other features of the Millennials are interesting, too.
     1. They prefer all things retro and they are the first generation to grow up with cell phones.
     2. Millennials get plenty of spending money from their parents to buy whatever they want.
     3. Millennials typically read book series, like *Goosebumps* and *Baby Sitters' Club*.
     4. Millennial humor is illustrated in the print cartoon *Calvin and Hobbes*.

Just as in the first two main points, Elvir writes the third main point using the same structure.

Conclusion

In summary, I have informed you about several key features that influenced the three most recent generations: Baby Boomers, Generation X, and Millennials. You can see how these three generations differ from one another, so imagine how their contrasting values and interests might clash in the workplace. Given the time constraints, I have provided you with only a few features of each generation. I would encourage you to read more about the generations. You might find it valuable in your workplace in the future. Which makes you wonder, what could the future hold for the next generation?

Elvir's conclusion begins with a clear summary of his three main points. He then activates the audience response by recommending that they read more about generational differences. His final question provides a strong sense of closure to the speech.

12f

The speaking outline. The **speaking outline**, the one you actually use to deliver your speech, is a pared-down version of your full formal outline. You construct the formal outline for an interested reader having no necessary prior knowledge of your topic. However, you write the speaking outline for yourself as a unique speaker. The only rule for the speaking outline is that it be *brief*.

Why is the speaking outline briefer than the formal outline?

- It is made up of essential words and phrases and serves as your speaking notes.

- If you spoke from a complete sentence outline, you might be tempted to read the speech, sacrificing eye contact and other vital interaction with your audience.

Important items are included in the speaking outline but not in the formal outline.

- *You can include directions to yourself about the delivery of the speech.* You could also note places where you want to pause, to slow down, to speak louder, or to use presentational aids.

- *You should include any supporting material you plan to use.* Quotations and definitions should be written in complete sentences, even though the rest of the outline is in words and phrases. Include just enough information to be able to cite each of your sources clearly and correctly.

- *Use keywords or phrases to remind you of each step in your introduction and conclusion.* Then try to deliver those crucial parts of the speech without referring to your notes.

Let's look at Elvir's speaking outline, which he created by using his formal outline.

12f

SAMPLE

Speech Outline

Given space constraints, we will show only the first main point of Elvir's speech.

I. Baby Boomers (1943–1960)
   A. General characteristics
      1. Worked 60 week
      2. "Me Generation"
      3. Equal playing field—civil rights
   B. Core Values
      1. Value work & involvement. Optimistic & team oriented.
      2. Personal gratification & personal growth

C. Other Features
   1. Buy and display whatever is trendy
   2. 1st generation credit cards
   3. Read: *Business Week, People*
   4. Humor: *Doonesbury*

PAUSE

(T: Baby Boomers produced Generation X)

II. Generation X (1960–1980)
   A. General Characteristics
      1. Need for feedback & flexibility, dislike close supervision ⟶ problems in workplace
      2. 1st "latch key" kids, 1st prevalent divorce ⟶ personally adept / comfortable with change
      3. Work to live, not live to work; Smola & Sutton (2002) X'ers less loyal & impt. on work

LOOK UP

   B. Core Values
      1. Self-reliant, pragmatic, & think globally. 1st Live Aid concert
      2. 1st generation to grow up using computers, VCRs, & cable television. Technological literacy.
   C. Other Features
      1. Multiple piercings, tattoos, functional clothing, Japanese cars
      2. Cautious, conservative with money
      3. Read: Spin, Wired, chat room dialogue
      4. Humor: Dilbert

SLOW DOWN

(Gen X is self-reliant, Millennials dependent upon parents)

III. Millennials (1980–2000)
   A. General Characteristics
      1. X'ers love M's; over-protected and busy
      2. More technologically savvy than other gens.
      3. Parent input important; parents cool
   B. Core Values
      1. Optimistic, confident, moral
      2. Civic duty, achievement, diversity
   C. Other Features
      1. All things retro and cell phones
      2. Parents give plenty money
      3. Read: Book series (Goosebumps, Baby Sitters' Club)
      4. Humor: Calvin and Hobbes

PAUSE

⟵ Delivery prompts are in capital letters so Elvir can see them at a glance and not confuse them with content prompts.
Transitions can be marked with a "T" or put in parentheses.

⟵ Although Elvir's speaking outline entries are abbreviated, many are parallel in structure.

12f

⟵ Elvir's speaking outline contains specific supporting materials such as facts, along with information about each source he needs to cite.

In this chapter, you have learned the following concepts to increase your communication competence.

12a Organizing the Body of Your Speech

- Organizing the speech includes creating an introduction, developing the main ideas of the speech body, and writing a conclusion. A clear organizational structure for your speech is important to help your listeners remember your main ideas and understand the topic.

- Public speakers employ a wide variety of organizational structures. Several patterns most commonly used are topical, chronological, spatial, causal, pro-con, and problem-solution.

- All of the patterns are useful for both informative and persuasive speeches, except problem-solution, which is appropriate only for persuasive speeches.

Competence. Can I distinguish between the different organizational patterns? Do I know which pattern would be most appropriate for my speech topic?

12b Developing Your Key Ideas

- After selecting an organizational pattern and arranging your main points, you need to develop each key idea.

- Your listeners will better comprehend and remember your speech if you *signpost*, *state*, *support*, and *summarize* each idea.

Competence. Do I understand the purpose of signposting? Do I use supporting materials to develop each of my main ideas? Do I summarize each idea before moving on to the next?

12c Connecting Your Key Ideas with Transitions

- A speaker moves from one idea to the next with the aid of a transition. A transition not only connects two ideas, but also indicates the nature of that connection.

- Four basic types of transitions are complementary, causal, contrasting, and chronological.

Competence. Do I know the purpose of a transition? Can I incorporate transitions into my speech to connect the main points?

12d Organizing the Introduction of Your Speech

- The introduction should achieve five goals: (1) get the attention of your audience; (2) state your topic or purpose; (3) stress the importance or relevance of your topic; (4) establish your credibility to speak on your topic; and (5) preview the key ideas you will develop in the body of the speech.

Competence. Can I identify different techniques that I can use to gain my audience's attention? Do I know how to create an effective preview statement?

12e Organizing the Conclusion of Your Speech

- An effective conclusion must do three things: (1) summarize your key ideas; (2) secure your listeners' commitment to your information and ideas; and (3) provide closure, or bring the speech to a satisfying psychological conclusion.

Competence. Do I know how to write an effective summary statement? Can I write a concluding sentence that provides closure for my audience?

12f Outlining Your Speech

- An outline serves several functions. There are also several types of outlines, including working outlines, formal outlines, and speaking outlines.

- Be sure to follow the stages of outlining so that you organize your speech properly and effectively.

Competence. Can I put together an appropriately structured outline? Can I distinguish between the three stages of outlines?

Review Questions

1. What are the six organizational patterns for structuring the main points of a speech?
2. Which of the six organizational patterns is most appropriate for persuasive speeches only?
3. List the 4 S's for developing each main point of your speech.
4. Explain the concept of signposting.
5. Name and define one of the four types of transitions.
6. What are the five objectives of an introduction?
7. Name one type of attention getter.
8. What is the difference between a preview statement and a summary statement?
9. What are the three goals of a conclusion?
10. Explain the differences between the three stages of speech outlines.

Discussion Questions

1. Is it possible to give an effective speech without an introduction?
2. Are there speaking situations in which the use of humor is completely inappropriate, even if the humor is not offensive?

Key Terms

causal division *p. 286*

causal transition *p. 294*

chronological division *p. 285*

chronological transition *p. 295*

circular conclusion *p. 303*

complementary transition *p. 294*

contrasting transition *p. 294*

direct question *p. 296*

formal outline *p. 308*

preview statement *p. 300*

problem-solution division *p. 288*

pro-con division *p. 287*

rhetorical question *p. 296*

signpost *p. 289*

spatial division *p. 286*

speaking outline *p. 312*

summary statement *p. 302*

topical division *p. 284*

transition *p. 293*

working outline *p. 308*

Delivering Your Speech and Using Presentational Aids

Your communication competence will be enhanced by understanding:

- how to use different methods of delivery to create the most effective speech;
- how you can develop the qualities of an effective speaker, thereby enhancing your communication competence;
- why elements of vocal and physical delivery can increase your competence as a public speaker;
- how to create a useful presentational aid to help you more effectively communicate your message to an audience.

13a Exploring the Basics of Delivery

Your manner of presenting a speech—through your unique voice, body, and language—forms your style of delivery. In other words, *what* you say is your speech content and *how* you say it is your **delivery**. Though poor delivery may diminish the impact of well-organized ideas, effective delivery can bolster those same ideas. Your delivery not only shapes your image as a speaker, but also changes your message in subtle ways.

Methods of Delivery

Before we survey the individual elements that make up delivery, it's important to know the possible methods of delivering a speech and the qualities that should mark the method you choose. There are four basic ways you can deliver your public speech.

Speaking impromptu. We engage in **impromptu speaking** whenever someone calls on us to express an opinion or unexpectedly asks us to "say a few words" to a group. In these informal situations, other people do not necessarily expect us to be forceful or well organized, and we are probably somewhat comfortable speaking without any preparation. The more important the speech is, however, the less appropriate the impromptu method of delivery. Although impromptu speaking is excellent practice, no conscientious person should risk a grade, an important proposal, or a professional advancement on an unprepared speech.

Speaking from memory. Speaking from memory is when we prepare a written text and then memorize it word for word. It is appropriate only on rare occasions. At best, a memorized speech allows a smooth, almost

13a

effortless-looking delivery because the speaker has neither notes nor a manuscript and can concentrate on interacting with the audience. For most of us, however, memorizing takes a long time. Concentration on the memory work you've done and your fear of forgetting part of the speech can also make you sound mechanical or programmed when reciting. For these reasons, speaking from memory is usually appropriate only for brief speeches, such as those introducing another speaker or presenting or accepting an award.

Speaking from manuscript. **Speaking from manuscript** occurs when a person delivers a speech from a complete text prepared in advance. Not only does this ensure that the speaker will not be at a loss for words, but is also essential in some situations. An address that will be quoted or later published in its entirety is typically delivered from a manuscript. Major foreign policy speeches or State of the Union addresses by U.S. presidents are always delivered from manuscript, because it is important that the speaker be understood, not misunderstood. Speeches of tribute and commencement addresses are also often scripted. Manuscript delivery may be appropriate for any speaking situation calling for precise, well-worded communication.

Having every word of your speech scripted may boost your confidence, but it does not ensure effective delivery. You must write the speech in a conversational style. The text of your speech requires a good deal of time to prepare, edit, revise, and type for final delivery. In addition, if you do not also take time to practice delivering your speech in a fluent, conversational manner and with appropriate emphasis, well-placed pauses, and adequate eye contact, you are preparing to fail as an effective speaker.

Speaking extemporaneously. The final method of delivery, and by far the most popular, is **speaking extemporaneously**, or from notes. This is the delivery style that is the focus of this text. Speaking from notes offers several advantages over other delivery methods.

13a

- **You can be natural and spontaneous.** You don't have to worry about one particular way of wording your ideas, because you have not scripted the speech.
- **You can relax.** You don't have to worry that you will forget something you have memorized.
- **You can adapt your speech to the audience.** If something you say confuses the audience, you can repeat it, explain it using other words, or use a better example to clarify it.

You can't experience the freedom that extemporaneous speaking permits unless you have taken the time to develop your speech content and organization and to analyze your audience.

When speaking either from notes or a manuscript, keep several practical points in mind:

- **Practice with the notes or manuscript you will actually use in delivering the speech.** Double- or even triple-space a speech manuscript and format text in a font size that's easy for you to see. Type sentences on the upper two-thirds of each sheet to help ensure better eye contact. You need to know where things are on the page so that you have to glance down only briefly.

- **Number your note cards or the pages of your manuscript.** Check their order before you speak. This will ensure that you can easily put your notes back together should you drop them on the way to deliver your speech.

- **Determine when you should and should not look at your notes.** Looking at your notes when you quote an authority or present statistics is acceptable. In fact, doing so may even convey to your audience your concern for getting supporting materials exactly right. However, do not look down while previewing, stating, or summarizing your key ideas. If you cannot remember your key points, what hope is there for your audience?

- **Devote extra practice time to your conclusion.** The last thing you say can make a deep impression, but not if you rush through it or deliver it while gathering your notes and walking back to your seat. Your goal at this critical point in the speech is the same as your goal for all your delivery: to eliminate distractions and to reinforce your message through your body, voice, and language.

To demonstrate that you are well prepared and to ensure contact with your audience, you may want to memorize your introduction and conclusion. If you deliver the body of your speech extemporaneously, look at your notes occasionally. Just don't look at your notes while you are stating or summarizing each main point. If you quote sources in your speech, you are, in effect, briefly using a manuscript. Finally, as an audience-centered speaker, you must be flexible enough to improvise a bit. If you are well prepared, this combination of delivery methods should look natural to your audience and feel comfortable to you.

Practice with the notes you will actually use to deliver your speech.

Number your note cards or pages of notes.

Determine when you should and should not look at your notes.

Devote extra practice time to your conclusion.

Qualities of Effective Delivery

As you begin to think about the way you deliver a speech, keep in mind three characteristics of effective delivery.

Effective delivery helps both listeners and speakers. You know what you want to say, but your audience does not. Your audience has only one chance to receive your message. Just as clear organization makes your ideas easier to remember, effective delivery can underscore your key points, sell your ideas, or communicate your concern for the topic.

The best delivery looks and feels natural, comfortable, and spontaneous. No one should notice how hard you are working to deliver your speech effectively. Some occasions and audiences require you to be more formal than others. In other situations, you may find yourself moving, gesturing, and using presentational aids extensively. You want to orchestrate all these elements so that your presentation looks and feels relaxed and natural, not strained or awkward. You achieve spontaneous delivery such as this only through practice.

Delivery is best when the audience is not aware of it at all. Your goal should be delivery that reinforces your ideas and is free of distractions. When the audience begins to notice how you twist your ring, to count the number of times you say "um," or to categorize the types of grammatical mistakes you make, your delivery is distracting them from what you are saying.

How can you help ensure effective delivery? Concentrate on your ideas and how the audience is receiving them. Pay attention to their interest in your speech, their understanding of your message, and their acceptance or rejection of what you are saying. If you notice listeners checking their watches, reading papers, whispering to friends, or snoozing, they are probably bored. At this point you can enliven your delivery with movement and changes in your volume. Such relatively simple changes in your delivery may revive their interest.

13a

But what if you notice looks of confusion on your audience's faces? Slow your rate of delivery, and use descriptive gestures to reinforce your ideas. If you observe frowns or heads shaking from side to side, you've encountered a hostile audience! There are ways to help break down the resistance of even an antagonistic group. Look directly at such listeners, establish a conversational tone, incorporate friendly facial expressions, and use your body to demonstrate involvement with your topic.

Applying Concepts DEVELOPING SKILLS | **Choosing Methods of Delivery**

You are a company spokesperson who is addressing reporters after an accident at one of your company's plants. Given the explanations of each method above, what method of delivery would be best in that situation? What if you were a keynote speaker at a banquet at your former high school? What method would you consider best in that situation?

13b Examining Elements of Vocal Delivery

Any prescription for effective delivery will include three basic elements: the *voice*, or vocal delivery; the *body*, or physical delivery; and *language*. Vocal delivery includes rate, pause, volume, pitch, inflection, voice quality, articulation, and pronunciation.

Rate and Pause

Your **rate** is the speed of your speaking. Rate can communicate something, intentionally or unintentionally, about your motives in speaking, your disposition, or your involvement with the topic. Your goal in a speech, therefore, should be to avoid extremely fast or slow delivery; you should instead use a variety of rates to reinforce your purpose in speaking and make you seem conversational.

Pauses or silences are an important element in your rate of delivery. You pause to allow the audience time to reflect on something you have just said or to heighten suspense about something you are going to say. Pauses also mark important transitions in your speech, helping you and your audience shift gears. Remember, though, that to be effective in a speech, pauses must be used intentionally and selectively. If your speech is filled with too many awkwardly placed pauses or too many vocalized pauses, such as "um" and "uh," you will seem hesitant or unprepared, and your credibility will erode quickly.

Volume Your audience must be able to hear you in order to listen to your ideas. **Volume** is simply how loudly or softly you speak. A person who speaks too loudly may be considered boisterous or obnoxious. In contrast, an inaudible speaker may be considered unsure or timid.

Adapt your volume to the size of the room where you speak. In your classroom, you can probably use a volume just slightly louder than your usual conversational level. When you speak before a large group, a microphone may be helpful or even essential. If possible, practice beforehand so that the sound of your amplified voice does not startle you.

Pitch and Inflection

Pitch refers to the highness or lowness of vocal tones, similar to the notes on a musical staff. Every speaker has an optimal pitch range, or key. This is the range in which you are most comfortable speaking, and your voice is probably pleasant to hear in this range.

Speakers who are unusually nervous sometimes raise their pitch. Other speakers think that if they lower their pitch they will seem more authoritative. In truth, speakers who do not use their normal pitch usually sound artificial.

A problem more typical than an unusually high- or low-pitched voice is vocal delivery that lacks adequate **inflection**, or changes in pitch. Someone who speaks without changing pitch delivers sentences in a flat, uniform pitch pattern that becomes monotonous. Indeed, the word *monotone* means "one tone," and you may have had instructors whose monotonous droning invited you to doze. Varied inflection is an essential tool for conveying meaning accurately.

Voice Quality

Voice quality, or timbre, the least flexible of the vocal elements, is the characteristic that distinguishes your voice from other voices. You may have called a friend on the phone and had difficulty telling him from his father or her from her mother or sisters. Most of the time, however, you recognize the voices of friends easily. In general, our individual voices are distinct. In fact, police investigators often use voice prints to identify and distinguish individual voices on tape recordings. You may notice that sometimes the clarity and resonance of your voice can be temporarily affected by colds, allergies, or strain.

Articulation and Pronunciation

The final elements of vocal delivery are articulation and pronunciation. **Articulation** is the mechanical process of forming the sounds necessary to communicate in a particular language. Most articulation errors are made from habit and take four principal forms: deletion, addition, substitution, and transposition.

- **Deletion.** Deletion is leaving out sounds, for example saying "libary" for "library" or "goverment" for "government."
- **Addition.** If you have heard someone say "athalete" for "athlete," you've heard an articulation error caused by the *addition* of a sound.
- **Substitution.** Examples of errors caused by the *substitution* of one sound for another are "kin" for "can" and "git" for "get."
- **Transposition.** *Transposition* is the reversal of two sounds that are close together. This error is the vocal equivalent of transposing two letters in a typed word. Saying "lectren" for "lectern" or "hunderd" for "hundred" are examples of transposition errors.

Articulation errors made as a result of habit may be so ingrained that you can no longer identify your mistakes. Your speech instructor, friends, and classmates can help you by pointing out articulation problems. You may need to listen to recordings of your speeches to locate problems and then practice the problem words or sounds to correct your articulation.

Pronunciation, in contrast to articulation, is simply a matter of knowing how the letters of a word sound and where the stress falls when that word is spoken. If you have any doubt about the pronunciation of a word you plan to use in a speech, look it up in a current dictionary and then practice the correct pronunciation out loud before the speech. Apply this rule to every word you select, including those in quotations. If you follow this simple rule, you will avoid embarrassing errors of pronunciation.

Applying Concepts DEVELOPING SKILLS | **Identifying Vocal Delivery Skills**

Go to YouTube and find a short speech. Using the qualities of vocal delivery discussed above, identify the strengths and weaknesses of the speaker's vocal delivery.

13c Understanding the Elements of Physical Delivery

Elements of physical delivery include appearance, posture, eye contact and facial expression, movement, and gestures.

Appearance

We all form quick impressions of people we meet based on subtle nonverbal signals. *Appearance*—in particular our grooming and the way we dress—is an important nonverbal signal that helps people judge us. Clothing not only influences our perceptions of others but also shapes our self-perception. You probably have certain clothes that give you a sense of confidence or make you feel especially assertive or powerful. You feel differently about yourself when you wear them. Dressing "up" conveys your seriousness of purpose to your listeners. It also establishes this same positive attitude in your own mind.

Posture

A public speaker should look comfortable, confident, and prepared to speak. You have the appropriate attire. Your next concern is your *posture*, the position or bearing of your body. The two extremes to avoid are rigidity and sloppiness. Don't hang on to or drape yourself across the lectern, if you are using one. Keep your weight balanced on both legs, and avoid shifting your weight back and forth in a nervous swaying pattern. Equally distracting is standing on one leg and shuffling or tapping the other foot. You may not realize that you do those things. Other people will have to point them out to you. Remember that for your delivery to reinforce your message, it must be free of annoying mannerisms.

Eye Contact and Facial Expression

Eye contact can carry many messages: confidence, concern, sincerity, interest, and enthusiasm. Lack of eye contact, on the other hand, may signal deceit, disinterest, or insecurity.

Your face is the most important source of nonverbal cues as you deliver your speech, and your eyes carry more information than any other facial feature. As you speak, you will occasionally look at your notes or manuscript. You may even glance away from the audience briefly as you try to put your thoughts into words. Yet you must keep coming back to the eyes of your listeners to check their understanding, interest, and evaluation of your message.

As a public speaker, your goal is to make eye contact with as much of the audience as much of the time as possible. The way to do this is to make sure that you take in your entire audience, from front to back and from left to right. Include all those boundaries in the scope of your eye contact, and look especially at those who seem to be listening carefully and responding positively. Whether you actually make eye contact with each member of the audience is immaterial. You must create that impression. Again, this takes practice.

Your facial expression must match what you are saying. The speaker who smiles and blushes self-consciously through a speech on date rape will simply

13c

not be taken seriously and may offend many listeners. If you detail the plight of earthquake victims, make sure your face reflects your concern. Your face should register the thoughts and feelings that motivate your words.

Movement

Effective *movement* benefits you, your audience, and your speech. First, place-to-place movement can actually help you relax. Moving to a visual aid, for example, can help you energize and loosen up physically. From the audience's perspective, movement adds visual variety to your speech, and appropriate movement can arouse or rekindle the listeners' interest. Most important, though, physical movement serves your speech by guiding the audience's attention. Through movement, you can underscore key ideas, mark major transitions, or intensify an appeal for belief or action.

Make certain that your movement is selective and that it serves a purpose. Avoid random pacing. Movement to mark a transition should occur at the beginning or the end of a sentence, not in the middle. Finally, bring the speech to a satisfying psychological conclusion, and pause for a second or two before gathering your materials and moving toward your seat in the audience.

Gestures

Gestures, movements of a speaker's hands, arms, and head, seem to be as natural a part of human communication as spoken language. Gestures not only punctuate and emphasize verbal messages for the benefit of listeners; they also ease the process of encoding those messages for speakers. According to Frick-Horbury and Guttentag (1998), people asked to communicate without gestures produce labored speech marked by increased hesitations and pauses. Such speakers also demonstrate decreased fluency, inflection, and stress.

If you don't normally gesture in conversation, force yourself to include some gestures as you practice your speech. At first you may feel self-conscious about gesturing. Keep practicing. Gestures that seem natural and spontaneous are well worth whatever time you spend practicing them. Not only do they reinforce your ideas and make you seem more confident and dynamic, but gestures, like movement, can also help you relax.

The combination of vocal and physical delivery will have an impact on the audience's perception of your speech. Delivery is a vital part of your public speech, and effective vocal and physical delivery are assets worth cultivating if you want to enhance your communication competence.

Cultural CONNECTIONS | Delivery Styles

When listening to speakers from another culture, it is important to consider their nonverbal cues, from a cultural perspective. Understanding cultural differences in nonverbal cues can enhance your communication competence. Here we will examine differences in eye contact and volume.

According to Tidwell (2009), Western cultures value direct eye contact, but not staring. Direct eye contact indicates a listener's interest in the speaker and the speaker's interest in communicating with the listener. Arab cultures value eye contact that is maintained longer than in Western cultures. Someone who communicates with an Arab and does not maintain prolonged eye contact is considered untrustworthy. In Asian, African, and Latin American cultures, avoiding eye contact is a sign of respect.

In the United States, African Americans use more eye contact when speaking than when listening. Whites use more eye contact when listening than when speaking (Tidwell, 2009).

With regard to volume, cultures differ on what is considered appropriate. Loud speaking volume indicates strength in Arab cultures, confidence in German cultures, and impoliteness and loss of control for Asian cultures.

Application

Based on the information above, how would you adapt your speaking style for a multicultural audience? How will your peer ratings of classmates' speeches be affected by your knowledge of cultural differences in delivery styles?

13d

13d Using Presentational Aids Effectively

Our language reflects the power of the visual message: "A picture is worth a thousand words." "I wouldn't have believed it if I hadn't seen it with my own eyes." As a speaker, you need not rely only on words to communicate your ideas precisely and powerfully. You can add force and impact to many messages by incorporating a visual dimension as well.

THE FOUR FUNCTIONS OF PRESENTATIONAL AIDS

Increases Message Clarity

Presentational aids give your speech greater clarity. They can specify the demographic breakdown of voters in a past election, illustrate the structure of an online course, or explain the process of monitoring and controlling air traffic. You can convey detailed statistical information more clearly in a simplified line graph than by merely reciting the data. Speeches using a spatial organizational pattern often benefit particularly from visual reinforcement.

Reinforces Message Impact

Presentational aids give your speech greater impact. Seeing may encourage believing; certainly, it aids remembering. Because they both hear and see the message, listeners are more fully involved in the speech. This greater sensory involvement with the message lessens the opportunity for outside distractions and increases retention.

Increases Speaker Dynamism

Presentational aids make you seem more dynamic. Gestures are an important part of your delivery. Using presentational aids forces you to move, to point, to become physically involved with your speech. Your gestures become motivated and meaningful, and, consequently, you appear more dynamic and forceful.

Enhances Speaker Confidence

Using presentational aids can increase your confidence. Clear, attractive presentational aids that you have practiced using can help you relax. Knowing that your presentational aids will enhance the clarity and impact of your message gives purpose to your movement and gestures (which will help burn off some of your nervous energy).

Plan Your Aids for Your Purpose and Audience

Before you begin to create your presentational aids to clarify and enliven your speech, ask yourself, "Will such aids make my presentation more effective?" A well-designed, appropriate presentational aid can add significantly to the effectiveness of the speech and the speaker. Consider the four functions of presentational aids as you determine whether to include presentational aids in a particular speech.

Determine the information to be presented visually. Complex or detailed sections of a presentation may be particularly appropriate for visualization. Be careful, however, not to use too many visual aids. The premium in a speech is on the spoken word. Multimedia presentations can be exciting; they may also be extremely difficult to coordinate. Handling too many objects or charts quickly becomes cumbersome and distracting.

Select the type of presentational aid best suited to your resources and speech. The information you need to present, the amount of preparation time you have, your technical expertise at producing the aid, and the cost involved will all influence the visual aid you select. If preparing quality presentational aids to illustrate your speech will take more time, money, or expertise than you have, you are probably better off without them. A presentational aid that calls attention to its poor production is a handicap, no matter how important the information it contains.

Ensure easy viewing by all audience members. A speaker addressing an audience of 500 would not want to display a videotaped presentation on a single television or computer monitor. A bar graph on a computer monitor or posterboard should be visible to more than just the first four rows of the audience. If possible, practice with your presentational aids in the room where you will speak. Position or project the aid and then sit in the farthest possible seat. (In an auditorium, make it the back row; people will not move forward unless forced to.) If you can read your presentational aid from that distance, it is large enough. If you cannot, either enlarge or eliminate the aid.

Create Effective Presentational Aids

In this section we'll offer guidelines for creating a variety of presentational aids that will help you communicate information clearly and simply. Michael Talman (1992), a graphics design consultant, compares a graphic in a presentation to "going by a highway billboard at 55 miles per hour. Its effectiveness can be judged by how quickly the viewer sees and understands its message" (p. 270). Limit the range of colors, as well as mute secondary visual elements—such as frames, grids, arrows, rules, and boxes—to clarify the primary information you want to convey (Tufte, 2001). Remember that the chief purpose of visual aids is to inform, not to impress, the audience.

We'll also offer guidelines that will help you construct a presentational aid that is professional in appearance. In the business and professional world, a hand-lettered poster, no matter how neatly done, is inappropriate. Professionals understand the importance of a good impression and are willing to pay graphics designers to help them create polished presentational aids. Today, however, the computer puts a galaxy of inexpensive, professional-looking design options at the fingertips of anyone willing to learn the programs. If you throw together a chart or graph the night before your speech, that is exactly what it will look like. Your hastily prepared work will undermine an image of careful and thorough preparation.

13d

PowerPoint. For many situations, especially in business, your audience will expect you to use presentational aids using the software package from Microsoft called PowerPoint. PowerPoint (PPT) allows you to create a computerized slide show in which you can display main points of your speech, facts and statistics, and pictures and objects, among other things. However, a bad PowerPoint presentation can ruin your speech and prevent your audience from understanding your message. The following guidelines will help you avoid this pitfall.

- **Limit amount of text.** The last thing you want to do as a speaker is lose your audience because they are reading your PPT slides rather than listening to what you are saying. Use bullet points or something similar to bring attention to the key points of your speech. Use key words and/or key phrases, but not full sentences when communicating your key points on each PPT slide.

- **Use graphic elements purposefully.** Are you planning to visually display facts and statistics? Use PPT slides to provide graphs and charts for visual learners in your audience. Use PPT slides to show photographic evidence of a problem you are describing or the components of an object you are explaining. Pictures and/or images should have a title on a PPT slide, but no words other than those needed for a person to glance at the slide and understand the information it presents.

- **Avoid distracting background design.** Many of the predesigned templates you have to choose from have background designs that you are very distracting. If you are going to use a background, be sure that its

Figure 13.1

Incorrect Use of Power Point Slide

In this figure you can see that the student used too many different fonts, too many fonts that are hard to read, and colors that are hard to read. In addition, there are too many words on the slide.

BABY BOOMERS (1943-1960)

× *Baby Boomers exhibit several defining characteristics.*
  + They are the first generation to work 60 hours per week.
  + Given the title the "Me" Generation, they are quite focused on their well-being and their looks.
  + They grew up in the era of the civil rights movement so equal rights for everyone is important to them.

× *Baby Boomers possess several core values.*
  + They are optimistic and team-oriented in the workplace.
  + They focus on personal growth by engaging in physical fitness, yoga, and self-help books

× *Several features are unique to the Baby Boomers.*
  + They buy trendy clothing and products to look "hip."
  + Baby boomers are the first generation to have credit cards.
  + Typically, they read magazines like *Business Week* and *People.*
  + Their humor is similar to the humor of *Doonesbury* cartoon.

design is consistent with the purpose of your speech. Suppose your informative speech topic was "No Child Left Behind Law." Which would be more appropriate for a background design? (a) A stack of books in bright colors with 1 + 1 = 2 written above it, or (b) a globe in the bottom right side of the screen? The correct answer is (a) because it is more relevant to your speech topic, education in the United States. The globe is virtually irrelevant. It is best to use a plain background if possible. The plain background is less distracting to the audience members, and as such, they are able to focus attention to your spoken message.

- **Choose text color and font wisely.** A combination of colors and texts makes your PPT slide look unorganized, not to mention hard to read. Use color combinations (background and text) that are easy to see. The easiest slides to read are those that have a light background and dark colored text. Yellow text is among the most difficult colored text to read on almost any background. Dark colored text on a dark colored background is nearly impossible to read. Use *serif fonts* (with the "legs" on the ends of the letters). Serif fonts include Times New Roman, **Cambria**, and **Garamond**. *Sans serif fonts* (without the "legs" on the tops and bottoms of the letters) are harder to read in long stretches, especially. Arial, Helvetica, and Geneva are all sans serif fonts. Ornate and unique fonts can be the most difficult to read, such as *Script* and **Haettenschweller**. Thus, you should avoid ornate or unique fonts if at all possible. Be sure to test your PPT slides on a friend or roommate to see if they notice any problems with the color of the text and/or background.

Figure 13.2

Appropriate Use of Power Point Slide

In this slide, the student uses black lettering and fonts that are easy to read. There are phrases rather than complete sentences.

BABY BOOMERS (1943-1960)

- **Defining Characteristics**
  + First generation to work 60 hrs/wk
  + "Me" Generation
  + Equal rights for everyone
- **Core Values**
  + Optimistic and team-oriented
  + Personal growth
- **Unique Features**
  + Buy trendy clothing and products
  + First generation with credit cards
  + Read magazines like *Business Week* and *People*
  + Humor similar to *Doonesbury* cartoon

- **Watch overuse of images.** The more images or graphics you have on a slide, the more distracting the slide is for your audience. Do not frivolously use images. In other words, do not use an image or graphic just to have something "eye-catching" on your PPT slide. Unnecessary and/or irrelevant images/graphics keep the audience from paying attention to your speech.

- **Avoid distracting effects.** PowerPoint has several features to make the wording on your slides appear distinct. However, most of the time, these features are merely a distraction to the audience. One useful feature, called "Custom Animation," enables you to bring in text when you want to and make it go away when you are finished with it. Use this feature simply and sparingly to show your key points on each slide as you address them in your speech. Be sure to use the *same* feature throughout the presentation and be sure that it is not distracting to the audience. Do not mix animation effects because you think it will keep the audience's attention. It will only prove to be a distraction.

Keep in mind that when you use PowerPoint, your PPT presentation should *aid* your audience in their understanding of the purpose of your speech. A wise use of PowerPoint will enhance your competence and credibility as a speaker. Free PowerPoint tutorials on how to use the software are available on the Internet.

Objects. For some subjects, displaying the actual object is the most effective way to make your speech understandable for your audience. *Objects* may be either *actual*, such as a hula-hoop, or *scaled*, such as an architect's model. Other three-dimensional presentational aids are, for instance, a scuba diver's oxygen tank and breathing regulator, a deck of tarot cards, a replica of the Statue of Liberty, or an MP3 player.

Objects can also include people or animals. You might enlist a volunteer to help you demonstrate tests for color blindness or bring in a Jack Russell terrier for a speech on that breed of dog. Objects used effectively give your speech immediacy and carry a great deal of impact.

Applying Concepts | **Using PowerPoint**
DEVELOPING SKILLS

Create a basic PowerPoint presentation with two to four slides listing your three favorite foods and three destinations (anywhere in the world) that you would like to visit, but have not yet been.

Graphic representations. For most subjects, however, it is not possible or practical to show the actual object to your audience. In these cases you must use a visual representation instead. Whether these graphics are used independently or as part of a PowerPoint presentation, you should prepare them with your audience in mind.

■ **Pictures.** In some cases, *pictures* can make a speaker's oral presentation more concrete and vivid. It is difficult to imagine how a speech on the artistic styles of Georgia O'Keeffe or Edward Hopper could be effective without pictures or prints of some of their paintings, since the actual paintings would not be available.

Make sure that you select pictures with size and clarity in mind. A small snapshot held up for audience view detracts from, rather than reinforces, the speaker's purpose. Pictures used as visual aids often must be enlarged. You can use a color copier to enlarge your pictures. If the room has a visual presenter, such as Elmo, you can project small pictures on a screen for easy audience viewing. You can also scan or copy your pictures and save them to a disk or a flash drive; then project them from a computer as a series of PowerPoint slides.

■ **Diagrams.** *Diagrams* are graphics showing the parts of an object or organization or the steps in a process. A diagram could show the features of a commercial spacecraft design, the organizational structure of the U.S. judicial system, or the steps in the lost-wax method of casting jewelry. The best diagrams achieve their impact by simplifying and exaggerating key points. For example, no diagram of manageable size could illustrate all the parts of a hybrid, gas-electric car engine. However, a carefully constructed diagram, whether drawn on posterboard or projected electronically, could isolate and label key parts of that engine design.

■ **Graphs.** *Graphs* can be used as presentational aids to illustrate some condition or progress. A **line graph** is useful in depicting trends and developments over time. A speaker might use a line graph to illustrate the rising cost of a college education over the past 20 years. Some line graphs trace two or more variables—income and expenditures, for example—in contrasting colors. A **bar graph** is useful in comparing quantities or amounts. A bar graph contrasting deficits and profits and showing their relative size, provides a clear, visual indication of economic health, particularly when income is represented in black and deficits in red. Notice how the graph in Figure 13.3 clearly shows increases of grade point averages at both public and private schools.

The **pie** or **circle graph** is helpful when you want to show relative proportions of the various parts of a whole. When using a pie graph, emphasize the pertinent "slice" with a contrasting color. Cheryl informed her

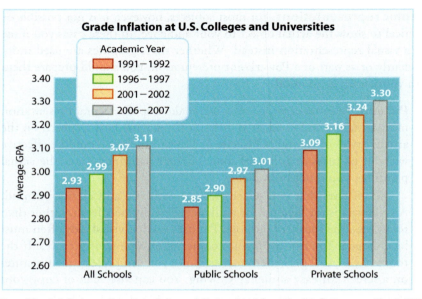

Figure 13.3
Bar Graph: Grade Inflation at U.S. Colleges & Universities

Source: Stuart Rojstaczer, March 2009.

From "Grade Inflation at American Colleges & Universities" from GradeInflation.com, March 2009. © Stuart Rojstaczer. Reproduced by permission.

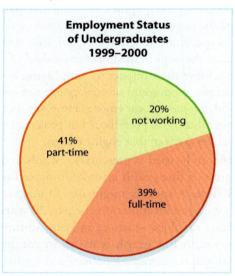

Figure 13.4
Pie Graph: Percentages of a Population

Source: National Center for Education Statistics, 2002.

classmates on how college students spend their time outside class. She rounded her statistics to the nearest percentage point and then constructed a pie graph (Figure 13.4). She used color for the slices representing students who worked either full- or part-time to emphasize that approximately 80% of all college undergraduates work to pay for part or all of their education.

- **Maps.** *Maps* lend themselves especially well to speeches discussing or referring to geographic areas. A speaker informing an audience about the genocide in Darfur might illustrate for the audience the location of Darfur, Sudan. Commercial maps are professionally prepared and look good, but they may be either too small or too detailed for a speaker's purpose. If you cannot isolate and project a section of the map for a large audience, prepare a simplified, large-scale map of the territory in question.

- **Handouts.** In addition to showing the graphic aid to the audience, you could hand out copies of presentational aids such as pictures, diagrams, graphs, charts, or maps to individual audience members. *Handouts* are appropriately used when the information cannot be effectively displayed or projected or when the audience needs to study or refer to the information after the speech.

- **Film, video, and audio aids.** *Film and video clips* are appropriate whenever action will enhance a visual presentation. With the widespread popularity of Web sites like YouTube, this type of presentational aid is becoming easier and cheaper to use. Keep in mind that some Web sites and YouTube clips are available for a short period and then are gone. Also, clips from films and videos can be lengthy. It is important that you, not a presentational aid, organize and present the ideas of your speech. Use only short video clips to illustrate your key ideas. Video and film are ideal for introducing viewers to aspects of various cultures.

   Audio aids include records, tapes, compact discs, and MP3 files, and certainly there is an audio dimension to films and videos. Speech topics on music lend themselves to audio reinforcement of the message. Audio aids need not be confined to music, however. An audience listening to a speech on Winston Churchill could benefit from hearing his quiet eloquence as he addressed Great Britain's House of Commons and declared, "I have nothing to offer but blood, toil, tears, and sweat." A speaker analyzing the persuasive appeals of radio and television advertisements could play pertinent examples.

No matter what type of aid you create, a conscientious speaker will spend hours preparing a speech; presentational aids are a part of that presentation. Just as you rehearse the words of your speech, you should rehearse referring to your aid, uncovering and covering charts, and advancing slides. In short, if you plan to use presentational aids, learn how before your speech;

13d

Applying Concepts
DEVELOPING SKILLS | Choosing a Presentational Aid

If you are giving a speech about the top three places to visit in Athens, Greece, which presentational aid would be most effective? Why? If you are giving a speech about constellations, which would be most effective? Why?

Using Graphic Photographs and/or Visual Images

Some speech topics lend themselves to the potential for using graphic photographs or visual images (print or video) that could be disturbing to some audience members. A speech persuading people to ban animal testing of human products could be more persuasive with photographs of injured animals (after they have had products tested on them). Whether it is informative or persuasive, a speech about the genocide in Darfur would be more powerful with images of burned villages and massacred citizens.

Before displaying a potentially disturbing presentational aid, you should provide a disclaimer that the image may be disturbing to some people and that they may choose to look away until you instruct them otherwise. But don't forget to tell them when you have removed the presentational aid from view.

Application

Is a disclaimer enough? Is it ethical for a speaker to use potentially disturbing presentational aids? Are there some images that would be ethical and acceptable and others that are too disturbing, thus making them unethical and unacceptable? What would you classify as too disturbing?

no audience will be impressed by how much you learn during the course of your presentation.

Speak Effectively Using Your Presentational Aids

Whether you are using presentational software, such as PowerPoint, or other presentational aids, you cannot afford to use them poorly. Let's explore some practical guidelines on how to use presentational aids in your public speech.

13d

Reveal the presentational aid only when you are ready for it. A presentational aid is designed to attract attention and convey information. If it is visible at the beginning of the speech, the audience may focus on it, rather than on what you are saying. Show your aid only when you are ready to discuss the point it illustrates.

If your presentational aid is on posterboard, cover it with a blank posterboard, or turn the blank side to the audience. At the appropriate time, expose the visual aid. If you are using projections, enlist someone to dim or turn the lights off and the projector on at the appropriate time.

Talk to your audience—not to the presentational aid. Whether you are using PowerPoint or MS Word or the Elmo, you should refrain from looking at the screen. You should *glance* at the screen to be sure that what you intend to be displayed is actually being displayed. Once you see that the correct information is on the screen, you should cease looking at the screen and look at the computer monitor instead. When you look at the screen, you are talking *into* the screen and *not* at your audience. Therefore, they will have a rather difficult time hearing you because the screen and wall will be absorbing your voice.

Don't read your presentational aids. Speakers who put too many words on their PP slides tend to read the slides to the audience. A typical audience member's thought is, "I can read this myself. Why does this speaker insist on reading it to me?" Additionally, when you have a lot of text on a PPT slide, the audience will *automatically* begin reading the slide *instead of* paying attention to your spoken word. If you practice delivering your speech using your PPT presentation, you should be able to avoid looking at the screen excessively and avoid reading the slides to the audience.

Know your slides. If you practice your delivery with your PPT presentation, then you will *know* the material on your slides. The slides then *enhance* your speech rather than distract from your speech. If you do not know what is on your slides, the audience will assume that you do not know much about your topic. As such, your credibility as a speaker will be diminished greatly.

Refer to the presentational aid. Speakers sometimes stand at the lectern using their notes or reading their manuscript, relatively far from their aid. Others carry their notes with them as they move to the aid, referring to them as they point out key concepts. Both cases give the impression that the speakers must rely on their notes because they do not fully understand what the presentational aid conveys.

A well-constructed presentational aid should function as a set of notes. The key ideas represented on the aid should trigger the explanation you will provide. When you practice using your presentational aid, use your aid as your notes.

Conceal the presentational aid after you have made your point. Once you proceed to the next section of your speech, you do not want the audience to continue thinking about the presentational aid. If the aid is an object or a posterboard, cover it. If you are using projections, turn off the projector or clear the computer screen.

13d

Bring a backup aid. Despite the advancement in technology, computers and projectors can break down. Therefore, it is always wise to have a backup plan for your presentational aid. You can print the PowerPoint slides and use a visual presenter, such as an Elmo, to project them. Today's high-tech visual presenters like the Elmo offer the advantage of enlarging and projecting visual aids without the work of preparing transparencies. No matter what, always come prepared for the worst-case scenario while hoping that the best one will be the case!

Applying Concepts
DEVELOPING SKILLS | **Improvising with large visual aids**

How could you follow the guidelines for using presentational aids, if you have a large object? For example, what if you were giving a speech about motorcycle safety and you had a helmet, leather jacket, gloves, etc.? How could you follow the guidelines but not keep the items in clear view?

Competence SUMMARY

In this chapter, you have learned the following concepts to increase your communication competence.

13a   Exploring the Basics of Delivery

■ There are four main methods for delivering speeches: impromptu, memorized, manuscript, and extemporaneous.

■ Effective delivery helps both listeners and speakers; looks and feels natural, comfortable, and spontaneous; and occurs when the audience is not aware of it at all.

Competence.   Can I explain the difference between each of the four methods of delivering speeches? Do I know how my speech benefits from effective delivery?

13b   Examining Elements of Vocal Delivery

■ Effective delivery includes three basic elements: the voice (vocal delivery), the body (physical delivery), and language (written words).

■ Vocal delivery includes rate, pause, volume, pitch, inflection, voice quality, articulation, and pronunciation.

Competence. Can I incorporate the three basic elements of effective delivery in my speech? In what ways can I improve my vocal delivery?

13c   Understanding the Elements of Physical Delivery

- The elements of physical delivery are appearance, posture, eye contact, facial expression, movement, and gestures.

Competence. In what ways can I improve my physical delivery?

13d   Using Presentational Aids Effectively

- Presentational aids increase message clarity, reinforce message impact, increase speaker dynamism, and enhance speaker confidence.
- Before your speech, you should determine what information you want to convey in a presentational aid, make sure that your aid communicates that information clearly and professionally, practice using your presentational aid, and be sure to properly position the aid so everyone in the audience can see it.
- A speaker can choose from among several presentational aids including PowerPoint presentations, objects, pictures, diagrams, graphs, maps, film and video clips, handouts, and audio and other aids.
- During your speech, reveal your aid only when you are ready for it, talk to your audience and not to your aid, refer to your aid and keep it in view until you can see that the audience sees the point, and then conceal it.

Competence. Can I identify the functions of presentational aids to help me choose which presentational aids will be most effective for my speech? Do I know how to prepare my speech effectively using my visual aid? Can I use my presentational aid appropriately during my speech?

Review Questions

1. What are the four methods of delivery?
2. Name the qualities of effective delivery.
3. How do pronunciation and articulation differ?
4. Explain the importance of two of the elements of physical delivery.
5. What are the four functions of presentational aids?
6. Explain two strategies for using presentational aids.

Discussion Questions

1. Is it possible for a speech to be effective with poor delivery?
2. Consider the best speech you have ever heard (the person need not be famous). What qualities made that the best speech you have heard?

Key Terms

articulation *p. 323*

bar graph *p. 333*

impromptu speaking *p. 318*

inflection *p. 323*

line graph *p. 333*

pauses *p. 322*

pie or circle graph *p. 333*

pitch *p. 323*

pronunciation *p. 324*

rate *p. 322*

speaking extemporaneously *p. 319*

speaking from manuscript *p. 319*

speaking from memory *p. 318*

voice quality *p. 323*

volume *p. 323*

Informative Speeches

Your communication competence will be enhanced by understanding:

- how to choose an appropriate informative topic that interests you and your audience;
- how to construct an effective informative speech so that you can convey knowledge to your audience;
- how to cite sources efficiently to enhance your credibility.

14a Speaking to Inform

Giving an effective informative speech poses at least three challenges that form the essence of informative speaking:

1. Choosing a topic you find personally interesting and that your listeners will find interesting or relevant
2. Finding adequate information to make you well informed about the topic
3. Organizing your information in the most fitting manner

We seek knowledge for three reasons: We want to *know*, *understand*, and *use* information. The goals of a **speech to inform**, in turn, are to impart knowledge, enhance understanding, or permit application.

- Suppose you decided to prepare an informative speech on the general subject of advertising. Your specific purpose could be to inform the audience about advertising in ancient times. Your listeners probably know little about this topic, and you can readily assume that your speech would add to their knowledge.

- Alternatively, you could inform the audience about how effective advertising succeeds. Using examples your audience already knows, you could deepen their understanding of advertising strategies and principles.

- If your purpose is to inform your listener about how they can prepare effective ads to promote a charity fund-raising event, your speech would help your listeners apply basic advertising principles.

When you prepare an informative speech, you must make sure that you don't slip into giving a persuasive speech. How can you avoid this problem?

14a

After all, a persuasive speech also conveys information. In fact, the best persuasive speeches usually include supporting material that is both expository and compelling.

Some topics are easy to classify as informative or persuasive. A speaker urging an audience not to use cell phones while driving is clearly trying to persuade; the speaker is attempting to intensify beliefs and either change or reinforce behavior. On the other hand, a speech charting the most recent options in cell phone technology is a speech to inform.

Sometimes speakers begin preparing a speech to inform, only to discover that during the speech construction process their objective has become persuasion. In other instances, speakers deliver what they intended to be an informative speech only to find that their listeners received it as a persuasive message. How can this happen? Let's look at the experience of one speaker, Sarah.

Sarah designed a speech with the specific purpose of informing the audience of the arguments for and against allowing women to serve in military combat. She took care to represent each side's arguments accurately and objectively. After speaking, however, Sarah discovered that some listeners who were previously undecided on the issue found the pro arguments more persuasive and now supported permitting women to serve in combat roles. But Sarah also learned that others in the audience became more convinced that women should be excluded from such roles. Did Sarah's speech persuade? Apparently for some audience members the answer is yes; they changed their attitudes because of this speech. Yet Sarah's objective was to inform, not to persuade.

In determining the general purpose of your speech, remember that both speakers and listeners are active participants in the communication process. Listeners will interpret what they hear and integrate it into their frames of reference. Your objectivity as a speaker will not stop the listener from hearing with subjectivity. As a speaker, though, you determine *your* motive for speaking. It is not to advocate specific beliefs, attitudes, and behaviors on controversial issues. Your objective is to assist your audience as they come to know, understand, or apply an idea or issue.

Applying Concepts
DEVELOPING SKILLS

Speaking to Inform

14a

Select an emotionally charged issue (political correctness, Internet filtering in public libraries, or legalization of drugs, for example). Brainstorm aspects of the issue that would be appropriate for an informative speech. State the specific purpose of the speech and briefly describe what you would discuss. In discussing your topic, point out what makes the speech informative rather than persuasive.

14b Classifying Informative Speech Topics

Experts identify several ways of classifying informative speeches. We offer a topical pattern that is based on the types of topics you can choose for your speech. As you read about these topic categories, keep two guidelines in mind.

- Approach each category of topics with the broadest possible perspective.
- Recognize that the categories overlap; the boundaries between them are not distinct.

The purpose of our categories is to stimulate, not to limit, your topic selection and development. As you begin brainstorming, consider information you could provide your listeners regarding people, objects, places, activities, events, processes, concepts, conditions, and issues.

Speeches about People

People are an obvious and abundant resource of topics for an informative speech. A speech about a person gives you an opportunity to expand your knowledge in a field that interests you while sharing those interests with your listeners. If you're a fan of animated films, an informative speech assignment gives you the option to discuss J. Stuart Blackton, one of the pioneers of American animation, or contemporary Japanese animator Hayao Miyazaki, creator of *Spirited Away, Howl's Moving Castle,* and *Ponyo on a Cliff by the Sea.*

Of course, you don't need to confine your topic to individuals associated with your major or areas of interest. You could interest and inform audiences by discussing the lives and contributions of people such as Dr. Guion ("Guy") Bluford, Jr., Pat Tillman, Angelina Jolie, Kurt Cobain, Jane Goodall, LeBron James, M. Night Shyamalan, Kenneth Cole, or Chesley B. "Sully" Sullenberger, III. You could also compare and contrast two or more individuals to highlight their philosophies and contributions, such as Rachel Carson and Ralph Nader, or Malcolm X and Martin Luther King, Jr.

Speeches about people are often organized chronologically or topically. Cary used a chronological pattern to trace the life and legacy of Christopher Reeve. She presented three main points:

    I. The actor

    II. The accident victim

    III. The activist

In her second key idea, Cary discussed the equestrian accident that left Reeve paralyzed in 1995. She described how this event transformed him from the roles he had portrayed as an actor to a more important role as an activist. His final performance would be not on a Broadway stage or a movie screen, but on an international stage as an advocate for medical research to discover cures for spinal cord injuries.

Speeches about Objects

Speeches about objects focus on what is concrete, rather than on what is abstract. Again, consider objects from the broadest perspective possible so that you can generate a maximum number of topic ideas. Topics for this type of speech could include electric cars, the Great Wall of China, "nanny cams," performance clothing, smart roads, or volcanoes.

Speeches about objects can use any of several organizational patterns. A speech on the Statue of Liberty could be organized spatially. A speech tracing the development of cyclones and anticyclones evolves chronologically. A speech on the origins, types, and uses of pasta uses a topical division.

Kevin used a topical organization for his speech on genetically modified (GM) animals, sometimes called designer animals:

    I. The process of designing animals

    II. Benefits of GM animals
       A. Medical uses
       B. Commercial uses

    III. Problems of GM animals
       A. Animal health issues
       B. Ethical issues

Speeches about Places

Places are an easily tapped resource for informative speech topics. These speeches introduce listeners to new locales or expand their knowledge of familiar places. Topics may include real places, such as historic sites, emerging nations, national parks, and planets. Topics may also include fictitious places, such as the Land of Oz or the Island of the Lord of the Flies. Speeches about places challenge speakers to select words that create vivid images.

To organize your speech about places, you would typically use one of three organizational patterns: spatial, chronological, or topical. A speech about the Nile, the world's longest river, is organized spatially if it discusses the upper, middle, and lower Nile. A presentation about your college could trace its development chronologically. A speech on Poplar Forest, Thomas Jefferson's getaway home, could use a topical pattern discussing Jefferson's architectural style.

Suppose you selected as your informative speech topic Ellis Island, the site of the chief U.S. immigration center from 1892 to 1954. You could use a spatial pattern to inform your audience about Ellis Island's Main Building: the

14b

Registry Room, the Baggage Room, and the Oral History Studio. A speech to inform listeners on the history of Ellis Island could be organized chronologically: years of immigration, 1892–1954; years of dormancy, 1954–1984; and years of remembrance, 1984-present. Or, it could use a topical organization and focus on these three main points: the process of immigration, the place of immigration, and the people who immigrated.

Speeches about Activities and Events

Activities are things you do at home, work, or school; by yourself or with friends; to learn, relax, or accomplish a required task. One source of speech topics is your hobbies, your interests, and your experiences. Topics that you already know well, and are willing to explore more fully, often enhance your credibility and energize your delivery.

If you're interested in dancing, a speech on krumping, sometimes called street dancing or clown dancing, could be lively and informative. You could use a topical pattern, informing your audience on these key points:

    I. The origins of krumping

    II. The purposes of krumping

    III. The style of krumping

    IV. The face-painting of krumping

Events are important or interesting occurrences. Examples of topics for a speech about an event include 9/11, the sinking of the *Titanic*, and the Woodstock festival. For a speech assignment not requiring research, you could speak about an event in your life you consider important, funny, or instructive, for example: "the day I registered for my first semester in college," "the day my first child was born," or "my most embarrassing moment."

Speeches about events typically use a chronological or topical pattern. For example, if your topic is the daring Great Train Robbery that took place in 1963, you could organize your speech chronologically, describing what happened before, during, and after those famous 15 minutes. Lisa used a topical organization in her speech on the "World's Longest Yard Sale." She excited her audience with an enthusiastic discussion of this 4-day event. More than 5,000 vendors spanned 450 scenic miles from Kentucky through Tennessee and into Alabama. Lisa divided her topic into two key ideas:

    I. Shopping
      A. Antiques
      B. Collectibles
      C. Furniture
      D. Food

II. Scenery
   A. Lookout Mountain Parkway
   B. Big South Fork National River
   C. Little River Canyon National Preserve

Speeches about Processes

A process is a series of steps producing an outcome. Your informative speech about a process could explain or demonstrate how something works, functions, or is accomplished. Informative speeches could be on such how-to topics as suiting up and entering a "clean room," using an automated external defibrillator, and making a good first impression.

Because a process is by definition a time-ordered sequence, speeches about processes commonly use chronological organization. For example, if your specific purpose is to inform your audience of the steps to a successful job interview, you could present these key ideas:

   I. Prepare thoroughly

   II. Arrive promptly

   III. Enter confidently

   IV. Communicate effectively

   V. Follow up immediately

Speeches about processes, however, are not confined to a chronological pattern. The best organization is the one that achieves the purpose of the speech. A student presenting a how-to speech on podcasting would likely choose a chronological pattern if the specific purpose is to explain the steps in the process. Another student might examine the process of podcasting more generally, using a topical pattern to discuss the equipment needed, the most popular file formats, the rapid growth of podcasts, or their effects on traditional broadcasters. Both speeches concern a process, but each uses an organizational pattern that's suitable for the speaker's specific purpose.

Speeches about Concepts

Speeches about concepts, or ideas, focus on the abstract, rather than the concrete. Whereas a speech about an object such as the Statue of Liberty may focus on the history or physical attributes of the statue itself, a speech about an idea may focus on the concept of liberty. Other topics suitable for informative speeches about concepts include ecotourism, concrete poetry, pirate radio, traumatic obsessions, artificial intelligence, and endangered languages.

14b

Speeches about concepts challenge you to make specific something that is abstract. These speeches typically rely on definitions and examples to support their explanations. Appropriate organizational patterns vary. A speech on Norse mythology could use a topical division and focus on key figures. Speeches about theories, particularly if they are controversial, sometimes use a pro-con division.

Speeches about Conditions

Conditions are particular situations: living conditions in a third-world country or social and political climates that give rise to movements such as witchcraft hysteria in Salem, McCarthyism, the women's movement, the civil rights movement, jihad, and national independence movements.

The word *condition* can also refer to a state of fitness or health. Speeches about conditions can focus on a person's health and, indeed, medical topics are a popular source of speeches. Informative speeches about crush syndrome, obsessive-compulsive disorder, and pre-eclampsia, for example, can educate listeners about these interesting conditions. A speaker could choose as a specific purpose "to inform the audience about the causes and treatment of repetitive stress injuries." Topical organization is appropriate for many speeches about specific diseases or other health conditions.

Jean became interested in the topic of autism. She gathered information from several organizations that conducted research and provided information on this developmental disability. Reviewing the FAQ links on several Internet Web sites, Jean selected four questions to organize the body of her speech:

    I. What is autism?

    II. What causes autism?

    III. How do you treat autism?

    IV. Is there a cure for autism?

Though the fourth question is closed, requiring only a yes or no answer, Jean used it as an opportunity to discuss types of research being conducted in search of a cure. At the conclusion of her speech, she gave her audience the URLs for the Autism Society of America and the Center for the Study of Autism Web sites, so that they could continue to learn more about this important topic.

Speeches about Issues

Speeches about issues deal with controversial ideas and policies. Topics appropriate for informative speeches on issues include the use of polygraphs as a condition for employment, uniform sentencing of criminals, freedom of expression versus freedom from pornography, stem cell research, and eliminating sugared soft drinks from school vending machines. Any issue being debated in your school, community, state, or nation can be a fruitful topic for your informative speech.

14b

You may be thinking that controversial issues are more suitable as topics for persuasive speeches, but they can also be appropriate for speeches to inform. Just remember that an informative speech on a controversial topic must be researched and developed so that you present the issue objectively.

Two common organizational patterns for speeches about issues are the topical and pro-con divisions. If you use a topical pattern of organization, it will be easier for you to maintain objectivity. If you choose the pro-con pattern, you may run the risk of moving toward a persuasive speech. A pro-con strategy—presenting both sides of an issue—lets the listener decide which is stronger. If your informative speech on an issue is organized pro-con, guard against two pitfalls: lack of objectivity and lack of perspective.

Speakers predisposed toward one side of an issue sometimes have difficulty presenting both sides objectively. If you feel strongly committed to one side of an issue, save that topic for a persuasive speech.

A second pitfall that sometimes surfaces in the pro-con approach is lack of perspective. Sometimes a speaker will characterize an issue as two-sided when, in reality, it is many-sided. For example, one student spoke on the issue of child care. He mentioned the state family-leave laws that permit mothers of newborn infants to take paid leaves of absence from work and fathers to take unpaid leaves while their jobs are protected. The speaker characterized advocates of such bills as pro-family and opponents as pro-business. He failed to consider that some people oppose such laws because they feel the laws don't go far enough; many state laws exempt small companies with fewer than 50 employees. If you fail to recognize and acknowledge the many facets of an issue in this way, you lose perspective and polarize your topic.

As you begin working on your informative speech, remember to select a topic that will benefit your listeners and then communicate your information clearly and memorably. Use the eight subject categories we have just explored to narrow and focus your topic.

As you go about selecting your topic, keep in mind this question: "How will the audience benefit from my topic?" Remember, your informative speech must help your audience know, understand, or apply information you provide.

Once you have selected a topic, ask yourself the following three questions:

1. What does the audience already know about my topic?
2. What does the audience need to know to understand the topic?
3. Can I present this information in a way that is easy for the audience to understand and remember in the time allotted?

If you are satisfied with your answers to these questions, your next step is to begin developing the most effective strategy for conveying that information.

Targeting an
Informative Topic

Generate a list of one informative topic for each of the eight speech categories discussed above. Evaluate the suitability of each topic by asking and answering the following questions: Does the topic interest me? Would the topic likely interest my audience? Will I be able to find sufficient supporting material on this topic? Can I develop a speech that is clearly informative rather than persuasive? Does this topic meet all the criteria for the assigned speech?

Place an asterisk (*) by each topic that received five yes answers. Continue to assess and narrow this short list until you've decided on the most appropriate topic for your speech.

TYPES OF INFORMATIVE SPEECHES

If your speech is about ...	Use ...	If your purpose is to ...
People	Topical organization	Explain various aspects of person's life
	Chronological organization	Survey events in person's life
Objects	Topical organization	Explain various uses for object
	Chronological organization	Explain how object was created or made
	Spatial organization	Describe various parts of object
Places	Topical organization	Emphasize various aspects of the place
	Chronological organization	Chart history of/developments in place
	Spatial organization	Describe elements or parts of the place
Activities and Events	Topical organization	Explain significance of activity/event
	Chronological organization	Explain sequence of activity/event
	Causal organization	Explain how one event produced or resulted from another
Processes	Topical organization	Explain aspects of the process
	Chronological organization	Explain how something is done
	Pro-con organization	Explore arguments for and against process
	Causal organization	Discuss causes and effects of process
Concepts	Topical organization	Discuss aspects, definitions, or applications of the concept
Conditions	Topical organization	Explain aspects of condition
	Chronological organization	Trace strategies or phases of condition
	Causal organization	Show causes and effects of condition
Issues	Topical organization	Discuss aspects of issue's significance
	Chronological organization	Show how issue evolved over time
	Pro-con organization	Present opposing viewpoints on issue

14b

14c Guidelines for Speaking to Inform

In the remainder of this chapter, we offer ten guidelines for the informative speech. Use them as a checklist during your speech preparation, and you will deliver an excellent informative speech.

Stress Your Informative Purpose

The primary objective of your informative speech is to inform. It is important for you to be clear about this, especially if your topic is controversial or related to other topics that are controversial. For example, if you are discussing U.S. immigration policy, gay marriage, or the role of women in religion, you must realize that some in your audience may already have some very strong feelings about your topic. Stress that your goal is to give additional information, not to try to change anyone's beliefs.

Be Objective

One of the most important criteria for an informative speech is objectivity. If you take a stand, you become a persuader. Informative speakers are committed to presenting a balanced view. Your research should take into account all perspectives. If, as you develop and practice your speech, you find yourself becoming a proponent of a particular viewpoint, you may need to step back and assess whether your orientation has shifted from information to persuasion. If you do not think you can make your speech objective, save the topic for a persuasive speech.

Nothing betrays the image of objectivity that is essential in an informative speech as quickly as the inappropriate use of language. For example, in an informative speech on the pros and cons of juvenile curfew laws, one student used language that revealed his personal opinion on the issue. Even when explaining the arguments for such laws, he described them as "silly," "costly," and "unenforceable." In an informative speech, your language should be descriptive, not evaluative or judgmental.

Be Specific

An informative speech gives you the perfect opportunity to tell your audience a lot about a little. Narrow your topic. Focus on specific people, objects, places, activities, events, processes, concepts, conditions, and issues. A "sports" topic could be narrowed to sports commentators, the history of AstroTurf, competitive team sports and male bonding, and so on. The more specific you are about your topic, your purpose, and the materials you use to

14c

support your speech, the more time you will save during your research. Your specific focus will also make your speech easier for the audience to remember.

Be Clear

If you choose your topic carefully and explain it thoroughly, your message should be clear. Do not choose a topic that is too complex or you run the risk of being too technical for most audiences. You would not be able to give your audience the background knowledge necessary to understand your presentation in the limited time you have. At the same time, be careful about using jargon. Impressing the audience with your vocabulary is counterproductive if they cannot understand your message. The purpose of informative speaking is not to impress the audience with complex data, but to communicate information clearly.

Be Accurate

Inaccurate information misinforms and has two negative consequences.

- **Inaccuracies can hurt your credibility as a speaker.** If listeners recognize misstatements, they may begin to question your credibility: "If the speaker's wrong about that, could there be other inaccuracies in the speech?" Accurate statements help you develop a positive image or protect one you have established earlier.
- **Inaccurate information can do potential mental or physical harm to listeners.** For example, you give an informative speech on the life-threatening reactions some people have to sulfites, a common ingredient in certain food preservatives. Your audience leaves worried about their health and the damage they may have suffered. You didn't mention that these reactions are rare. Your misinformation has harmed your audience. If audience members are unaware of factual errors, they may form invalid beliefs or make unwise decisions.

You must also accurately cite your sources. Some speakers assume that because they do not take a controversial stand in an informative speech, they need not cite sources. An informative topic may require fewer sources than you would use to establish your side of a debatable point; however, demonstrating the truth of your ideas and information is important.

Limit Your Ideas and Supporting Materials

Do not make the mistake of thinking that the more information you put into a speech, the more informative it is. If you overload your audience

14c

with too much information, they will stop listening. Remember the adage that "less is more." Spending more time explaining and developing a few ideas will probably result in greater retention of these ideas by your listeners.

Be Relevant

As you research your topic, you will no doubt discover information that is interesting but not central to your thesis. Because it is so interesting, you may be tempted to include it. Don't. If it is not relevant, leave it out. To avoid this problem and to keep yourself on track, write out your central thesis and refer to it periodically. When you digress from your topic, you waste valuable preparation time, distort the focus of your speech, and confuse your audience.

Use Appropriate Organization

There is no one best organizational pattern for informative speeches. Choose the pattern that is most appropriate to your topic and specific purpose. However, some patterns are inappropriate for an informative speech. While a pro-con approach is appropriate, a pro-con—assessment strategy moves the speech into persuasion. If you have any doubt that your organization is informative rather than persuasive, check with your instructor.

Use Appropriate Forms of Support

As with persuasive speeches, speeches to inform require appropriate supporting materials. These materials should come from sources that are authoritative and free from bias. If you discuss a controversial issue, you must represent each side fairly. For example, if your specific purpose is to inform your audience on the effects of bilingual education, you must research and present information from both its proponents and its critics.

Use Effective Delivery

Some speakers have a misconception that delivery is more important for a persuasive speech than for an informative speech. Regardless of the type of speech, show your involvement in your speech through your physical and vocal delivery. Your voice and body should reinforce your interest in and enthusiasm for your topic. Your delivery should also reinforce your objectivity.

14c

EYEON**ETHICS** | Managing Bias in an Informative Speech

Leon is president of a campus fraternity. He feels he is an expert on the subject of Greek life at his school, so he decides to use his observations and personal experiences as the basis for an informative speech on the pros and cons of joining fraternities and sororities. However, Leon fears that if he reveals that he is a fraternity president, his listeners will assume that he is not presenting objective information—so he does not mention it.

Application

Is it ethical for Leon to avoid mentioning his fraternity affiliation or the fact that he is a fraternity president? Is it possible for him to give an unbiased presentation of both sides of the issue? In general, is it ethical for speakers who are strongly committed to an organization, cause, or position to give informative speeches on related topics? If so, what obligations do they have to their audience?

14d Citing Your Sources

To acknowledge the sources you read in gathering information for your speech, you will need to provide "oral footnotes" for ideas and supporting materials in your speech that are not your own. Doing so accomplishes two goals.

- **Enhance your credibility.** Clear source citations enhance the credibility of what you say by demonstrating that experts and data support your position.

- **Guide listeners to your sources.** Clear source citations help interested listeners find published sources that they might wish to read or study.

Let's look at how to cite sources in your speech by answering some frequently asked questions about oral source citations, or "oral footnotes."

Question: How do you "orally footnote" sources as you deliver your speech?

Answer: Your instructor may require more or less information in oral source citations than we do, so be sure to check.

OUR GENERAL RULE: Give only the information necessary to build the credibility of the source, but enough information to help listeners find your source if they wish to do so.

Question: Do you need to include *all* the information that was in your bibliographic entry for the source?

Answer: No. Only the most active listener would remember the title and page numbers of a journal article or the publisher of a book that you cite, for example.

Question: Is there any information not in your bibliography that you *should* mention as you cite a source?

Answer: Yes. To establish the credibility of any source you name, you need to explain at least briefly that individual's qualifications. You can usually find such information somewhere in the book, magazine, journal, or Web site you are using. If not, check a biographical database.

If the author is a newspaper or magazine staff writer, you do not need to name that individual.

If the publication has a corporate author (a group, committee, or organization), just mentioning the name of the group or organization is probably sufficient.

The date of publication may be extremely important to building credibility on a current topic. For periodicals published weekly or for online magazines that are frequently updated, specify the date, month, and year that the material was published or that you accessed it.

INEFFECTIVE AND EFFECTIVE ORAL FOOTNOTES

Instead of saying:	Say this:
"Studs Terkel says in his book *Will the Circle be Unbroken?* ..."	Studs Terkel, Pulitzer Prize-winning oral historian, says in his 2001 book *Will the Circle be Unbroken?* ..."
"According to an article I found on the Lexis/Nexis Academic database ..."	"According to an article in the July 18, 2005, issue of the *Roanoke Times and World News* ..."
"Leigh T. Hollins says in his article in the journal *Fire Engineering* ..."	"Leigh T. Hollins, a certified EMT and battalion chief in the Manatee County, Florida, fire department, says in his article in the June 2005 issue of the journal *Fire Engineering* ..."
"According to statistics from the Bureau of Labor Statistics ..."	"According to figures I found on the U.S. Department of Labor's Bureau of Labor Statistics Web site on March 3, 2005, ..."
"I found an article at memory.loc.gov/ammem/jrhtml/jr1940.html ..."	"On March 12th of this year, I found an article entitled 'Breaking the Color Line: 1940–1946.' It's a link from the Recreation and Sports collection of the Library of Congress's Web site *American Memory* ..."

Question: Do I need to cite the entire Web address of a Web site that I am using as supporting material?

Answer: Orally footnoting Internet sources poses special challenges. Though it is never acceptable to say just, "I found a Web page that said ..." or "I found this on Yahoo," most listeners will not remember a long URL that you mention. If the URL is simple and easily recognizable, mention it: "pbs.org," "cnn.com," or "espn.com," for example. Identifying the sponsor of a Web site is important. If you cannot identify the group or individual who published and maintains the site, you may need to look for a better source.

In each case, the oral footnote that takes a few more words identifies the source more clearly and more specifically, and would reinforce the speaker's credibility. Advice for citing books, articles, and other types of sources is contained in following table.

SELECTING INFORMATION FOR ORAL FOOTNOTES

If you are citing:	Tell us:
A magazine/journal article	That it is an article, the title of the magazine or journal, the author's name and credentials (if other than a staff writer), and the date of the publication.
A newspaper article	That it is an article, the name of the newspaper, the author's name and credentials (if other than a staff writer), and the date of the issue you are citing.
A Web site	The title of the Web page; the name of the individual, agency, association, group, or company sponsoring the site; and the date of publication, last update, or the date you accessed it.
A book	That it is a book, the author's name(s) and credentials, the book's title, and the date of publication.
An interview you conducted	That you interviewed the person, the person's name, and his or her position or title.
A TV or radio program	The title of the show, the channel or network airing it, and the date of the broadcast.
A videotape or DVD	The title of the tape or disk.
A reference work	The title of the work and the date of publication.
A government document	The title of the document, the name of the agency or government branch that published it, and the date of publication.
A brochure or pamphlet	That it is a brochure; its title; the name of the agency, association, group, or company that published it; and the date of publication (if available).

**Applying Concepts
DEVELOPING SKILLS** | **Evaluating Source Citations**

Using the speech that you chose for the previous Applying Concepts/ Developing Skills box, assess the speaker's citation of sources. Did the speaker cite sources? If so, were they cited properly? If not, where could the speaker have added source citations?

14e Outlining Your Informative Speech

As discussed in chapter 12, your outline will progress through several stages. You start with the working outline, and when you have chosen an organizational pattern, you can begin constructing the formal outline. The final outline is the speaking outline, which you use to deliver your speech. See how Elvir Berbic went from his speaking outline (found in chapter 12) to his speech. Below is a transcript of his speech.

Informative Speech

What a Difference a Generation Makes

Elvir Berbic, Radford University, Radford, Virginia

We're living in an age when multiple generations are working side by side in the workplace. According to Zemke, Raines, and Filipczak, authors of the 2000 book *Generations at Work*, generational differences can create problems in the workplace. Everyone in this room may not be from the same generation. I'm a member of the Millennial generation, and I have read extensively about generational differences. Because all of you are part of one of the generations that I'll discuss today, I think you will find the information interesting, too.

Elvir's topic is apparent by the end of the first paragraph. He also establishes his credibilty and links the topic to his audience.

A generation is defined by historians Neil Howe and William Strauss in their book *Millennials Rising* written in 2000 as a "society-wide peer group," born over approximately the same time period, "who collectively possess a common persona" (p. 40). Each generation is characterized by defining historical events, such as 9/11, that happen in their formative years. These events shape the attitudes, beliefs, and values of a generation. The Vietnam War, the Space Shuttle Challenger explosion, and the Columbine shootings are defining moments for each of the three generations I will discuss. Drawing from Ron Zemke's insightful book, *Generations at Work*, today I'm going to explain several key features that characterize the three most recent generations: Baby Boomers, Generation X, and Millennials.

This section of the introduction previews the three main points that he will develop in the body of the speech.

The first generation that I'll talk about is the Baby Boomer generation, who were born between the years 1943 and 1960. There are several defining general characteristics of the Baby Boomers. They were the first generation to work 60 hours a week. Baby Boomers are often referred to as the "Me Generation" because they are focused on making themselves better. They go to the gym, get plastic surgery, and purchase self-help material. The Boomers fought for civil rights and diversity. They wanted to create an equal playing field for everyone.

Here Elvir begins to apply the "4 S's" to his first point. He signposts ("first") and states the idea (Baby Boomer generation). He supports his points with facts and examples.

These general characteristics were born from the core values of Baby Boomers. In the workplace, boomers value hard work and involvement. They are optimistic and team oriented. Both in and out of the workplace, they are concerned with personal gratification and personal growth.

Several other features of Boomers will help us to distinguish them from the other two generations. They buy whatever is trendy, including clothing, plastic surgery, and electronic gadgets. Boomers are the first generation to acquire credit card debt. Boomers typically read *Business Week* and *People* magazine. Their sense of humor is similar to that found in the print cartoon *Doonesbury*.

14e

The Baby Boomer generation produced the second generation I'll discuss: Generation X. Generation X includes people born between 1960 and 1980. Let's look at the general characteristics of X'ers. In the workplace, X'ers need feedback and flexibility. They are not fond of close supervision in the workplace, which can cause problems. Remember that the Boomer parents worked long hours, so the X'ers came home from school each day to an empty house, making X'ers the first generation of "latch key" kids. As the first generation to see an increase in parental divorce, they are comfortable with change. In response to the overtime hours that they saw their parents work, X'ers work to live, not live to work. In a study published in 2002, researchers Smola and Sutton report that X'ers are less loyal to the company they work for and they place less importance on work life than Boomers.

The core values of the X'ers mirror their general characteristics. They are self-reliant and pragmatic. X'ers witnessed the first Live Aid concert, which made them think globally given its emphasis on world hunger. X'ers are the first generation to grow up using computers, VCRs, and cable television. This explains why they value technological literacy.

Some of the other features of the X'ers further extend our understanding of their generation. They began the trends of multiple piercings and tattoos. Unlike their Boomer parents, they prefer functional clothing and Japanese cars. They are cautious and conservative with their money. X'ers typically read *Spin*, *Wired*, and chat room dialogue. The print cartoon *Dilbert* appeals to their sense of humor.

While Generation X is characterized as self-reliant, the final generation I'll discuss, the Millennials, is much more dependent on their parents. Millennials were born between the years 1980 and 2000. The general characteristics of the Millennial are in stark contrast to the characteristics of their parents, the X'ers. Having absent parents, X'ers were determined to make sure their children knew they were loved. As a result, the Millennials are often over-protected by their parents, who keep the Millennial child's calendar full from morning to night. Millennials are more technologically savvy than any previous generation. What their parents think is important to Millennials. In fact, they think their parents are cool.

The core values of the Millennials reflect their close relationships with their parents. They are optimistic, confident, and moral. They value civic duty, achievement, and diversity.

Other features of the Millennials are interesting, too. They prefer all things retro. They are the first generation to grow up with cell phones. Millennials get plenty of spending money from their parents to buy whatever they want. Millennials typically read book series, like *Goosebumps* and *Baby Sitters' Club*. Millennial humor is illustrated in the print cartoon *Calvin and Hobbes*.

In this section, Elvir reiterates the timeline by stating that the Boomers produced the X'ers. He then signals the beginning of the next main point.

He also uses facts and examples to support his main idea.

You can see that Elvir is continuing with the same pattern of subpoints that he used in the previous main idea.

To introduce his third main point, Elvir connects the second and third main points and signposts (final) the third main point.

Elvir continues to follow the same pattern of subpoints that he used in the previous two main points.

14e

In summary, I have informed you about several key features that influenced the three most recent generations: Baby Boomers, Generation X, and Millennials. You can see how these three generations differ from one another, so imagine how their contrasting values and interests might clash in the workplace. Given the time constraints, I have provided you with only a few features of each generation. I would encourage you to read more about the generations. You might find it valuable in your workplace in the future. Which makes you wonder, what could the future hold for the next generation?

In his conclusion, Elvir signals the end (in summary), and reviews the three main points of his speech. He also ties the conclusion back to the attention-getter in the introduction.

Now that they are intrigued by the information he presented, Elvir suggests that his audience read more about generations. The final question that he poses to his audience helps him end with an impact.

Competence SUMMARY

In this chapter, you have learned the following concepts to increase your communication competence.

14a Speaking to Inform

- An informative speech requires you to research a subject of your choice, synthesize data from various sources, and pass it on to your listeners.
- Your goals as an informative speaker are to expand listeners' knowledge, assist their understanding, or help them apply the information you communicate.

Competence. Can I choose a topic, synthesize data, and deliver the information to an audience? Do I understand the goals of an informative speech?

14b Classifying Informative Speech Topics

- Classifying informative speeches by subject gives you an idea of the range of possible topics and the patterns of organization each subject typically uses.
- Informative speeches can be about people, objects, places, activities and events, processes, concepts, conditions, and issues.

Competence. Can I create a list of several potential speech topics given the list of categories provided in this chapter?

14c   Guidelines for Speaking to Inform

- To develop and deliver an effective informative speech: (1) Let your audience know that your purpose is to inform. (2) Be objective in your approach to the topic and the language you use. (3) Be specific. (4) Be clear. (5) Be accurate. (6) Limit the ideas and supporting material that you try to include. (7) Be relevant. (8) Use the pattern of organization best suited to achieving your specific purpose. (9) Use appropriate forms of support. (10) Use lively, effective speech delivery.

Competence.   Can I incorporate the guidelines into my informative speech so that it is as effective and interesting as possible?

14d   Citing Your Sources

- If you use supporting materials that others have developed, you must cite them in your speech by providing "oral footnotes." You should offer enough information to establish the credibility of the source without overwhelming the listener.

Competence.   Do I know how to cite sources properly in my speech?

Review Questions

1. What are the three challenges of an informative speech?
2. What are the three goals of an informative speech?
3. Name three categories of informative speech topics.
4. Why is objectivity important in an informative speech?
5. List and explain four of the guidelines for speaking to inform.
6. What is an oral footnote?
7. How do you cite a newspaper article in an informative speech?

Discussion Questions

1. How could you change a persuasive speech topic into an informative speech topic and maintain objectivity? Give an example of a topic that could fulfill both a persuasive and an informative speech requirement.
2. Why do you need to cite sources in your speech? Do highly credible people need to cite sources? Why or why not?

Persuasive Speeches

Your communication competence will be enhanced by understanding:

- how we persuade in order to enhance your ability to influence others;
- how to use the types of persuasive speeches to help you determine your primary objective when you work on your speech;
- how Monroe's motivated sequence helps you to structure your persuasive speech so that it is more organized and effective;
- when to use each form of persuasive argument and how well-constructed arguments can increase your persuasiveness.

15a Understanding the Importance of Persuasion

Persuasion is the process of influencing another person's values, beliefs, attitudes, or behaviors. You can change, instill, or intensify your listeners' values, beliefs, attitudes, and behaviors. Your goal is to move your listeners closer to your position. Remember, when you speak to persuade, you are speaking to listeners who may oppose, be indifferent to, or support your position. The information you gather and the assumptions you make about your audience before your speech determine the strategy you use as you develop your remarks.

Persuasion does not necessarily require power. Power implies authority or control over another. Persuasion is more accurately equated with *influence*. As a speaker you try to influence the audience to adopt your position. You probably have little power over your listeners, and they have the freedom to reject your message. The concept of persuasion as influence means that you can bring about change whether or not you are the more powerful party in a relationship.

Many students preparing persuasive speeches make the mistake of thinking that they must change their audiences' opinions from "oppose" to "favor," or vice versa. Persuasion occurs any time you move a listener's opinion in the direction you advocate, even if that movement is slight.

As a Speaker

Delivering a persuasive message will challenge and benefit you in several ways. It will require you to select an issue you think is important and to communicate your concern to your audience. Voicing your beliefs will demand that you confront their logic and support; in other words, you must test the validity of your ideas. That process, in turn, will require that you gather supporting materials and draw valid inferences from them as you develop your arguments. Approached seriously and researched energetically, a persuasive speech assignment can develop both your critical thinking and speech-making skills. Change can occur when people speak and audiences are moved.

The persuasive speaker tries to move the audience to his or her side of an issue. As a speaker, your goal should be to establish a common perspective and tap values your listeners share, not to manipulate or trick your audience.

As a Listener

As a listener, you also benefit by participating in the persuasive process. A speaker can make you aware of problems around you and show how you can help solve them. You hear other points of view and, consequently, may better understand why others have beliefs different from yours. A speech that challenges your beliefs often forces you to reevaluate your position. Participating as a listener also heightens your critical thinking and improves your ability to explain and defend your beliefs. As a listener you have an opportunity to judge how others use persuasive speaking techniques, thus enabling you to improve your own persuasive speaking. Finally, you, the critical listener, have a right and an ethical responsibility to choose whether or not you are persuaded.

| **Applying Concepts** **DEVELOPING SKILLS** | Noticing Persuasion in Your Daily Life |

List on a sheet of paper the messages aimed at persuading you that you have heard, read, or seen during the past 24 hours. These messages may come from friends, family members, politicians, religious leaders, advertisers, newspapers, magazine columnists, television commentators, and so forth. In what way did each message attempt to influence you? Of all of the messages you were able to list, which type of influence did you identify as most often used?

15b Identifying Types of Persuasive Speeches

An effective persuasive speech may change what people believe, what people do, or how people feel. Persuasive speeches, then, may be divided into speeches to convince, to actuate, or to inspire. Understanding these divisions can help you determine your primary objective as you work on your speech, but keep in mind that persuasive speeches often include two or more objectives. For example, if your purpose is to get your audience to boycott fur products, you must first convince them that your cause is right. We usually act or become inspired after we are convinced.

Speeches to Convince

In a **speech to convince**, your objective is to affect your listeners' beliefs or attitudes. Each of the following specific purpose statements expresses a belief the speaker wants the audience to accept:

- To convince the audience that "hate speech" is constitutionally protected
- To convince the audience that hybrid cars are worth the extra money in the long run
- To convince the audience that there is a constitutional right to privacy

The speaker's purpose in each of these speeches is to establish belief, not to secure action.

Speeches to Actuate

A **speech to actuate** may establish beliefs, but it always calls for the audience to act. The specific purpose statements listed here illustrate calls for action:

- To move, or actuate, the audience to donate nonperishable food to a local food bank
- To move the audience to spay or neuter pet cats and dogs
- To move the audience to begin a low-impact aerobic workout program

You can see from these examples that the speaker wants to secure action from the audience members through changing or reinforcing their beliefs.

Speeches to Inspire

A **speech to inspire** attempts to change how listeners feel. Examples include commencement addresses, commemorative speeches, eulogies, and pep talks. Some specific purposes of speeches to inspire are these:

- To inspire the audience to honor the service of fallen fire fighters
- To inspire the audience to appreciate those who made their education possible
- To inspire listeners to give their best efforts to all college courses they take

The purposes of inspiration are usually noble and uplifting. These speeches typically have neither the detailed supporting material nor the complex arguments characteristic of speeches to convince or to actuate.

Applying Concepts DEVELOPING SKILLS | **Identifying Persuasive Speech Types**

Select a persuasive speech from *Vital Speeches of the Day*, YouTube, or another source. Identify the specific purpose of the speech and explain the type of persuasive speech that your sample illustrates.

15c Examining Persuasive Speaking Strategies

As far back as the era of Ancient Greece, there is evidence of people giving advice on how to be an effective persuasive speaker. Aristotle devoted much space in his classic work *The Rhetoric* to the subject. He discussed three modes of persuasion: *ethos*, *logos*, and *pathos*. These three modes remain an important foundation for understanding persuasive speaking (Cooper, 1960). What do these terms mean and how can they help you as you prepare a persuasive speech?

- **Ethos** refers to speaker credibility and derives from the character and reputation of the speaker.
- **Logos** refers to logical appeal that relies on the form and substance of an argument.
- **Pathos** is emotional appeal that taps the values and feelings of the audience.

Any speech is shaped by the speaker, the message, and the audience. Each variable affects the finished product. After all, no two people will give the same speech on the same topic to the same audience. Your strategy for each speech must be based on your unique situation and your own creativity.

Establish Your Credibility

As a speaker, your first source of persuasion is your own credibility, or ethos. **Credibility** is simply your reputation, and it helps determine how your listeners evaluate what you say. Research confirms that the higher your perceived credibility, the more likely the audience is to believe you (Benjamin, 1997).

Speaker credibility is fluid, varying according to your listeners. You possess only the credibility your listeners grant you. Credibility also varies according to time. Your credibility before, during, and after your speech may change.

15c

A speaker having high credibility can more successfully persuade than a speaker having low credibility. Clearly, you need to pay careful attention to your credibility at each stage in order to deliver a successful persuasive speech. How do you enhance your image? Credibility is comprised of competence, trustworthiness, and dynamism. If your audience believes that you possess these qualities, you can be effective in persuading them.

Convey competence.   How can you get your audience to see you as knowledgeable and worthy of their trust? Four strategies will help you establish an image of *competence* on your subject.

1. **Know your subject.** To speak ethically, you must be well informed about your subject. You will discover that the more you read and listen, the easier it is to construct a message that is both credible and compelling.

2. **Document your ideas.** Document your ideas by using clear, vivid, and credible supporting materials to illustrate them. Though your listeners may not expect you to be an expert on your topic, they need assurance that facts or experts corroborated what you say. Providing documentation supports your statements and increases your believability.

3. **Cite your sources.** You need to tell your listeners the sources of your information. Citing sources enhances the credibility of your ideas by demonstrating that experts support your position. It also requires that your sources be unbiased and of good quality.

4. **Acknowledge any personal involvement or experience with your subject.** Listeners will probably assume that you have an edge in understanding color blindness if you let them know you are color-blind. They will probably make the same positive assumption if you have diabetes and are speaking on diabetes.

Convey trustworthiness.   *Trustworthiness* is attributed to both you and your subject. In other words, we should trust you as an individual (you are honest in what you say), and we should trust you with your topic (you are unbiased in what you say). A speaker can demonstrate trustworthiness in two ways:

1. **Establish common ground with your audience.** If listeners know that you understand their values, experiences, and aspirations, they will be more receptive to your arguments. You increase your persuasiveness when you identify with your listeners.

2. **Demonstrate your objectivity in approaching the topic.** The information and sources you include in your speech should demonstrate thorough, unbiased research. One student gave his speech on cigarette

smoking, arguing that its harmful effects were greatly exaggerated. He relied on studies sponsored by the tobacco industry. He undermined his image of trustworthiness because he limited his research to sources the audience considered biased on the topic.

Convey dynamism.   *Dynamism* is a quality closely associated with delivery that conveys both confidence and concern. We enjoy listening to speakers who are energetic, vigorous, exciting, inspiring, spirited, and stimulating. If you appear tentative or unsure of yourself, the audience may doubt your conviction. To the extent that you can strengthen your verbal, vocal, and physical delivery, you can enhance your image of confidence and, hence, your credibility.

Dynamism also demonstrates a concern for the audience and a desire to communicate with them. If your delivery seems flippant, distracted, or detached from the audience, your listeners will assume that you are not concerned about the topic or about them. On the other hand, conveying enthusiasm for your topic and your listeners communicates a strong positive message.

Focus Your Goals

A common mistake many beginning speakers make is to seek dramatic change in the listeners' values, beliefs, attitudes, and behaviors. The speaker who can accomplish this is rare, particularly if he or she seeks change on highly emotional and controversial issues such as gay marriage, gun control, or capital punishment. Therefore, appeal to logos, or logic, as you consider the following guidelines when determining your persuasive speech goals.

Limit your Goals.   Keep in mind that the more firmly your audience is anchored to a position, the less likely you are to change their attitudes. It is unrealistic for you to expect dramatic change in a person's beliefs and values in a 5- to 10-minute speech. Instant conversions occur, but they are rare.

Which of the following specific purpose statements is the more limited and reasonable goal?

> To persuade the audience that exposure to violent video games promotes aggression

> To persuade the audience that habitual exposure to violent video games promotes aggression in children

15c

The second statement is more limited and potentially more persuasive. Select a realistic goal and channel your efforts toward achieving it. Remember that persuasion is more likely if your goals as a speaker are limited, rather than global.

Argue incrementally.   Persuasion is more permanent if you achieve it incrementally, or one step at a time. This principle becomes more important if your audience is likely to hear counterarguments to your position. When your listeners hear another speaker attack one of your arguments later, they may lack sufficient evidence to counter those attacks; as a result, what you accomplished may be only temporary. Your goal should be to "inoculate" your listeners to possible counterarguments. The stronger your arguments, the greater the likelihood that you will bring about enduring change in your audience's opinions. If you know your audience already has been exposed to counterarguments, you may need to address those arguments before introducing your own.

Connect with Your Listeners

Persuasion is more likely if a speaker establishes common ground with the audience. Using an appeal to pathos, you are probably more easily persuaded by people similar to you than by those who are different. We may reason that individuals having backgrounds like ours will view situations and problems as we would. Furthermore, we believe that people who share our beliefs will investigate an issue and arrive at a judgment in the same manner we would if we had the time and the opportunity.

One way to increase your persuasion, then, is to identify with your listeners. Explain how you and your audience share similar experiences or attitudes so that they feel that they can relate to your speech. You can relate to them as fellow college students or as residents of the same town.

Four principles of persuasion should guide how you establish common ground with your audience. Each of these principles requires you to understand your listeners as a result of some careful audience analysis.

Assess listeners' knowledge of your topic.   Persuasion is more likely if the audience lacks information on the topic. In the absence of information, a single fact can be compelling. The more information your listeners possess about an issue, the less likely you are to alter their perceptions.

Arturo applied this principle in a speech to persuade his audience that auto insurance companies should not be allowed to set rates based on drivers' credit ratings. Few of his listeners knew that the practice occurred. Yet, by citing just a handful of credible sources (ethos), Arturo proved that the practice increased beginning in the mid-1990s, had been adopted by 92% of insurers by 2001, and was "nearly universal" by March 2002. As a result, drivers with the worst credit ratings paid rates that were, in some cases, 40% higher than those with the best ratings.

New and surprising information such as this can have great persuasive impact. Of course, this principle also has significant ethical implications.

Ethical speakers will not exploit their listeners' lack of knowledge to advance positions they know are not logically supported.

Assess how important your audience considers your topic.   Ken, Andrea, and Brad gave their persuasive speeches on the same day. Ken's purpose was to persuade the audience to support the school's newly formed lacrosse team by attending the next home game. Andrea's topic concerned the increasing number of homeless adults and children in the city. She told the class about Project Hope, sponsored by the Student Government Association, and asked everyone to donate either a can of food or a dollar at designated collection centers in campus dining halls or in the Student Center. Finally, Brad advocated legalization of marijuana, citing the drug's medical and economic potential.

Which speaker do you think had the most difficult challenge? In answering this question you must consider the audience. Persuasion is related to how important the audience considers the topic.

The perceived importance of a topic may *increase* the likelihood of persuasion. Listeners who viewed combating hunger as a more important goal than supporting the lacrosse team were probably more persuaded by Andrea and may have contributed to Project Hope.

On the other hand, just as the importance of a topic can work for you as a persuasive speaker, it can also work against you and *decrease* the likelihood of persuasion. It is surely easier, for example, for someone to persuade you to change brands of toothpaste than to change your religion. The reason is simple: Your religion is more important to you. Brad probably had a tougher time persuading his listeners than did either Ken or Andrea. Legalizing marijuana probably ran counter to some deeply held audience opinions, and the intensity of those beliefs and values may have made them more resistant to Brad's persuasive appeals. The importance of an issue will vary according to each audience member, and you need to take this into account as you prepare your persuasive appeal.

Motivate your listeners.   People change their values, beliefs, attitudes, and behaviors when they are motivated to do so. To be an effective persuader, you must discover what motivates your listeners. This requires an understanding of their needs and desires. How can you do this? You can enhance your persuasive appeal by following three steps.

1. Identify as many of the needs and desires of your listeners as possible.
2. Review your list, and select those that your speech satisfies.
3. As you prepare your speech, explain how the action you advocate fulfills audience needs.

If you discover that your speech does not fulfill the needs or desires of your listeners, then you have probably failed to connect with these listeners. They may receive your speech with interest, but those listeners probably will not act on your message. As you discover the needs and desires of the listeners, you can more appropriately choose arguments based on ethos, pathos, and logos. If the audience is familiar with your topic, logical appeals (logos) are not going to be effective. Instead, you may find that emotional appeals (pathos) are more effective in persuading the audience to act.

Relate your message to listeners' values.   Persuasion is more likely if the speaker's message is consistent with listeners' values, beliefs, attitudes, and behaviors. People want to establish consistency in their lives. We expect coherence between our beliefs and actions, for example. In fact, we will call someone a hypocrite if he or she professes one set of values, but acts according to another. Your ability to persuade is thus enhanced if you request an action that is consistent with your audience's values.

Use this principle of consistency in constructing your persuasive appeal. For example, we have had students who persuaded their classroom audience to oppose the use of animals in nonmedical product testing. They first identified the beliefs that would cause a person to challenge such tests—for example, product testing harms animals and is unnecessary. Next they showed their audience that they share these beliefs. Once they accomplished that, the speakers then asked their listeners to act in accordance with their beliefs and boycott companies that continue to test cosmetics on animals.

Organize Your Arguments

Immediately after your speech, chances are that your audience will remember only 50% of what they heard. A speech that is poorly organized in the first place has even less chance of surviving in the minds of audience members. Using the organizational strategies presented in chapter 12 can enhance your appeal to their sense of logos and increase your listeners' retention of your message.

Keep in mind that persuasion is more likely if arguments are placed appropriately. Once you have determined the key arguments in your speech, you must decide their order. To do that, you must know which of your arguments is the strongest. Assume for a moment that your persuasive speech argues that the public defender system needs to be reformed. Assume, too, that you are using a problem—solution organization. Your first main point and the arguments supporting it could be:

I. The public defender system is stacked against the defendant.
   A. Public defenders' caseloads are too heavy.
   B. Public defenders have too little experience.
   C. Public defenders have inadequate investigative staffs.

In previous *Cultural Connections*, we have examined cultures through the qualities of individualism and collectivism and high context and low context. Individualistic cultures tend to be low-context communicators, while collectivistic cultures tend to be high-context communicators.

You may recall that individualistic cultures prefer direct communication characterized by explicit and precise language. According to Koeman (2007), in advertising, individualism is illustrated by "the dominance of rational cues like communicating product information, explicit reference to competing brands, and stressing the functional value of the product" (p. 226).

Collectivistic cultures prefer indirect communication, which is characterized by ambiguous language that requires shared meaning among the communicators. Koeman (2007) states that advertisements in collectivistic cultures "make use of a more indirect communication style … based on associations with a certain person or lifestyle and subjective features of the product advertised" (p. 226).

Gudykunst (1998) classified cultural values reported by Schwartz (1992) in terms of individualism and collectivism. Individualistic cultures value stimulation (excitement and novelty), hedonism (pleasure for oneself), power (social status and prestige), achievement (personal success), and self-direction (independent thought). Collectivistic cultures value tradition (respect and acceptance of customs), conformity (restraint of actions that might violate social expectations or norms), and benevolence (preservation and enhancement of well-being of people with whom one associates) (Koeman, 2007).

Application

Knowing some of the cultural values of collectivistic cultures, how would you incorporate those values if you were giving a persuasive speech on the importance of recycling to an audience largely comprised of people from a collectivist culture? How would you change your persuasive arguments if you were giving the same speech to a largely individualistic audience?

One of these three arguments will probably be stronger than the other two. You may have more evidence on one; you may have more recent evidence on it; or you may feel that one argument will be more compelling than the other two for your particular audience. Assume that you decide point B is your strongest. Where should you place it? Two theories of argument placement are the *primacy and recency theories.*

Primacy theory.   **Primacy theory** recommends that you put your strongest argument first in the body of your speech to establish a strong first impression. Because you are most likely to win over your listeners with your strongest argument, this theory suggests that you should win your listeners to your side as early as possible. Primacy theorists tell you to move your strongest argument to the position of point A.

Recency theory.   **Recency theory**, on the other hand, maintains that you should present your strongest argument last, thus leaving your listeners with your best argument. They would have you build up to your strongest argument by making it point C.

15c

If your listeners oppose what you advocate, you may want to present your strongest argument first. Moving them toward your position early in the speech may make them more receptive to your other ideas. If your audience already shares your beliefs and attitudes and your goal is to motivate them to action, you may want to end with your most compelling argument. Both primacy and recency theorists generally agree that the middle position is the weakest. If you have three or more arguments, therefore, do not place your strongest argument in a middle position. When you sandwich a strong argument between weaker ones, you reduce its impact.

Support Your Ideas

You can use examples, narration, comparison, contrast, statistics, and testimony to give your ideas credibility. Well-supported ideas benefit your speech in two ways. First, they provide an ethical underpinning for your position. Ethical speakers test their ideas for validity and support and share that support with their listeners. Second, well-supported ideas enhance your credibility. Using quality evidence, citing your sources, and employing valid reasoning increase your credibility (ethos) as a speaker (Gass & Seiter, 1999).

EYEONETHICS | Biased Sources: To Use or Not to Use

You probably wouldn't be surprised that a Gallup study sponsored by Motorola found that people who use cellular phones are more successful in business than those who don't, or that a Gallup poll sponsored by the zinc industry revealed that 62% of Americans want to keep the penny coin. These are just two examples that *Wall Street Journal* writer and editor Cynthia Crossen uses in her book, *Tainted Truth: The Manipulation of Fact in America*, to illustrate the difficulty of distinguishing between neutral research and commercially sponsored studies.

Assume that you are preparing to give a speech on hormone replacement therapy to counteract the effects of aging. Through an electronic database search, you find a study that shows the hormone melatonin prevents cancer, boosts the immune system, and improves the quality of sleep. When you look for the source, you see that the study was sponsored by a pharmaceutical company that produces melatonin.

Application

What course of action should you follow? Should you disregard the findings because the study was commercially sponsored, use the findings without mentioning the study's sponsor, mention the findings and acknowledge the study's commercial sponsorship, or treat the findings in some other way? How could the use of the findings affect your credibility?

Enhance Your Emotional Appeals

As we have seen, pathos is the appeal to emotions. Among the emotions speakers can arouse are anger, envy, fear, hate, jealousy, joy, love, or pride. When speakers use these feelings to try to influence you, they are using emotional appeals.

Because some of the emotions listed above seem negative, you may consider emotional appeals as unacceptable or inferior types of proof. Perhaps you have even heard someone say, "Don't be so emotional; use your head!" It is certainly possible to be emotional and illogical, but keep in mind that it is also possible to be both emotional and logical. Is it wrong, for example, to be angered by child abuse, to hate racism, or to fear chemical warfare? We don't think so. The strongest arguments combine reason with passion. Logos and pathos should not conflict but complement each other.

Jessica Jones (2004) began her persuasive speech by relating a personal narrative she remembered from her childhood:

> I was four years old; my sister was only two. It was not long after we reached my grandma's house that the phone rang. I could hear ambulance and police sirens head toward the highway as tears were forming in my mom's eyes. There had been a car accident. My dad was rushed to the hospital; his little Fiesta car was totaled. He had been hit on the passenger side by a man driving a station wagon, and, fortunately, both my dad and the other driver survived. Because the other driver fell asleep at the wheel, my dad went to the hospital instead of coming home that night to his family.

Jessica quoted several sources with examples and statistics related to driver fatigue, including these powerful statistics:

> Drowsy driving is estimated to cause about 20 percent of [all vehicle] accidents, 1.2 million a year, more than drugs and alcohol combined. It accounts for an astonishing five percent of all fatal crashes, and 30 percent of fatal crashes in rural areas.

Did Jessica construct a logical argument? Yes. She presented examples and statistics to support her position. Did she construct an emotional argument? Again, yes. She tapped her listeners' need for safety and their compassion for those who have suffered because of drowsy drivers. Logos and pathos coalesced to form a compelling argument.

Use the following four guidelines to develop and enhance the pathos of your persuasive speech.

Tap audience values. The first, and probably most important, guideline for developing emotional appeals is to *tap audience values*. As we have mentioned repeatedly, you must conduct careful audience analysis before you can deliver an effective speech. Demonstrate in your speech how your audience's values support your position. The more attached listeners are to the values a speaker promotes, the more emotional is the appeal. Part of your responsibility as a speaker is to make that connection evident to your listeners.

Use vivid examples. A second strategy for enhancing emotional appeals is to use vivid, emotionally toned examples. An example may not be sufficient to prove your point, but it should illustrate the concept and generate a strong audience feeling. Notice how the following student used visual examples to enhance the pathos of his speech.

Duncan selected as the specific purpose of his speech to persuade the audience to become members of Amnesty International. He had joined the organization because he felt that, as an individual, he could do little to help end torture and executions of prisoners of conscience throughout the world. As part of a concerted worldwide effort, however, he saw the opportunity to further social and political justice. His speech included ample testimony of persecution coupled with statistical estimates of the extent of the problem.

Duncan wanted to infuse his speech with convincing emotional appeals to support the data. After presenting the facts, he paused and spoke these words to his listeners:

> In the last four minutes you've heard about the anguish, the pain, the suffering, and the persecution experienced by thousands of people, simply because they want to be free and follow their consciences. I want you not only to *hear* of their plight, but also to *see* it.

Duncan pushed the remote control button of a slide projector and proceeded to show five slides of people brutalized by their own governments. He did not speak, but simply showed each slide for ten seconds. After the last slide, he spoke again:

> They say a picture is worth a thousand words. Well, these pictures speak volumes about man's inhumanity to man. But these pictures should also speak to *our consciences*. Can we stand back, detached, and do nothing, knowing what fate befalls these individuals?

Duncan then told the audience how they could become involved in Amnesty International and begin to make a difference. Duncan's speech had a powerful effect because he touched his audience's emotions with vivid examples.

Use emotive language   Duncan also employed pathos by using a third technique: he used emotive language, such as "the anguish, the pain, the suffering, and the persecution …" Nowhere can words be more powerful than when they work to generate emotional appeals.

Use effective delivery.   Finally, you should use effective delivery to enhance emotional appeals. When a speaker's verbal and nonverbal messages conflict, we tend to trust the nonverbal message. For that reason, speakers who show little physical and vocal involvement with their speeches usually come across as uninterested or even insincere. When you display emotion yourself, you can sometimes generate audience emotion.

It is important to remember that these three modes of persuasion—ethos, logos, and pathos—all work to enhance your persuasive appeal. The best persuasive speeches combine all three. Effective persuaders are credible, present logically constructed and supported arguments, and tap the values of their listeners.

| Applying Concepts **DEVELOPING SKILLS** | Assessing Speaker Credibility |

Using the speech that you located for the previous Applying Concepts Developing Skills box, assess the speaker's credibility in terms of his or her competence, trustworthiness, and dynamism. Did the speaker use emotional appeals? If so, describe one emotional appeal used by the speaker.

15d   Using Monroe's Motivated Sequence

One type of persuasive speech, the speech to actuate, provides an interesting challenge to speakers. They must move their listeners to action using a progression of motivated steps. In the 1930s, Alan Monroe developed one of the most popular patterns for organizing the superstructure of a speech to actuate. Called "the motivated sequence," this pattern is particularly appropriate when you discuss a well-known or easily established problem. **Monroe's motivated sequence** includes the following five steps, or stages: attention, need, satisfaction, visualization, and action.

Attention

Monroe argued that speakers must first command the *attention* of their listeners. Suppose your geographic area is experiencing a summer drought.

You could begin your speech with a description of the landscape as you approached your campus a year ago, describing in detail the green grass, the verdant foliage, and the colorful, fragrant flowers. You then contrast the landscape of a year ago with how it looks now: bland, brown, and blossomless. With these contrasting visual images, you try to capture the audience's attention and interest. You can also use any of the suggested attention getters from chapter 12 (page 296).

Need

A speaker's second objective is to establish a *need*. For example, your speech on the drought could illustrate how an inadequate water supply hurts not only the beauty of the landscape, but also agricultural production, certain industrial processes, and, ultimately, the economy of the entire region.

Satisfaction

When you dramatize a problem, you create an urgency to redress it. In the *satisfaction* step of the motivated sequence, you propose a way to solve, or at least minimize, the problem. You may suggest voluntary or mandatory conservation as a short-term solution to the water shortage crisis. As a longer-range solution, you might ask your audience to consider the merits of planting grasses, shrubs, and other plants requiring less water. You could advocate that the city adopt and enforce stricter regulations of water use by businesses or that it develop alternative water sources.

Visualization

Monroe argued that simply proposing a solution is seldom sufficient to bring about change. Through *visualization*, Monroe's fourth step, a speaker seeks to intensify an audience's desire to adopt and implement the proposed solution. You could direct the audience to look out the window at the campus and then ask if that is the scenery they want. More often, though, you create word pictures for the audience to visualize. Without adequate water, you could argue, crops will die, family farms will fail, industries will not relocate to the area, and the quality of life for everyone in the area will be depressed. In contrast, you could refer to the landscape of a year ago, the image you depicted as you began your speech. The future can be colored in green, red, yellow, and blue, and it can represent growth and vitality.

Action

The final step of the motivated sequence is the *action* you request of your listeners. It is not enough to know that something must be done; the audience must know what you want them to do, and your request must be within their power to act. Do you want them to join you in voluntary conservation by watering their lawns in the evening when less water will evaporate or by washing their cars less frequently? Are you asking them to sign petitions pressuring the city council to adopt mandatory conservation measures when the water table sinks to a designated level? Conclude your speech with a strong appeal for specific, reasonable action.

Applying Concepts | **Using Monroe's**
DEVELOPING SKILLS | **Motivated Sequence**

Find an infomercial on YouTube or some other Internet source. Trace the persuasive argument of the infomercial using the Monroe's Motivated Sequence. Be sure to label each of the five steps of the sequence.

MONROE'S MOTIVATED SEQUENCE

ATTENTION STEP
Gain audience's attention

NEED STEP
Provide evidence of the problem

SATISFACTION STEP
Suggest solutions to the problem

VISUALIZATION STEP
What life would be like with or without your solution

ACTION STEP
Tell audience what they can do to help

15e Constructing a Persuasive Argument

Before you can prove your case you must understand the structure of arguments and how those arguments are organized in your speech. Earlier in this chapter, we referred to this type of persuasive appeal as *logos*. Let's see how all this works.

Structuring sound arguments is an important skill for the public speaker. Developing your own persuasive arguments exercises your critical thinking skills.

You may offer proof by arguing from example, analogy, cause, deduction, or authority. The type of argument you select will depend on your topic, the available evidence, and your listeners. You may combine several types of argument in a single persuasive speech. Knowing how to construct and test arguments will also help you as you listen to the speeches of others and increase your communication competence.

Argument by Example

Argument by example is an inductive form of proof. **Inductive argument** uses a few instances to assert a broader claim. For example, we hear friends complain of problems with a particular make of car and decide not to buy that model. A speaker relates several examples of corruption in city hall, and we conclude that political corruption is widespread. These are examples of inductive reasoning.

How can you test whether an argument by example is sound? Argument by example is valid only if you can answer yes to each of the following four questions.

Are the examples true?   Hypothetical or imaginary examples can clarify a point, but they do not prove it. Only when true examples are presented should you proceed to the next question.

Are the examples relevant?   Suppose a speaker presents the following evidence in her speech on homelessness: "According to police reports published yesterday, city police picked up three individuals who were found sleeping in the park this past weekend. So, you can see that even in our city homelessness is a serious problem." Do these examples really support the claim? Did these individuals not have homes? Had they passed out? Were they there for other reasons? Until you can answer these questions, you cannot assume that they were homeless. The examples must relate to the specific claim.

Are the examples sufficient?   A speaker must present enough examples to prove an assertion. In general, the greater the population for which you generalize, the more examples you need. Three examples of homelessness may be statistically significant in a small town, but that number is far below average for many large cities.

Are the examples representative?   Was the weekend typical? How did it compare with other weekends, weekdays, or seasons? To prove the argument, the speaker must present examples that are true, relevant, sufficient, and representative.

Argument by Analogy

An **analogy** is a comparison. *Argument by analogy* links two objects or concepts and asserts that what is true of one will be true of the other. Argument by analogy is appropriate when the program you advocate or oppose has been tried elsewhere. Some states have lotteries, no-fault insurance, and the line-item veto; others do not. Some school systems allow corporal punishment, offer magnet programs, and require a passing grade for participation in extracurricular activities; others do not. A speech defending or disputing one of these programs could demonstrate success or failure elsewhere to establish its position.

Jon argued that pharmacists should not have the right to refuse to fill patients' prescriptions, even for moral or religious reasons. Notice how he used argument by analogy to support his position:

> The June 4, 2005, *Ledger Times* reminds us that in many ways pharmacists are like bus drivers and airline pilots. It would be outrageous for a pilot who disapproved of gambling to refuse transport to Las Vegas-bound passengers who wanted to visit casinos. Or for a bus driver, disturbed [by] tax dollars [that] went to a lavish new football stadium rather than a decrepit public school to refuse to let sports fans off at the arena. Professional pharmacists hold a state-conferred monopoly on medications. In that respect, they are public servants. Their role calls for neutrality on the job—whether they prefer to or not.

Do you find Jon's argument persuasive? The key to this pattern is the similarity between the two entities. In testing the validity of your argument by analogy, you need to answer this question: "Are the two entities sufficiently similar to justify my conclusion that what is true of one will be true of the other?" If not, your reasoning is faulty. This question can best be answered by dividing it into two questions.

Are the similarities between the two cases relevant?   For example, suppose you used argument by analogy to advocate eliminating Friday classes during summer school on your campus as State U has done. The facts that both schools have similar library facilities and the same mascot would be irrelevant. Equivalent student enrollments, numbers of commuting students, and energy needs are highly relevant and can be forceful evidence as you build your case.

15e

Are any of the differences between the two cases relevant?   If so, how do those differences affect your claim? If you discover that, your college has far fewer commuter students than State U does, this difference is relevant to your topic and will undermine the validity of your claim.

Argument by Cause

Argument by cause connects two elements or events and claims that one produced the other. Causal reasoning takes two forms—reasoning from effect to cause and from cause to effect. The difference between the two is their chronological order.

An *effect-to-cause argument* begins at a point of time (when the effects are evident) and moves back in time (to when the cause occurred). When you feel ill and go to the doctor, the doctor will usually identify the symptoms (the effects) of the problem and then diagnose the cause. The doctor is problem solving by reasoning from effect to cause.

In contrast, *cause-to-effect argument* begins at a point of time (when the cause occurred) and moves forward (to when the effects occurred or will occur). Doctors reason from cause to effect when they tell patients who smoke that this habit may result in emphysema or lung cancer.

Rachel used a cause-to-effect argument in her speech on the lack of safety in nursing homes:

CAUSE

In 1965 the Fire Marshals Association of North America begged Congress to require sprinklers in all nursing homes. Forty years and 12 failed proposals later, Congress has yet to act. On December 16, 2005, *USA Today* reveals that there are 16,000 nursing homes that violate fire safety standards annually. Twenty-three thousand fires are reported every year. Four states—Massachusetts, Minnesota, Montana, and Hawaii—set no fire safety standards, only six states require fire sprinklers, and less than half require smoke alarms that alert authorities.

EFFECT

These statistics lead up to an average of at least one fatal fire every month, much like the one that occurred just before the holidays as reported by the Associated Press on December 13, 2005, where two were killed in a Michigan fire and dozens more injured. Fires in nursing homes are all too common, and with more than 1.6 million residents in need of assisted-living arrangements, the danger is real.

When you argue by cause, test your reasoning to make certain it is sound. To do this, ask yourself the following three questions.

Does a causal relationship exist? For an argument from cause to effect or effect to cause to be valid, a causal relationship must exist between the two elements. Just because one event precedes another does not mean that the first caused the second. One student argued that the scholastic decline of American education began with, and was caused by, the Supreme Court's decision outlawing mandatory school prayer. We doubt the connection.

Could the presumed cause produce the effect? During the highly inflationary times of the late 1970s, one student gave a speech arguing that various price hikes had contributed to the high inflation rate. She provided three examples: The cost of postage stamps had increased 87.5%, chewing gum 100%, and downtown parking meter fees 150%. While she was able to document the dramatic percentage increase in the prices of these products, her examples had more interest than impact. The examples did not convince her audience that these increases by themselves significantly influenced on the inflation rate.

Could the effect result from other causes? A number of causes can converge to produce one effect. A student who argues that next year's increased tuition and fees are a result of the college president's fiscal mismanagement may have a point. But other factors may have made the tuition increase necessary: state revenue shortfalls, decreased enrollment, cutbacks in federal aid, and so on. Speakers strengthen their arguments when they prove that the alleged cause contributed substantively to producing the effect and that without the cause, the effect would not have occurred or the problem would have been much less severe.

Argument by Deduction

Ben began his speech on time management with the following statement:

> All of us are taking courses that require us to be in class and to study outside class. In addition, many of us are members of social, academic, religious, or career-oriented clubs and organizations. Some of us work. All of us like to party! Crowded into our school and work schedules are our responsibilities to friends and family members. In short, we're busy!
>
> College is a hectic time in our lives. Sometimes it seems that we're trying to cram 34 hours of activity into a 24-hour day. In order to survive this schedule and beat the stress, college students need to develop effective time-management skills. You are no exception! If you listen to my speech today, you will learn how to set realistic goals, meet them, and still have time to socialize with friends and get a good night's sleep. Sound impossible? Just listen closely for the next eight minutes.

15e

Ben used two types of arguments in his introduction. He opened by *arguing from example*, providing several instances to make his case that college life is busy. He then used deductive reasoning to make the speech relevant to each member of the audience. A **deductive argument** moves from a general category to a specific instance. In this sense, deductive arguments are the reverse of argument by example. To see why that's true, consider the structure of a deductive argument.

Deductive arguments consist of a pattern of three statements (a major premise, a minor premise, and a conclusion) called a **syllogism**. The *major premise* is a claim about a general group of people, events, or conditions. Ben's major premise was this: "College students need to develop effective time-management skills."

The *minor premise* places a person, event, or condition into a general class. Ben's minor premise could be phrased like this: "You are a college student."

The *conclusion* argues that what is true of the general class is true of the specific instance or individual. Ben concluded that each college student in his audience needed to develop effective time-management skills.

Use the following steps to check the structure of your deductive argument.

1. State your major premise.
2. Say "because," and then state your minor premise.
3. Say "therefore," and then state your conclusion.

The resulting two sentences should flow together easily and make sense. Ben could have tested the clarity of his argument by saying the following: "College students need to develop effective time-management skills. *Because* you are a college student, *therefore* you need to develop effective time-management skills." Notice that if the two premises are true and relate to each other, the conclusion must also be true.

Argument by Authority

Argument by authority differs from the four other forms of argument we have discussed. To see how it is different, consider the following example from Lynn's speech:

> I believe that every student should be allowed to vote for Outstanding Professor on Campus, rather than having the award determined by a select committee of the faculty. And I'm not alone in my opinion. Last year's recipient of the award, Dr. Linda Carter, agrees. The President of the Faculty Senate spoke out in favor of this proposal at last week's forum, and the Student Government Association passed a resolution supporting it.

Argument from authority uses testimony from an expert source to prove a speaker's claim; its validity depends on the credibility the authority has for the audience. In this example, Lynn did not offer arguments based on example, analogy, cause, or deduction to explain the validity of her position. Instead, she asserted that two distinguished professors and the SGA agreed with her. She asked her audience to believe her position based on the credentials of the authority figures who endorsed her claim. Her rationale was that her sources had access to sufficient information and had the expertise to interpret it accurately; thus, we should trust their conclusions.

An argument based on authority is only as valid as the source's credibility. To test your argument, ask and answer two questions: (1) *Is the source an expert?* (2) *Is the source unbiased?*

Testing the arguments you use and hear others use is crucial to effective, ethical speaking and listening. See "Constructing a Persuasive Argument" for a summary of the tests of argument.

CONSTRUCTING A PERSUASIVE ARGUMENT

Argument by Example
(inductive argument)

Answer these questions:
- Are the examples true?
- Are the examples relevant?
- Are the examples sufficient?
- Are the examples representative?

Argument by Analogy
(comparison)

Answer these questions:
- Are the similarities between the two cases relevant?
- Are the differences between the two cases relevant?

Argument by Cause
(one element produces the other)

Answer these questions:
- Does a causal relationship exist?
- Could the presumed cause produce the effect?
- Could the effect result from other causes?

Argument by Deduction
(general cases to specific incident)

Use syllogism:
- State major premise.
- State minor premise.
- State your conclusion.

15e

Argument by Authority
(expert source as evidence)

Answer these questions:
- Is the source an expert?
- Is the source unbiased?

Using the speech you selected for the first two Applying Concepts/Developing Skills applications, assess the speaker's use of arguments. Which of the five types of arguments could you identify in the speech? Were the arguments logical?

15f Evaluating a Persuasive Speech

SAMPLE

Persuasive Speech

Volunteering

Rushdat Hale, Radford University, Radford, Virginia

Specific purpose: To persuade the audience to be involved with community service.

Central Idea: Volunteering takes little time and provides personal health benefits

How many of you like to do things that make you feel real good? [Rushdat pauses as classmates begin raising their hands.] Ah, that's what I thought. During my speech, I want to convince you to do something not just because it's a good thing to do, but because doing it will make you feel good. What's this "good thing"? It's volunteering.

The U.S. Bureau of Labor Statistics estimates that between September 2007 and September 2008, almost 25% of Americans volunteered through various organizations. I have volunteered for several worthy causes over the years, and I can assure you that this has been one of the more rewarding parts of my life. If you're not part of that 25%, I want to encourage you to make that commitment. If you already volunteer, I encourage you to continue and to enlist others.

So today, let's ask and answer three questions: First, how does volunteerism help others? Second, how does volunteerism help us? And finally, how can we volunteer?

← ATTENTION

In her introduction, Rushdat uses *direct question* as her attention getter. She mentions that volunteering will be beneficial for her audience and she mentions her own experience with volunteering (to enhance her credibility). Finally, she previews the main points of her speech.

(First, how does volunteering benefit others?)

Recently, a friend of mine told me he'd rather send a million dollars to Cambodia than spend a thousand dollars here helping Americans because Americans can fend for themselves. This cannot be further from the truth. With these days of high unemployment rates and budget cuts, we need volunteers to step up and help those in need.

Megan DeMarco, staff writer for *The Philadelphia Inquirer,* on August 6, 2009, detailed the plight of non-profit organizations during a recession. Many programs designed to help the needy have seen their budgets slashed and are in need of more volunteers. Volunteerism is one way of helping others in our communities.

Volunteering, however, not only benefits others, it also benefits us. So, let's answer a second question: What is in it for me?

A 2007 study conducted by the Corporation for National and Community Service found a strong relationship between volunteering and good health. The study documented that those who volunteer have lower mortality rates, greater functional ability, and lower rates of depression later in life. This doesn't surprise DeMarco who also reported that people who are unemployed find comfort in helping others in need.

Last August, one of my cousins came to visit. She went with me to one of my charitable organizations—a food program that serves people in the Roanoke and Vinton areas. My cousin is a computer programmer who works hard the whole week and then usually sleeps in on Saturdays. As she was helping out that day, I could see that she was excited and really getting into it. She was interacting with people and she was beaming. So at the end of the day, I asked her, "How did you feel about volunteering today?" And she said: "I was so happy. I had no idea volunteering could make me feel this good. I thought I was doing myself a favor by sleeping in on Saturdays. But today, I was out here not only helping people, I was helping myself." And that's what volunteering can do for you!

It's been well documented that volunteering gives you social and health benefits. According to DeMarco's article in *The Philadelphia Inquirer* dated August 6, 2009, people who are unemployed find comfort in helping others in need.

In a 2007 study on the health benefits of volunteering conducted by the Corporation for National and Community Service, there is a strong relationship between volunteering and good health. The research concluded that those who volunteer have lower mortality rates, greater functional ability, and lower rates of depression later in life.

You've heard how volunteering can help society and can benefit you. Are you ready to volunteer your time and talent to a charitable organization? If so, you need to take two steps. First, find the time to volunteer. Now, I know some of you are thinking, "I'm a college student. I work part-time. I hang out with my friends. When am I going to find the

---

[Transition] Signpost and Statement

NEED

Rushdat asserts that every community has *needs* for which volunteer opportunities exist. She uses *narrative* as a supportive material to show that some people do not believe that Americans could need help. Then she provides references to reiterate the need for volunteers in America.

[Transition] Signpost and Statement

SATISFACTION

Rushdat seeks to *satisfy the need* for volunteers by offering specific reasons why volunteering is beneficial.

She provides *statistics* as supporting material (number of volunteers, number of people served).

VISUALIZATION

After proposing the solution, Rushdat poses a counterargument and then refutes it with *statistics*. She asks her audience to visualize ways they can find the time to volunteer.

15f

time to volunteer?" It's easier than you think. A 2008 Bureau of Labor Statistics study indicated that Americans spend over five hours per day engaged in leisure and sports activities, such as exercising and watching TV. Think about the time you spend emailing, text messaging, and talking on the cell phone. Couldn't you spare at least one hour per week helping others in need? I can assure you many charitable organizations will even let you volunteer less than an hour—maybe just once a month. Someone's life will be better because of the time you give.

Once you find the time, you then need to find a place to volunteer. ← **[Transition] Signpost and Statement**
This is your easiest task.

You're just a few keystrokes away from locating your cause. Tonight, ← **ACTION**
"Google" two organizations: "Volunteer Match" and "Network for Good." **In her conclusion, Rushdat provides**
These sites will match your interests with the kinds of volunteering activities **with information about how the**
that are comfortable for you. For example, you can indicate that you want to **audience can *act* by volunteering in**
work with an environmental organization or a children's organization. **their community.**

Opportunities abound for volunteering right here in the New River **She uses a *narrative* and *statistics* as**
Valley. For example, the New River Community Action volunteers work at **supporting materials.**
clothing and food banks, distribute flyers and posters, and pick up
donations. If working in our community interests you, go to www.swva.
net/nrca and enlist as a volunteer. According to their web site that I
accessed on June 10, 2009, the New River Valley Community Action
served 12,171 people in the NRV supported by 1,115 volunteers who
worked 46,034 hours just in the years 2007–2008!

In summary, you now know that volunteering benefits yourself and ← **Conclusion: She** signals the end,
others, and you know how to find some of the places to volunteer. reviews the main points **of the**
Remember that volunteering does not need to take a lot of your free time— **speech, and encourages people to**
even just an hour each month. Join the 25% of Americans who volunteer **go out and volunteer (end with an**
and reap the personal benefits from your efforts. You'll be glad you did. **impact)**

Sources:

Bureau of Labor Statistics, U.S. Department of Labor (2008, July). American
time use survey — 2008 results. Retrieved on August 18, 2009, from
http://www.bls.gov/news.release/atus.nr0.htm

Bureau of Labor Statistics, U.S. Department of Labor (2009). Volunteering
in the United States, 2008. Retrieved August 18, 2009,
from http://www.bls.gov/news.release/volun.nr0.htm

The Corporation for National & Community Service, Office of Research
and Policy Development. (2007). The health benefits of volunteering:
A review of recent research. Retrieved June 10, 2009,
from http://www.nationalservice.gov/pdf/07_0506_hbr.pdf

DeMarco, M. (6 August, 2009). Recession drives spike in volunteerism.
The Philadelphia Inquirer, A01.

New River Community Action. (2009). Volunteers. Retrieved on June 10,
2009, from http://www.swva.net/nrca/volunteer.htm

15f

Competence SUMMARY

In this chapter, you have learned the following concepts to increase your communication competence.

15a Understanding the Importance of Persuasion

- Persuasion is the process of influencing another person's values, beliefs, attitudes, or behaviors.
- The information you gather and the assumptions you make about your audience before your speech determine the strategy you use as you develop your remarks.

Competence. Can I identify the different forms of influence? Do I understand why it is important to know these forms of influence?

15b Identifying Types of Persuasive Speeches

- Three types of persuasive speeches are speeches to convince, to actuate, or to inspire.

Competence. Do I know the purpose of each of the three types of persuasive speeches? Upon listening to a persuasive speech, could I label it as one of the three types of persuasive speeches?

15c Examining Persuasive Speaking Strategies

- Three modes of persuasion, discussed at least as early as the time of Aristotle, are *ethos*, *logos*, and *pathos*.
- The higher your perceived credibility, the more likely the audience is to believe you. *Competence*, *trustworthiness*, and *dynamism* are three components of a speaker's credibility.
- You are more likely to persuade if your goals are limited rather than global, if you achieve your goals incrementally, if you establish common ground with the audience, and if your message is consistent with listeners' values, beliefs, attitudes, and behaviors.
- Well-supported ideas provide an ethical underpinning for your speech and enhance your ethos for the audience. Increase your persuasiveness by enhancing the emotional appeals of your message.

Competence. Can I explain the three modes of persuasion? Do I know the components of credibility? Can I explain the strategies for enhancing my persuasive speech?

15d Using Monroe's Motivated Sequence

- Persuasive speeches are more effective if they follow logical steps.
- Monroe's motivated sequence contains five steps: attention, need, satisfaction, visualization, and action.

Competence. Do I know how to implement each of the five steps of the Monroe's motivated sequence?

15e Constructing a Persuasive Argument

- In your speech, you can argue from example, analogy, cause, deduction, or authority. The type of argument you select will depend on your topic, the available evidence, and your listeners.
- An inductive argument uses a few examples to assert a broader claim, while a deductive argument moves from a broad category to a specific instance.

Competence. Do I know how to construct each of the five forms of argument? Can I distinguish between inductive and deductive reasoning?

Review Questions

1. What is persuasion?
2. What are the three types of persuasive speeches?
3. Explain each of the three modes of persuasion.
4. What are the components of credibility?
5. List the strategies for enhancing your persuasive speech.
6. Explain the five steps of the Monroe's motivated sequence.
7. What are the five forms of argument?
8. What is a syllogism?

Discussion Questions

1. Locate a political advertisement on the Internet. Which form(s) of argument does it use? Which form of argument do you think is most often used in political ads? Why?
2. Monroe's motivated sequence was created in the 1930s. Explain why you think it has been popular for almost a century?
3. Locate a speech that you feel includes examples of unethical emotional appeals. Explain why the emotional appeals are questionable.

Key Terms

analogy *p. 381*

credibility *p. 367*

deductive argument *p. 384*

ethos *p. 367*

inductive argument *p. 380*

logos *p. 367*

Monroe's motivated sequence *p. 377*

pathos *p. 367*

persuasion *p. 364*

primacy theory *p. 373*

recency theory *p. 373*

speech to actuate *p. 366*

speech to convince *p. 366*

speech to inspire *p. 366*

syllogism *p. 384*

Special Occasion Speeches

We can all count on being called on to deliver a speech on some special occasion. To speak your best at these times, you must consider the customs and audience expectations in each case. You may also not have much time to prepare for special occasion speeches, as sometimes you are called on to give a speech at the last minute.

SPEECH OF INTRODUCTION

One of the most common types of special occasion speeches is the *speech of introduction*—a speech to introduce a featured speaker (not yourself).

The following guidelines will help you prepare such a speech of introduction:

- **Keep focus on person being introduced.** The audience has not gathered to hear you. Keep your remarks short, simple, and sincere.

- **Be brief.** If you can, request and get a copy of the speaker's résumé. This will give you information to select from when preparing your introductory remarks. Highlight key information only.

- **Establish the speaker's credibility on the topic.** Present the speaker's credentials. As you prepare, ask and answer questions such as: What makes the speaker qualified to speak on the subject? What education and experiences make the speaker's insights worthy of our belief?

- **Create realistic expectations.** Genuine praise is commendable, just be careful not to oversell the speaker.

- **Establish a tone consistent with the speaker's presentation.** Would you give a humorous introduction for a speaker whose topic is "The Grieving Process"? Of course not. On the other hand, if the evening is designed for merriment, your introduction should help set that mood.

SPEECH OF PRESENTATION

The *speech of presentation* confers an award, a prize, or some other form of special recognition on an individual or a group. Such speeches are typically made after banquets or parties; as parts of business meetings or sessions of a convention; or at awards ceremonies. When you give a speech of presentation, let the nature and importance of the award being presented, as well as the occasion on which it is being presented, shape your remarks.

The following guidelines will help you plan this special-occasion speech:

- **State the purpose of the award or recognition.** If the audience is unfamiliar with the award or the organization making the award, begin by briefly explaining the nature of the award or the rationale for presenting it. In contrast, an award having a long history probably needs little explanation.

- **Focus your speech on the achievements for which the award is being made.** Don't attempt a detailed biography of the recipient. Because you are merely highlighting the honoree's accomplishments, the speech of presentation will be brief, rarely more than five minutes and frequently much shorter.

- **Organize the speech based on whether audience already knows who has won.** If they do not know the award winner, capitalize on their curiosity. Let ambiguity about who will receive the honor propel the speech and maintain the audience's attention.

  If the audience knows in advance the name of the person being recognized, begin the speech with specifics and end with more general statements that summarize the reasons for the presentation.

- **Compliment the entire group of nominees.** It is polite and expected that you announce all the nominees in your presentation before announcing the winner.

ACCEPTANCE SPEECH

At some point in your life, you may be commended publicly for service you have given to a cause or an organization. An *acceptance speech* is a response to a speech of presentation. When a recipient acknowledges the award or tribute, he or she provides closure to the process.

A gracious acceptance speech usually includes four steps:

- **Thank the person or organization bestowing the award.** You may wish to name the group sponsoring the award, the person who made the presentation speech, and commend what the award represents. Your respect for the award and its donor authenticates your statement of appreciation.

- **Compliment your peers as a group rather than individually.** If you are accepting a competitively selected award, and especially if your competitors are in the audience, acknowledge their qualifications and compliment them.

- **Thank those who helped you achieve the honor.** Whether you are an accomplished pianist, vocalist, artist, athlete, or writer, you have usually had someone—parents, teachers, or coaches—who invested time, money, and expertise to help you achieve your best.

- **Accept your award graciously.** Humility breeds respect.

SPEECH OF TRIBUTE

A *speech of tribute* honors a person, a group, or an event, and it can be one of the most moving forms of public address. A special form of the speech of tribute is the *eulogy*, a speech given for those who have recently died.

Five guidelines will help you write a eulogy or any other speech of tribute:

- **Establish noble themes.** Remember to focus on the positive. A speech of tribute celebrates what is good about a person; it is not an occasion for a warts-and-all biography. You must be careful, however, not to exaggerate a person's accomplishments. To do so may undermine your speech by making it seem insincere or unbelievable.

- **Develop the themes of your speech with vivid examples.** Anecdotes, stories, and personal testimony are excellent ways of making your speech more vivid, humane, and memorable.

- **Express the feelings of the audience assembled.** The audience needs to be a part of the occasion for any speech of tribute. If you are honoring Mr. Crenshaw, a former teacher, you may speak for yourself, but you can also speak for your class or even all students who studied under him. The honoree should feel that the tribute expresses more than one person's view.

- **Create a memorable image of the person being honored.** Your speech not only honors someone, it also helps audience members focus on that person's importance to them.

- **Be genuine.** If you are asked to deliver a speech of tribute about someone you do not know, you may want to decline respectfully. The personal bond and interaction you develop in getting to know someone well is essential for a speech of tribute.

SPEECH TO ENTERTAIN

The three main purposes of speaking are to inform, to persuade, and to entertain. Although many informative and persuasive speeches contain elements of humor, the speech designed specifically to entertain is special because it is often difficult to do well.

The *speech to entertain* seeks to make a point through the creative, organized use of the speaker's humor. The distinguishing characteristic of a speech to entertain is the entertainment value of its supporting materials. It is usually delivered on an occasion when people are in a light mood: after a banquet, as part of an awards ceremony, and on other festive occasions.

If you combine the following five guidelines with what you already know about developing a public speech, you will discover that a speech to entertain is both challenging and fun to present.

- **Make a point.** Frequently, the person delivering a speech to entertain is trying to make the audience aware of conditions, experiences, or habits that they take for granted.

- **Be creative.** To be creative you must make sure that your speech to entertain is your product, and not simply a replay of another performer. Your speech to entertain should give your audience a glimpse of your unique view of the world.

- **Be organized.** The speech to entertain must have an introduction, body, and conclusion. It must convey a sense of moving toward some logical point and achieving closure after adequately developing that point. Failure to organize your materials will cause you to ramble, embarrassing both you and your audience.

- **Use appropriate humor.** Most people associate entertainment with lots of laughter and feel that if the audience is not laughing a good deal they are not responding favorably to the speech. Some subjects that entertain us don't result in waves of laughter, however. Your humor should be adapted to your topic, your audience, the occasion, and your own personal style.

- **Use a spirited delivery style.** Your personality, timing, and interaction with the audience are essential to making a speech to entertain lively and unforgettable.

Guidelines for Using Humor

For speeches of entertainment, humor is often a necessary component. Good humor makes your speech memorable. However, you should consider the range of things that entertain you, from outrageous antics to quiet, pointed barbs.

The following four suggestions should guide your use of humor.

- **Be relevant.** Good humor is relevant to your general purpose and makes the main ideas of your speech memorable.

- **Be tasteful.** What delights some listeners may offend others. Do the best job you can in analyzing your audience, but when in doubt, err on the side of caution. Remember, humor that is off-color is off-limits.

- **Be tactful.** Avoid humor that generates laughter at the expense of others. Humor intended to belittle or demean a person or group is unethical and unacceptable. For that reason, most sexist or ethnic humor should also be off-limits.

- **Be positive.** The tone for most occasions featuring speeches to entertain should be festive. People have come together to relax and enjoy each other's company. Dark, negative humor is usually inappropriate as it casts a somber tone on the situation.

IMPROMPTU SPEECH

The *impromptu speech*, one with limited or no advance preparation, can be intimidating. You have not had time to think about the ideas you want to communicate. You begin speaking without knowing the exact words you will use. You have not practiced delivering your speech. Don't panic! By now you have a pretty good understanding of how to organize, support, and deliver a speech. You have practiced these skills in prepared speeches. All this practice will help you in your impromptu speech.

If you follow these four guidelines, you should be ready for almost any impromptu speech that comes along.

- **Speak on a topic you know well.** The more you know about your topic, the better you will be able to select relevant ideas, organize them, and explain them as you speak. In addition, your confidence will show in your delivery.

- **Make the most of the time you have.** Don't waste "walking time" from your seat to the front of the room worrying. Instead, ask yourself, "What do I want the audience to remember when I sit down? What two or three points will help them remember this?"

- **Focus on a single or a few key points.** Too many key points will make your speech sound scattered and disorganized.

- **Be brief.** An impromptu speech is not the occasion for a long, rambling discourse. Say what you need to say, and then be seated.

Applying Concepts
DEVELOPING SKILLS

Analyzing an Award Acceptance Speech

Find an award acceptance speech on YouTube. You will likely find something for a recent music awards program or a movie awards program. Watch the speech and write down the guidelines that the person used and the guidelines that they did not use.

Group Presentations

Why study group work as a part of public speaking? The answer is that groups often make presentations in the workplace (either internally or in public), and the quality of those presentations depends on how well the group members have functioned together.

For most of your work in this class, you have operated alone. You selected, researched, and organized your speech topics. You have practiced and delivered these speeches standing alone in front of your classmates. Your individual work continues in a group. You must still present, support, and defend your ideas, but now you must also work competently with the other members of your group in order to complete the presentation.

PREPARING A GROUP PRESENTATION

Although there is no one correct way to prepare for a team presentation, the following suggestions will help you work more efficiently and produce a more effective product.

- **Brainstorm about the Topic.** Through brainstorming, you will discover what team members already know, and you will uncover numerous ideas for further research. In addition to providing content, brainstorming also serves a relationship function. By giving all members an opportunity to participate, brainstorming gives you a glimpse of your peers' personalities and their approaches to group interaction. You get to know them and they get to know you. Maintaining an atmosphere of openness and respect during this first meeting gets the team off to a good start. Once you have generated a list of areas concerning your topic, you are ready for the second step.

- **Do Some Exploratory Research.** Through brainstorming, you will discover areas that need further investigation. The second phase is individual research. While there may be some merit in each person selecting a different topic to research, research roles should not be too rigid. Rather than limiting yourself by topic, you may wish to divide your research by resource. One member may search the Internet, another the library's databases, while a third may interview a professor who is knowledgeable about the topic, and so forth. It is important that you not

STEPS IN PREPARING A GROUP PRESENTATION

1. Brainstorm about the Topic *

2. Do Some Exploratory Research

3. Discuss and Divide the Topic into Areas of Responsibility *

4. Research Your Specific Topic Area

5. Draft an Outline of Your Content Area

6. Discuss How All the Information Interrelates *

7. Finalize Presentation Procedures *

8. Plan the Introduction and Conclusion of the Presentation *

9. Prepare and Practice Your Part of the Presentation

10. Rehearse and Revise the Presentation *

* Denotes those steps requiring group interaction;
the other steps can be done individually.

restrict your discovery to the list of topics you have generated. Exploratory research is also a form of brainstorming. As you look in indexes and read articles, you will uncover more topics. Each team member should try to find a few good sources that are diverse in scope.

■ **Discuss and Divide the Topic into Areas of Responsibility.** After exploratory research, your team should reconvene to discuss what each member found. Which expectations did your research confirm? Which were contradicted? What topics did you find that you had not anticipated? Your objective at this stage is to decide on key areas you wish to investigate. Each person should probably now be given primary responsibility for researching a particular area. That person becomes the content expert in that area. While this approach makes research efficient, it has a drawback. If one person serves as a specialist, the team gambles that he or she will research thoroughly and

report findings objectively. If either assumption is not valid, the quantity of information may be insufficient and its quality contaminated. An alternative approach is to assign more than one person to a specific area.

■ **Research Your Specific Topic Area.** Using the strategies discussed in chapter 11, research your topic area. Your focus should be on the quality of the sources you discover, not on quantity. While your primary goal should be to gather information on your topic, you should also note information related to your colleagues' topics. As you consult indexes, jot down sources that may be helpful to another team member. If you are researching a relevant Internet source that could benefit another the group member, email him or her the URL. Team members who support each other in these and other ways make the process more efficient and, hence, more enjoyable. This usually results in a better product.

Planning the Group Presentation

Meet with your presentation group to decide on a topic idea. Use the process of effective decision making that you learned in chapter 8 to help you to create a list of potential topics and choose the best topic for your presentation.

Then once your group has chosen a topic, draw up a plan for how you will proceed. In other words, as a group, determine how you will incorporate each of the remaining steps in preparing a group presentation and write down your conclusions. Use your written statements as a way of guiding your group through the creation and delivery of your group presentation.

■ **Draft an Outline of Your Content Area.** After you have concluded your initial research but before you meet again with your team, construct an outline of the ideas and information you've found. This step is important because it forces you to make sense of all the information you have collected, and it will expedite the next step when you will share your information with group members.

■ **Discuss How All the Information Interrelates.** You are now ready to meet with your group. Members should summarize briefly what they have discovered through their research. After all have shared their ideas, the team should decide which ideas are most important and how these ideas relate to each other. There should be a natural development of the topic that can be divided among the group members.

■ **Finalize Presentation Procedures.** The speaking order should already be determined.

There are, nevertheless, certain procedural details that the group must decide. Will the first speaker introduce all presenters or will each person introduce the next speaker? Where will the participants sit when they are not speaking: facing the audience or in the front row? The more details you decide beforehand, the fewer distractions you will have on the day you speak.

■ **Plan the Introduction and Conclusion of the Presentation.** A presentation should appear to be that of a group and not that of four or five individuals. Consequently you must work on introducing and concluding the group's comments, and you must incorporate smooth transitions from one speaker's topic to the next. An introduction should state the topic, define important terms, and establish the importance of the subject. A conclusion should summarize what has been presented and end with a strong final statement.

■ **Prepare and Practice Your Part of the Presentation.** As part of a group presentation, you will need to refer to your colleagues' comments and perhaps even some of their supporting materials. The team presentation may also impose physical requirements you have not encountered as a speaker, such as using a microphone, speaking to those seated around you in addition to making direct contact with the audience, or speaking from a seated position.

■ **Rehearse and Revise the Presentation.** Independent practice of your portion of the presentation is important, but that is only one part of rehearsal. The group should practice its entire presentation. Group rehearsal will not only make participants more confident about their individual presentations but also give the group a feeling of cohesion.

DELIVERING A GROUP PRESENTATION

A group presentation is more than just a collection of individual speeches on the same topic. By coordinating your team's content and delivery, you will enhance your collective credibility and message impact. Consider the following guidelines to create a polished and proficient group presentation.

- **Dress appropriately.** All presenters should be well groomed and dressed up, rather than "dressed down."

- **Introduce the presentation and group members.** Provide an agenda for your presentation. What will listeners learn and who will present each section? Will one person introduce all team members at the beginning, or will each person introduce the next speaker?

- **Incorporate smooth transitions from one person to the next.** A seamless presentation requires planning and practice.

- **Have one person design and produce all presentational aids.** This will ensure that their design and appearance are consistent.

- **Have one person display all presentational aides except when he or she is speaking.** Assigning one person to handle and project all the aids will help make the presentation flow smoothly and consistently.

- **Assign someone to keep time and provide other signals to the group.** Use subtle but clear time signals so that team members do not exceed their time limits. This person may also signal when presenters are speaking too softly or too rapidly.

- **Conclude the main presentation.** Often the person who introduced the presentation also concludes it.

- **And, of course, practice, practice, practice, both individually and as a group.**

Following the procedures described in this module will ensure that your group presentation is carefully planned, conscientiously researched, adequately supported, and competently delivered. More than that, however, your presentation will also demonstrate spontaneity, goodwill, and the camaraderie that will likely have developed if members of your group have functioned effectively and productively together.

accommodation   Giving in to someone else's wishes (or demands) in order to resolve the conflict.

achievement goal   The outcome that the group intends to produce.

active listening   The process of paraphrasing a speaker's message and conveying understanding of that message back to the speaker.

affection   The basic human need to be liked and esteemed.

agenda   A pre-set plan for members to follow during a meeting.

aggressive   When one person intentionally inflicts psychological or physical harm on an opponent with the goal of winning the argument.

analogy   A comparison used in a speech.

argumentativeness   A willingness to verbalize and defend a viewpoint.

articulation   The mechanical process of forming the sounds necessary to communicate in a particular language.

artifacts   Objects that convey information about us.

assertiveness   The willingness to stand up for your rights without infringing on the rights of others.

assigned leader   Appointed by someone outside of the group.

assumed leader   Emerges from the communication within the group.

asynchronous   Computer-mediated communication forms that allow you to send and receive messages when the other person is not logged in or able to receive the information.

attitude   An expression of approval or disapproval of something or someone.

audience disposition   How listeners are inclined to react to a speaker and his or her ideas.

audience-specific apprehension   Anxiety felt by a person depending on the audience involved in the setting.

authority rule   A decision is made by the group leader rather than the entire or majority of the group.

autonomy-connection dialectic   Dialectic regarding the amount of time the dyad spends together or apart.

avoidance   Occurs when you refuse to confront conflict or manage it.

bar graph   Visual aid that is useful in comparing quantities or amounts.

behavior   An overt, observable action, or how we act.

behavioral conflict   Involves control over tangible issues, such as resources or interests.

belief   Something you accept as true that it is usually stated as a declarative sentence.

brainstorming   Creating a list of all of the ideas that come to your mind without evaluating or censoring any of them.

breadth and depth   The number and variety of topics covered in self-disclosures.

captive audience   An audience that feels required to be present and may have an unfavorable attitude toward the speaker.

causal division   Speech organizational pattern in which you trace a condition or action from its causes to its effects, or from effects back to causes.

causal transition   A cause-and-effect relation between two ideas in a speech.

certainty   A close-minded behavior and unwillingness to consider any other perspective.

channel   The mechanism used to transmit a message.

chronemics   The use of time to communicate.

chronological division   Speech organizational pattern that organizes a speech according to a time sequence.

chronological transition   Shows the time relationships between ideas during a speech.

circular conclusion   A conclusion in which the final statement echoes or refers to the attention-getting step of the introduction.

clarity   The exactness of a message.

climate   The tone of an interaction.

closed questions   Questions that can be answered with a yes, a no, or a short answer.

coercive power   Power based on a person's ability to persuade by punishing or threatening someone.

cognitive restructuring   An approach to reducing anxiety that requires speakers to restructure their thinking and focus on positive rather than negative self-statements.

cohesiveness   The bonds among group members that provide a sense of togetherness.

collaboration   When both parties in the conflict get what they want.

communication   The process of sharing meaning through a continuous flow of symbolic messages.

communication apprehension   Fear or anxiety associated with either real or anticipated communication with another person or persons.

communication appropriateness   The determination of whether or not a communicative behavior is suitable to the given context in which the behavior was enacted.

communication competence   The ability to communicate effectively and appropriately within a given communication context.

communication context   The environment in which a person is communicating and the number of people with whom that person is interacting.

communication effectiveness   The accomplishment of desired outcomes in a communicative interaction.

communicator   Each person participating in a communication interaction.

comparison   The process of depicting one item—person, place, object, or concept—by pointing out its similarities to another, more familiar item.

competition   When you assert your own rights with little (or no) concern for the other person.

complaining   Stating something that you do not like.

complementary transition   Adding one idea to another, thus reinforcing the major point of the speech.

compromise   When each party gives up a little in order to resolve conflict.

computer-mediated communication (CMC)   A wide variety of interpersonal contexts using digital technology.

confirmation   Statements acknowledging the presence and acceptance of those with whom they are communicating.

conflict   When the goals of interdependent people are incompatible and at least one person communicates to the other(s) about the incompatibility.

conflict aftermath   The residual effects of the communication and behaviors that occurred during the conflict episode.

conflict stage   The second stage of decision making during which group members begin discussing the situation and suggesting solutions.

connotative meaning   The emotional association that a particular word has for an individual listener.

consensus   Group members are willing to support a given decision or solution.

contempt   Takes criticism one step further and adds *intention* to hurt or to insult a person with a personal attack.

content conflict   Emphasizes tangible issues, such as money, events, or people.

content dimension   The words in the message that are communicated.

context-specific apprehension   Anxiety about communicating that exists only in certain contexts (such as in interpersonal or public speaking settings).

contrast   Links two items by showing their differences.

contrasting transition   Shows how two ideas differ in a speech.

control   A defensive behavior in which you communicate that you know how the other person should act, think, or feel.

costs   Things you sacrifice for the relationship.

credibility   The dependability or believability of a speaker or that speaker's sources.

criticism   Attacking a person's personality or character.

cultural schemata   Pockets of knowledge (schemata) based on ethnic heritage and familial experiences.

decision emergence   The third stage in decision making when group members begin to formulate a solution to the situation.

decision making   The process of choosing among options that already exist.

deductive argument   An argument that moves from a general category to a specific instance.

defensive climate   An environment in which communication is likely to be negative and communicators do not feel comfortable communicating freely.

defensiveness   When a person is compelled to explain the motives for his or her behavior.

delivery   how you say the words of your speech using vocal qualities and gestures that shape your image as a speaker.

demographics   Descriptive characteristics of your audience, such as age and sex.

denotative meaning   The dictionary definition of a word.

description   A supportive behavior using objective statements that do not assign blame in the situation.

direct aggression   Personal attacks ranging from teasing and swearing to physical violence.

direct question   A question that seeks a public response.

disconfirmation   When you ignore the presence of others and who they are as persons.

displaced conflict When you direct the conflict toward the wrong person.

distributive agreements Conflict solutions that "distribute" the benefits unevenly.

empathy Feeling as the other person feels, or putting yourself in another person's shoes.

environment The context in which communication occurs.

equality A supportive behavior that lets the other person know that you respect him or her and that you do not consider yourself superior.

equilibrium theory Theory that states that the more intimate the relationship, the closer you allow the person into your personal space.

ethics The standards we use to distinguish right from wrong, or good from bad, in thought and behavior.

ethos Speaker credibility that derives from the character and reputation of the speaker.

evaluation A defensive behavior in which the communicator judges (positively or negatively) the other person and/or places blame on that person.

example A specific illustration of a category of people, places, objects, actions, experiences, or conditions.

expectancy What you predict or expect to occur.

expectancy violations theory Theory that explains why you react to people in different ways based on their nonverbal communication.

expert opinion Someone who is considered an expert on the topic makes the decision for the group.

expert power Power based on a person's knowledge of a subject.

external noise (also physical noise) Anything outside of the communicators that interferes with the reception of the message, such as environmental noise.

false conflict Occurs when you perceive a conflict when none exists.

feedback A response to a communicated message.

felt conflict The emotional impact of the perceived conflict.

formal outline A complete sentence outline reflecting the full content and organization of your speech.

formation phase Phase of group development in which group members get to know each other, and the primary emphasis is on socioemotional concerns.

functional approach Emphasizes emergent leadership, which means that a different leader emerges as the group moves from task to task.

general norms Norms that direct the behavior of the group as a whole.

general purpose One of the following purposes of a speech: to inform, to persuade, or to entertain.

generalization A statement in which you categorize something or someone as representative of an entire group.

goal An objective that a group or individual strives to achieve.

group communication Between 3 and 15 individuals with interdependent goals and an assigned or assumed leader meet and interact over time.

group culture The personality and beliefs of the group.

groupthink A phenomenon that limits open communication and adversely affects the quality of decision making when group members fail to exercise independent judgment.

gunnysacking When you keep minor conflicts with another person to yourself, but then unload them all at one time during a major conflict.

halo effect The process of inferring additional positive qualities about someone based on a known positive quality.

haptics The use of touch to communicate.

hearing The continuous, natural, and passive process of receiving aural stimuli.

high self-monitor People who are able to go into a particular context and change their behavior to match the appropriateness of the context.

high-context culture Much of the communication information in the culture is implicitly conveyed by the context of the situation.

hot button issues Areas of interest that create enthusiasm in the person with whom you are talking.

hyperpersonal communication Online communication that is more intimate and social than that found in equivalent, offline interactions.

identity management The deliberate use of nonverbal cues to help form and manage others' perceptions of you.

impromptu speaking Speaking without advance preparation.

inclusion The desire to be wanted.

indirect communication When you hint or imply something that you want someone to do rather than asking directly.

inductive argument Argument that uses a few instances to assert a broader claim.

inflection Changes in the pitch of your voice.

information power Power based on the ability of a group member to influence others because of the information he or she possesses.

integrative agreements   Based on the assumption that there is a way to approach a conflict so that both parties benefit from the solution.

internal noise (or psychological noise)   A communicator's thoughts that keep that person from paying attention to a message.

interpersonal communication   Communication that takes place between two people.

interpersonal schemata   Pockets of knowledge (schemata) identifying other people's characteristics and how you react to them.

intrapersonal communication   Cognition or thought; communicating with oneself.

jargon   The special language of a particular activity, business, or group of people.

kinesics   The use of body movements, or gestures, to communicate.

latent conflict   When underlying conditions are present that could cause conflict.

leader   A person who influences people and their behaviors.

leadership   Communication that modifies or influences the behaviors of others in order to accomplish a common group goal.

legitimate power   Power based on the authority or title held by the person.

line graph   A visual aid used to depict trends and developments over time.

listening   The intermittent, learned, and active process of giving attention to aural stimuli.

logos   Logical appeal that relies on the form and substance of an argument.

low self-monitor   A person who does not change their behavior as they encounter different contexts.

low-context culture   The information between communicators is stated explicitly.

maintenance functions   Behaviors that influence the interpersonal relationships among group members and the overall climate of the group.

maintenance goal   An objective of the group to strengthen or maintain the group.

majority rule   The group votes and the solution chosen by a numerical majority (50% + 1) of group members is suggested to be implemented.

manifest conflict   Occurs when conflict is communicated.

mass communication   Interactions that take place when a sender transmits a message to many people—often hundreds of thousands to billions—who cannot be gathered in one place.

meaning   The relationship between the symbol (typically a word) and the thing that it represents.

message   Any verbal and nonverbal information transmitted from one communicator to another.

minority rule   A small number of group members make decisions for the whole group.

minutes   Summary statements in an agenda about items of discussion from the previous meeting.

misplaced conflict   When people argue about the wrong issues.

Monroe's motivated sequence   Persuasive speech organizational approach that includes five steps: attention, need, satisfaction, visualization, and action.

moral conflict   Exists when there are moral implications involved in the conflict.

mutual influence   The result when nonverbal feedback produces changes in another person's communication.

narration   Storytelling or the process of describing an action or series of occurrences.

need   A strong desire that must be met for a person to feel a sense of satisfaction.

need for control   The need to have some influence in what occurs in your environment.

neutrality   A defensive behavior which includes statements of indifference.

noise   Anything that interferes with the reception of the message.

nonassertiveness   An unwillingness to manage conflict.

nonsubstantive conflict   Occurs when there is no real issue involved.

nonverbal messages   Messages that are sent without using words.

normative conflict   Exists when there is some question regarding the rules and norms of the relationship.

norms   Informal rules for general behavior and role expectations.

olfactics   The use of smell to communicate.

open questions   Questions that invite longer answers and can produce a great deal of information.

openness-closedness dialectic   Dialectic that involves the amount of self-disclosure expressed between the two people in the relationship.

orientation   The first stage of decision making when group members familiarize themselves with the task.

other-imposed prophecies   Your predictions about others' behavior cause you to act toward them as if the prediction were true.

paralanguage   Includes tone of voice and utterances, which are vocal but not verbal.

passive aggression   Communicating your dissatisfaction with something in a disguised manner.

pathos   Emotional appeal that taps the values and feelings of the audience.

pauses   Brief silences used strategically for emphasis in a speech.

perceived conflict   Occurs when one or both parties become aware of their incompatible goals.

perceived self   The person you believe you are.

perception   The process of assessing information in your surroundings.

perception checking   Asking others for clarification or validation of your perceptions.

perceptual accentuation   When you see only what you expect and want to see.

personal appearance   How you look in terms of physical appearance and clothing.

personal goal   An outcome that an individual group member strives to achieve.

personality conflict   Conflict that involves behaviors or beliefs and values.

persuasion   Process of influencing another person's values, beliefs, attitudes, or behaviors.

pie   (or circle graph) Visual aid that is helpful when you want to show relative proportions of the various parts of a whole.

pitch   The highness or lowness of vocal tones.

plagiarism   The false assumption of authorship; the wrongful act of taking the product of another person's mind and presenting it as one's own.

podcast   A previously recorded and sometimes scripted speech, message, or radio or television broadcast.

power   The ability to influence the behavior of others.

power distance   The degree to which members of a culture accept unequal distributions of power among its members.

powerless speech mannerisms   Words and phrases that deflate the strength and confidence of your message.

pragmatic rules   Guide the context of words.

predictability-novelty dialectic   Dialectic that reflects the amount of change versus routine in a dyad's relationship.

presenting self   Your public image, or the perception you want others to have of you.

preview statement   Part of the speech introduction in which you "tell us what you're going to tell us."

primacy effect   Explains the impact of first impressions—what we see or hear first exerts the most influence on our perception.

primacy theory   States that the strongest argument should come first in your speech to establish a strong first impression.

primary group (or socially-oriented group)   Exists to fulfill our basic needs for inclusion and affection.

problem orientation   Suggests to the other person that you work together on a solution to the problem.

problem solving   A multistep process used by a group to create a plan to move from an undesirable state to a predetermined goal.

problem-solution division   Speech organizational pattern where you first establish a compelling problem and then present a convincing solution.

pro-con division   Speech organizational pattern that presents both sides of an issue by explaining the arguments for and arguments against a position.

production phase   When the group has reached socioemotional maturity and is able to focus on task concerns.

pronunciation   Knowing how the letters of a word sound and where the stress falls when that word is spoken.

protection theory   Theory that states that your personal space is defined by you and how safe you feel having people of varying relationship levels close to your body.

provisionalism   Supportive communication messages indicating a willingness to hear all sides of the story before making a judgment.

proxemics   The use of space to communicate.

pseudo-listening   Pretending to listen.

psychographics   The psychological characteristics of the audience such as values, beliefs, attitudes, and behaviors.

public speaking   Interactions that take place when one person speaks face to face with an audience.

punctuation   The act of placing emphasis on a particular communicative or behavioral event.

rate   The speed of your speaking.

real conflict   An actual conflict situation in which both parties acknowledge that they have incompatible goals.

recency effect   What occurs most recently exerts more influence on our perceptions.

recency theory   States that you should present your strongest argument at the end of a speech leaving your audience with your best argument.

referent power   Power based on the attraction or likeability of a person as perceived by group members.

reinforcement stage   The final stage of decision making occurs when group members reinforce their ability to come to a decision and to reach their primary goal.

relational conflict Involves relational issues such as control and power.

relational dialectics Suggests that relationships are influenced by opposing forces (or tensions) that change throughout the lifespan of the relationship and are managed through communication between relational partners.

relational schemata Pockets of knowledge (schemata) that deal with how you view relationships.

relationship dimension The role(s) that each person plays in an interaction; influences the interaction.

research The process of gathering evidence and arguments you will need to understand, develop, and explain your subject.

reverse halo effect When you infer additional negative qualities about someone based on a known negative quality.

reward power Power based on a person's ability to reward compliance.

rewards Include both tangible benefits and intangible benefits.

rhetorical question Stimulates thought but is not intended to elicit an overt response.

ritual questions A series of easy-to-answer questions that allow you to gather basic information about the other person.

role A set of behaviors that serve a particular function within a group.

role norms Norms that direct behavior for specific roles within the group.

schemata Pockets of knowledge used by your brain to organizes stimuli.

secondary groups (or task-oriented groups) Focused on doing work, such as accomplishing a task or solving a problem.

secret tests Presenting another person with inconspicuous challenges that will provide proof of commitment to your friendship or romance.

selective attention Individuals select different stimuli from those competing for their attention.

selective exposure When we consciously expose ourselves to certain viewpoints that are consistent with our own.

selective listening Paying attention to the speaker only when the topic of conversation changes to something that interests you.

selective perception When you attend to some stimuli and not others.

self-awareness The extent to which you know yourself.

self-centered functions of roles Behaviors that represent a hidden agenda on the part of the person exhibiting the behavior.

self-concept How you describe yourself subjectively.

self-disclosure Voluntarily revealing information about ourselves to another to aid in the development and management of interpersonal relationships.

self-esteem The value that you place on yourself.

self-fulfilling prophecy When you make a prediction about the outcome of a situation and you act on that prediction as if it were true, thus making the predicted outcome more likely to occur.

self-monitoring Reading the environment and adjusting communication accordingly.

self-schemata Pockets of knowledge (schemata) used to organize stimuli based on your own personality traits.

semantic noise Interference that occurs when a conversational partner misunderstands or misinterprets something that a partner said.

semantic rules Linguistic rules that guide the meaning of words.

sidetracking Allowing something that someone says to distract you.

signpost A word such as *initially*, *first*, *second*, and *finally* that allows the listeners to indicate a change from one point to another point.

silencers Used to prevent the continuation of the argument.

simultaneous interaction The act of sending and receiving messages, both verbal and nonverbal, at the same time.

situation schemata Pockets of knowledge (schemata) that refer to the appropriateness of a behavior in a given context.

situation-specific apprehension Anxiety about communicating in particular settings or with certain people.

situational (or contingency) approach Suggests that the best leadership style depends on the nature of the situation.

small talk A conversational tactic whose purpose is to gain basic information that will help you to make a connection with someone.

social comparisons When you judge yourself against your peers, siblings, friends, and others.

social information and deindividuation (SIDE) theory Theory that states that because of the lack of nonverbal cues and visual anonymity, CMC users become deindividuated (person is merely text on a screen) in relational formation.

social information processing theory Theory that assumes that people adapt to the medium that they have available for communication.

social penetration theory Describes relational development based on self-disclosure.

spatial division Speech organizational pattern in which your main points are organized according to their physical proximity or geography.

speaking extemporaneously The most popular method of delivery in which the speaker uses brief notes.

speaking from manuscript A speech delivered from a complete text prepared in advance.

speaking from memory A speech that is prepared as a written text and then memorized word for word.

speaking outline The outline you actually use to deliver your speech that is a pared-down version of your full formal outline.

specific purpose Statement used in the speech creation process that includes three parts: the general purpose, the audience, and the goal.

speech to actuate Speech that may establish beliefs but always calls for the audience to act.

speech to convince Speech with an objective to affect your listeners' beliefs or attitudes.

speech to entertain Designed to make a point through the creative, organized use of humorous supporting materials.

speech to inform Objective is to impart knowledge enhance understanding, or permit application.

speech to inspire A speech that attempts to change how listeners feel.

speech to persuade Seeks to influence either beliefs or actions.

spontaneity Messages that are instantaneous and free from deception or manipulation.

stage-hogging When you turn the topic of conversation away from what the speaker is discussing and toward yourself.

states (as in state schemata) An individual's physical or emotional conditions (such as anger).

statistics Collections of numerical data.

stereotyping When you react to a person by assuming he or she is a representation of a generalization.

stonewalling An avoidant behavior that occurs when you cease to communicate with the other person.

strategy A defensive communication message that is deliberately deceptive or manipulative.

style approach Examines whether the leader could choose a way of communicating (or a style) that would increase effectiveness.

substantive conflict Deals with issues that are potentially harmful to the relationship.

summary statement Part of a speech conclusion in which you "tell us what you told us."

superiority A defensive behavior in which you communicate as though you are better than the other person.

supportive climate An environment in which communication is likely to be positive and the communicators feel comfortable communicating freely.

syllogism A pattern of three statements (a major premise, a minor premise, and a conclusion) used in deductive arguments.

symbol Stands for something else.

synchronous Forms of CMC that allow you to communicate directly and immediately with another person or groups of people.

syntactic rules Dictate what letters can go together to form a word.

systematic desensitization A method in which you engage in the activity that creates anxiety until you become less anxious in that situation.

taboo topics Those topics that you and your relational partner avoid because of the negativity that they create.

task An action or activity that the group performs to help them reach a goal.

task function Behaviors that affect the task output of the group.

territoriality Nonverbal cue used to "protect" your space or things.

testimony Sometimes called quotation, this is a method in which you quote or paraphrase the words and ideas of others.

thesis statement A one-sentence synopsis that presents the central idea of the speech.

topical division Organizational pattern in which the speech is divided by aspects, or subtopics, of the subject.

trait apprehension When a person feels a general sense of anxiety in all communication settings.

trait approach The approach to examining leadership that believes that there are certain physical and psychological traits of leaders.

transition A statement connecting one thought to another in a speech.

uncertainty   An uneasiness or anxiety about another person or your relationship with that person.

uncertainty reduction theory (URT)   Theory that explains the exchange of information between two people to create understanding and reduce uneasiness or anxiety.

universals (or axioms) of communication   Rules or principles of communication interaction that is true of any human communication in any context.

unreal conflict   When one person misperceives a conflict situation or that the conflict doesn't really exist.

valence   The positive or negative value assigned to an unexpected behavior.

value   A judgment of what is desirable or undesirable, right or wrong, and is usually stated in the form of a word or phrase.

visualization   Method to reduce nervousness in which you visualize yourself delivering an effective—not a perfect—presentation.

vivid   Speeches should provide supporting materials that are striking, graphic, intense, and memorable.

voice quality (or timbre)   The least flexible of the vocal elements that distinguishes your voice from other voices.

volume   How loudly or softly you speak.

voluntary audience   An audience that has assembled of its own free will and usually has a favorable attitude toward the speaker.

words   Symbols that are conventionally agreed upon to represent certain things, people, and events.

working outline   The first outline of the speech-making process that consists of a list of aspects of your chosen topic.

REFERENCES

Adams, D. (1979). *A hitchhiker's guide to the galaxy.* New York: The Ballantine Publishing Group.

Adler, R.B., & Elmhorst, J.M. (1999). *Communicating at Work: Principles and Practices for Business and the Professions (6th Ed.)*, p. 241. Boston: McGraw.

Altman, I., & Taylor, D. (1973). *Social penetration: The development of interpersonal relationships.* New York: Holt, Rinehart & Winston.

Anderson, P. A. (1993). Cognitive schemata in personal relationships. In S. Duck (Ed.), *Individuals in relationships: Understanding relationship processes series, Vol. I* (pp. 1–29). Newbury Park: CA: Sage.

Anonymous. (2004, November 15). "Not another meeting!" *USA TODAY*, D1.

Aries, E. (1998). Gender differences in interaction. In D. J. Canary & K. Dindia (Eds.), *Sex differences and similarities in communication* (pp. 65–81). Mahwah, NJ: Erlbaum.

Association of American Colleges and Universities (2006, November/December). Percentage of business leaders who want colleges to "place more emphasis" on essential learning outcomes. Retrieved August 3, 2009, from http://www.aacu.org/leap/businessleaders.cfm

Bacon, D.R., Stewart, K.A., & Silver, W.S. (1999). Lessons from the best and worst student team experiences: How a teacher can make a difference. *Journal of Management Education, 23*(5), 467–488.

Balter, M. (3 Oct. 2001). First 'speech gene' identified. *Academic Press Daily InSight*, American Association for the Advancement of Science, 7 Sept. 2002 www.academicpress.com/insight/10032001/grapha.htm.

Barber, C. L. (1965). *The story of speech and language.* New York: Crowell.

Barker, L., Edwards, E., Gaines, C., Gladney, K., & Holley, F. (1980). An investigation ofproportional time spent in various communication activities by college students. *Journal of Applied Communication Research, 8,* 101–109.

Barnlund, D.C. (1970). A transactional model of communication. In K. K. Sereno & C. D. Mortensen (Eds.), *Foundations of communication theory* (pp. 83–102). New York: Harper and Row.

Bass, B. M. (1981). *Stogdill's handbook of leadership: A survey of theory and research.* New York: The Free Press.

Baxter, L. A. & Wilmot, W. W. (1985). Taboo topics in close relationships. *Journal of Social and Personal Relationships, 2,* 253–269.

Baxter, L. A. (1993). The social side of personal relationships: A dialectical analysis. In S. Duck (Ed.), *Social context and relationships* (pp. 139–165). Newbury Park, CA: Sage.

BBC Monitoring Worldwide Media (2009, April 2). New US study identifies emerging threats to Internet freedom. Supplied by BBC Worldwide Monitoring. Retrieved June 7, 2009, from the Lexis Nexis database.

Benjamin. J. (1997). *Principles, elements, and types of persuasion.* Fort Worth: Harcourt. http://www.bls.gov/news.release/volun.nr0.htm

Berger, B., Reber, B. H., & Heyman, W. C. (2005). *Illuminating the path to success in public relations.* Paper presented at the International Communication Association annual meeting, New York, NY.

Berger, C. R., & Calabrese, R. J. (1975). Some explorations in initial interaction and beyond: Toward a developmental theory of interpersonal communication. *Human Communication Research, 1,* 99–112.

Boothman, N. (2000). *How to make people like you in 90 seconds or less.* New York: Workman.

Bosson, J. K, & Swann, W. B., Jr. (2001). The paradox of the sincere chameleon: Strategic self-verification in close relationships. In J. Harvey & A. Wenzel (Eds.), *Close romantic relationships: Maintenance and enhancement* (pp. 67–86). Mahwah, NJ: Lawrence Erlbaum Publishers, Inc.

Bryson, B. (1990). *The mother tongue: English & how it got that way*. New York: Avon.

Burgoon, J. K., & Hale, J. L. (1988). Nonverbal expectancy violations: Model elaboration and application. *Communication Monographs, 55*, 58–79.

Canary, D. J., & Emmers-Sommer, T. M. (1997). *Sex and gender differences in personal relationships* (pp. 1–23). New York: Guilford Press.

Chiu, R . K., & Babcock, R. D. (2002). The relative importance of facial attractiveness and gender in Hong Kong selection decisions. *International Journal of Human Resource Management, 13*(1), 141–155.

CNN.com (6 June 2002, 18 June 2002). *'Jihad' dropped from Harvard student's speech*. http://fyi.cnn.com/2002/f...dnews/05/31/Harvard.jihad.ap/index.html

Cody, M. J. (1982). A typology of disengagement strategies and an examination of the role intimacy, reactions to inequity and relational problems play in strategic selection. *Communication Monographs, 49*, 148–170.

Conville, R. L. (1991). *Relational transitions: The evolution of personal relationships*. New York: Praeger.

Coonan, C. (2009). China walls off net. Daily Variety (4 June 2009): 4. Retrieved June 7, June 2009, from the LexisNexis database.

Cooper, L. (1960). *The rhetoric of Aristotle*. New York: Appleton.

Cronin, M., Olsen, R., & Stahl, J. (1992). *Mission possible: Listening skills for better communication*, computer software, Oral Communication Program, Radford University, Radford, VA.

DeVito, J. A. (2009). *The interpersonal communication book* (12th ed.). Boston: Pearson Education.

Dewey, J. (1910). *How we think*. Boston: Heath.

Dindia, K. (2006). Men are from North Dakota, women are from South Dakota. In D. J. Canary & K. Dindia (Eds.), *Sex differences and similarities in communication*(2nd ed). (pp. 3–21). Mahwah, NJ: Erlbaum.

DiYanni, R., & Hoy, P.C. (2001). *The Scribner Handbook for Writers* (3rd ed., p. 196). New York: Longman.

Eaves, M. H., & Leathers, D. G. (2003). Context as communication: McDonald's vs. Burger King. In K. M. Galvin and P. J. Cooper (Eds.), *Making connections: Readings in relational communication* (3rd ed.) (pp. 143–153). Los Angeles, CA: Roxbury.

Ekman, P., & Friesen, W. (1975). *Unmasking the face*. Englewood Cliffs, NJ: Prentice Hall.

Felmlee, D. H. (1998). Fatal attraction. In B. H. Spitzberg & W. R. Cupach (Eds.), *The dark side of close relationships* (pp. 3–31). Mahwah, NJ: Lawrence Erlbaum Associates, Publishers.

Fenton, S., & Reposa, G. (1998). Evaluating the goods. Technology & Learning, 23–32.

French, J. P. R., Jr., & Raven, B. (1960). The bases of social power. In D. Cartwright & A. Zander (Eds.), *Group dynamics* (pp 607—623). New York: Harper & Row.

Frick-Horbury, D., & Guttentag, R. E. (1998). The effects of restricting hand gesture production on lexical retrieval and free recall. *American Journal of Psychology*, pp. 45–46.

Gabor, D. (2001). *How to start a conversation and make friends* (2nd ed.). New York: Fireside.

Gass, R. H., & Seiter, J. S. (1999). *Persuasion, social influence, and compliance gaining*. Boston: Allyn & Bacon.

Gates, B. (2005). High schools are obsolete: Teaching kids what they need to know. *Vital Speeches of the Day*, 396–397.

Gibb, J. R. (1961). Defensive communication. *Journal of Communication, 11*, 141–148.

Gottman, J. (1994). *Why marriages succeed or fail … and how you can make yours last*. New York: Simon and Schuster.

Grassian, E. (2006). Thinking critically about Web 2.0 and beyond. Retrieved August 15, 2009, from UCLA College Library. www.library.ucla.edu/libraries/college/11605_12008.cfm

Gray, J. (1992). *Men are from Mars, women are from Venus: A practical guide for improving communication and getting what you want in your relationships*. New York: HarperCollins.

Gray, J. (1997). *Mars and Venus on a date: A guide for navigating the 5 stages of dating to create a loving and lasting relationship*. New York: HarperCollins.

Gruber, J. (2001). Heart disease in women. *Winning Orations*, 15. Coached by Judy Santacaterina.

Gudykunst, W.B. (1998). *Bridging differences: Effective intergroup communication*. Thousand Oaks, CA: Sage Publications.

Hall, E. T. (1982). *The dance of life: The other dimension of time*. New York: Doubleday.

Hall, E.T. (1990). *The hidden dimension*. New York: Anchor Books.

Hawkins, K. W., & Stewart, R. A. (1990). Temporal effects of leadership style on state communication anxiety in small task-oriented groups. *Communication Research Reports, 7*(1), 3–8.

HNN Staff (6 June 2002, 18 June 2002). So what does jihad really mean? *History News Network*. www. historynewsnetwork.org/articles/article.html?id=774.

Hofstede, G. (2001). *Culture's consequences: Comparative values, behaviors, institutions, and organizations across nations* (2nd ed.). Thousand Oaks, CA: Sage.

Howe, N., & Strauss, W. (2000). *Millennials rising: The next great generation*. New York: Vintage Books.

InformationWeek (2006, November 2). China: Net Censorship? Not Here; China does not censor the Internet—no way, no how, said a Chinese official attending the Internet Governance Forum in Athens, Greece. Retrieved April 20, 2008, from General OneFile. Gale. Radford University Library.

Jablin, F. (1981). Cultivating imagination: Factors that enhance and inhibit creativity in brainstorming groups. *Human Communication Research, 7*, 245–258.

Jakobson, R. (1964). Closing statement: Linguistics and poetics. In T. A. Sebeok (Ed.), *Style in language* (pp. 350–374). Cambridge: MIT Press.

Jamieson, K. H. (1995). *Beyond the double bind: Women in leadership*. New York: Oxford University Press.

Janis, I. L. (1982). *Groupthink: Psychological studies of policy decisions and fiascoes* (2nd ed.). Boston: Houghton.

Jenson, A. D., & Chilberg, J. C. (1991). *Small group communication: Theory and application*. Belmont, CA: Wadsworth.

Jones, J. J. (2004). Are you guilty? *Winning Orations*. Coached by Barbara F. Sims. Mankato, MN: International Oratorical Association.

Kanter, R.M. (1977). *Men and women of the corporation*. New York: Basic.

Kim, Y. Y., & Paulk, S. (1994). Intercultural challenges and personal adjustments. In R. L. Wiseman & R. Shuter (Eds.), *Communication in Multinational Organizations* (pp. 117–120). Thousand Oaks, CA: Sage.

Knapp, M. L. (1978). *Social intercourse: From greeting to goodbye*. Needham Heights, MA: Allyn & Bacon.

Koeman (2007). Cultural values in commercials: Reaching and representing the multicultural market? *Communications: The European Journal of Communication Research, 32*(2), 223—253.

Koesten, J. (2004). *Family communication patterns, sex of subject, and communication competence.* Communication Monographs, *71*(2), 226–244.

Lea, M., & Spears, R. (1992). Paralanguage and social perception in computer-mediated communication. *Journal of Organizational Computing, 2*, 321–341.

Leggett, G., Mead, C.D., Kramer, M, & Beal, R.S. (1991). *Prentice Hall Handbook for Writers* (11th ed., pp. 417–418). Upper Saddle River, NJ: Prentice Hall, [We have drawn on examples these authors use in their excellent section on connecting language.]

Lemon, S. (2007, March 19). China tightening net access control, U.S. says. *Computerworld, 41*(12), 20–21. Retrieved April 20, 2008, from General OneFile. Gale. Radford University Library.

Lester, J. S. (1994). *The future of white men and other diversity dilemmas*. Berkeley, CA: Conari Press.

Library Tutorial—Evaluating Information Resources (2005, September 15). Retrieved on August 15, 2009, from McConnell Library, Radford University. http://lib.radford.edu/ tutorial/IX/index.asp

Lindey, A. (1952). *Plagiarism and originality* (p. 2). New York: Harper.

Loeb, M. (2006). Backstabbers beware: Trust is most important way to get ahead. *Foxnews.com Market Watch*. Accessed December 22, 2006.

Lulofs, R .S. & Cahn, D. D. (2000). *Conflict: From theory to action* (2nd ed.).Boston: Allyn and Bacon.

Lutz, W. (1997). *The new doublespeak: Why no one knows what anyone is saying anymore*. New York: HarperCollins, Publishers, Inc.

Luxen, M. F., & Van de Vijver, F. J. R. (2005). Facial attractiveness, sexual selection, and personnel selection: When evolved preferences matter. *Journal of Organizational Behavior, 27*(2), 241–255.

Lyons, L. (2003). Which skills hold the secret to success at work? Part II. Retrieved August 3, 2009, from http://www.gallup.com/poll/9115/Which-Skills-Hold-Secret-Success-Work-Part.aspx

Maggio, R. (1991). *The bias-free word finder: A dictionary of nondiscriminatory language*. Boston: Beacon.

Maggio, R. (1997). *Talking about people: A guide to fair and accurate language*. Phoenix, AZ: Oryx.

Martinet, T. (2004). Ribbons: Functions or fashion. *Winning Orations*, 79. Mankato, MN: Interstate Oratorical Association. Coached by Christina Ellis.

Mayer, L. V. (1994). *Fundamentals of voice and diction*, 10th ed. Dubuque, IA: Brown.

McCroskey, J. C. (1982). Oral communication apprehension: A reconceptualization. In M. Burgoon (Ed.), *Communication yearbook 6* (pp. 136–170). Beverly Hills, CA: Sage.

McCroskey, J.C. (1984). The communication apprehension perspective. In J. A. Daly & J. D. McCroskey (Eds.), *Avoiding communication:*

Shyness, reticence, and communication apprehension (pp. 13–38). Beverly Hills, CA: Sage.

McCroskey, J. C., & Richmond, V. P. (1988). Communication apprehension and small group communication. In R. S. Cathcart & L. A. Samovar (Eds.), *Small group communication: A reader* (5th ed.) (pp. 405–419). Dubuque, IA: Wm. C. Brown.

McCroskey, J. C., & Wright, D. W. (1971). The development of an instrument for measuring interaction behavior in small groups. *Speech Monographs, 38,* 335–340.

Meinen, J. (2006). Untitled Speech, *Winning Orations,* 17. Coached by Dan Smith. Mankato, MN: Interstate Oratorical Association.

Miller, A. N. (2002). An exploration of Kenyan public speaking patterns with implications for the American introductory public speaking course. *Communication Education, 51*(2), 168–182.

National Association of Colleges and Employers (2005). Job outlook 2005. In Career Development and Job-Search Advice for New College Graduates. http://www.jobweb.com

National Communication Association (1998). How Americans communicate, conducted by Roper Starch. http://www.natcom.org/research/poll/how-americans-communicate.htm

Parshall, G. (22 Sept. 1995). A 'glorious mongrel.' *U.S. News & World Report, 48.*

Patton, B. R., & Downs, T. M. (2003). *Decision-making group interaction* (4th ed.). Boston: Allyn and Bacon.

Pondy, L. R. (1967). Organizational conflict: Concepts and models. *Administrative Science Quarterly, 12,* 296–320.

Pruitt, D. G., & Rubin, J. Z. (1986). *Social conflict: Escalation, stalemate, and settlement* New York: Random House.

Publication Manual of the American Psychological Association, 5th ed. (2001). Washington, DC: American Psychological Association.

Quirk, M. (2006). The Web police: Internet censorship is prevalent not just in China but throughout the world. Can the Web be tamed? *The Atlantic Monthly, 297.*4, 50–51. Retrieved April 20, 2008, from General OneFile. Gale. Radford University Library.

Rabby, M. K., & Walther, J. B. (2003). Computer-mediated communication effects on relationship formation and maintenance. In D. J. Canary & M. Dainton (Eds.), *Maintaining relationships through communication: Relational, contextual, and cultural variations* (pp. 141–162). Mahwah, NJ: Lawrence Erlbaum Associates, Publishers.

Reis, H.T. (1998). Gender differences in intimacy and related behaviors: Context and process. In D.J. Canary & K. Dindia (Eds.), *Sex differences and similarities in communication: Critical essays and empirical investigations of sex and gender in interaction* (pp. 203–231). Mahwah, N.J.: Lawrence Erlbaum Associates, Publishers.

Resnick, R. (2006). The nursing home catastrophe, *Winning Orations,* 1. Coached by Josh Miller. Mankato, MN: Interstate Oratorical Association.

Ripley, A. (2001, October 29). Grief lessons. *Time,* 69.

RoAne, S. (1997). What do I say next? Talking your way to business and social success. New York: Warner Books.

Schilder, J. (1992). Work teams boost productivity. *Personnel Journal, 71*(2), 67–72.

Schullery, N. M., & Gibson, M. K. (2001). Working in groups: Identification and treatment of students' perceived weaknesses. *Business Communication Quarterly, 64*(2), 9–30.

Schutz, W.C. (1958). *Firo: A three-dimensional theory of interpersonal behavior.* New York: Rinehart.

Schwartz, S. (1992). Universals in the content and structure of values. In M. Zanna (Ed.), *Advances in Experimental Social Psychology* (Vol. 25). New York: Academic Press.

SMART Technologies, ULC. (copyrighted 2004). *The state of meetings today.* Retrieved May 18, 2009, from http://www.effectivemeetings.com/meetingbasics/meetstate.asp

SMART Technologies, ULC. (copyrighted 2004). Effectivemeetings.com (accessed 18 May 2009). *The state of meetings today.* http://www.effectivemeetings.com/meetingbasics/meetstate.asp.

Smola, K.W., & Sutton, C.D. (2002). Generational differences: Revisiting generational work values for the new millennium. *Journal of Organizational Behavior, 23*(4), 363–382.

Socha, T. J. (1997). Group communication across the life span. In L.R. Frey & J.K. Barge (Eds.), *Managing group life: Communicating in decision-making groups* (pp. 3–28). Boston: Houghton Mifflin.

Sorensen, G., & McCroskey, J. C. (1977). The prediction of interaction of behavior in small groups: Zero-history versus intact groups. *Communication Monographs, 44,* 73–80.

Sorensen, S. M. (1981). *Group-hate: A negative reaction to group work.* Paper presented at the Annual Meeting of the International Communication Association (Minneapolis, MN).

Speak For Success (2007). Single breakthrough skill is key to success for executive women. News Release, June 11, 2007. www.speakforsuccess.com/docs/ExecWomen SurveyRelease.pdf

Spitzberg, B.H. (1994). The dark side of (in)competence. In W. R. Cupach & B. H. Spitzberg (Eds.), *The dark side of interpersonal communication* (pp. 25–49). Hillsdale, NJ: Lawrence Erlbaum.

Stanger, K. (2008, June 12). Criteria for Evaluating Internet Resources. Retrieved August 15, 2009, from Bruce T. Halle Library, Eastern Michigan University. http://www.emich.edu/ halle/evaluating_internet.html

Stewart, J. (2006). *Bridges not walls: A book about interpersonal communication*, 9th Ed. Boston, MA: McGraw-Hill.

Talman, M. (1992). *Understanding Presentation Graphics*. San Francisco: SYBEX.

Tannen, D. (1990). *You just don't understand*. New York: Balantine.

Techweb (14 January 2009). China Internet use exceeds global average. Retrieved June 7, 2009, from the LexisNexis database.

The London Eye (29 April 2009). Interesting things you never know about the London Eye, Retrieved 11 August 2009. www.londoneye.com/Explorethe LondonEye/InterestingFacts/ Default.aspx

The New Zealand Herald (4 June 2009). Hard to raise a Twitter on eve of anniversary. Retrieved 7 June 2009, from the LexisNexis database.

Thomas, K. W. (1976). Conflict and conflict management. In M.D. Dunnett (Ed.), *The handbook of industrial and organizational psychology*. Chicago: Rand McNally.

Thomas, K., & Kilmann, R. H. (1974). *Conflict mode instrument*. Tuxedo, NY: XICOM, Inc.

Tidwell, C. H., Jr. (2009). Nonverbal Communication Modes. Retrieved on June 15, 2009, from Google Scholar. http://www.andrews.edu/~tidwell/bsad560/ NonVerbal.html

Titsworth, B. S. (2004). Students' notetaking: The effects of teacher immediacy and clarity. *Communication Education*, 317.

Tufte, E. R. (2001). *The visual display of quantitative information (2nd ed.)*. Cheshire, CT: Graphics Press.

Walther, J. B. (1992). Interpersonal effects in computer-mediated interaction: A relational perspective. *Communication Research, 19*, 52–90.

Walther, J. B. (1996). Computer-mediated communication: Impersonal, interpersonal, and hyperpersonal interaction. *Communication Research, 23*, 342–469.

Wartella, E. (1996, November 23). *The Context of Television Violence*. Arnold Lecture presented at the Speech Communication Association Annual Convention, Marriot Hotel & Marina, San Diego.

Watzlawick, P., Beavin, J. H., & Jackson, D. D. (1967). *Pragmatics of human communication: A study of interactional patterns, pathologies, and paradoxes*. New York: W.W. Norton.

Whitley, M. (1997). "Involuntary Commitment Laws," *Video User's Guide for the Allyn & Bacon/AFA Student Speeches Video I, pp. 43–45*. Boston: Allyn & Bacon.

Wood, W., & Eagly, A. H. (2002). A cross-cultural analysis of the behavior of women and men: Implications for the origins of sex differences. *Psychological Bulletin, 128*, 699–727.

Yum, Y., & Hara, K. (2006). Computer-mediated relationship development: A cross-cultural comparison. *Journal of Computer-Mediated Communication, 11*, 133–152.

Zemke, R., Raines, C., & Filipczak, B. (2000). *Generations at work: Managing the clash of Veterans, Boomers, Xers, and Nexters in your workplace*. New York: AMACOM.